SKEPTICISM IN EARLY MODERN ENGLISH LITERATURE

This ambitious account of skepticism's effects on major authors of England's Golden Age shows how key philosophical problems inspired literary innovations in poetry and prose. When figures like Spenser, Shakespeare, Donne, Herbert of Cherbury, Cavendish, Marvell, and Milton question theories of language, degrees of knowledge and belief, and dwell on the uncertainties of perception, they forever change English literature, ushering it into a secular mode. While tracing a narrative arc from medieval nominalism to late seventeenth-century taste, the book explores the aesthetic pleasures and political quandaries induced by skeptical doubt. It also incorporates modern philosophical views of skepticism: those of Stanley Cavell, Ludwig Wittgenstein, Roland Barthes, and Hans Blumenberg, among others. The book thus contributes to interdisciplinary studies of philosophy and literature as well as to current debates about skepticism as a secularizing force, fostering civil liberties and religious freedoms.

ANITA GILMAN SHERMAN is Associate Professor of Literature at American University, Washington, DC. She is the author of *Skepticism and Memory in Shakespeare and Donne* (2007) and has published articles on Montaigne, Garcilaso de la Vega, Thomas Heywood, W. G. Sebald, and others.

SKEPTICISM IN EARLY MODERN ENGLISH LITERATURE

The Problems and Pleasures of Doubt

ANITA GILMAN SHERMAN

American University

CAMBRIDGE
UNIVERSITY PRESS

University Printing House, Cambridge CB2 8BS, United Kingdom

One Liberty Plaza, 20th Floor, New York, NY 10006, USA

477 Williamstown Road, Port Melbourne, VIC 3207, Australia

314–321, 3rd Floor, Plot 3, Splendor Forum, Jasola District Centre, New Delhi – 110025, India

79 Anson Road, #06–04/06, Singapore 079906

Cambridge University Press is part of the University of Cambridge.

It furthers the University's mission by disseminating knowledge in the pursuit of education, learning, and research at the highest international levels of excellence.

www.cambridge.org
Information on this title: www.cambridge.org/9781108842662
DOI: 10.1017/9781108903813

© Anita Gilman Sherman 2021

This publication is in copyright. Subject to statutory exception and to the provisions of relevant collective licensing agreements, no reproduction of any part may take place without the written permission of Cambridge University Press.

First published 2021

A catalogue record for this publication is available from the British Library.

ISBN 978-1-108-84266-2 Hardback

Cambridge University Press has no responsibility for the persistence or accuracy of URLs for external or third-party internet websites referred to in this publication and does not guarantee that any content on such websites is, or will remain, accurate or appropriate.

For Davis

Contents

Acknowledgments		*page* viii
Introduction: Secularizing Skepticism?		1
1 Visionary, Interrupted: Spenser's Skeptical Artwork		32
2 Fantasies of Private Language: Shakespeare's "The Phoenix and Turtle" and Donne's "The Ecstasy"		74
3 Conformity / Neutrality in Lord Herbert of Cherbury		92
4 The Skeptical Fancies of Margaret Cavendish: Reoccupation		137
5 The Enchantments of Andrew Marvell: Skepticism and Taste		176
Afterword: Experience in Crisis: Milton's *Samson Agonistes*		225
Bibliography		235
Index		263

Acknowledgments

This book has been so long in the making that it is doubtful I can remember all those who had a hand in its formation. That said, it is a pleasure to review in memory the individuals and institutions that have helped me. I am most grateful to those who read portions of the book at various intermediate stages: Brandi Adams, Reid Barbour, William M. Hamlin, Rebeca Helfer, Eugene Hill, Ben LaBreche, Greg Miller, Debapriya Sarkar, and above all Theodore Leinwand who read the entire typescript. The readers for Cambridge University Press also made invaluable suggestions; they will recognize their contributions.

The National Endowment for the Humanities sponsored a Summer Institute on Medieval and Early Modern Philosophy in 2015 that mixed rigor and collegiality in exemplary fashion; I owe thanks to Peter King, Marcy Lascano, Calvin Normore, and Robert Pasnau. The Shakespeare Association of America hosted seminars in which I drafted various ideas in this book; I give special thanks to Judith Anderson, James Bednarz and Jennifer Vaught. The National Humanities Center hosted a Summer Institute on the lyric poetry of Andrew Marvell in 2012; Nigel Smith presided over a week of scholarship and interchange that continues to inform my work. The Texas Institute for Literary and Textual Studies (TILTS) held a symposium in 2010 on religious conflict and violence in early modern England during which I presented my initial pages on Herbert of Cherbury. The Folger Shakespeare Library awarded me a short-term fellowship in 2014 for work on Cavendish. I will not soon forget holding those beautiful folios in the cool penumbra of the Paster reading room during that steamy July.

I also want to thank audiences at various venues where I delivered papers: the International Milton Congress in 2004, the Southeastern Renaissance Conference in 2006, the University of Maryland in 2008, the Sixteenth-Century Society Conference in 2009, the Rocky Mountain Renaissance and Medieval Association Conference in 2011, and the

Renaissance Society of America and the George Herbert Society in 2017. Angela Balla, Douglas Bruster, Daryl Gless, Andrew Hadfield, Anne-Marie Miller-Blaise, Gerard Passanante, Robert L. Reid, Andrew Shifflet, and Richard Strier stand out in memory for having helped me refine my ideas after those talks. Others whose advice I took include William Rogers Brubaker, Lara Dodds, Christopher Highley, David Lawrence, Jonathan Loesberg, Julie Park, David Pike, David Sacks, Matthew Seal, and Richard C. Sha. I also want to credit those who participated in the special session on skepticism in the seventeenth century that I organized at the Modern Languages Association Convention in 2013 and those who attended the seminar on theatrical skepticism that Lauren Robertson and I co-hosted at the Shakespeare Association of America in 2019.

Thanks to the University of Texas Press for permission to reprint a revised version of what became Chapter 3, first published as "The Politics of Truth in Herbert of Cherbury" by Anita Gilman Sherman from *Texas Studies in Literature and Language*, vol. 54, no. 1 (Spring 2012), pp. 189–215 (Copyright © by the University of Texas Press. All rights reserved). Thanks to Fordham University Press for permission to reprint "Fantasies of Private Language in Shakespeare's 'Phoenix and Turtle' and Donne's 'Ecstasy'" from *Shakespeare and Donne: Generic Hybrids in the Cultural Imaginary*, ed. Judith Anderson and Jennifer Vaught (Fordham University Press, 2013), pp. 169–184. Thanks to Taylor & Francis for permission to reprint a portion of "The Sceptic's Surrender: Believing Partly" from *The Routledge Companion to Shakespeare and Philosophy*, ed. Craig Bourne and Emily Caddick Bourne (Routledge, 2019), pp. 350–359. Thanks to the Folger Shakespeare Library for permission to reprint the engraved frontispiece of Margaret Cavendish's 1668 *Playes* and a woodcut illustration from Jan Van der Noot's 1569 *A Theatre for Worldlings*. No set of acknowledgments would be complete without thanking the extraordinary libraries that make this kind of academic work possible: not only the Folger Shakespeare Library, but also The Bender Library at American University, my home institution, and the Milton S. Eisenhower Library at The Johns Hopkins University.

I miss the brilliance, the sense of humor, and the unflagging support of the late Marshall Grossman whose graduate seminars introduced me to many wonderful poems, among them, Andrew Marvell's "Upon Appleton House."

Finally, thanks are due to my wonderful family whom I tried not to neglect while immersed in this project.

Introduction
Secularizing Skepticism?

At the start of *Hamlet*, uncertainty hovers in the air. The soldiers of the watch at Elsinore feel uneasy, unsettled by a ghost they have encountered on previous nights. They summon Hamlet's friend, Horatio. As Horatio approaches the battlements, the soldiers chide him for having "ears / That are so fortified against our story" (I.i.29–30). Evidently, his philosophical allegiance to stoicism (with its valuing of reason) predisposes him to skepticism about spirits, omens, and auguries. One soldier grumbles, "Horatio says 'tis but our fantasy, / And will not let belief take hold of him" (I.i.21–22). Horatio confirms his reputation for rational doubt with a dismissive, "Tush, tush, 'twill not appear" (I.i.28). He resists the soldiers' report, but not for long, as the ghost soon enters. "It harrows me with fear and wonder," Horatio confesses (I.i.42). His companions urge him to address the apparition, but the ghost "stalks away," offended, they surmise, causing Horatio to "tremble and look pale" (48, 51). "Is not this something more than fantasy?" one soldier rebukes Horatio.

Horatio spends the rest of the scene trying to process his experience. Having initially scoffed at their report, he now concedes, "Before my God, I might not this believe / Without the sensible and true avouch / Of mine own eyes" (54–56). Devotees of *Othello* and *Much Ado About Nothing* know that ocular proof is problematic in Shakespeare. Shakespeare takes a skeptical view of the senses, considering them unreliable avenues to knowledge, and literally recommends "consensus" among senses and people before acting on a hypothesis. Horatio's eyewitness may therefore be flawed although being shared increases its likelihood. Horatio may fall into the category of a doubting Thomas – a person of shallow faith who requires tactile evidence before he is willing to believe in the reality of spirits.

Recognizing that what he has seen may be significant, Horatio entertains possibilities of what the ghost might mean. Although he concedes that he "know[s] not" why the ghost has appeared, he ventures that it "bodes some strange eruption to our state," ascribing this hypothesis to "the gross and scope of my opinion" (I.i.66–68). Like a good humanist student, Horatio weighs alternatives, turning to history, both current and ancient, in his effort to understand. His disquisition on Denmark's troubled history with Norway – extended in Q2 with an account of bloody omens marking the eve of Julius Caesar's assassination – is suddenly interrupted by the ghost's return. "Stay, illusion!" Horatio commands (I.i.108). Unsure what this illusion is or means, he implores it more formally this time, pleading repeatedly "speak" and "speak to me." Horatio may be confounded by the ontological status of the illusion, but he is willing to interact with it, as if it were real, on a provisional basis. Then the cock crows and Horatio says of the ghost, "it started like a guilty thing / Upon a fearful summons" (129–130). He is remembering folklore about ghosts. "I have heard," he explains, that at the cock's crowing "th'extravagant and erring spirit hies / To his confine; and of the truth herein / This present object made probation" (135–137). Horatio entertains a story of cause and effect, relating the timing of the ghost's disappearance to his compulsory return to his abode, interpreted as a zone of punishment. The soldier, Marcellus, gives a Christian coloring to Horatio's hypothesis, adding

> Some say that ever 'gainst that season comes
> Wherein our saviour's birth is celebrated
> The bird of dawning singeth all night long;
> And then, they say, no spirit can walk abroad,
> . . . .
> So hallowed and so gracious is the time.
> (I.i.139–145)

Horatio replies, "So have I heard, and do in part believe it" (146). This may be a tactful concession to Marcellus's feelings, but it is also sincere. Horatio is rueful, even wistful that faith eludes him. He is not ready to embrace the Christian folklore about the seasonal fluctuation of erring spirits.

Nevertheless, the encounter with the specter has changed Horatio. He has abandoned his resistance to the idea of ghosts, but he is not prepared to let belief take hold of him. He occupies an epistemologically intermediate condition, neither disbelieving nor believing, but suspended in between. Although he is poised precariously between the entertainment of propositions and assent, Horatio is receptive to new evidence – up to a point. As Hamlet famously says, "There are more things in heaven and earth, Horatio, / Than are dreamt of in our philosophy" (I.v.168–169).

Q2 offers a key variant on the line, substituting "your" for "our" philosophy. Either way, Hamlet implies that the philosophy they have imbibed at Wittenberg has made Horatio skeptical of an enchanted universe alive with spirits.

Too often skepticism is considered a cynical reflex associated with atheism and disbelief. But as the opening scene of *Hamlet* illustrates, skepticism permits of degrees, waning and waxing in response to new evidence, often comprising an intermediate stage in the formation of beliefs and convictions.[1] Skepticism and belief are intertwined in complex ways affecting rationality.[2] Skeptical doubt is not an ideological position, then, so much as an epistemological condition constantly in process and subject to change. This book aims to show the vitality and creativity of skeptical doubt for literary production in early modern England by discussing neglected aspects of skepticism in signature texts. Instead of understanding skepticism as an existential dead end or arid philosophical problem, a "fortuitous imbroglio" as Hegel called it, or an insidious force evacuating the world of spirit and enchantment, I argue that for certain early modern writers skepticism proves to be an aesthetic boon – a fertile source of literary invention, offering mind-opening possibilities.[3] Its aesthetic ramifications in turn have political implications that go beyond a celebration of diversity, multiplicity or perspectivism.[4]

Scholars disagree about whether skepticism tends left or right, toward radical stances and free speech (*parrhesia*) or toward passivity and conformity. If ties are found to neo-Stoicism or Tacitus, skepticism is often deemed conservative; while if ties are found to Epicureanism and to Lucretius, it is deemed liberal and emancipatory. Activism or detachment, toleration or fanaticism, republicanism or absolutism, a Machiavellian *Realpolitik* or the embrace of diversity and community – all these stances are said to be shaped by skepticism.[5] When it comes to literature, the jury

---

[1] For further discussion of degrees of belief in Shakespeare, see Sherman (2019).
[2] See, e.g., Neto and Paganini's collection (2009), especially section 2 on the relations between skepticism and the Protestant Reformation (63–123); Popkin's seminal work (2003), especially xxi–16, 64–79, 112–127; Stephens (2001) on the relation of belief and resistance to skepticism (26–31, 99–102).
[3] *The Phenomenology of Mind* (1967), B.IV. B.2.249.
[4] Coined by Nietszche in *The Genealogy of Morals*, "perspectivism" has become a critical commonplace for describing the polyphony of multiple perspectives constitutive of skepticism in Cervantes's work; see, e.g., Castro (1925), Spitzer (2015), and others.
[5] On the political work of skepticism, see, e.g., Bredvold (1934); Burke (1990); Dykstal (2001); especially 77–104; Greenblatt (2011); Kahn (1985); Laursen (1992); Laursen and Paganini's collection (2015) surveys political responses to skepticism ranging from conformity to libertinism; Lom (2011), 11–29; Oakeshott (1996); Tuck (1993); Zerba (2012), Part 3, especially 164–236,

is also out on skepticism's effects. Some find skepticism in the radical nihilism of Renaissance tragedy, identifying the skeptical dictum that nothing can be known (*nihil scitur*) as a source of tragic despair.[6] Others focus on links between skepticism and traditions of debate, specific rhetorical techniques or a digressive style.[7] The wandering of Montaigne's essays, it is said, captures the testing and assaying quality of skepticism.[8] While these analyses are insightful, they sometimes fall short of a holistic approach to skeptical art.

Skepticism should be seen more broadly as a philosophical, psychological, aesthetic, and political phenomenon that informs a stance toward the world. Only then can skepticism's full impact as a secularizing force be felt and assessed. Today when secularism is an inflammatory political issue the world over and when the skepticism promoted by intellectual elites is blamed for cultural relativism and for a resurgence of fundamentalist piety, populist politics, and anti-Western ideologies, it is instructive to revisit the seventeenth century.[9] Toleration was hard-fought for in the seventeenth century and by no means inevitable.[10] Now, when intolerance is once more prevalent and notions of truth increasingly under siege, it is timely to show the many ways skepticism manifests itself in works from the golden age of English literature. By investigating the literary fortunes of skepticism in the seventeenth century, this book contributes to current debates about the role of the arts and the humanities in fostering polities that endorse civil liberties and religious freedoms. The cultural role of art in mediating and thinking through the religious wars and political conflicts of that distant time has much to teach us, our advances in technology notwithstanding. It is therefore important – even urgent – to understand the aesthetic pleasures and ethical dilemmas incited by literary forms

---

examines the politics of skepticism in Cicero, Machiavelli, and Montaigne. See the end of Chapter 3 in this book for discussion of Oakeshott and Tuck.

[6] See Dollimore (1984), 9–29, 83–108, 163–181.

[7] See Altman (1978) who attributes the tradition of debate *in utramque partem* visible in drama to the medieval *quaestio* and before that to the Ciceronian dialogue. See Charles Schmitt (1972) for continuities between *disputatio in utramque partem* and Ramism's approach to rhetoric. See Skinner (1996) for *paradiastole*, a technique of redescription said to foster a skeptical outlook. See Cave (2009) for *antiperistasis*, a variant on oxymoron involving risky intellectual moves that gesture outward only to retreat to safety, thereby disturbing orthodoxies while retaining an orthodox appearance.

[8] On skeptical styles, see, e.g., Giocanti (2001); Minazzoli (1998).

[9] See Annas and Barnes (1985) for an elegant refutation of the conflation of skepticism with relativism (98).

[10] On the growth of toleration in the seventeenth century, see, e.g., Curley (2005); Jordan (1932–40); Levine (1999); Zagorin (2003); Zweig (1951).

Secularizing Skepticism?

conducive to skepticism. After all, it is these pleasures that help literature insinuate itself unpredictably into hearts and minds, motivating a range of social and political actions.

Studies of Renaissance skepticism have tended to neglect its devious pleasures, focusing instead on the rediscovery and circulation of skeptical texts from Antiquity; the different branches of skepticism (chiefly, Cicero's Academic skepticism versus Pyrrho's more stringent version) together with their connection to Stoicism; the influence of skepticism on the Enlightenment; and the effects of skepticism on other fields, mainly science but also historiography.[11] Literary histories of Renaissance skepticism are few and far between. Most address a single genre, usually drama thanks to its dialogic nature, or a single author, most often Montaigne or Shakespeare.[12] Surprisingly little has been written about the ways the structural problems inherent in philosophical skepticism affect the lives and texts of a range of literary figures, as they seek to address its challenges.[13] This book offers a new literary history of skepticism in England, centered on problems involving cognition, aesthetics, and politics. The writers discussed here – among them, Spenser, Shakespeare, Donne, Herbert of Cherbury, Cavendish, Marvell, and Milton – seldom, if ever, call themselves skeptics, but all feel compelled to engage with what the philosopher Stanley Cavell calls "the threat" or "temptation" of skepticism with its ethical and existential dilemmas.

While the book could have discussed a host of other seventeenth-century English playwrights, prose writers, poets, and political theorists famous for their skeptical stances toward the world, I have limited my scope to texts that I believe best illustrate key topics that remain under-theorized as regards skepticism. Hence, each chapter deals with a particular topic, problem, or cluster of problems, attendant on skepticism.

---

[11] See, e.g., Floridi (2002); Hamlin (2001); Matytsin (2016), especially 1–36, 233–274; Rosin (1997) surveys the sources of skeptical thought in his second chapter, noting that "if one had no access to the prime sources for information on classical skepticism, Erasmus's edition of Galen certainly could provide the basic tenets of the position" (75). Charles Schmitt (1972) traces the influence of Cicero's *Academica* from Antiquity through the sixteenth century, noting how it wanes after the publication of the writings of Sextus Empiricus (73–77); Smith and Charles (2017), especially 103–124.

[12] See, e.g., Aggeler (1998); Millicent Bell (2002); Bradshaw (1987) analyzes "the exploratory, interrogative effect of Shakespeare's perspectivism" (x); John D. Cox (2007); Demonet and Legros (2004); Engle (2000); Hamlin (2005, 2014); Hiley (1992); Hillman (2007); Kellogg (2015); Kuzner (2016); Pierce (1993); Lauren Robertson (2016); Sherman (2007); Srigley (2000); Strier (2000).

[13] Exceptions include Bredvold (1934) with his sensitive treatment of Dryden; Caldwell (2016); Spolsky (2001); Wiley (1952).

These include (1) engagements with nominalism, (2) fantasies of private language, (3) illusions of neutrality, (4) parodies of sovereignty, and (5) exercises in aesthetic discrimination. The chapters are organized chronologically, opening with Edmund Spenser's translations of Du Bellay (1569) and closing with Andrew Marvell's *Poems* (1681). Although each of the chapters can be read independently, reading them sequentially helps highlight recurrent threads that weave the book's argument. One thread is skepticism's tempestuous relationship with language, enamored of its baroque multiplicity, jealously questing for its truth, but checked by disappointment. Hear the absurd *cri de coeur* of Shakespeare's misanthrope, Timon of Athens: "Let ... language end" (5.2.105)! Another recurrent thread is the skeptical attraction to the sublime – that overwhelming experience of awe and dread inspired by the vastness of the unknown. Attracted to objects and encounters that defy understanding, the skeptical seeker (*zetetikos*) is transported by complex emotions, feeling at once incapable and exalted, ignorant and superbly inventive.[14] Intertwined with these divergent preoccupations – the skeptical appropriation of the nominalist desire for a science of language fitted to experience and the emotional susceptibility to the sublime – a third thread recurs throughout these pages: a heightened attention to beauty following from the skeptic's obsession with unreliable appearances. In Herbert of Cherbury's case, this beauty is figured in idealized terms: a harmonious unity, proto-Kantian in its disinterested autonomy. In Marvell's case, by contrast, beauty is figured in the myriad fluctuations of the everyday.[15] Either way, the skeptic's attention to beauty leads to questions of aesthetic

---

[14] The reemergence of the category of the sublime in early modernity has elicited reams of erudite commentary, much of which centers on exploring the sublime as an aesthetic and experiential hallmark of modernity. Robert Doran (2015), for example, claims that the discourse of the sublime contributes to secularization in the early modern period inasmuch as "the sublime is a bourgeois appropriation of aristocratic subjectivity," serving "to exalt the bourgeois individual through the aesthetic" (20). Patrick Cheney (2018) argues that the classical sublime is integral to the formation of the modern author. Cheney shows that Longinus's *On the Sublime* (ca. first century AD) had a widespread influence long before its mid-seventeenth-century translations into the vernacular (9–15). Adapting David Sedley's work (2005) on the skeptical sublime, Cheney's analyses of Marlowe and Spenser disclose how the mind's "titanic struggle with doubt" issues in "sublime authorship" (107). For an insightful taxonomy of the sublime, structured around Longinus, Edmund Burke, Immanuel Kant, and Jean-François Lyotard, see forthcoming work by Patrick Gray (n.d.). The structural affinity of the sublime and skepticism is evident in the following definition: "The sublime is the sudden and unsettling experience of the contingency of one's own frameworks of meaning and understanding" (Porter 2016, 140).

[15] Adapting Ernst Cassirer's analysis (1932), Luc Ferry (1993) dubs these two approaches 'rationalist' and 'sentimental,' arguing that this opposition defines the history of aesthetics from its beginnings in the seventeenth century.

discernment. By tracing an intellectual arc from nominalism to aesthetic taste and exploring the political quandaries attached to skeptical doubt, these chapters endeavor to capture the skeptical pulse at the heart of modernity.

My goal is to transmit a sense of the complexity of skepticism, the way its many facets influence conditions of human possibility represented in literature: fantasies of intimacy and experiences of loneliness, theories of language and ideals of governance, notions of mind and norms of conduct, ideas of war and worship, God and the supernatural, nature and nurture, as well as rules for judgment and aesthetic evaluation. My historical approach – a combination of intellectual history and literary analysis – does not preclude competing, modern philosophical views of skepticism. Philosophers and theorists like Giorgio Agamben, Roland Barthes, Hans Blumenberg, Stanley Cavell, Martin Heidegger, Charles Taylor, and Ludwig Wittgenstein, among others, figure in these pages because they themselves address the upheavals and innovations of seventeenth-century Europe in addition to illuminating the ideas and texts under discussion.

Yet, before embarking on this endeavor, I need to define skepticism and address its contingent relation to secularization. These terms are often discussed in isolation from one another, while sometimes they are treated interchangeably as each purports to explain the same phenomenon – modernity – but from a different vantage point. I hope to dispel misunderstandings by offering historically respectful definitions that defamiliarize each term. Then I offer an overview of each chapter. The definitions and overview will help clear a path for analysis of key sixteenth- and seventeenth-century texts.

**

What is meant by skepticism? At a minimum – and as an initial working definition – skepticism means a commitment to inquiry through a process of questioning. As John Donne memorably puts it in "Satire III", "Doubt wisely, in strange way / To stand inquiring right, is not to stray" (77–78). This skeptical stance often translates into the perspectivism mentioned earlier whereby conflicting viewpoints are juxtaposed in a bid to understand difference. In Renaissance writers skepticism often manifests itself in affection for techniques that destabilize visual perception and for paradoxes and puzzles that dislodge the certainties of the "dogmatists."[16] Despite this

---

[16] On Renaissance paradox, see Colie (1966).

fondness for cerebral games, skepticism involves humility before the mysteries of the universe and other people, often expressed through protestations of ignorance and an anti-intellectual suspicion of academic learning and rationality.

I complicate this definition in several ways. First, I include medieval antecedents, thereby emphasizing historical continuities. Until recently the scholarly consensus was that Renaissance skepticism burst onto the European scene thanks to the publication in 1562 of Henri Estienne's Latin translation of the Greek *Outlines of Skepticism* by Sextus Empiricus, a second-century philosopher and compiler of ancient skeptical lore. But, as Henrik Lagerlund (2009) declares, "we now know that this is wrong and that the history of skepticism must be rewritten" (1). Lagerlund points out that Cicero's *Academica* circulated widely throughout the Middle Ages, as did Augustine's refutation, *Contra Academicos* (10). Furthermore, a translation of Sextus was made in the late thirteenth century.[17] By the late fourteenth century, several manuscripts of Sextus were available – presumably the source of the skeptical arguments confuted in the first three books of Gianfrancesco Pico della Mirandola's 1520 *Examen Vanitatis*.[18] Lagerlund shows that skeptical problems preoccupied thinkers throughout the Middle Ages, especially in the late thirteenth and early fourteenth centuries. For two hundred years, many European university scholars engaged with "skepticism of a much more problematic sort" than that introduced by Sextus (27). Lagerlund's findings challenge the implicit periodization separating Renaissance doubt from putative medieval piety. Yet Lagerlund sounds a note of caution: "how this is related to and had an impact on Renaissance and Early Modern skepticism is not known yet, but must be a future area of research" (1).[19] I suggest that even if medieval skepticism was resisted by Renaissance humanists and poets, medieval investigations into language and mental fictions invigorated the poetic creativity of Renaissance humanists, contributing to their exuberant flights of linguistic imagining as well as to their philosophical thought.

---

[17] See Wittwer (2016). [18] See Floridi (2002).
[19] Lagerlund echoes Schmitt (1972, 197): "A major question, which to the best of my knowledge has not been faced, is: 'What influence did this nominalistic tendency toward skepticism have in the Renaissance?'" (9). For Lagerlund, the influence, if it exists, hinges on "largely unstudied" commentaries to Aristotle's *Posterior Analytics* (27). Cf. Pasnau (2013) on the neglected importance of the *Posterior Analytics*.

A few intellectual historians have also challenged the standard narrative of origins and emergence attached to skepticism and centered on Sextus. Less cautious than historians of philosophy about drawing connections, they have had no qualms asserting that late medieval skepticism is a precursor of early modern skepticism. In Louis Dupré's account of European intellectual history, for example, the signal event triggering modernity is nominalism. Following Etienne Gilson, Dupré argues that nominalism inaugurates "the fragmentation of the ontotheological synthesis" of the high Middle Ages such that the orders of nature and grace become separated (1993, 11).[20] The separation of nature in turn permits the cultivation of scientific curiosity. As Michael Gillespie puts it, Francis Bacon "confronts and accepts the nominalist vision of the world and attempts to find a solution to its fundamental problems" (2008, 39). In this view, nominalism enables skepticism, which prompts an attention to method focused on the observation of facts; this leads to empiricism and science. Similarly, Hans Blumenberg declares, "Only after nominalism had executed a sufficiently radical destruction of the humanly relevant and dependable cosmos could the mechanistic philosophy of nature be adopted as the tool of self-assertion" (1983, 151).[21]

Historians of philosophy tend to balk at these sweeping generalizations. William Courtenay (2008) goes so far as to deny that there was a nominalist school, while Katherine Tachau (1982) argues that William of Ockham – the theologian most often invoked by intellectual historians as the preeminent nominalist – had very little influence, his ideas barely circulating outside his Oxford college.[22] While these scholars are surely right that *grands récits* premised on continuity are as difficult to prove as those premised on rupture – especially given the tendency among early modern thinkers to revile and ridicule the scholastics – it stands to reason that differing philosophical viewpoints may have subsisted side by side,

---

[20] Like Dupré, who mourns the passing of Aquinas's ontotheological synthesis, Toulmin suffers from nostalgia for "Cosmopolis," attributing the demise of the concept of "an overall harmony between the order of the heavens and the order of human society," not to nominalism, but to other factors, among them, Descartes' method as well as the assassination of Henri IV in 1610 (1990, 67).

[21] Other intellectual historians linking nominalism and Renaissance skepticism include Funkenstein (1986), Gregory (2012), Oberman (1960, 1963, 1974) and Rosin (1997, 47–78). See Chapter 4 for further discussion of Blumenberg.

[22] But see Normore on the seventeenth-century interest in medieval nominalism as shown in, e.g., Obadiah Walker's *Artis Rationalis ad mentem Nominalium* (1673) and Johannes Salabert's *Philosophia Nominalium Vindicata* (1651) (2017, 122–123). See also Biard who observes that debates about mental language persisted well into the sixteenth century and beyond, noting that Leibniz in 1670 "praises 'the nominalist sect, the most profound of all the scholastics, and the most consistent with the spirit of our modern philosophy'" (2014, 673).

occasionally mingling, despite the polarizing postures taken. As Calvin Normore suggests, many sixteenth-century thinkers adopted nominalist positions without giving credit to nominalism's "founding fathers," even as some tried to reconcile conflicting views (2017, 128).[23] Hence, my efforts in this book to backdate skepticism, giving late medieval thinkers a role in introducing some of the questions that fascinate early modern writers.

Second, my understanding of skepticism goes beyond perspectivism and inquiry by showing the spectrum of emotions – from paralysis to passion – resulting from susceptibility to skeptical doubt. Here Stanley Cavell's definition of skepticism is useful because it reinstates a narrative of rupture with respect to emotion. He contrasts the despairing, hyperbolical tenor of modern skepticism inaugurated by Descartes with the healing tranquility offered by Sextus and other Pyrrhonists. Cavell thinks of skepticism as a psychological worldview: "the human disappointment with human knowledge" (1979, 44). This approach allows him to define skepticism as "dissatisfactions with finitude" involving "an idea of life as inadequate to the demands of spirit" (2005, 44). He argues that what distinguishes modern skepticism from its earlier, Stoic manifestations is that "skepticism is a function of our now illimitable desire" (2003, 3). It produces a way of inhabiting the world, full of yearning for ideals and absolutes issuing from frustration with things as they are. "Skepticism is not," Cavell elaborates, "the discovery of an incapacity in human knowing but of an insufficiency in acknowledging what in my world I think of as beyond me, or my senses" (2005, 22). That insufficiency in acknowledging the beyond can manifest itself in attitudes of avoidance – averting the gaze from, say, the demands of love – or in wild longing. "A passionate utterance," he notes, "is an invitation to improvisation in the disorders of desire" (2005, 19). Extreme desire issues from the limitations of acknowledgment. While investigating skepticism's moods in art, Cavell posits that "if tragedy is the working out of a scene of skepticism, then comedy in contrast works out a festive abatement of skepticism, call it an affirmation of existence" (2005, 26). The role of genre in expressing or abating skepticism is crucial to his philosophical literary criticism.

Cavell recognizes that his post-Cartesian approach to skepticism, rocked as it is by emotion, marks a sea-change from the approach of the ancients

---

[23] Of "the cursus of sixteenth-century Nominalism," Normore says, "the story begins in semantics and ends in theology and ecclesiastical politics" (2017, 130). He adds of the *via Nominalium*, "Many of its views, however, lived on, and many of its characteristic theses appear in the work of scholastics and *novatores* alike and played a central role in shaping the philosophy and the physics of the seventeenth century" (133).

with their avowed therapeutic goals. In his *Outlines of Scepticism* Sextus Empiricus, a physician, declares, "The aim of Sceptics is tranquillity in matters of opinion and moderation of feeling in matters forced upon us" (1.xii.30). "Tranquillity," he explains, "is freedom from disturbance or calmness of soul" (1.iv.10). It helps one cope with "the rashness of the Dogmatists" (1.x.20). Tranquility (*ataraxia*) is attained, Sextus argues, through the equipollence (*isostheneia*) achieved thanks to the suspension of judgment (*epoché*). Suspended judgment, he adds, "is a standstill of the intellect, owing to which we neither reject nor posit anything" (1.iv.10). Hence his definition of skepticism: "an ability to set out oppositions among things which appear and are thought of in any way at all, an ability by which, because of the equipollence in the opposed objects and accounts, we come first to suspension of judgment and afterwards to tranquillity" (1.iv.8). Sextus goes on to offer techniques for setting up balanced oppositions, crediting these to his skeptical predecessors, among them Aenesidemus.

The Modes of Aenesidemus, with their aim of inducing emotional calm, have a distinguished genealogy, going as far back as Plato. They are critical to Renaissance writers, who use them in examples and figures of speech to attack the faculty of judgment and to point out flaws in the human sensorium. Montaigne, for one, is especially attracted to the tenth mode relating to variations in custom and law as he thinks through the contingency of social and doctrinal arrangements in his war-torn France. Seeking to demonstrate how skeptics "oppose custom to custom," Sextus observes that "Ethiopians tattoo their babies, while we do not" and "Indians have sex with women in public, while most other people hold that it is shameful" (1.xiv.148). Similarly, as regards law, "we say that in Persia homosexual acts are customary, while in Rome they are forbidden by law" (1.xiv.152). The point is that confronted with these opposed state of affairs, the skeptic must perforce suspend judgment, unable to know what is right or natural. A comparable dilemma obtains with perception.[24] The five senses are unreliable in furnishing truthful data about the world. "When we have stared for a long time at the sun and then bend over a book, we think that the letters are golden and moving around" (1.xiv.45), Sextus writes, seizing on the skeptical problem of the after-image even as he echoes Lucretius' famous image of the dust motes whirling in sunlight like atoms and letters (*elementa*).[25] The mutability of visual phenomena gives rise to a set of much-quoted examples like the bent stick or the dove's

---

[24] See Clark (2007), chapter 8, especially 271–280.   [25] *De rerum natura* II.114–128.

neck with its iridescent plumage (1.xiv.119–120).²⁶ These come from the fifth mode, "the one depending on positions and intervals and places," which details the shifting appearances, not only of the oar and the feathers, but also of the colonnade, the boat, and the tower that appears round from a distance but square close at hand (1.xiv.118). These tropes resurface in unexpected ways and places – in Marvell's "Garden" where "like a bird," his soul "waves in its plumes the various light," or in *A Midsummer Night's Dream* when Theseus describes the "tricks" of "strong imagination" when "in the night, imagining some fear, / How easy is a bush supposed a bear" (V.i.22–23).²⁷ Again, the point is that, given perceptual variability and human difference, it is wisest to suspend judgment.

Third, my analysis of skepticism insists on the range of social, economic, and political affiliations produced by skeptical sympathies. Taken together, the following sketches of two self-described skeptics from the mid-seventeenth century illustrate the sociological complexity of skepticism and the way it confounds current expectations of religious and political alignments. The sketches also illustrate the difference between what we might call first-wave and second-wave skepticism. William Walwyn (1600–1681), a leader of the Levellers and canny politician, was an avowed admirer of Montaigne, citing the *Essayes* in his own political and religious writings. As a partisan of Montaigne with his emphasis on deceptive appearances and the variability of custom, Walwyn exemplifies first-wave skepticism with its focus on doubt and the inability to achieve certainty. Knowing no foreign languages thanks to an irregular education and early apprenticeship as a "weaver" (2), he was an autodidact who read widely in translation. His library favored "humanist, particularly sceptical writings, ancient and modern" that included Plutarch, Seneca, Lucian, Machiavelli, Montaigne, and Charron. These "sceptical and humane authors," Nigel Smith (1992) explains, helped Walwyn "arrive at a unique radical religious and political position" that envisioned "toleration for the sake of a complete liberty of conscience" (145). Although Walwyn was a deeply religious man, devoted to Scripture, his radical beliefs earned him enemies and six months' imprisonment. From jail in 1649 he exhorted his persecutors to read Montaigne's "Apology for Raymond Sebond" and "Of Cannibals," saying: "Go to this honest Papist, or to these innocent Cannibals, ye Independent Churches, to learn civility, humanity, simplicity of heart;

---

[26] See Plato; Cicero; Lucretius; reprised by Sextus and again by Augustine, among others. See Annas and Barnes (1985).
[27] For the ludic effects of skeptical tropes, see, e.g., Darmon (2015) on Cyrano de Bergerac.

yea, charity and Christianity" (1989, 400). Walwyn suggests that exposure to Montaigne's skepticism will lead to Christian compassion. He is interested in skepticism as a means of achieving an inclusive and ethical society rather than as a methodological tool for managing knowledge, demarcating the little that can be known from the vastness of the unknown.

Although chronologically contemporary with Walwyn, Joseph Glanvill (1636–1680) exemplifies second-wave skepticism with its Baconian emphasis on skeptical questioning as an empirical tool enabling the discovery of nature's secrets.[28] Instead of dwelling on the futility of investigating deceptive appearances as a Montaignean might do, Glanvill and his experimentalist cohort – including such luminaries as Robert Boyle, author of (among other things) *The Sceptical Chymist: Or, Chymico-Physical Doubts & Paradoxes* (1661) – insist on observation as a means to an end, namely ascertaining the truth behind appearances. A Fellow of the Royal Society, rector of the Abbey Church at Bath, prebendary of Worcester and finally chaplain to Charles II, Glanvill penned tracts advocating the epistemological modesty of skepticism, among them *Scepsis Scientifica: or, Confest Ignorance, the way to Science* (1665).[29] In it he describes the infirmities of the human intellect in a Montaignean vein, lamenting that "we are as much strangers to our selves, as to the inhabitants of America" (*SS* C3). The strangeness of the self disturbs him, and he longs for "unmoved *apathy* in opinionative uncertainties." The ancient skeptics, he relates, "affected an indifferent aequipondious *neutrality* as the only means to their *Ataraxia*, and freedom from *passionate* disturbance" (*SS* 168). But despite his professed admiration for Montaigne (*SS* C3), for the neutrality of suspended judgment, and his advocacy of skepticism as an antidote to fanaticism, Glanvill is not a Montaignean in spirit. Unlike Montaigne, who derided the arrogance and cruelty of witch hunts, Glanvill believed in witchcraft and defended his convictions in *A Blow at Modern Sadducism* (1668) and *Sudducismus Triumphatus* (1681). His skepticism compassed faith in things unseen, meaning not only a celestial realm inhabited by angels but also an invisible dimension swayed by Satanic forces. His insistence that the mysteries of nature should inspire a cautionary, skeptical doubt about the

---

[28] Others prefer to call this "mitigated" or "constructive" skepticism. See, e.g., Hamlin (2005, 107–108); Larmore (1998, 1155–1164); Popkin (2003, 132–154); Van Leeuwen (1963).

[29] "For the prepossessions of *sense* having (as is shewen) so mingled themselves with our Genuine Truths, and being as plausible to appearance as they; we cannot gain a true assurance of any, but by suspending our assent from all, till the deserts of each, discover'd by a strict enquiry, claim it" (*SS* 55).

structures of reality led him to stake all on the dense population of the supernatural world.[30]

These examples attest to the appeal of skepticism across social class. While Glanvill courted the aristocracy, frequenting elite intellectual circles, Walwyn, by contrast, styled himself a man of the people, engaging in radical politics that included widening the franchise. As regards social divisions, it is worth remembering Keith Thomas's observations about the records of the ecclesiastical courts, among other sources. Thomas surmises that skepticism – defined, for him, as indifference or hostility to established religion manifested in heterodox beliefs – was alive among the rural populace of England and not only among educated people or city-dwellers with access to the bookstalls at Paul's Cross (1971, 159–173).

These examples may suggest that I will proceed like those early modern readers who worked through contradictory passages of Scripture by tabulating examples – *in bono et in malo*.[31] While it may be tempting to classify Walwyn as a good skeptic and Glanvill as a bad one, my concern is not with passing judgment on authors, but rather with showing how skeptical sympathies are translated into the pleasures of art. Yet the question remains: does skepticism have a dark side? For some, the answer is an unequivocal no.[32] For them, skepticism means enlightenment and a tradition of critique that ushers in liberalism and democracy. For others, the verdict on skepticism is mixed; disenchantment, anomie, passivity, and weakness follow in its wake, together with an abandonment of civic responsibility. Yet often, feelings of smallness, ignorance, and uncertainty flip over, by way of compensation perhaps, and become transformed through writing. Skeptical doubt may then induce literary experiences of sublime grandeur, demands for perfection, dreams of alternate worlds, brainy thought-experiments, and other assertions of selfhood. These imaginative forays into counter-factual conditions have aesthetic consequences and political repercussions that the following chapters explore.

**

What is meant by secularization? Although the following pages do not explicitly address secularization as a theme, it is nevertheless important to

---

[30] Glanvill's work on Sadducism influenced Cotton Mather, who was involved in the Salem witch trials.
[31] See Kaske (1999) on early modern Biblical reading practices.
[32] See, e.g., Sim who views skepticism as "a positive, life-enhancing attitude," promoting egalitarianism, democracy, freedom, and the generosity of philanthropy (2006, 162).

define the term at the outset because secularization is often considered a socio-political consequence of skepticism and hence persists as an implicit context for literary engagements with skepticism. After surveying a wide range of definitions, historian Peter Burke offers his "simple working definition": secularization is "the process of change from the interpretation of reality in essentially supernatural, other-worldly terms to its interpretation in terms which are essentially natural and focused on this world" (1979, 294). Similarly, theologian Harvey Cox defines it as "the loosing of the world from religious and quasi-religious understandings of itself, the dispelling of all closed worldviews, the breaking of all supernatural myths and sacred symbols," adding that "secularization simply bypasses and undercuts religion and goes on to other things" (1965, 1–2). Sometimes, as Cox's wording suggests, secularization is portrayed as an inevitable trans-historical force, on a par with Hegel's Spirit, when in fact its contingency needs to be recognized.[33] Recently, under pressure from events suggesting the compatibility of a technological society with theocratic aspirations, scrutiny of narratives of secularization has resumed. Gordon Graham, for example, shows "important empirical difficulties" in the "urbanization and industrialization" explanation of secularization, even as he dismisses the term as an invention of nineteenth-century intellectuals (2007, 34, 40). Blair Worden concedes that "secularization is a large and treacherous word," but nevertheless detects a "shift of emphasis from faith to conduct" in late seventeenth-century England in response to "the sense, across the doctrinal and ecclesiological spectrum, that the theological disputes of the interregnum had discredited religion, and that if religion were to be saved, moral reformation must take the place of doctrinal conflict" (2001, 20, 40, 39). In short, secularization is a disputed term.[34]

I address secularization because skepticism – the subject of this book – is usually assumed to be both an agent and a symptom of secularization understood as a "trend" or "general tendency" of modernity (Calhoun et al., 2011, 10). Indeed, the narrative intertwining skepticism, secularization and modernity is so well established, even entrenched, that it was

---

[33] Pankakowski (2013, 241), citing Hans Joas.
[34] The literature on secularization is vast. Sociologist Jose Casanova, for example, offers a sophisticated analysis, distinguishing "the secular" and "secularism" from "secularization," and differentiating three "subtheses" in the "theory" of secularization (Calhoun et al., 2011, 60). Philip S. Gorski gives a structural overview of the debate, arguing that secularization theory needs to be understood as "a *family* of theories of religious change" featuring "a process of religious and cultural rationalization" (2000, 141, 144). See also, e.g., Asad (2003), Bruce (2011), Taylor (2007), and Wilson (2016).

unquestioned for most of the twentieth century. Skepticism was often deemed synonymous with "disenchantment," the Weberian term associated with the so-called secularization thesis.[35] Recently, however, the new visibility of religious extremism in the heart of modern, secular states has cast doubt on this causal paradigm. The absence of skepticism among these technologically savvy religious groups has put secularists on the defensive and caused a revaluation of the historical narrative twinning skepticism with the emergence of Western modernity. Many literary historians have been quick to point out that most seventeenth-century writings – be it the poetry of George Herbert or John Milton, the religious lyrics of John Donne or the allegories of John Bunyan, not to mention innumerable sermons – are profoundly religious and out of step with the alleged *Zeitgeist* of secularization. The imaginative world of these texts is not the least bit disenchanted – devils, trials and temptations, the hope of salvation, and the conviction of sinfulness are as alive in them as in any medieval ones. For example, in his book about the prevalence of belief in angels, Joad Raymond declares of John Locke and Margaret Cavendish, "These late seventeenth-century writings do not indicate a process of secularization" (2010, 12). Yet Raymond admits on the next page that although he contests "some versions of the narrative of the disappearance of angels," he does not offer "an alternative narrative of transition" (13). Somehow, angels dropped out of literary and philosophical discourse, he concedes, but secularization wasn't why. The case of Glanvill, a skeptic with a stout belief in angels, suggests that skepticism wasn't why either. Yet skepticism, properly understood, supplements and complicates narratives of secularization and disenchantment thanks both to its dim view of rationality and its entangled relation to belief.

As Brian Cummings has argued, modern understandings of secularity have simplified our view of the past, setting up stark oppositions between religion and the secular, the sacred and the profane, when in fact, "both in the past and in our own society, the secular and the religious ... intersect in creative and profound ways" (2013, 3, 4–5). Ditto with skepticism: intersectional and creative. Misunderstandings arise, Cummings observes, in part because the secular is attached to *grands récits* that elicit suspicion: not only Max Weber's disenchantment thesis, but also Jacob Burckhardt's rise of the individual, Nietzsche's pronouncements about the death of

---

[35] See *Die Entzauberung* in Max Weber, "Science as a Vocation." The concept of disenchantment has also been contested and reappraised; see, e.g., Bennett (2001) discussed at the start of Chapter 5; Bilgrami (2014); Walsham (2008).

God, and Heidegger's nostalgia for a pre-technological age. Sjoerd Griffioen has recently looked at three of these *grands récits* – by Hans Blumenberg, Peter Berger, and Marcel Gauchet. Arguing that secularization qualifies as an "essentially contested concept," a phrase coined by Walter B. Gallie to describe "normative, open-ended concepts on which universal agreement cannot be attained," Griffioen claims that each narrative should be understood, not as an objective history, but as a *Geistesgeschichte*, "a speculative history with a moral" belonging to "'the critique-of-modernity' tradition" (2015, 186–187). Analyzing the work of Blumenberg, Berger, and Gauchet, he believes, will illuminate the contemporary debate about secularism, exposing its assumptions.

In his overview of the secularization debate, Griffioen identifies two major positions: the proponents of post-secularism (a term launched by Jürgen Habermas) who observe that religion is not going away, given the increased visibility of religion in politics, and the defenders of what Charles Taylor calls "subtraction stories," that is, theories that see Weberian disenchantment as a good thing liberating the mind from the shackles of superstition and obscurantism. Subtraction stories, which are premised on a notion of enlightenment that involves the casting off of religion as an oppressive ideology, date at least as far back as Herbert of Cherbury and his conspiratorial views of ancient Egyptian priestcraft. Post-secularists have a more benign take on religion than subtractionists, arguing that "modernity came into being *through* Christianity rather than in spite of it" (2015, 189). As Griffioen puts it, "All post-secularist accounts share in the conceptual problematization of 'secularization' and argue that it should no longer be perceived as an inevitable process or the simple overcoming of religion by the evaporation of a collective illusion" (2015, 189).

Kathleen Davis takes a more combative approach to secularization, arguing that the secularization thesis is a mystified narrative with an ideological agenda that, in turn, rests on and consolidates yet another mystified narrative, namely, the periodization dividing the Middle Ages from modernity. As she puts it, "theories of modernity rely upon the legitimacy of secularization to shore up the period divide" (2008, 6–7). Taking aim at theorists as diverse as Johannes Fabian, Antonio Negri, Reinhard Koselleck, and Dipesh Chakrabarty, Davis proceeds to delegitimize secularization in an effort to dismantle the medieval / modern divide. Both are belated constructions, she points out, imputing different temporalities to epochal mind-sets, thereby unwittingly abetting imperialist designs and justifications for social violence. As she succinctly says, "the claim to separate out the 'religious' from the 'secular' is above all a bid for sovereignty" (2008, 78). Davis's chief complaint against this intellectual history is that it forecloses possibilities, especially much-needed "rethinking of sovereignty" as well as "new political forms and alternate temporalities" (2008, 81, 96).[36]

The resurgence of political theology in early modern studies also takes up the secularization thesis. Political theology explores the transfer of theological concepts to the political realm, especially the way this transfer affects the vexed issue of sovereignty.[37] Indeed, the rhetoric of transfer opens a key question – how best to describe the linguistic carry-over from theology to politics? Is it best to speak of a residual trace, an unconscious analogy, a structural resemblance or homology, a transposition, a strategic appropriation, historical mimicry, or a functional reoccupation of now-empty metaphors? In studying the political fiction of the king's two bodies, Ernst Kantorowicz noted that English jurists "unconsciously rather than consciously" borrowed theological ideas, taking the mystery of "the Two Natures of the God-man" and adapting this duality to definitions of kingship (1957, 19). Kantorowicz understood this process of transfer and analogy as one of unconscious adaptation.[38] In his *Political Theology*, Carl Schmitt declared that "all significant concepts of the modern state are secularized theological concepts," adding that "the exception in jurisprudence is analogous to the miracle in theology" (1985, 36). Yet, in his *Legitimacy of the Modern Age* (1966), Hans Blumenberg, the philosopher of culture, disagrees, objecting to the methodological bias toward continuities, as if modernity were no more than an extension of the Middle Ages, dressing up old concepts in new clothes. Blumenberg contends that Schmitt mistakes "analogies," "metaphorical borrowings" and other forms of "historical mimicry" for "transformations." He insists that Schmitt's sovereign decision "is not the secularization of the *creation ex nihilo*," arguing that political theology simplifies the complexities of secularization. Instead, Blumenberg proposes that we analyze texts using "reoccupation"

---

[36] My objection to Davis's analysis is twofold. The first is that she slants her definition of secularization as "a break with the sacred" because she needs the rhetoric of rupture (which she decries) to level her attack (2008, 81). (Brian Cummings does the same.) The second is that like Karl Löwith and before him Wilhelm Dilthey and Hegel, she sees secularization as endorsing a prescriptive notion of progress that construes time as a quasi-eschatological script.

[37] See, e.g., Hammill and Lupton (2012); the 2018 issue of the *Journal of Early Modern Cultural Studies* devoted to "the varieties" of political theology; Kahn (2014). Funkenstein considers the impact on science of the secularization of theology, writing of "the *dialectical* anticipation of a new theory by an older, even adverse, one; and the *transplantation* of existing categories to a new domain – employing them under a new perspective" (1986, 14).

[38] One important subset of these German secularization narratives addresses the political theology of early modern England, inasmuch as Shakespeare and Hobbes serve as key examples.

(*Umbesetzung*) and "metaphorology" as ways of dealing with linguistic continuities in the face of political changes like secularization. Rather than thinking in terms of systems, he suggests we take a case-by-case approach, looking at "the requirements of the situation in which the choice is being made" (93).[39]

These disagreements about secularization and its relation to skepticism should not cause us to abandon the term secular; rather, they should prompt us to use it with more sensitivity to its historical nuances. Secular derives from *saeculum*, the Latin for century, age, or epoch. Early in the history of Christianity, it served to distinguish parish clergy, who worked in the world's time, from those who cloistered themselves and devoted their lives to prayer and thoughts of eternity. Secular thus denoted a lay ministry, a form of religiosity reaching out to the world. Peter Burke points out that it carried "pejorative overtones in the Middle Ages ... the idea being that monks were the true 'religious,' while parish priests were mere 'secular' clergy" (1979, 295). Although hardly a cloistered monk, Martin Luther also uses it pejoratively, associating the secular with the sword and contrasting it with the kingdom of God. "God has ordained the two governments," Luther explains in 1523, "the spiritual, which by the Holy Spirit under Christ makes Christians and pious people, and the secular [*weltlich*] which restrains the unchristian and wicked so that they must needs keep the peace outwardly, even against their will. So Paul interprets the secular sword" (1961, 370). For Luther and for Calvin, secular authority – or temporal authority, depending on the translation of *weltlich* – includes the church along with the state, as it too is a worldly institution with disciplinary powers.

When Milton speaks of "secular chains" in Sonnet 16, he is attacking the overweening reach of established religion and arguing for the separation of church and state. While "secular chains" may seem like an oxymoron given current associations of the secular with liberty, the phrase makes sense when we remember that Parliament in 1641 drafted an Act for Removal of Ecclesiastics from Secular Office (16 Car. 1, c.27), which said that "bishops and other persons in holy orders ought not to be entangled with secular jurisdiction, the office of the ministry being of such importance that it will take up the whole man; and for that it is found by long experience that their intermeddling with secular jurisdiction hath

---

[39] See my Chapter 4 for Blumenberg's concept of reoccupation in relation to the skepticism of Margaret Cavendish.

occasioned great mischiefs and scandal."[40] A decade later, the specter of a state church had not been laid to rest. When Milton sent his sonnet to Oliver Cromwell in May 1652, he wanted Cromwell to oppose any settlement that would impose religious uniformity. Milton urges Cromwell to resist "new foes ... threatening to bind our souls with secular chains." The closing couplet confirms the cruelty of these secular foes: "Help us to save free Conscience from the paw / Of hireling wolves whose Gospel is their maw." The wolves are "the clergy who on March 29, 1652 asked Parliament to establish the English Church on broad Protestant principles but with a State-salaried and State-controlled ministry" (1957, 160–161). Milton (along with Roger Williams, Sir Henry Vane and others) hated the idea of a state church. He rejected Luther's endorsement of the church as a disciplinary institution because he prized liberty of worship.

While these examples show that in the sixteenth and seventeenth centuries the adjective secular was used differently from our current parlance, they nevertheless reveal a feature that continues to be crucial to our understanding of the term: its jurisdictional force. Secular by definition demarcates an area or space apart from the spiritual.[41] Although the contours of this jurisdictional difference may vary with place and time – and, as the examples above illustrate, may occur within a given religion's purview – secular operates in opposition to another kind of jurisdictional sphere, often understood as one more private and personal like conscience. The intangible sense of faith underwriting membership in the invisible church or, as Luther might put it, in the kingdom of heaven, functions as the counterpart and contrary of membership in the visible church. This results in some slippage, as the secular is opposed to the inviolability of a person's interior space and thus becomes mapped onto a public / private distinction. (We see this in Milton's case.) Hence, the widespread view that secularization at once produces and constitutes the privatization of religion.[42]

---

[40] Cited in Sommerville (1992, 121).
[41] See Christiaan van Adrichem's account of spaces in the Temple at Jerusalem, the entry to which is described as the "Holy Secular": "THE IEWES ILE. The which also is called the *Entery*, the *Haule*, the *Holy Secular*, & *Solomon's Porch*, being the thirde parte of the temple" (1595, 46).
[42] But see Gorski who, instead of singling out jurisdiction as the key structural feature of secularization, focuses on differentiation, de-differentiation and re-differentiation: "If secularization is defined as the differentiation of religious and nonreligious roles and institutions, the centuries after the Reformation can actually be seen as an era of radical *de*-secularization. This raises an important question: If the Reformation led to de-differentiation, how are we to explain the *re*-differentiation that followed?" (2000, 159).

In his comprehensive account of secularization in early modern England, C. John Sommerville shows how faith intensified in the private sphere even as public spaces became increasingly secular; individual spirituality expanded even as sacred space shrank. For Sommerville, Henry VIII's jurisdictional power play triggers the foundational event in the secularization of England: his dissolution of the monasteries and redistribution of church property. This was accompanied by the suppression of what Sommerville calls "a polycentric if not polytheistic religion" (1992, 25). Shrines, holy wells, and sacred trees were prohibited as centers of devotion, along with pilgrimages to wonder-working relics or images. As Sommerville explains, "Under the more consistent monotheism of Protestantism, the area of the sacred narrowed" (1992, 73). The state-sponsored mandate to limit worship to designated buildings diminished the jurisdiction of the church and expanded that of the state. In the 1590s, jurisdictional struggles also played out in the court system.[43] Litigation against alleged abuses of the *ex officio* oath resulted in curtailing the jurisdiction of the ecclesiastical courts and expanding that of the common law courts. As Sir Edward Coke noted, commenting on a set of complaints issued by the bishops in 1605, "the humour of the time is growne to be too eager against all ecclesiastical jurisdiction" (Brooks, 2008, 114).

The use of space inside churches also changed, as activities bearing on the life of the community but not specifically on worship had to find other venues. Sommerville notes that "the alehouse or tavern assumed a new prominence as feasts, fraternity meetings, pageants, ales, and games were banished from the church" (1992, 139). While this reverential attitude to ecclesiastical space was intended to enhance spirituality, in the long run it contributed to secularization, as the effect was to sequester religion from ordinary life. The consequences of stipulating *adiaphora* were also paradoxical. The effort to separate indifferent things (such as ceremonies) from essentials in matters of worship participated in the jurisdictional impulse of secularization, the idea in this case being to narrow down the points of doctrine over which to fight. What began as an effort to mediate confessional conflict by finding common ground ended up isolating an inoffensive set of core principles and reducing the varieties of religious expression.

When scholars like Sommerville speak of the "paradoxes" of secularization, they often mean that the Reformation, despite the zeal of its proponents and often because of it, contributed unwittingly to the demise of religiosity. Peter Burke counts among "the unintended consequences" of

---

[43] See Brooks (2008), chapter 5.

the Reformation, and especially of its religious conflicts, "the revival of secular philosophies" like skepticism, Stoicism, and Epicureanism (1979, 299). Charles Taylor adds "exclusive" humanism to the list, following from deism (2007, 19, 27), while Ada Palmer sees deism following "the inadvertent secularizing seeds planted by humanists" (2017, 967). Brad Gregory argues that the Protestant emphasis on religious liberty has the unintended consequence of prizing "the right to religious unbelief" (2012, 188), while Michael McKeon locates the "paradox" of secularization in its "structural instability" (1987, 65, 87). Starting with Löwith's idea that secularization "may imply a faithful accommodation or translation of the sacred to the profane world," McKeon adds that it may also result in "mistranslation" (1983b, 206). "Reformation amounts to deformation" (1987, 65), he suggests, although eventually problems dissipate as "secularization attains the status of a relatively unquestioned good" (1983b, 206).

Gradually, the word secular begins to lose its religious associations, although this is by no means a smooth or obvious process. Not until the mid-nineteenth century did the terms "secularism" and "secularist" arise, coined by free-thinkers in response to the slur of being called atheists or infidels (Asad, 2003, 23). Thus, it is helpful when Charles Taylor isolates at least three contemporary meanings of secular. The first two – "secularized public spaces" (which can encompass social media, political institutions like Congress, or gathering places like Tahrir Square) and "the decline of belief and practice" – are widely acknowledged (2007, 20). Hence, he focuses on what it means to experience "secularity 3" whereby belief in God is "one option among others," this plurality of possibilities forming the background for the conditions of the "search for the spiritual" (2007, 3). Taylor thus shifts the terms of the so-called secularization narrative, since he sees secularity as the framework for new forms of religiosity rather than as a historical force crushing the remnants of faith.

Although I cannot single-handedly disentwine skepticism from secularization narratives, I hope to pick it loose. Skepticism's distrust of human reason and its compatibility with religious belief should weaken its connection to secularization without severing it. I am tempted to suggest – although it would be misleading – that skepticism escapes jurisdictional strictures (unlike secularization), spreading into all spheres of life. In the broadness of this claim, I would be following the lead of some language theorists regarding nominalism. Nicholas Hudson, for example, states that the "insight" achieved in the seventeenth century "that human knowledge was inseparable from the conventions of language represents a direct continuation of the logic of nominalism" (1997, 287). Christoph Bode agrees, arguing that "Ockham pointed the way that Hobbes, Berkeley and Wittgenstein were to explore later on: *the meaning is in the usage* – and therefore it can only be *made*, and it's not *there*, and it's not *stable*" (1997, 310). Similarly, Lea Formigari identifies "a thread" leading from "the semiotic logic of the Late Middle Ages all the way to the 17th-century 'scientific revolution,'" specifically to "Locke's paradigm, the starting point of modern language theories" (2004, 80).[44] However, I cannot make such sweeping claims for skepticism's eventual dominance although it may share some of nominalism's approaches, questions, and concerns.

Instead, I think the presence of skepticism in seventeenth-century English literature may offer a parallel to the privatization argument regarding faith and spirituality. Just as religiosity becomes increasingly internalized, less a matter of culture than of conscience, so skeptical doubt shifts its focus toward the end of the seventeenth century toward the private examination of subjective experience in all its phenomenological complexity. Skepticism continues to inform literary satire, of course, and through satire to criticize aspects of the public sphere. Nevertheless, skepticism can and often does retreat to an inward forum preoccupied with aesthesis. From having offered a tool for legislating among domains of discourse and knowledge pertaining to cosmology, natural philosophy, and medicine, skepticism curtails its ambitions and becomes bourgeois: intimate, if never comfortable. The path from metaphysics to taste, from skeptical thought-experiments about God to self-conscious meditations about art, is arguably analogous to the arc traced by some secularization narratives: from culture to faith or from theological dispute to moral reformation.[45] McKeon suggests as much when he traces "the momentum of historical consciousness … carrying individuals and groups through the implacable progress of skeptical thought from positivistic objectivity to solipsistic subjectivity" (1987, 87). Although only intermittently addressed in the following pages, secularization narratives shadow the literary history of skepticism offered here.[46]

**

---

[44] Ockham and Locke, Formigari observes, share the belief that universals are merely mental signs, although she concedes that Ockham's view of the universal as an *intentio* diverges considerably from Locke's view of it as a *conceptus* (2004, 81).
[45] See Sommerville (1992); Worden (2001).
[46] Although debating the merits and demerits of the secularization thesis is outside the scope of this project, I take to heart Davis's warning against eliding "a theory of history and the historical change it purports to examine" (2008, 87).

My aim, then, is to limn the contours of the skeptical literary imagination in the seventeenth century – a *mentalité* that is by definition open to non-normative thinking, although not necessarily to alternate temporalities and new political forms.[47] As William M. Hamlin notes, skepticism has a "protean ability to surface in new forms and guises," adding that "its hostility to the unexamined and its openness to the unseen rendered it both fascinating and instrumental to the literary imagination" (2005, 245–246). This book accordingly lays out a panoply of possibilities that skepticism makes available to writers, shaping their modes of thought and expression.

In Chapter 1 I investigate the synergies of skepticism and nominalism. I do this to address the scholarly lacuna regarding medieval skepticism identified by Lagerlund, but also to understand how these overlapping philosophical currents might manifest themselves in literature. Edmund Spenser is an ideal candidate for this study for several reasons. Spenser affects a late medieval style, channeling linguistic archaisms and modeling himself partly on Chaucer, an author often considered an exemplar of literary nominalism.[48] His philosophical explorations are eclectic and various in keeping with his wide-ranging intellect. While scholars have documented the influence of Neoplatonism, Epicureanism, Christian humanism, and classical skepticism on Spenser's thought, his fascination with epistemology and metaphysics also owes something to late medieval theology.[49] After all, if Spenser delights in reviving obsolete words, musty characters, and the beauties of allegory itself, might he not also enjoy renewing dated modes of philosophical discourse, whose hoary aura might go some way to mask, if not neutralize, more controversial topical associations? Consider Red Cross Knight's difficulty in distinguishing Una and Duessa: truth from falsehood. The Knight's confusion is often framed in terms of the Reformation debate about images and the role of visual experience in arriving at spiritual or transcendent truths. While it is useful to remember that the Reformation's emphasis on *sola scriptura* implies a "denigration of vision" (Knapp, 2011, 48), other discursive contexts also underwrite the shift toward a language-centered worldview. Some medieval theories of cognition were deeply suspicious of pictures in the

---

[47] Similarly, skepticism is more likely to express itself by reoccupying traditional literary forms – allegory, essay, epic, lyric, dialogue or satire – than by inventing new ones.
[48] For nominalism in Chaucer, see, e.g., Keiper (1997), Knight (1965), Peck (1978), and Utz (1995). See also Gillespie's claim that Petrarch offers "a notion of individuality that is prefigured in if not derived from nominalism" (2008, 67).
[49] Grogan observes that Spenser follows "primarily a medieval model" for the mind (2009, 81).

mind, preferring speculations about mental language (*oratio mentalis*) and posing thought-experiments about delusion, error, and after-images. Spenser's interest in questions of deception, in the limits of knowledge, in exercises of power, in counterfactual forays, and in problems of contingency coincides with the interests of medieval thinkers grappling with skepticism.

The chapter explores moments in Spenser's oeuvre when his speaker has a transient, but sublime vision of something meaningful and seemingly true: often a temple, sometimes a woman (a *madonna angelicata*) or group of female figures.[50] These visions have been interpreted variously, often as a poetic rapture aligned with a Neoplatonic ascent to eternal Forms or Ideas. Taking a different angle, I relate these visions to Heidegger's meditations on the origins of the work of art and his longing for the holism of Antiquity. Heidegger's sense that the work of art opens up a concealed world, bringing it into presence, helps us approach Spenser's own understanding of his task: specifically, the role of the artist's imagination in creating visions that mask the truth – eliciting the viewer's doubts – and yet lead to it. I also relate Spenser's dream-visions to the medieval debate about universals and particulars with its questions about the status of mental objects and the cognitive process of abstraction. While the relation of universals and particulars may strike some as a discursive context of merely antiquarian interest, the topic was relevant in Spenser's time, even more so than today when, *mutatis mutandis*, it continues to engage non-representational artists anxious to redeem their work from accusations of escapism and political apathy. Consider an abstract expressionist like Robert Motherwell (1915–1991) who, in describing the School of New York, concedes that "a dangerous tendency of such artists ... is solipsism, the idea that what is most real is what one finds to be most real in one's own mind" (2007, 94–95). Motherwell, therefore, insists on abstraction's connection to historical reality, arguing:

> The "pure" red of which certain abstractionists speak does not exist, no matter how one shifts its physical contexts. Any red is rooted in blood, glass, wine, hunters' caps, and a thousand other concrete phenomena. Otherwise we should have no feeling toward red or its relations, and it would be useless as an artistic element (55).

Sounding like a late medieval theologian parsing Aristotle's secondary qualities while negotiating the problem of universals, Motherwell asserts

---

[50] See Nohrnberg, 1976, 77.

that pure red cannot be divorced from its particular instances; its social, mineral and botanical contexts persist in our emotional faculty. Like Motherwell, but informed by his scholastic education, Spenser understands the liabilities associated with sublime visions – their tendency to awaken skepticism – and resists the charges of historical amnesia leveled against allegorical abstractions.

Thus, Spenser is not only wrestling with the towering examples of Ariosto, Tasso, and Ficino, with Calvinist theology and Ramist pedagogical reforms; philosophically, he is also working through the lingering effects of the epistemological and linguistic turn of the late Middle Ages, especially when he launches his critique of human understanding. Taking nominalism into account thus complicates Spenser's humanist attitude to skepticism. He finds inspiration not only in skeptical tropes focused on the variability of custom and the deceits of the senses, but also in late scholastic debates about how thinking works. His attention to nominalism and the problem of universals encourages a more cerebral, language-based approach to problems of representation. Perhaps Spenser's life-long meditation on the role and status of poetry acquired some of its urgency from a need to distance himself from scholastic theories of language.[51]

My Chapter 2 pursues this linguistic turn by considering the skeptic's desire for a perfect and private language. Private languages depend on ostensive definition and highlight the process of naming: the idea that a subject labels a discreet sensation with a private name and thereby creates a universe of private truths. Wittgenstein, who coined the term private language for a phenomenon with a long prior history addressed, among others, by nominalist logicians, felt it was an oxymoron since languages were by definition communal outgrowths premised on mutually agreed upon conventions. Wittgenstein's insight that the desire for private language emerges from the need to defeat skepticism informs my analysis of two metaphysical poems. Shakespeare's "The Phoenix and Turtle" and Donne's "The Ecstasy" explore fantasies of absolute intimacy between

---

[51] But see Fallon who implies that Spenser is a "realist" owing to his practice of allegory; "the layering of reality upon which allegory depends is eliminated" in nominalism, he says (1991, 177). Fallon argues that nominalism ultimately weakens allegory. By contrast, Kahn's take on allegory is suggestive of nominalism. Kahn follows Walter Benjamin in viewing allegory as "the linguistic mode that calls attention to the arbitrariness or conventionality of signification" and emphasizes the "contingent relation between material signs and their significance" (2007, 111). I think Spenser's allegories benefit from his awareness of the unstable status of mental objects in nominalism and from his allegiance to the grammars of poetic language.

lovers by entertaining the dream of a private language given the limitations and customs of speech. These poems, however, veer in different directions. Shakespeare paradoxically creates the semblance of a private language via a winged, virtuoso tour of poetic genres, while Donne finds solace for skepticism's "loneliness" (44) in the body's erotic expressions of love.

Lord Herbert of Cherbury occupies an important if anomalous position in the alternative history of skeptical problems outlined here. In *De veritate* Cherbury, attracted to Bacon's new science but constrained by his scholastic training, develops a metaphysical epistemology in his efforts to defeat skepticism. Richard Popkin, the preeminent historian of skepticism, describes Cherbury's work as "an attempted answer to the problem of knowledge raised by the sceptics, which contains an elaborate method for establishing accurate or true appearances and concepts, and then offers the Common Notions as the long-sought criterion for judging the truth of our most reliable information" (2003, 132). Popkin gives an overview of *De veritate*, pointing out flaws in argumentation, but he neither situates the work in terms of Cherbury's other writings nor does he pursue a biographical approach, investigating how Cherbury's philosophical commitments affect his political choices. I study Cherbury to further this book's exploration of the ethics and aesthetics of seventeenth-century skepticism. Chapter 3 thus focuses not only on his criteria for truth of perception (conformity and consent), but also on moments of truth in his life – especially the siege of his castle in Wales during the Civil War. It suggests that his epistemology affected his conduct at a time of crisis, arguing that Cherbury's philosophy of mind leads to aesthetic and political neutrality. The chapter proposes that neutrality follows from engagements with skepticism, a consequence seldom discussed except, for example, by Roland Barthes.

Chapter 4 argues that Margaret Cavendish's engagements with skepticism manifest themselves in rhetorical strategies of reoccupation – a term I borrow from the philosopher Hans Blumenberg who uses it to understand the way seventeenth-century thinkers coped with the unresolved questions they inherited as part of the nominalist legacy of the Middle Ages. Reoccupation is a far more aggressive way of coping with uncertainty than neutrality, as it involves the takeover of roles, tropes, plot devices, and other textual conventions deemed inadequate or hollow. My discussion of reoccupation in Cavendish follows that of neutrality in Cherbury because, despite many obvious differences, the trajectories of their lives as aristocrats and philosophers share similarities. Although Herbert came from one of England's most powerful noble families and

Margaret Lucas came from gentry, her marriage to William Cavendish, earl and later duke of Newcastle, made her identify with the aristocracy. Both suffered during the Civil Wars when their estates were sequestered and pillaged. Both were disgruntled with their sovereign, wishing that their services (William's military services as a general, in Margaret's case) had been more fully appreciated and better rewarded. Both felt entitled to participate in the philosophical discussions of the day, sending their books to the likes of Descartes and Hobbes. Both self-published their work in elegant folios that they dedicated to the universities of Oxford and Cambridge and sent to their libraries. And both cultivated their image as eccentrics: Herbert for his cantankerous personality and far-out religious ideas, Cavendish for the "singularity" of her strange outfits and her philosophical pretensions. While Herbert is often considered radical, having later been dubbed the father of deism, his secularity is less extreme than Cavendish's. Unlike Herbert, who seeks commonalities among the varieties of religious belief in an effort to secure irenic cooperation from the devout, Cavendish has the Machiavellian temerity to imagine societies where religious belief is, if not "an option" as Charles Taylor puts it (2007, 3), at best perfunctory and merely strategic.

Chapter 4 tracks Cavendish's engagements with skepticism through her textual moves – at once sincere and satirical – to reoccupy conceptual vacancies, a term adapted from Hans Blumenberg's philosophy of culture. Because Cavendish's philosophical response to the skepticism of Descartes and Hobbes has been extensively studied, the chapter focuses on reoccupation in her fiction. In *The Blazing World*, for example, Cavendish's avatars take over leadership, performing parodies of sovereignty with their capricious commands, bejeweled regalia, ecclesiastical supremacy, military might, and will to self-commemoration. Cavendish designs this novella of reoccupation – often deemed a utopia and an early foray into science fiction – as a vehicle for her responses to the work not only of Hobbes and Descartes, but also of Francis Bacon and Van Helmont, among others. Once "the new philosophy" had been assimilated, after having called all in doubt as John Donne wrote in "The Anniversaries," outer space in all its terrifying sublimity fires contemporary imaginations.[52] For some, including Cavendish, the impulse to reenchant the universe follows hard upon Descartes's bleak view of nature and matter – inert *res extensa*. Natural philosophy and metaphysical theories flourish in

---

[52] Once people "could feel secure in the post-Copernican universe," Monk observes, they begin to regard "space as an attribute of God" (1935, 1).

the wake of Descartes.[53] New translations of Lucretius compound this effect, as Lucretian atomism envisions a world pullulating with energy and deviant desire, inspiring theories of vitalist materialism.[54] While Cavendish is hardly alone in spinning fantasies of alternate worlds and interplanetary travel, she is exceptional in her overt self-representation as an author bent on reenchanting a disenchanted world. She asserts herself by reoccupying conceptual vacancies in the cosmic and philosophic landscape through skeptical literary interventions.

Chapter 5 takes up the enchanting skepticism of Andrew Marvell, arguing that his appreciation for the modes of Aenesidemus, especially their treatment of disproportion and scale, leads to the exquisite aesthetic sensibility characteristic of the man of taste. Marvell has gone down in history as "an early Whig hero" and a champion of religious toleration, taking his fight both to Parliament and to the radical underground with his anonymous, but hugely popular satirical polemics (Bardle, 2012, 61). The "great distance" Marvell travelled "from the circumspect observer of 1650" to the "gradual discovery of a fully public voice" in his final years as a politician and satirist reveal, according to McKeon, "a hard-won but permanent confidence in the powers of a 'positive' secularization, in the efficacy of human inventiveness to achieve ethical and spiritual ends" (1983b, 226). My chapter on Marvell does not end on as triumphant a note. I barely touch on Marvell's career as an embattled politician for liberty of conscience and freedom of speech because this aspect of his skepticism has been well documented elsewhere.[55] Instead of looking at the distance Marvell travelled from circumspect observer to committed MP for Hull, I track his evolving engagements with skepticism. I argue that Marvell's skepticism helps to hone an aesthetic sensibility attuned to the sublime effects of fluctuating appearances, a skeptical apprehension of the sublime that contributes to the emergent culture of taste so important in the eighteenth century. Giorgio Agamben's musings on taste support the connection I make between skepticism and aesthetics since he sees taste as "an excessive sense, situated at the very limit of knowledge and

---

[53] For example, the philosopher Anne Conway (1996) conceives a fully enchanted, baroque universe populated with myriad invisible beings, all seeking enlightenment and union with the Godhead. Christian Cabbalists and Quakers made their mark on Conway, as did the folk healer, Valentine Greatrakes known as "the stroker," whose cures Andrew Marvell went out of his way to attend (Hutton 2004).

[54] For vitalist materialism, see, e.g., Rogers (1996); Fallon (1991).

[55] See, e.g., Chernaik and Dzelzainis (1999), especially 23–74; Patterson (1978).

pleasure," explaining that "aesthetics takes as its object a knowledge that is not known" (2017, 51, 66).

While the emergence of the theorization of aesthetic experience in the late seventeenth century is widely accepted, its causes are debated.[56] Does it arise from the vogue in conduct manuals attesting to new social mobility – an outgrowth perhaps of Baldassare Castiglione's advice to courtiers that they practice *sprezzatura*? On this view, aestheticism is attached to disciplines of civility and snobbery, forming part of the behavior recommended for ambitious intellectuals and social climbers. Does it develop from a concern with decorum and proportionality – topics of long-standing interest to rhetoricians and architects? Can it be seen as evolving from Hobbes's idea of discretion? Should the French get credit for inaugurating aesthetic pronouncements with their Neoclassical views? Boileau fascinates Dryden and is a contemporary of Marvell. Or should Italian theorizations of art get precedence? The rise of aesthetics, we are told, coincides with programs of national and cultural reform whereby standards of art help define the identity of newly formed nation-states. It develops in tandem with capitalism, together with the spike in trade and circulation of consumer goods at the end of the seventeenth century.[57] Simon Gikandi has argued, for example, that the discourse of taste emerges alongside the slave trade as Europeans strive to codify aesthetic standards in order "to negate" the brutality of their commerce and regimes of repression (2011, 21).

While these accounts are convincing and valuable, they underplay skepticism's role in the development of aestheticism. Adorno and Horkheimer, however, identify this connection when they argue that skepticism is associated with urban elites who privilege interiority and creature comforts. Adorno thinks of "aesthetic nominalism" as a major force in history, associating it with "the rise of the novel" and the "progressive particularization" immanent in art (1997, 199, 201). Using Montaigne as his exemplum, Horkheimer considers "subjectivism" as an

---

[56] See, e.g. Bourdieu (1989); Largier (2009); Reiss (1997, 196); Noggle (2012); and Croce (1956): "The study of the expressive, aesthetic, linguistic faculty would, however, have found an appropriate occasion and a point of departure in the secular debate between nominalism and realism, which could not avoid touching to some extent the relations between the word and the flesh, thought and language" (178).

[57] See, e.g., McKeon (1983a, 1987); Minor (2006) on Italian theorizations of taste; Moriarty (1988) on France. Ferry distinguishes between "classical aesthetics and those of sentiment" only to observe that whether they single out reason or feeling as "the principle of the judgment of taste," both "fulfill the movement towards the subjectivization of the Beautiful begun by the classicists in the wake of Cartesianism" (1993, 45).

expression of "the bourgeois spirit" (1993, 278); he describes "action" in skepticism as "a matter of taste or a question of individual cleverness" (284), treating taste and wit as interchangeable ethical criteria unmoored from truth. While I agree with them that skepticism fosters individualism, I focus on the way it encourages a monadic phenomenology that contributes to an obsession with appearances and their shifting contours.

Because skepticism is often linked with a will to achieve depth – a desire to get to the heart of things, to understand mechanism, to dissect and anatomize, to penetrate the real or to rend the veil – it is important to understand how it can also lead to superficial pleasures and libertine diversions.[58] Fluctuations, ephemera, the play of light on a dove's neck are not merely challenges to the scientific observer, a question of accuracy in recording or empirical rigor. For some, on the contrary, attesting to the delights and subtleties of perceptual flux becomes an aesthetic goal rather than a means to a scientific end. Andrew Marvell's poetry shows how a skeptical sensibility – passionately engaged with the events of his day, never detached or careless or neutral although occasionally baffled and confused – is drawn to explorations of surface and exercises of aesthetic discrimination.

Finally, my Afterword considers the crisis of experience in *Samson Agonistes*, John Milton's sublime closet drama. Samson's uncertainties about God's plans and his difficulties interpreting his own heart capture the plight of the *viator* in a world with a *deus absconditus*. Samson craves self-knowledge and communion with God, but his desires are stymied. Baffled by his own inner promptings and unable to tolerate this opacity, he tries his strength against the columns of the temple of the Philistines. These columns are all too solid – unlike Spenser's early temples floating in mid-air before suddenly disintegrating. But like Spenser's visions, Samson's will to destroy has apocalyptic resonance. His skeptical doubts occasion a triumph of violence. This sublime ending – its atmosphere of dread and horror subdued by twisting rhetorical summations – captures the dialectic of skepticism and the sublime that is one of my recurring themes. The illegibility of individual experience – with its engaging, explosive possibilities – seems a fitting *envoi* for a book about skeptical doubt in early modern English literature.

---

[58] See, e.g., Hillman (2007); Picciotto (2010); Watson (2006), especially 18–25, 51–66.

CHAPTER I

Visionary, Interrupted
Spenser's Skeptical Artwork

With her wicked gift for communicating the feel of certain experiences, Virginia Woolf describes the "difficulty" of Edmund Spenser's poetry: "monotony. The verse becomes for a time a rocking horse; swaying up and down; a celestial rocking horse, whose pace is always rhythmical and seemly, but lulling, soporific. It sings us to sleep; it lulls the teeth of the mind." And yet, by way of compensation, Woolf explains, we discover "the sense that we are confined in one continuous consciousness, which is Spenser's; that he has saturated and enclosed this world, that we live in a great bubble blown from the poet's brain." Spenser challenges us "to think poetically," Woolf adds, although she is the first to admit this is not easy: "we are removed four hundred years from Spenser; and the effort to think back into his mood requires some adjustment, some oblivion, but there is nothing false in what is to be done" (1986, VI. 490).[1] My aim is to think back into Spenser's mood and modes of poetic consciousness by considering his philosophical moment – a transitional time characterized by a fascination with epistemological questions, that is, questions about knowledge and ways of knowing.

Spenser is obsessed with the elusiveness of knowledge, as his well-known investigations into the duplicity of appearances attests. My purpose is not to revisit the question or extent of his skepticism, epistemological, theological, political, or otherwise.[2] Instead, this chapter presents an important, but neglected, philosophical context for Spenser's doubts about the status of mental fictions that, in turn, forms part of my larger argument about skepticism's relation to language and aesthetic experience. Before

---

[1] Woolf's description of Spenser's poetry echoes Coleridge's remarks on *The Faerie Queene* (1818): "It is truly in the land of Faery, that is, of mental space. The poet has placed you in a dream, a charmed sleep, and you neither wish, nor have the power, to inquire where you are, or how you got there" (2014, 683).
[2] See, e.g., Greenlaw (1920); Hashhozheva (2014); Nuttall (2005); Ramachandran (2009, 2010); Skulsky (1981).

Visionary, Interrupted: Spenser's Skeptical Artwork 33

Figure 1   Temple of Hera, Paestum, 2015 (author photo)

exploring the philosophical urgencies that infuse Spenser's poetry, however, I offer an anecdote about temples that may help illuminate his representations of the elusiveness of knowledge.

One spring day in 1959, the American abstract expressionist painter, Mark Rothko, was touring the Greek ruins at Paestum in Italy (Figure 1). Rothko was picnicking "in a shady patch inside the shell of the Temple of Hera" with family and friends when two Italian boys accosted their group, offering themselves as guides, and asked whether he had come to paint the temples.

Should we infer that the boys asked this question because Rothko had equipment nearby, an easel or a sketchbook? The source doesn't say. But here's the punch-line. In answer to the boys, Rothko replied (relying on his friend's teenage daughter to translate): "Tell them that I have been painting Greek temples all my life without knowing it" (2006, 137).[3] If we take Rothko at his word and believe that his art aspires to represent all

---

[3] See Glenn Most for Rothko's invention of "a new, Lucretian mode of sublime painting" (2012, 261).

that Greek temples evoke in the Western imagination, then we find ourselves – passing through Plato and Nietzsche, the philosophers whom Rothko most often cites – in Heideggerian country.

For Martin Heidegger also visits the temples at Paestum, arguing that they exemplify the truth of the work of art. "The temple, in its standing there, first gives to things their look and to men their outlook on themselves" (1971, 42). It doesn't matter, Heidegger says, that "the world of the work that stands there has perished," given that "world-withdrawal and world-decay can never be undone" (1971, 40). What matters is that "the temple-work, standing there, opens up a world and at the same time sets this world back again on earth" (1971, 41). In these lines Heidegger captures what Rothko's alleged epiphany gestures at: nostalgia for, hence a prizing of, the arrival at truth. He is hearkening back to a less self-conscious time when art governed people's existence, disclosing the truth of their world to themselves – a time preceding the alienation wrought by skepticism with its privileging of detached observation.[4] Heidegger's holistic phenomenology includes a cluster of terms about the quest for truth that has resonance for Spenser.[5] Take the word for truth, *aletheia*, with its root, *lethe*, conjuring the river of forgetfulness; it is understood literally as a process of un-forgetting and figuratively as a process of un-concealing whereby beings emerge into "radiant self-showing" (Korab-Karpowicz n.d., 5). This process of disclosure involves an opening up of the world whereby the hidden ground of being comes into presence (*Anwesen*). In Heidegger's lexicon, this is figured as arrival at a clearing (*eine Lichtung*), a word evoking both "an open place" in a forest and a moment of luminosity or clarity (1971, 51).

How does this account of art as temple-work bear on Spenser? We might begin by saying that ancient temples preoccupied Spenser all his life, only he realized this from the first.[6] We might add that, despite a shared

---

[4] Heidegger focuses "on two crucial historical moments in Western humanity's changing historical understanding of art – a kind of before and after, as it were, which contrasts the fullness of what has been possible with the narrowness of what is currently actual. Heidegger is thus primarily concerned to show, first, how the ancient Greeks encountered art in a non-aesthetic way (and so enshrined it in their temples), and second, how art is typically understood and experienced by us late moderns" (Thomson, 2019, 3.1).

[5] For resonances between Spenser and Heidegger, also see Elizabeth Bieman (1988), 11, 261, 264, 274–275; Gordon Teskey (1996), 143–145; (2003), 346–350, 355–357; (2007), 115–117.

[6] Critics variously interpret Spenser's temples. Angus Fletcher, for example, notes that "throughout *The Faerie Queene* Spenser counterpoints visions of temples inside labyrinths, labyrinths inside temples" so as "to create for narrative a dilated threshold, an instantaneous crossing from labyrinthine confusion and excess to a templar clarity and restraint." Fletcher adds, "The liminal crossover between these two 'spaces' marks the moment of prophetic vision" (1991, 124).

preoccupation with forgetfulness, concealment and disclosure, together with a predilection for forest clearings, Spenser is less defensive about his desires than Rothko or Heidegger and therefore more susceptible to the phenomenological thrills of deferral and dissatisfaction. Early on, he is drawn to the temple-work of Joachim Du Bellay, ushering its elusive truths into the open through his exercise of translation. Later, in the "November" eclogue of *The Shepheardes Calender* and when Colin Clout conjures a vision of the Graces dancing in *The Faerie Queene*, the poet has experiences of voluptuous presence so fleeting that they intensify our cravings for beauty and knowledge. Finally, in the *Mutabilitie Cantos*, Spenser achieves a version of the skeptical sublime as if recognizing that his own temple-work in that poem cannot bridge the chasm of Western metaphysics, that rift between subject and object that Heidegger deplored and single-handedly proposed to close.[7] In other words, because Heidegger's philosophical project combats a metaphysics in league with skepticism, his lexicon can illuminate the tensions imbuing poetry that struggles with problems of knowledge, truth, and fullness of being.[8]

That Spenser's poetry captures the sophisticated philosophical questioning of the late sixteenth century has long been acknowledged. In Lodowick Bryskett's *A Discourse of Civill Life* (ca. 1586), a fictional Spenser is imagined as engaging in a discussion about "the order or maner of knowledge" (1972, 125). Bryskett's persona observes that "it is sayd, that sense is busied about things particular, and that only things universall are knowne" (1972, 124). But the fictional Spenser seems less interested in the distinction between universals and particulars than in the ailments besetting the soul: "But how cometh it to passe (replied Maister *Spenser*) that the soule being immortall and impassible, yet by experience we see dayly,

---

[7] Just as the sublime manifests itself in various ways – as an effect of rhetorical power (e.g., Longinus), as a response to the grandeur of nature (e.g., Burke), as the mind's capacity to compass the unknown (e.g., Kant) or as the effort to present the unpresentable (e.g., Lyotard) – so too does the skeptical sublime. As we shall see, the cosmos in *The Mutabilitie Cantos* is at once awe-inspiring and domesticated by mythological language. Mutabilitie feels equal to challenging the gods, yet the poet/narrator is overcome with the magnitude of the unpresentable. Spenser evokes various forms of sublimity even as he puts them in skeptical parentheses, signaling the limitlessness of the unknown. See Ramachandran (2009, 2010) and Most (2012). As Robert Doran observes, echoing Suzanne Guerlac, what's remarkable is the relative "stability" of the sublime across time and space despite these varied manifestations (2015, 9).

[8] Charles B. Guignon explains Heidegger's strategy for dispelling the threat of skepticism: "The epistemologically motivated distinctions of subject and object, person and thing, inner and outer, and mental and physical are held in abeyance. ... And when the doubtful ontological assumptions that underlie the Cartesian model are called in question, the implications of skepticism for our plain epistemic situation are also deflated" (1983, 61).

that she is troubled with Lethargies, Phrensies, Melancholie, drunkenesse, and such other passions, by which we see her overcome, and to be debarred from her office and function" (274). Bryskett's Spenser wants to anchor their colloquy in passions that frustrate the soul's ability to attain divine knowledge.[9] While Bryskett's Spenser is hardly a rounded character – he is memorable, if at all, for his brief remarks on *The Faerie Queene* and for a sharp question or two – his mostly silent presence at this Irish gathering nevertheless attests to a concern with modalities of knowledge.[10] In fact, Spenser may have been more interested in the question of universals and particulars than Bryskett allows. After all, in *Areopagitica*, Milton calls Spenser "a better teacher than Scotus or Aquinas," a comment that puts Spenser in the company of angelic doctors pursuing metaphysical themes (1957, 728–729). While Milton may have meant this as a biting compliment, I take his point that Spenser dramatized issues pertinent to Scholastic theology – not only the Aristotelian virtues touted at the start of *The Faerie Queene* but also problems of cognition and truth.

Spenser's poetic pursuit of truth and beauty bears revisiting because it offers an early modern glimpse into the aesthetics of skepticism. Take his early fascination with the status of visions (hallucination or rents in the veil?); his repeated chartings of the journey from the fallen world of deceitful appearances to the realm of Patterns, Ideas, and Forms; even his repeated evocations of dancing nymphs or temples. All these share something of Rothko's or even Cezanne's obsessive revisiting of a theme, as they return to the canvas in pursuit of yet another manifestation of graceful bathers, the Mont Saint-Victoire or an ever darker mood.[11] To convey the intensity of Spenser's yearning for a language that will capture the philosophical dimension of his artistic projects, it is not enough to invoke the Neoplatonism of Marsilio Ficino, Leone Ebreo, Baldassare Castiglione, let alone the upwardly mobile energies of Spenser's careerism. Neither the ecstasies of the poet's Neoplatonic *furor* nor the mystic's

---

[9] Bryskett's Spenser's question about the soul matches Socrates' version of the soul's struggles in Spenser's translation of *Axiochus* (1966, X. 29–30). See Judith Anderson's analysis of Bryskett's Spenser's concerns, linking them to mortalism and "to Mutability's directly challenging the soul's immortality" (2010, 264).

[10] "The occasion of the discourse grew by the visitation of certaine gentlemen coming to me to my little cottage which I had newly built neare unto Dublin at such a time, as rather to prevent sicknesse, then for any present griefe, I had in the spring of the yeare begunne a course to take some physicke during a few days" (1972, 5–6).

[11] Rothko considered Cezanne a precursor, observing that "he indicated the direction in which later art developed: toward a plastic equivalent to Plato's notions of abstract ideas" (2004, 41). See also Merleau-Ponty (1993) on "Cezanne's Doubt."

longing for union with the divine can account for Spenser's life-long inquiry into the numinous conditions of mental experience. To understand Spenser's acts of thinking in his poetry, especially in his quasi-dream visions, it is also necessary to consider the skeptical questions posed by late medieval philosophy.[12]

Late medieval philosophy was preoccupied with many issues, among them the relationships of language, thought, and reality given God's freedom and power. As Dominik Perler explains, medieval authors "made methodological use of skepticism," appealing to skeptical arguments so as "to work out a satisfying account of knowledge, to defend it against rival accounts, and to test its explanatory force" (2014, 385). At the universities Aristotle dominated the curriculum, especially as interpreted by Porphyry – his *Isagoge* is a commentary on Aristotle's *Organon* – and by Boethius's commentary and translation of Porphyry. These works stimulated discussion about universals, particulars, and related topics such as the operation of abstraction, the grammar of mental language, and the ontological status of concepts and fictional entities.[13] Spenser would have had opportunities to encounter texts addressing these issues, some of them by so-called nominalists and some by their opponents like Duns Scotus. The descriptive catalogues of Cambridge University libraries report that between 1569 and 1576 Spenser could have read texts by Pierre d'Ailly, Bartholomaeus Arnoldi of Usingen, John Buridan, and Johannes von Wesel. At Pembroke, his own college, he could have read texts by William of Ockham, Gabriel Biel, Peter Olivi, and Henry of Ghent.[14] Some of these *nominales* had endured persecutions. As late as 1474, Louis XI "forbade the teaching of nominalism in Paris," requiring that an oath be taken on pain of exile and no degree (Thorndike 1944, 355). A defense of nominalism was issued in response to the king's edict, detailing the history of these persecutions going back to Ockham and up to the present day

---

[12] Compare Alastair Fowler who argues that "the flexible metaphysics of Neoplatonism suited [Spenser's] temperament and art as Scholasticism would never have done" even as he concedes "that Neoplatonic forms are only a subset of the range of structures composing this encyclopedic yet Christian epic" (1977, 238). For Neoplatonism as a response to Pyrrhonian skepticism, see Lloyd Gerson on cognition and "self-thinking" in Plotinus (2014, 268–272).

[13] Antoine Compagnon summarizes: "Porphyre ... fut en effet le premier, dans sa lecture d'Aristote, à s'interroger sur l'existence des universaux, et les nominalistes découvrirent la question chez Boèce" (1980, 41).

[14] See Kaske (1999) for Spenser's access to books in Cambridge libraries (6). Nicholas Hudson observes that scholastic texts "still formed the backbone of university logic courses" (1997, 284) in Locke's day. Hudson argues that Locke "both knew and strongly supported the major principles of nominalism advanced by Ockham and developed by later authors such as [Lorenzo] Valla and [Marius] Nizolius" (1997, 285).

(Thorndike 1944, 355–360). Summoned to Avignon and excommunicated in June 1328, Ockham wrote anti-papal polemics to the end of his life. This dissent and conflict with authorities was not forgotten. Martin Luther boasted, "My master Occam was the greatest dialectician." In February 1520 when defending himself against charges of heresy, Luther declared, "I demand arguments not authorities. That is why I contradict my own school of Occamists, which I have absorbed completely" (Oberman 1989, 120).[15] Copies of Luther abounded in Cambridge libraries. Spenser could well have been introduced to nominalist questions through his reading of Luther and Calvin. Although the nominalists never banded together to form a school and the extent of their influence is debated, this chapter argues that the skeptical quality of their inquiries emerges obliquely in Spenser's work. But before delving into Spenser's poetry for traces of late medieval philosophy, I touch on certain Scholastic and nominalist questions regarding cognition and language that may have intrigued him.

Chimeras in the Mind or Words?

What is the proper object of the human intellect? Is it God? (Henry of Ghent) Is it being, *ens*? (Duns Scotus) Is it the material world? (Aquinas) How does the human intellect operate? For Aquinas the answer involves abstraction.[16] The human intellect acquires concepts by abstracting from the data acquired through sensory perception. Taking his cue from Aristotle's notions of substance and accidents, Aquinas suggests that the concept of color can be abstracted from an apple (*ST*, Q 85, Art.1). Similarly, the concept of human nature can be abstracted from the encounter with individual human beings. As Robert Pasnau points out, abstraction for Aquinas is "a matter of selective attention, singling out some one feature while ignoring others" (2006, 45). However, the operation transforming perception into cognition involves a tricky causal chain that cognitive scientists today might compare to the process of encoding

---

[15] Steven Ozment speculates "whether, beyond Gerson, Wessel, Gansfort, and Biel, the young Luther might be said to represent a genuine synthesis of these diverse traditions. A devotee of medieval spirituality, he was trained in the Ockhamist tradition. Before he posted his 95 theses against indulgences, he critically annotated Tauler and Biel, edited the *Theologia Deutsch*, and fathered a disputation against scholastic theologians (Scotus, Ockham, d'Ailly, and Biel) ... Rejecting the basic axioms of both mysticism and nominalism, he still maintained parallel conclusions" (1974, 91).

[16] See Pasnau (2006).

information (Stump 1999, 170). To summarize Aquinas crudely, particulars in the world emit "sensible species" that travel through the air and impress themselves on the sense organ where they in turn become "phantasms" in the brain from which the intellect abstracts "intelligible species" that in turn enable the formation of universals.[17] "Phantasms," Eleonore Stump explains, "are responsible for the mental images one has in imagining as well as in all sensory cognition" (1999, 171). The tricky causal sequence is necessary, among other reasons, because "knowledge is in inverse ratio to materiality" such that "the more immaterially a being receives the form of the thing known, the more perfect is its knowledge" (*ST*, Q 85, Art. 2). In Aquinas there are degrees of knowledge, as Spenser would have recognized, and perfect knowledge is the goal. As we shall see, Spenser's allegories, with their selective attention to certain traits, share features with abstraction, understood as the process by which particulars shed their materiality so that perfect knowledge results.

Although not the first to harbor doubts about species, William of Ockam is credited with having declared these intermediary entities superfluous; hence, the fame of his razor and his moniker, *Venerabilis Inceptor*. Ockham applies his proverbial razor to the scholastic apparatus of entities mediating between intellect and reality, shaving away the doctrine of *species* abstracted from sensuous *phantasms* and leaving in its stead the clean lines of language: universals are concepts related to the order of words rather than to a transcendent order of being.[18] Along with other philosophers working after Aquinas, he distinguishes between intuitive and abstractive cognition. But Ockham's version of intuitive cognition is stark. "I say," he asserts, "that a thing itself is seen or apprehended immediately, without any intermediary between itself and the [cognitive] act" (*Sent.* I.27.3, quoted in Pasnau 2002, 229). By curtailing the causal chain, this doctrine preempts the possibility of mistaken apprehensions – those errors of perception and interpretation that fascinated Spenser. Ockham's stark account of intuitive cognition does little to explain how "epistemic contact is achieved," leading Stump to compare Ockham's account of our

---

[17] See Leen Spruit for a detailed account of "species" in Aquinas (1994, I. 156–174). Spruit argues that for Aquinas intelligible species "is an unconscious and structural principle, rather than a mere copy of a cognitive object – thereby breaking new ground towards a non-circular theory of knowledge acquisition" (173).

[18] Spruit explains that while Ockham's overt "targets are Thomas and Duns Scotus," his actual quarrel is with "the Arabic interpretation of the Neoplatonic theory of emanation" (1994, I. 293). Aspects of Neoplatonism thus inform nominalist innovations.

cognitive faculties to "a black box" (1999, 194–195).[19] Despite the failure to explain epistemic contact, Ockham's view of intuitive cognition informs the widespread view that nominalism embraces experience, producing a new sense of immediacy relevant to literature and fiction-making, as we shall see.[20]

Ockham, however, did not arrive at his razor-wielding, samurai act overnight. Early in his career, he subscribed to the notion of a *fictum* or "thought-object," shadowy entities that doubtless intrigued Spenser (1964, 45).[21] These *ficta* come about through a process that he compares to an artist's activity:

> For just as the artist who sees a house or building outside the mind first pictures in the mind a similar house and later produces a similar house in reality which is only numerically distinct from the first, so in our case, the picture in the mind that we get from seeing something outside would act as a pattern. For just as the imagined house would be a pattern for the architect, if he who imagines it had the power to produce it in reality, so likewise the other picture would be a pattern for him who forms it. And this can be called a universal, because it is a pattern and relates indifferently to all the singular things outside the mind. ... And in this way a universal is not the result of generation, but of abstraction, which is only a kind of mental picturing. (1964, 44)[22]

The familiar analogy of the draftsman at his drawing board explains that "universals" are "patterns" while "abstraction" is nothing more than "mental picturing." This language of picturing or representation with its assumption of resemblance would have been congenial to Spenser not least because it coexists alongside the claim that *ficta* are semantic universals in that they can be predicated of many things.[23] "Propositions are composed out of *ficta*," Pasnau explains (1997, 280–282). In this early phase, Ockham distinguishes a *fictum* from a *figmentum* or impossibility like

---

[19] Spruit also uses the black box metaphor to describe cognitive processes in Ockham (1994, I. 298).
[20] "However it is defined, nominalism entails the ontological thesis of the singularity of being; thus, there are only individuals. ... The nominalist denies that beings can take on any such forms or degrees of being: for the nominalist, in contrast to what the Neoplatonist tradition suggested, anything that is, is singular – and consequently it is so by itself, without the need to be individualized out of natures or essences" (Biard 2014, 666).
[21] Pasnau observes "that Ockham does not treat considerations of parsimony as decisive against *ficta* ... Ockham's attitude seems to be that nonreal entities don't count as much against parsimony as do real entities" such as species (1997, 83).
[22] *Ordinatio*, D. II, Q. viii, *prima redactio*.
[23] Pasnau notes that the notion of resemblance in play is "special" and "obscure": "An objectively existing *fictum* would be actually like the external things it represents if it were to have subjective existence. This is an obscure counterfactual claim to make" (1997, 279).

"a chimera and a goat-stag" (1964, 45). The chimera or goat-stag was a paradigmatic epistemological problem likely known to Spenser. The Greeks also puzzled over the status of a hybrid conjured from sensory fragments but with no corresponding object in reality.[24] Despite Ockham's allegiance to the direct apprehension of reality, his speculations about the status of these unreal, but intentional thought-objects might well have interested Spenser.[25]

Later, Ockham abandons the *fictum* and *figmentum,* disowning the view arguably germane to Spenser that there is "another little world made up of thought-objects" (1964, 146).[26] Historians of philosophy debate the reasons for this shift, surmising, for example, that it may have been prompted by the arguments of Peter Aureol and William Crathorn regarding the classic skeptical case of the bent stick in the water. Pondering the cognitive status of that fictive entity, Ockham concludes that at least in the case of illusions, if not hallucinations, "no inner object is required" (Pasnau 1997, 282). Instead, he takes up the notion of a *qualitas impresa* that issues in a *habitus* or disposition to act. According to this *actus*-theory, "concepts, rather than being the objects of certain cognitive acts, are directly identified with these very acts themselves" (Panaccio 2004, 8). In this more functional account, the act of abstraction and the abstract universal become identical. Claude Panaccio describes this as merging: "The terminology of the mental sign appropriately merges at this point with that of the *notitia* or cognition, to provide a clear-cut answer to the old problem of universals" (2004, 10).

The shift from an imagistic to a semantic account of mind so formative for Spenser's poetic genius caused consternation among Ockham's contemporaries.[27] They recognized that the jettisoning of species was "a major step" (Tachau 1982, 416).[28] Peter Aureol, for example, explains "the

---

[24] See Doyle (1995).
[25] "Despite his advocacy of direct realist theories of perception, Ockham cannot take the same view of intellectual cognition. The immediate objects of intellect, when intellect is concerned with universals, are mental entities" (Pasnau 1997, 279–280). See also Marilyn McCord Adams (1977).
[26] *Quodlibeta* III, *q.* 3. Pasnau argues that "Ockham abandoned *ficta* not so much because he came to have doubts about the concept of fictive existence but because he decided he could give an account of conceptual thought without relying on inner representations beyond the act itself" (1997, 82). See Leff on the chronology of Ockham's evolving views of *ficta* (1975, 78–102).
[27] Leff describes the shift as "the substitution of a logical for a metaphysical order" (1976, 12). Spruit agrees: "The gist of Ockham's new paradigm is an (epistemo-)logical model of knowledge acquisition competing with an older account chiefly couched in terms of a (meta-)physical process" (1994, I. 298).
[28] Biard notes that the nominalist semiological reformulation of Aristotelian categories is "delicate … because it has consequences for the doctrine of transubstantiation" (2014, 670).

evidently imagistic aspects of sensation and intellection" by positing the formation of "apparent, objective images (the *esse apparens*) as the central fact of conceptualization" (Tachau 1982, 398). Robert Holcot proposes to reconcile conflicting theories by giving the controversial term 'species' a plethora of synonyms: "in the intellect they are 'concepts' or 'words'; in the memory they are 'species', 'idol', 'image' or 'exemplar'" (Tachau 1982, 415). Problems emerge of interest not only to philosophers but also to later poets like Spenser. What causes cognitive error and mistakes of memory? Not only does the ancient skeptical trope of the stick bent in water come up, but so does the status of after-images and other illusions. Further, how does one pass from apprehension of a singular to apprehension of a mental proposition? In other words, how does one get from the sight of one's pet curled up by the door to the sentence, "The cat is on the mat"?

Thanks partly to the vogue of terminist logic, it was felt necessary to isolate the mechanisms by which sensory input switches into semantic terms. For William Crathorn, the switch occurs in the posterior ventricle of the brain, the site of memory. Here the 'stored' species generates a "mental word," also known as a generated cognition (*notitia genita*), which in turn impresses itself on the middle ventricle where the soul can access it (Tachau 1982, 421). Katherine Tachau believes that resistance to Ockham's non-representational theory of knowledge in the years following his death stems partly from widespread attachment to the "light-metaphysics" associated with an emanationist Neoplatonism (1982, 442). Although she deems his efforts "to dislodge the species from discussions of perception" a failure (1982, 440) and insists there was no Ockhamist "school," she shows that the questions he raised about epistemology and psychology stimulated the best minds of the fourteenth century.[29] In the sixteenth century and beyond the complex relays among images and words captured in these theories proved fruitful for poetic minds like Spenser's.

Spenser's poetry grapples sensuously with debates about mental language sparked by Ockham and his colleagues. These debates continue. Scholars today consider whether Ockham anticipates Noam Chomsky's idea of a universal grammar or current developments in cognitive

---

[29] But see Oberman who disputes the notion that "Scotism" and "Ockhamism" were limited to "a merely academic setting" and argues for "the rapid spread of nominalist ideas" throughout Europe via sermons (1974, 12). Certainly, "the shift in emphasis from a culture of visuality to one centered on the word (however incomplete)" has been often studied (Knapp 2011, 54).

science.[30] But whereas Chomsky views this grammar as innate, Ockham is skeptical about the existence of "deep structures." Ockham rejects the view that universals are substances (*SL* 1.15). Instead, he argues that the universal is "an intention of the soul capable of being predicated of many" (*SL* 1.15). As a subject of predication, a universal is no more than a semantic sign. Although written and spoken discourse is conventional and internal discourse is universal and natural – the medium through which the transparent minds of angels communicate, no less – mental language nevertheless parallels spoken and written language (Yrjönsuuri 2006, 104). As a committed Aristotelian, Ockham believes that "the conceptual structure of the mental language corresponds to the structure of reality" – an idea surely encountered by Spenser in the course of his studies at Cambridge (Yrjönsuuri 2006, 109). Because mental language "rises from what the real structure of the world is like ... learning to think means learning the universal language" (Yrjönsuuri 2006, 113). The notion of a meta-language that is not innate but rather learned (that is, acquired through experience), yet nevertheless natural and connected to things in the world suggests an understanding of internal discourse that is at once representational and schematic. What are the implications of this nominalist view of language and cognition not just for poets but also for the world in which they lived?

Many have interpreted Ockham's work as a watershed moment. For them, the severe abstract universal, heir to chimeras and goat-stags, unleashes the enormity of an epistemic shift. According to Louis Dupré and Brad Gregory, among others, Ockham's understanding of universals as semantic predicates diminishes the transcendent status they enjoy in Aquinas's system because he reduces them to collective nouns in the intellect. "Henceforth ideality belongs exclusively to the mind" (1993, 40), Dupré laments, reiterating that "Ockham's theory carries the immanence of conceptual forms to a point where intuitive knowledge becomes entirely established within the mind" (1993, 81). Ockham himself writes, "A universal is a mental content of such nature as to be predicated of many things ... only a mental content or a conventional sign is a universal" (1964, 39–40). Gregory sees this development as catastrophic, asserting that "metaphysical univocity in combination with Occam's razor opened a path that would lead through deism to Weberian disenchantment and

---

[30] See, e.g., Normore (1990) who finds similarities with Jerry Fodor's work on the language of thought (67).

modern atheism" (2012, 41).[31] In Heiko Oberman's view, by contrast, the *via moderna* of nominalism allows people "to avoid the basic fallacy of the old philosophy, namely, obfuscating reality with preconceived ideas instead of allowing experienced reality to shape thought" (2003, 33). Oberman believes nominalism leads to "the vital scepticism which we have come to acknowledge as prerequisite for a sound scientific attitude" (1960, 69). William J. Courtenay (1984) suggests more cautiously that nominalism be considered a philosophy of language.[32] Given this more limited understanding, Ockham's "major breakthrough" is the development of a meta-language.[33] But regardless of how we evaluate nominalism's impact on the history of the West, it is notable that Ockham presides over a debate about the status of mental objects that fascinated many, including Spenser, even as his own philosophical trajectory registers ambivalence about things in the mind and marks a shift to *verba*. When Ockham relinquishes his *fictum*-theory in favor of an *actus*-theory, a picture of the mind as a storehouse of images recedes, replaced by that of a semantic mind furnished with a system of propositions devised to capture the complexities of syntax and grammar. This system of natural signs connects the mind to reality and the soul to God in ways that would have resonated for godly poets like Spenser.[34]

Structures of Nominalist Feeling

The skeptical methodology of late medieval nominalism manifests itself, not only in debates about mental objects and mental language, but above all in debates about God's power, a subject that no devout Christian could afford to overlook, let alone godly poets. Can God change the past? some asked. Can God command a person to hate Him? Can God deceive us?

---

[31] See also Richard Weaver who blames Ockham for the demise of truth and transcendence in the West, dubbing him a type of Macbeth in whom "the powers of darkness were working subtly ... in the seemingly innocent form of an attack upon universals" (1948, 3).

[32] Courtenay in "Nominalism and Late Medieval Religion" (1984), citing E. A. Moody's work (53).

[33] Wilfrid Sellars (1970, 62), cited in Panaccio (1999, 66). Hudson elaborates: "Like Frege, Russell and the young Wittgenstein, he [Ockham] stressed the deficiencies of natural (i.e. ordinary) language, and sought to isolate a lucid and simple idiom for the use of philosophy" (1997, 286).

[34] Emphasizing the voluntarism of nominalist theology and anticipating later developments in the philosophy of language, Ozment argues that nominalist discourse is "a willed verbal relation" whereby "the mind 'legislates' universals as tools to handle perceived species and genera" (1974, 80). In the quest for knowledge leading to salvation the *viator*'s best hope are these "freely fashioned verbal 'conventions'" (1974, 78). Nicholas Hudson argues, by contrast, that this is John Locke's radical innovation (1997, 291). Most scholars agree that Ockham retained the notion of "natural" signs with respect to concepts.

Could God have chosen to become incarnate as a stone or irrational creature, even an ass? Since preserving God's omnipotence is a priority for these theologians, the only limit on God is the law of non-contradiction. God's theoretical capacity for deception has recently led scholars to dub the cluster of problems following from this hypothesis as "demon skepticism."[35] Unlike Descartes who raises the possibility of a deceiving God in his *Meditations* only to quickly dismiss it on the grounds of God's goodness and truth, some medieval theologians were quite willing to explore the implications of a God who might find it strategic to induce false beliefs in rational creatures.[36] This leads to lively investigations of counterfactual possibilities that highlight the contingent nature of things as they actually are – a habit of mind characteristic of skeptical inquiry as the case-studies in this book show.

These skeptical thought-experiments about the extent of God's power often turn on the distinction between *potentia absoluta* and *potentia ordinata*, a distinction that colored the view of several Renaissance poets, as we will see. The question of how to speak about things God cannot do was tackled by exploring the difference between *posse* and *velle*: God's capacity and God's volition. As William Courtenay explains, thinkers as far back as Peter Damian (1067) considered that "the realm of possibility open to God is not exhausted by or limited to what God has chosen to do" (1984, 2). Anselm developed this line of thought by emphasizing God's freedom to act, including his freedom to bind himself to the laws of nature. By the thirteenth century, the focus was not on divine inability so much as on "God's relationship with the world, a relationship based on covenant and self-commitment"(1984, 6). Theologians like Aquinas preferred to dwell on the "appropriateness and reliability of the established order of things" ordained by God (1984, 7). Trouble arose when canon lawyers in the late thirteenth century used the *absoluta /ordinata* distinction to draw analogies to the Pope's sovereignty and his self-binding decision to obey ecclesiastical laws. This had the political effect of framing *potentia absoluta* "as a type of action rather than [as] a neutral sphere of unconditioned possibility" (1984, 12). Duns Scotus was responsible for the migration into theology of this legal, constitutional view of sovereignty. Scotus's insistence "on God's ability to act outside and against his established law allowed *potentia absoluta* to appear as a form of extraordinary divine action, *supra legem* (1984, 13). Ockham pushed back against this view, arguing

---

[35] See, e.g., essays by Klima in Klima and Hall (2011).
[36] See, e.g., Perler (2010) and Marilyn McCord Adams (1970).

that *potentia absoluta* was not a sphere of action, but rather of unrealized total possibility. As Courtenay explains, "Ockham would never have applied the distinction to the papacy if he thought it would encourage absolutist behavior" (1984, 15).[37] After Ockham, nominalists chose to investigate the realm of future contingents and counterfactuals, *secundum imaginationem*, opened up by *potentia absoluta* (1984, 15).[38]

What are the consequences for poets and intellectuals like Spenser of this voluntaristic way of thinking about divine power, combined with the nominalist priority on individuals? According to Heiko Oberman, this outlook contributes to a sense of "distance between God hidden and God revealed" (1960, 57) together with "hunger for reality" (1960, 62). The sense of distance is partially captured in the tag line: "*finiti et infiniti nulla proportio.*" The absence of proportion or relation between the human creature and the hidden God, the *deus absconditus*, together with the view of the individual as a wayfarer (*viator*), contributes to a feeling of autonomy. Ockham himself declares that "it is the experience of the contingent character of our world which 'necessitates' the freedom of man."[39] While Oberman is not prepared to say that this ushers in "a *new* historical consciousness" (1960, 52), his claims about nominalist anthropology suggest the emergence of what Raymond Williams might call a new "structure of feeling" oriented around autonomy.[40] As Oberman sees it:

> The supernatural world, instead of accompanying and nourishing the *viator*, has receded and has become a hemisphere, a dome. This dome shuts out the world of God's non-realized possibilities and provides room on the inside for man's own realm, in which he, as the image of God, thinks and acts. (1960, 63)

"The dome-motif" enables the wayfarer "to find his own way, unhampered by the supernatural world" (1960, 68). He is free to investigate the laws of

---

[37] The politics issuing from nominalism are as vexed as those issuing from skepticism. It is too simple to assume that the voluntarism attached to nominalism issues in authoritarian politics, Joan Bennett notwithstanding (1989, 8–9, 11–12).

[38] See Normore (1983).

[39] "... *inquirendum est quomodo et unde contingat contingentia in rebus; pro quo sit ista conclusio: contingentia effectus praesupponit libertatem alicuius causae agentis*" (I *Sent*. D 38, q 1, a 7), cited in Oberman 1960, 64.

[40] See Williams 1977, 128–135, especially: "... a social experience which is still in process, often indeed not yet recognized as social but taken to be private, idiosyncratic, and even isolating, but which in analysis (though rarely otherwise) has its emergent, connecting, and dominant characteristics, indeed its specific hierarchies" (1977, 132). For the importance of voluntarism to the emergence of autonomy in modern moral philosophy, see Schneewind (1998), especially 22–36, 250–251, 509–515.

nature through experimentation because secondary causes belong to the realm of *potentia ordinata*. In this way voluntarist theology transforms physics: "If God is no longer tied to creation by 'deterministic' causation but related to it by volition, i.e., by his personal decision, then all metaphysical arguments based on necessary causal links – as is indeed typical of Aristotle's cosmology and Aquinas's *via antiqua* – lose their cogency, if not their credibility" (Oberman 1987, 28). When the ordained order is a product of God's will, its contingency is uppermost such that one cannot reason from secondary causes in the world below to the First Cause in the world above. The dome interferes.[41]

Thus Oberman distinguishes vertical from horizontal aspects of the theological distinction between *potentia absoluta* and *potentia ordinata*. The vertical aspect creates "an eschatological openness" that reminds him of Joachim of Fiore's millenarianism and reminds me of Spenser (1960, 58). It emphasizes "the directness of God's acting," even as it inflames faith, inciting the wayfarer to "transcend the dome" (1960, 62–63).[42] God is now "a covenant God" who makes the wayfarer "responsible for his own life, society and world, on the basis and within the limits of the treaty or *pactum* stipulated by God" (1974, 15). The horizontal aspect encourages independent reasoning related to the "criticism of the hierarchy of knowledge" implicit in nominalism's embrace of experience (1960, 62). These spatio-temporal dimensions of a nominalist worldview – eschatological openness to the world above and a "quest for immediacy" in the world below (1960, 62) – converge in the psyche and transform social experience, generating a heady mix of "loneliness" (1960, 68), longing, aspiration, and stubborn inquiry evident in the poetic endeavors of Spenser, among others.[43] Politically, this revisioning of "the relationship between the sacred and the secular" means "presenting coordination as an

---

[41] Oberman elaborates: "If there does not exist a metaphysically necessary ladder along which the first cause has to 'connect with' the second cause, the laws of nature can be derived no longer from illuminating the physical world from 'above,' but from this world itself" (1987, 28).

[42] Oberman explains the anti-Platonic thrust of nominalism, saying "that in the vertical dimension our reality is not the lowest emanation and level in a hierarchy of being which ascends in ever more real steps to the highest reality, God" (1974, 13). The anti-Platonic implications of nominalism have consequences for the way the sublime is experienced and represented. With respect to the vertical dimension, the *viator* feels insignificant, overcome by the terrifying grandeur of the abyss separating him from God. With respect to the horizontal dimension, he feels challenged by the limits of the knowable and ready to pit his mind against them. Adapting Porter's terminology, I define the nominalist sublime as consisting of "two sublimities" at "their troubling point of juncture" such that "felt incommensurability" rules (2016, 392–393).

[43] Contingency, Oberman explains, "is understood in two directions, embracing both the vertical relation God-world-man and the horizontal relation world-man-future" (1974, 13).

alternative to subordination and partnership of persons instead of the hierarchy of being" (1974, 15).

How did these emergent structures of feeling generated by metaphysical debate affect the artistic imagination? Nearly a century ago Charles Homer Haskins compared the *Summa Theologica* of Thomas Aquinas to the great gothic cathedrals (1927, 358). Erwin Panofsky went further, arguing that nominalism and mysticism – "two extremes" that were "opposite aspects of the same thing" – led to "aesthetic subjectivism" such that "the energies of High Scholasticism" were "channeled into poetry and, ultimately, humanism" (1951, 11–14).[44] Panofsky, like Oberman, saw nominalism, mysticism, and humanism as different expressions of a "mental habit" primed for a sensory–spiritual immediacy (1951, 27).[45] He understood the architectural space of certain Gothic cathedrals as "wildly pictorial" thanks to nominalism (1951, 43). With regard to literature, nominalism also often serves as shorthand to describe a growing interest in the phenomenology of individual experience.[46] This new empirical sensibility suggests, to Hugo Keiper, for example, that nominalist literature is dialogic and polyphonic, open to heterogeneous voices (1997, 48–49). Similarly, Terence Cave argues that late medieval nominalism and Renaissance

---

[44] But see Ozment who observes that "mysticism and nominalism appear to be diametrically opposed in their basic ideological bents. Nominalists are finally confined to the penultimate, connoisseurs of time and history. Mystics, by contrast, look to an eternal covenant behind historical covenants…" (in Trinkaus 1974, 91).

[45] Oberman considers nominalism and humanism to be "parallel movements" because both focus on "the freedom and autonomy of man" (1960, 70). He believes "the too often isolated conception of man's freedom in the Renaissance should be analyzed in direct connection with its [Nominalist] epistemology." He observes that "in both systems man ends up going his own way – be it in a horizontal or vertical direction" (1960, 62).

[46] For the wide range of critical interpretations, consider this sampling. Compagnon sees nominalism behind the shift in Montaigne's use of pronouns – from "we" to "I" – adding that Montaigne's fideism puts him closer to Ockham and the French nominalists, Nicolas d'Autrecourt, Jean de Mirecourt, and Jean Gerson, than to skeptics or Pyrrhonians (1980, 23). Randall views nominalism as spelling the demise of analogy. Ockham's "understanding of the universe implies that analogy is impossible," he says, adding that "literary images in the late Middle Ages and throughout the Renaissance continued to depend on the analogical relationships of perfect and imperfect, but often these images reflected the troubled nature of the analogical edifice itself" (1996, 46). By contrast, Penn suggests, as regards John Wyclif, "the possibility that nominalism, far from rendering analogy and allegory unworkable … may have contributed positively to its development" (in Keiper et al., 1997, 186). Silver describes Sir Thomas Browne's "loose nominalism": "on the one hand, presumptively literal usage which makes the world commensurate with the fantasies of human intellection, and on the other, tropological usage which abundantly imagines the divine without predicating any identity between 'real' things and its figures. … Words here function like semiotic building blocks, fitted together contingently and according to their nominal compatibility as signs, in a kind of syntactic accretion" (1990, 99, 101). I see convergences between the practice of allegory and debates about universals and their relationship to particulars.

skepticism share a view of "discourse" as "fluid, erratic, always potentially mendacious" (2009, 17). These contemporary-sounding assessments of nominalism's effects on literature should come as no surprise given the recent tendency, one critic wryly notes, to treat "late medieval nominalism as a historical precedent – and, therefore, a reassertion – of prevalent modern/postmodern perceptions."[47]

Other scholars focus on the theological distinction between *potentia absoluta* and *potentia ordinata* to mount arguments about sovereignty and autonomy in early modern texts. Ullrich Langer, for example, argues that the freedom and willfulness of Renaissance fictions emerge from the remoteness and incomprehensibility of the nominalist God. In his view, Joachim Du Bellay's refusal of Renaissance Rome in the *Regrets* and his idealization of France and ancient Rome issue from a sense of sovereignty and autonomy constitutive of nominalism (1990, 150). Likewise, Clément Marot's lyric staging of his own relationship as a poet–courtier to the king rehearses notions of sovereignty and autonomy negotiated in nominalist theology (1990, 67–70). As Langer puts it, "The nominalist God's *potentia absoluta* is a way of preserving the nonnecessary origin of any order, and the sense of continuing dependence on that order" (1990, 192). Nominalism thus brings out not only the contingency of the sublunar order, but also of the courtier–poet's precarious position in that order. It helps crystallize the subversive idea that things could have been otherwise.

Building on Ullrich Langer's exploration of nominalism's effects on Du Bellay and Marot, in the next sections I look at a few of Spenser's translations of their poetry. But instead of dwelling on the dynamics of power as Langer does, I address issues of epistemology – abstraction, concepts, fictional entities, and *oratio mentalis* – in the conviction that late medieval philosophy's preoccupation with the ontological status of mental objects had effects on Spenser's literary imagination. In the last part of the chapter, I attend to the structures of feeling sketched out by Oberman to revisit *The Mutabilitie Cantos*. Critics have long described Spenser's vast archaeological appetite – his desire to digest and incorporate into his own text past authors, motifs, genres, and diction.[48] Spenser's desire to tap into and

---

[47] Richard Utz (1995, 27). Utz mentions, among others, Theodor Adorno, John Gardner, Fredric Jameson, Stephen Knight, Julia Kristeva, Richard Rorty, and J. Stephen Russell (1995, 27–29).
[48] For example, Angus Fletcher observes: "As we read our way *into* Spenser, his figures grow large with another size, of dull reverberations, by alluding to other cultures, other religions, other philosophies than our own" (1964, 273). Also see, among others, Barkan (2000); Berger (1968); Maley (2001).

revivify traditions that may have been perceived as under siege or out of style also embraces late medieval nominalism.[49]

Translating Temple-Work

Early in his poetic career, in his schoolboy translations, Spenser tackles Joachim Du Bellay's *Songe* – visions fraught with enigmatic symbolism that harrow the passive spectator before vanishing into thin air. Each dream has an apocalyptic quality, reminiscent of the Book of Revelation; antique monuments and colossal figures overwhelm the speaker with their sublime grandeur before disappearing (Figure 2). As if a veil has been rent, the dreamer witnesses a spectacle of otherworldly significance. When the intense moment of fullness passes, the speaker experiences perplexity and sadness. He is not lost so much as at a loss to decipher the Manichean allegory he has glimpsed: violent powers set loose, destroying emblematic figures and structures, but whether for good or ill is unclear. If these dreams were simply thrusting pagan idols before Spenser's Protestant readers, then their destruction would warm the cockles of their iconoclastic hearts. But the dreamer, with whom we identify, is not joyful; instead he is perplexed and mourns the spectacle of desecration. Already in his adolescence, Spenser is drawn to ruptures in the fabric of everyday life that permit moments of cosmic insight.[50]

At these apocalyptic moments, Spenser interrogates the meaning and status of his visions – abstract universals glimpsed in a flash of poetic rapture. Consider Spenser's translation of Du Bellay's fourth sonnet in the *Songe*: an evocation of a triumphal arch so beautiful and otherworldly that the poet is devastated when it crumbles before his eyes.[51] In Du Bellay's French, in Spenser's unrhymed 1569 translation for Jan Van der Noot's *Theatre for Worldlings*, and in the rhymed version for his 1591 *Complaints*, the poem begins with "Je vis" or "I saw." The poet gradually guides our

---

[49] Nuttall argues that Spenser was the "central engine" of "an aesthetic" of "alienated medievalism" popular in Elizabeth's time (2005, 216–217). He suggests that this alienation operates as a religious distancing device, creating a space for irony and wit at the expense of popish and Gothic things (219); it is, in effect, a subtle "substitute for iconoclasm" (224). In my view, Spenser's attention to late medieval philosophical questions is not alienated so much as engaged.

[50] But see Rebeca Helfer who argues that in the *Complaints*, Spenser downplays Van der Noot's emphasis on eschatology, muting the end-times in favor of historical time, such that ruins become "a place for remembering the past anew" (2012, 62).

[51] See McCabe: "The image of the triumphal arch in the fourth epigram, for example, may be regarded as the archetype of all the ill-fated triumphal buildings – such as the palace of Lucifera – which recur throughout *The Faerie Queene*" (1989, 63).

Figure 2 Woodcut, Jan Van der Noot, *Theatre for Worldlings*, 1569 (courtesy of the Folger Shakespeare Library)

eyes, showing us ivory columns emerging from metallic bases and abutting in alabaster chapters and crystal friezes, culminating in "the double front of a triumphal Arke," Spenser's phrase in both versions. Yet there is a curious omission in his translations of the first stanza that speaks to Spenser's ambivalence regarding the ontological status of the vision. Du Bellay writes:

> Je vis élevé sur colonnes d'ivoire
> Dont les bases étaient du plus riche métal
> A chapiteaux d'albâtre et frises de crystal
> Le double front d'un arc dressé pour la mémoire.
> (1967, 51)

"Un arc dressé pour la mémoire" – an arch erected for memory – suggests that it has a commemorative purpose like the obelisk in the preceding sonnet and also a mnemonic purpose of the sort attached to memory theaters. If the dreamer is encouraged to fix the ornamental features of the arch in his mind in the manner advised by the "art of memory," then this diminishes the eschatological dimension of the vision and reduces it to a stage-set operating as an *aide-mémoire*. Perhaps Spenser resists Du Bellay's phrase, "pour la mémoire," because it instrumentalizes, even as it internalizes, the figure of the arch, a quasi-nominalist move. Spenser prefers to keep the arch floating in an ambiguous space, at once inside the dreamer's head and outside, beyond the veil of illusion. He improves on Du Bellay's poem by keeping the focus on an architectonic structure so "faire" – "si beau" – that it defies human craftsmanship, thereby intimating its otherworldly origins.

Similarly, in his translation of the sonnet's sestet, Spenser mutes Du Bellay's nominalism, resisting his implication that the vision is a figment in the mind. In 1569 he renders the opening line of the sestet, "L'ouvrage ne montrait un artifice humain" as "The worke did shewe it selfe not wrought by man." He drops the French word, *artifice*, with its connotations of artistic craftsmanship and replaces it with the earthier English notion of wroughtness. But by 1591, when he retranslates the same French verse, the emphasis shifts to the speaker's wistfulness regarding the superiority of divine making: "No worke it seem'd of earthly craftsman's wit, / But rather wrought by his owne industry, / That thunder-dartes for *Jove* his syre doth fit." The word, wrought, is still there, but flanked by the wit, craft, and industry belonging to Vulcan – and here both Du Bellay and Spenser hint at their epic aspirations, as the Homeric *ekphrasis* of Achilles' shield is dimly recalled. My point is that by omitting the phrase, "pour la mémoire," and by bringing out what Heidegger would call "the workly character of the art work" (1971, 28), Spenser champions the divine origins of art, even as he witnesses a sublime example of divine craftsmanship inexplicably falling to dust. In this way, the act and exercise of translating Du Bellay lead Spenser to confront the status of cognitive representations.[52]

Another translation from Du Bellay reveals Spenser's attraction to questions of epistemology. In Sonnet 27 of the *Antiquités*, Du Bellay suggests that for architects and builders the rubble of empire still sets the standard: "Ces vieux fragments encore servent d'exemples" (1967, 44). Spenser translates this line in *The Ruines of Rome* as "Yet these olde fragments are for paternes borne." Substituting "pattern" for "example" is significant. Example is secular, historical and ethical in its connotations, whereas pattern, like form, has a Neoplatonic flavor oriented toward the aesthetic. Like an archetype, a pattern is a thing of beauty and perfection, whereas an example need only constitute a benchmark. Perhaps because Spenser never visited Rome, he is less ambivalent than Du Bellay about the city and more inclined to idealize it. Rome may be a *fictum* or *figmentum* on a par with Jerusalem or Athens.[53] Or perhaps he is of Heidegger's mind when it comes to the remains of ancient temples – that "truth is set to work in such a work" (1971, 37).

Similarly in Sonnet 5, Spenser downplays Du Bellay's ambivalence about the value of pagan literatures, with a discreet word change taking the verse in a more epistemological direction. Du Bellay's concluding tercet reads:

> Mais ses écrits, qui son los le plus beau
> Malgré le temps arrachent du tombeau,
> Font son idole errer parmi le monde.
> (1967, 30)

To describe the posthumous life of the classics as an idol erring through the world seems almost churlish. To be sure, idol can be read in a Petrarchan rather than Reformation context and "errer" can be interpreted as wandering rather than erring, but surely the suggestion of pagan error haunting the world clings to this description of Roman "écrits."

---

[52] See Barkan (2000) and Coldiron (2002) for different takes on Spenser's translations of Du Bellay.
[53] A vision of the heavenly Jerusalem concludes the sonnet sequence beginning with Spenser's translations of Du Bellay's dreams of Rome's crumbling empire in *A Theatre for Worldlings* (1569).

Spenser's translation of the tercet substitutes "appeare" for "errer":

> But her brave writings, which her famous merite
> In spight of time, out of the dust doth reare,
> Doo make her Idole through the world appeare.

Spenser could have ended the sonnet with the word *err* if he had wanted to conclude with a touch of doctrinal piquancy; instead, he juxtaposes "world" and "appeare" so as to foreground the philosophical problem of appearances. "Idole" operates here as it does in the "Hymn to Heavenly Beautie" where Spenser describes Anacreon's *ekphrasis* of Venus as "that Idole of his fayning thought" (l. 223). It may also have a whiff of Robert Holcot's nonchalant philosophical usage when he treats idol, image, and exemplar as interchangeable synonyms for entities in the mind.

Insofar as Spenser is inclined to aestheticize otherworldly visions, transmuting them into representations of poetic inspiration, it is arguable that he is engaging with Neoplatonism and its figure of the poet as an ecstatic mystic. Yet I want to trouble this view, suggesting that Spenser is also dealing with ontological problems of immediacy and ideality contested in this period. Rome's architectural emblems should be seen as abstract universals captivating the poet's consciousness, not only as metonymies for empire. While Anne Lake Prescott may be right that "reading Spenser reading du Bellay reading Rome is a dizzying exercise in multiple uncertainties" (1996, 132), surely one point of repair is that his meditations on classical temples show Spenser wrestling, not only with the enigmas of historical change, but also with the ontological status of imaginative experience and mental sights.

Abstraction in "November"

Spenser's aestheticizing of epistemological problems can also be seen in his free translation of one of Clément Marot's elegies where he puts into practice Aquinas's method of abstraction. He erases the historical particulars of Marot's poem so as to arrive at larger, general truths. Aristotelian induction combines with a Platonic reverence for ideal forms. But the abstracted ideal is no sooner apprehended than it takes a nominalist turn, exposed both as a *fictum* and as a linguistic artifact.[54] To support this

---

[54] Peter Sacks discusses the convergence of skepticism and aestheticization in *The Shepheardes Calender* when he writes of E. K.'s commentary that "perhaps the most interesting feature of the gloss is this disconcerting skepticism regarding almost every figure in the poem. By skepticism I mean the insistence on the figure as figure, thereby checking the reader from any completion of reference. We

claim, I compare The Song of Dido, comprising the core of the "November" eclogue in *The Shepheardes Calender*, and Marot's pastoral elegy for the Queen-Mother, its avowed literary model.

In the "Argument" preceding "November," E. K. advertises the superiority of what follows, saying: "*This Aeglogue is made in imitation of Marot his song, which he made upon the death of Loys the frenche Queene. But farre passing his reache, and in myne opinion all other the Eglogues of this booke.*" The eclogue then opens with Thenot, an older shepherd, challenging Colin Clout to a singing contest. Can Colin Clout compose an elegy for Dido, whom Thenot mourns, as beautiful and as moving as the poem Colin sang about Rosalind when she jilted him? In other words, can Colin give voice to Thenot's sorrow with the same emotional conviction he once gave his own? Colin accepts the dare, framing it as a problem of skill and knowledge: "Yet as I conne, my conning I will strayne" (l. 52). Colin then recites fifteen stanzas that describe how the whole world grieves for Dido before climaxing in his vision of the resurrected Dido walking in the Elysian fields. This moment has multiple resonances – for Neoplatonism, for Petrarchism, for Christian pastoral, for the tradition of the *madonna angelicata*, and more. But while the burst of Christian Platonism toward the end of Spenser's pastoral cycle has long elicited commentary, it is seldom discussed as a sign of epistemological trouble.[55] Yet *The Shepheardes Calender* as a whole has often been considered a skeptical work, thanks partly to its veiled criticisms of the queen's ecclesiastical policies. The dirge for Dido may well veer into political allegory, betraying skepticism about the queen.[56] But it also offers evidence of the epistemological challenges of representing truth and beauty. Dido's apotheosis does not deliver the beatific plenitude it summons with its incantatory rhythms. Instead it offers a vision of "numinous" womanhood

---

are told that the eclogues are a labor of concealment; that the names are pseudonyms shadowing hidden identities; that such figures as Pan, Niobe, Atlas, Endymion, Titan and the Fates are all dependent on the 'feigning' of poets and are all susceptible to an array of interpretations. The gloss is like an odd mirror containing the poem's reflection of its fictions. This curious, potentially undermining relation is crucial to almost all Spenser's work" (1985, 51).

[55] The Song of Dido's epistemological dimensions emerged for me after reading Marshall Grossman on John Donne's *Anniversaries*. Grossman argues that *The Anniversaries* chart a progression from "representation" to "contemplation" understood "as a movement inward that is also a fall from metaphysical ontology into the beginnings of a critical epistemology." Grossman's sense of "the epistemological–subjective tradition around which history is formed" may well derive from nominalism's modes of intellectual engagement (1998, 166–167).

[56] Cf. "For it is only if we consider Dido as a dark foreboding of what Elizabeth might become that the formal structure of the *Calender*, and indeed the entire project it represents, becomes fully intelligible" (Patterson 1987, 121).

so internalized and transient that it undermines the transcendence of universals and ideal forms.[57]

Spenser makes several choices in The Song of Dido, the net effect of which is to move the poem away from historical particulars and toward abstraction. For starters, he strips Dido of any historical identity. By contrast with Marot's shepherdess, whom he identifies by name, title and maternal relation to the reigning king, Dido is a riddle. E. K. goes out of his way in the "Argument" preceding the eclogue to point out that she is mysterious, remarking that "the personage is secrete, and to me altogether unknowne." This teasing invitation to affix an identity on Dido does not preclude the fact that Dido remains conspicuously devoid of identifying features: a universal abstracted from a phantasm. The most one learns is that she made her home in Kent since the shepherds who mourn her "on Kentish downes abyde" (l. 63). One likewise learns that a "greate shepheard" called Lobbin mourns her with special intensity, he having been one of her favorites. If one looks for details of a plastic and visual sort to anchor her in a material landscape, one discovers that she "entertayned" her fellow shepherds with "cakes and cracknels" (l. 96), "curds and clouted Creame" (l. 99). But the echo of Colin Clout's name in the adjective, "clouted," detracts from the reality of the detail. Dido's favors to Lobbin are dictated by the demands of genre rather than by her individuality. "Nosegayes," "colourd chaplets," "knotted rushrings," and "gilte Rosemaree" have a cumulative effect that is ornate and intricate, but empty of personality. By contrast, in Marot's eclogue, the shepherd–poet (also called Colin) mentions the Queen's pet parrot as waiting for her in Paradise: "Son Papegaye, qui partit avant elle" (l. 212). Colin recalls how rich fathers brought their daughters to be educated by the Queen-mother and how she instructed them in virtue under the shade of a great oak. He also alludes to her role in the negotiations of the Treaty of Cambrai in 1529. As H. S. V. Jones puts it in the 1966 variorum edition of Spenser's Works, "Compared with Spenser, the French poet offers a much more circumstantial description" (ed. Greenlaw 1966, 401).

The move away from what Mark Rothko calls "illustrative anecdote" toward abstractive "myth" also shows in Spenser's representation of nature (2004, 95). Whereas Marot's eclogue derives much witty charm from his onomastic catalogue of grieving cities, regions, and rivers, nature in "November" is pared down to floods, flocks, and beasts. In keeping perhaps with the nominalism Langer ascribes to him, Marot revels in

---

[57] See Krier on "the culturally rich *topos* of a numinous woman beheld" (1990, 7).

geographical names, enjoying the melody and musicality of empirical particulars:

> Coignac s'en coigne en sa poictrine blesme:
> Rommorantin la perte rememore:
> Anjou faict jou: Angolesme est de mesme.
> Amboyse en boyt une amertume extreme:
> Le Meine en maine ung lamentable bruyt:
> La pauvre Touvre arrousant Angolesme
> A son pave de Truites tout destruict.
>   (158–164)

This patriotic and punning catalogue has no analogue in "November." Its absence is all the more conspicuous given that later in the marriage of rivers in Book IV of *The Faerie Queene* and in *The Mutabilitie Cantos*, Spenser personifies local topography in celebration of his country; no doubt Marot's rivers lingered in his mind. That said, the effect of this omission in "November" is to leave the elegy to Dido strangely bereft of specificity. The absence of intimate detail gives the poem an abstract ethereality.[58]

Spenser's ritualized approach to the Song's refrain heightens the self-induced aspects of Colin's effort to achieve a vision of truth and beauty through philosophical abstraction. While both poems move from mortality to eternity and from particular to universal in the turn from lament to consolation typical of elegy, Spenser's is more formal and focused than Marot's. After eleven variations on the refrain "O hevie herse ... O carefull verse," the poem devotes a stanza to the transition from earthly grief to Christian hope and having shifted from minor to major key, resumes the refrain, now felicitously reprised as "O happy herse ... O joyfull verse." This is repeated four times. By contrast, Marot's use of the refrain seems embryonic and undeveloped. "Chantez mes vers" is irregularly spaced and sporadic, appearing only five times, before suddenly shifting key and modulating to "Cessez mes vers," which appears only twice. Marot's

---

[58] In translating Marot, Spenser adopts the approach to abstraction theorized in Hans-Georg Gadamer's aesthetics. As if he were channeling an abridged version of Aquinas, Gadamer writes: "What we call a work of art and experience (*erleben*) aesthetically depends on a process of abstraction. By disregarding everything in which a work is rooted (its original context of life, and the religious or secular function that gave it significance), it becomes visible as the 'pure work of art.' In performing this abstraction, aesthetic consciousness performs a task that is positive in itself" (1960, 85).

If we follow Gadamer's reasoning, then The Song of Dido's transmutation of Marot is an allegory of aesthetic cognition, enacting the process of abstraction constitutive of aesthetic consciousness.

injunction to silence terminates the lyrical call to mourning.[59] In Spenser's refrain, however, the turn from "heavie herse" to "joyfull verse" signals Colin's quest for mystical transport. Mysticism, as Panofsky and Oberman remind us, speaks to that hunger for contact that likewise marks nominalism.

Yet Colin's desire for an almost ecstatic union with Dido is no sooner articulated than frustrated. The immediacy of his "I see thee blessed soule, I see" vanishes, and the distance between his vantage point and hers reemerges in the wistful tone of his repeated "there's": "There lives shee with the blessed Gods in blisse, / There drincks she *Nectar* with *Ambrosia* mixt" (194–195). The eclogue signals that for all his efforts to sustain a vision of a transcendent ideal, Colin is not wholly successful.[60] Dido remains remote. As if Colin were overcome by nominalist heartache, Dido's perfections seem abstract and conventional, as empty as the shining cities and imperial monuments that light up Spenser's dream-visions before crumbling to dust. At best she is a *fictum* in the mind, more likely an armature of words.

Some critics accuse Colin's elegy of emotional evasiveness and cold technical proficiency designed to showcase the skills of the poet more than the attributes of the shepherdess ostensibly memorialized.[61] They endorse my sense that a skeptical testing of abstraction is occurring when Colin Clout sacrifices feeling to elegance and mourning to musicality. Certainly, the intimacy of Marot's vision of heavenly consolation brings out the extent to which The Song of Dido is aestheticized. What's striking is that even Thenot – the eclogue's embedded audience – gives the elegy a lukewarm reception, qualifying his praise with unsettling briskness:

> Ay francke shepheard, how bene thy verses meint
> With doolful pleasaunce, so as I ne wotte,
> Whether rejoyce or weepe for great constrainte?
> Thyne be the cossette, well hast thow it gotte.

---

[59] Pigman says of Marot's "abrupt reversal": "there is something charmingly defiant in this neglect of transition, but the two parts of the poem are hardly unified" (1985, 84).

[60] Compare Cheney who sees this moment as an instance of Spenser's "heroic sublime" because "the poet must keep wing with the soul's ascent. ... Transport takes the form of transcendence, and transcendence takes the form of vision, as the poet witnesses the soul's immortalizing entry into Elysium" (2018, 88). Elsewhere, however, Cheney notes that Spenser solves "the problem of the sceptical sublime, according to which the mind's encounter with the ineffable object produces doubt" (2018, 107).

[61] Berger comments on "the subordination of grief to art and its disappearance into art" (1987, 399). Sacks notes "the highly stilted and theatrical beginning" and "the dogged alliteration and labored syntax," all of which contribute to an "impression of remoteness" (1985, 49, 48).

>   Up *Colin* up, ynough thou morned hast,
>   Now gynnes to mizzle, hye we homeward fast.
>   (203–208)

Colin's sad song has produced a voluptuous commotion inside Thenot, the mixture of pleasaunce and constraint awakening his sensibilities. But his mind moves quickly to other things, his squeamishness about wet weather uppermost in his mind. Moreover, he accidentally on purpose withholds the "greater gifts" that he planned to bestow if Colin's rhymes were "as rownd and rufull" as the ones formerly sung in honor of Rosalind; the cosset is Colin's *faute de mieux* reward. Why does Spenser choose to frame the Song of Dido with Thenot's equivocal remarks? Perhaps he wishes to close on a note of rueful irony, foregrounding Thenot's polite but inadequate response, so as to intimate how precarious a power art has. On the one hand, Spenser showcases a "patterne" of Christian pastoral. On the other, he wonders skeptically what function it serves. What if temple-work (in Heidegger's phrase) neither consoles nor reforms? It may well reveal a world, but it barely holds Thenot's attention.

Poetic Thinking on Mount Acidale

Spenser often refracts his distress about audience response through the rustic persona of Colin Clout, using these moments to think philosophically about poetry's relationship to experience and knowledge. In Book 6 of *The Faerie Queene*, devoted to exploring the virtues of courtesy, the "Elfin Knight," Sir Calidore, blunders into the lyric ecstasy that Colin has conjured with his pipe. It is as if Calidore has wandered into the vibrant sonorities of Spenser's *Epithalamion* – or as if he has encountered that venturesomeness of song that Heidegger associates with Orpheus and the Open: "poets whose song turns our unprotected being into the Open" (1971, 137). The unprotected being of the listener flourishes with the song. At first Sir Calidore stands to the side, mesmerized by the concentric circles of nymphs and graces, spying on the woodland ballet of naked girls. Anticipating the knight's distracting effect, the epic narrator tells Colin in the imperative voice to stay focused on his beloved and continue piping undeterred:

>   Pype iolly sheapheard, pype thou now apace
>   Unto thy love, that made thee low to lout;
>   Thy love is present there with thee in place,
>   Thy love is there advaunst to be another Grace.
>   (VI.x.16)

But Sir Calidore, not content to be "rapt with pleasaunce" and "resolving, what it was, to know, / Out of the wood he rose, and toward them he did go" (VI.x.17). He desires to pluck the heart out of the mystery he has stumbled on. But we learn that "resolving ... to know" is a problem, disruptive and discourteous:

> But soone as he appeared to their vew,
>   They vanisht all away out of his sight,
>   And cleane were gone, which way he never knew;
>   All save the shepheard, who for fell despight
>   Of that displeasure, broke his bag-pipe quight,
>   And made great mone for that unhappy turne.
>   But *Calidore*, though no lesse sory wight,
>   For that mishap, yet seeing him to mourne,
> Drew neare, that he the truth of all by him mote learne.
>   (VI.x.18)

Calidore's maladroit intrusion destroys the vision of beauty and grace that Colin has created through his art.[62] Out of pique, Colin smashes his bagpipe and then begins to "mourne," explaining, "For being gone, none can them bring in place, / But whom they of them selves list so to grace" (VI.x.20). "They" are those "fugitive gods" whose "trace" (Heidegger explains) poets "bring to mortals" (1971, 138).

Insofar as Colin's vision constitutes a climax of aesthetic insight and represents the fragility of inspiration in all its plenitude, it illuminates the artist's desire for beauty and harmony. But this Orphic moment cannot last in part because Spenser is an ironizing skeptic at least as much as a proto-Heideggerian. Just as Colin is descanting on the beauties of his sweetheart – an historical individual surrounded by a chorus of allegorical universals dancing their praise – the author's historically situated voice intrudes with an arch apology:

> Great *Gloriana*, greatest Majesty,
> Pardon thy Shepheard, mongst so many layes,
> As he hath sung of thee in all his dayes,
> To make one minime of thy poore handmayd,
> And underneath thy feete to place her prayse.
>   (VI.x.28)

---

[62] "By the ancient logic of pastoral the piper and the Graces must now stand for poetry itself, Arcadia is the place of innocence and Calidore, that walking embodiment of courtesy, is enemy to both" (Nuttall 2005, 224).

The poet hails the historical Queen Elizabeth, asking her pardon for daring to exalt his lowly beloved (a musical "minime," "thy poore handmayd") in a text dedicated to her. The artist's self-consciousness about his epic project disrupts the dialogue with Calidore; his historical position as a courtier and servant ironizes the textual integrity of his work. The Orphic moment also collapses because Colin, for all his powers of concentration, cannot sustain his fantasy in the presence of a vapid, though admiring, Calidore. That art may be no more than a "picture in the mind," as William of Ockham would say (1964, 44), is an anguishing discovery, felt every time an artist encounters a reader or spectator who falls short. The vision on Mount Acidale is, to echo Virginia Woolf, a great bubble blown from the poet's brain, at risk of puncture from profane passers-by.

The scene of poetic thinking staged on Mount Acidale may be interpreted as an illustration of Heidegger's *Lichtung* – a clearing in the forest open to light that is, in Charles Taylor's words, "the space of expression itself" (1995, 120). After all, the "place" on Mount Acidale is described as an "open greene" (VI.x.11) bordered by a "wood" (VI.x.4). The activity disclosed is poetic creation, lyric language made visible. Taylor treats language and *Lichtung* as almost interchangeable terms, explaining that "language opens a clearing" such that "the human agent is 'the shepherd of Being'" (1995, 121).[63] This is "a de-onticizing move," according to Taylor, because the clearing designates a space "between interlocutors" that reveals the relational embeddedness of *Dasein* (1995, 116–117). As Heidegger puts it, "In the midst of beings as a whole an open place occurs. There is a clearing, a lighting. ... Only this clearing grants and guarantees to us humans a passage to those beings that we ourselves are not, and access to the being that we ourselves are" (1971, 51).[64] Heidegger explains that this open place of song is elusive for man, if not for Orpheus: "The hard thing consists not only in the difficulty of forming the work of language, but in the difficulty of going over from the saying work of the still covetous vision of things, from the work of the eyes, to the 'work of the heart'" (1971, 136). Colin may aspire to Orphic powers and momentarily attain them in his poetic frenzy, but Calidore remains a covetous spectator, full of "greedy fancy" for the shepherd's "discourses" (VI.x.29).

---

[63] Taylor cites Heidegger's "Letter on Humanism," *Wegmarken* (Frankfurt, 1949, 1967) (1995, 328, 338).

[64] Thomson explains: "A clearing redirects our attention from entities to being, that usually unnoticed ontological light through which things ordinarily appear. Seeing differently, Heidegger thus suggests, can turn an apparent dead-end into the occasion for an ontological epiphany" (2019, 3.3).

While Colin may be at one with his creation, *Dasein* inhabiting *Lichtung*, Calidore is a voyeur with a will to know a foreign thought-object. His goal-driven intellectual approach contrasts with the poet's presencing of song.[65]

Gordon Teskey has brilliantly described the "form" of *The Faerie Queene* as a "continual, dynamic adjustment to its changing understanding of itself . . . thought thinking itself while continually changing its mind and giving itself ampler room in which to explore" (2007, 115). Building on Heidegger, among others, to communicate the quality of the poem's thinking, Teskey distinguishes between two models or rather "moments." The first involves moments of arrest, "inviting us to grasp some state of affairs before it slips away" (2007, 114); the keyword here is grasping, as in apprehending a concept but also handling a tool with a designated function. The second model is open-ended, exploratory, practicing a relaxed form of "continual questioning" that Teskey likens to Heidegger's *Gelassenheit*, or letting-go (2007, 114, 116). Teskey understands the virtue of courtesy thematized in Book VI as enacting the second form of poetic thinking because courtesy includes hospitality: welcoming the strange and the stranger. Courtesy, he believes, is central to the poetic thinking implied in Heidegger's "*In-die-Nähe-hinein-sich-enlassen,* letting-oneself-into-nearness," a "self-surrender, which allows one to approach without seizing, and to think by being open to what reveals itself of its own accord" (2003, 357). When describing Spenser's "project" in *The Faerie Queene*, Teskey speaks of "an intellectual action" and "delicate, courteous probing of the unknown" (2003, 357). It is part of the irony of the scene on Mount Acidale – as well as of the knight's education – that Calidore ruins the moment when Colin Clout is grooving into nearness of the graces with his poetic piping (*In-die-Nähe-gehen*). Calidore recognizes his rudeness and begs "pardon" for the "luckeless breach" he has made to Colin's "blisse" (VI.x.29).

The bumbling knight models the first kind of poetic thinking, which is premised on the dichotomy between subject and object on which the skeptical problematic depends. Resolving to know, he falls into the trap of the subject who wishes to grasp the object of thought and in the course of that aggressive move breaks the spell. As if he had learned from other characters in *The Faerie Queene* misled by their sensory experience,

---

[65] Baldine Saint Girons captures something of Colin's phenomenological experience on Mount Acidale so long as one substitutes the graces for the nocturne as an emblem of the artist's desire: "Aussi bien fallait-il arriver à penser la nuit non comme quelque chose qui subsisterait tel un objet, mais au contraire, comme un événement qui se produit au-dehors de moi, mais aussi en moi, quant *je deviens la nuit*" (2004, 287).

Calidore worries about the ontic status of what he sees. Faced with the "straunge sight" of a hundred naked women dancing, he "wist not what to weene" and entertains four possibilities: "Whether it were the traine of beauties Queene, / Or Nymphes, or Faeries, or enchaunted show, / With which his eyes mote have deluded beene" (VI.x.17). The elfin knight is not so naïve or infatuated with pleasure as not to consider that his eyes might be deceiving him. His skepticism about the object of sight leads him to inquiry.

Calidore is a descendant of the dreamers in Spenser's translations from the French: beneficiaries of a beautiful and mysterious vision the meaning of which they struggle to grasp. On Mount Acidale the sights to be grasped are no longer temples and other architectural metonymies, but rather nymphs, graces, and centrally, Colin Clout's beloved – an individual among mythical figures and allegories. The sense of eschatological crisis may have faded, replaced by the plenitude of aesthetic experience; yet all these visions are artworks, issuing from the poet–dreamer's mental labor, and all vanish at the slightest jar – fragile as a hallucination although each discloses a world. As Heidegger says, "towering up within itself, the work opens up a *world* and keeps it abidingly in force" (1971, 43). While Spenser might doubt the presumption of abidingness, reminding Heidegger of mutability's sway, he would surely share Heidegger's sense of the artwork as engaged in unconcealing and disclosure. He might even appreciate the anti-Platonist thrust of Heidegger's rhetorical question: "Who could maintain the impossible view that the Idea of Temple is represented in the building?" (1971, 36). Yet unlike Heidegger, Spenser feels no urgency to abandon the polarity between subject and object. Colin's vision of the dancing graces oscillates like a nominalist hologram – at once a Botticellian picture and a festival of heightened language. This suggests Spenser's lingering fascination with Scholastic metaphysics. Like a conflicted nominalist, he wants it both ways: aesthetic experience at once internalized and transcendent; pictures in the mind operating as universals but also capturing the reality of at least one beloved individual limned in words. Like the early Heidegger who wrote his thesis on Duns Scotus and the nominalist logic of Thomas of Erfurt before reacting against his younger self's "subjectivism" (Taylor 1995, 114), Spenser never fully escapes from nominalist structures of feeling and their skeptical consequences.[66]

---

[66] Taylor cites *Die Kategorien-und Bedeutungslehre des Duns Scotus*, in *Frühe Schriften* 280. As S. J. McGrath says, "The *Habilitationsschrift* introduces us to a Heidegger at home in the Middle Ages,

Mutability and the Nominalist Sublime

Spenser expresses himself poetically, pictorially, and epistemologically in ways that attest to his engagement with skeptical problems, including those following from nominalist debates. While the vision on Mount Acidale conjures the glory and fragility of language in action, only pausing to interpellate the Queen, *The Mutability Cantos* – perhaps the last written part of his allegedly unfinished epic poem – more fully explore questions of divine power and contingent norms. They bear traces of those nominalist structures of feeling outlined by Oberman. These include the subject's autonomy and God's sovereignty, horizontal explorations beneath heaven's "dome," and vertical longings for relationship with the divine. Because nominalism wishes, above all, to preserve God's freedom and power to have ordered things differently (*potentia absoluta*), it follows that the established order of things (*potentia ordinata*) is contingent. This awareness of contingency can inform a range of emotional postures taken in dialectical response to uncertainty: humility and hubris, detachment and passion, reality hunger and eschatological openness.[67] In *The Mutabilitie Cantos* we see, above all, "the speculative fascination exerted by the theological predicates of absolute power and freedom" typical of nominalism (Blumenberg 1983, 160). The cosmic scale of his fascination with power and freedom allows Spenser to broach the sublime – understood here as a special category of aesthetic experience involving dread and awe at the grandeur of the ravages of both nature and culture.

The relation of skepticism and the sublime has been theorized in recent years.[68] David Sedley, for example, contends that "two early modern phenomena, the rise of the sublime as an aesthetic category and the emergence of skepticism as a philosophical problem, are interrelated" (2005, 8). By locating the emergence of the sublime, not in the late seventeenth or early eighteenth century as usually happens, but in the late sixteenth century with Montaigne, Sedley aims to recover the structure of their "close but unstable cohabitation" (2005, 3). Montaigne, he claims, inaugurates the experience of the skeptical sublime when he records his impressions of Rome in 1580–1 in his *Journal de Voyage*. Du Bellay's work shaped Montaigne's expectations of Rome. But Montaigne rejects the

---

discovering in its labyrinthine metaphysics rich disclosures of historical life and prefigurations of phenomenological concepts" (2006, 43).
[67] "The distinction [between *potentia absoluta* and *ordinata*] is not understood unless presented as 'dialectics'" (Oberman 1987, 28).
[68] See Chapter 5 for more on the skeptical sublime.

Mutability and the Nominalist Sublime

discourse of wonder (*admiratio*) predominant in Du Bellay. Faced with the challenge of conjuring the grandeur of empire from the experience of rubble, Montaigne makes an imaginative leap that requires its own aesthetic category: the sublime. Like Spenser who also wrestles with Du Bellay's temples, Montaigne "depicts an interactive relation between the retreat of epistemological and moral authority and the advancement of a certain notion of aesthetic experience" (Sedley 2005, 42). That notion of aesthetic experience, I believe, emerges not just from Pyrrhonist doubt, but also from the skepticism fostered by nominalist questions and late Scholastic debates.

As an allegory, Mutability operates like one of those "instantly viewed universal[s]" described by Nuttall: "half-concept, half-image, the universal which is ... an instance of itself" (1967, 36).[69] She enacts restlessness, impatience, and indignation. Headstrong and changeable by definition, Mutability feels entitled to shape her own destiny and rule over others, behaving like one of those autonomous subjects described by Oberman. At first her reach is horizontal, as she subdues the sublunar world, breaking the laws of Nature, Justice and Policy (VII.vi.6).[70] But then her aspirations turn skyward in her bid to transcend the dome and confront divine authority. As the narrator recounts,

> And now, when all the earth she thus had brought
> To her behest, and thralled to her might,
> She gan to cast in her ambitious thought,
> T'attempt th'empire of the heavens hight,
> And *Iove* himself to shoulder from his right.
> (VII.vi.7)

Full of self-assertion, Mutability rebels against Jove's sovereignty. She flaunts her freedom to challenge prevailing conceptions of cosmic political order, insisting on their contingency. Having caused mayhem on earth and perverted Nature's orderly statutes (VII.vi.5), she seeks an unmediated encounter with the Olympian deities. Her hunger for immediate experience is typical of nominalism, even as she functions like an "instantly viewed" abstract universal.

---

[69] Consider Ockham: "Every universal is one particular thing and ... is not a universal except in its signification, in its signifying many things" (1974, 1. 14). Might not this view of universals have implications for allegory?

[70] Brown compares Mutability to "a Marlovian overreacher" (2010, 276). Marlovian overreachers may be acting out in response to nominalist structures of feeling inasmuch as they feel empowered to act outside the law, modeling their sovereignty on God's *potentia absoluta*; see Langer on *lex regia* versus *lex digna* (1990, 153–158).

Mutability's journey through the vastness of the universe approaches the sublime. She travels through the elemental and planetary spheres separating her from ultimate power. Canto VI rehearses her vertical flight:

> And first, she past the region of the ayre,
> And of the fire, whose substance thin and slight,
> Made no resistance, ne could her contraire,
> But ready passage to her pleasure did prepare.
> (VII.vi.7)

Shooting up through air and fire, she climbs to the Circle of the Moon, arriving at "a bright shining palace" where she enters through "silver gates" to find Cynthia "sitting on an Ivory throne . . . / Drawne of two steeds, th'one black, the other white, / Environd with tenne thousand starres around" (VV.vi.8–9). The ensemble is dramatic: a nocturnal voyage pausing at a dazzling, moonlit shore. But a storm is in the offing as the Moon and Mutability quarrel about precedence:

> Meane-while, the lower World, which nothing knew
> Of all that chaunced here was darkned quite;
> And eke the heavens, and all the heavenly crew
> Of happy wights, now unpurvaide of light,
> Were much afraid, and wondred at that sight;
> Fearing least *Chaos* broken had his chaine,
> And brought againe on them eternall night: (VII.vi.14)

As Milton doubtless appreciated, the overall effect of this *mise-en-scène* is sublime – a shadowed world below while up above the celestial forces clash in peril of "the wrathfull Thunders wrack" (VII.vi.12).

No sooner is this sublime cosmos evoked than it is called into skeptical question thanks to a rhetorical move exposing the canto's crafted textuality; picture and language collide, evoking scholastic debates about the hybrid status of mental fictions. The intrusion of the word, Author, abruptly defuses the threatening storm in an "ironic reversal" typical of the skeptical sublime's economy (Noggle 2001, 6). Hearing about the trouble below, Jove orders Hermes to deal with its instigator, even as he concedes that a rebellious "Author" might well have emerged from his own Olympian precincts:

> Him to attache, and down to hell to throwe;
> But, if from heaven it were, then to arrest
> The Author, and him bring before his presence prest.
> (VII.vi.16)

The meta-narrative word, Author, aligning Spenser with Mutability, draws us up short, breaking the illusion of sublimity along with our suspension of disbelief. The incongruous picture of Hermes manacling "The Author" and marching him/her into Jove's court reminds us again of history and the way the censoring state apparatus can puncture the "great bubble blown from the poet's brain." This moment marks (as Colin Burrow would say) "a potential antagonism between power and poetry" (2001, 233); it may also parody (as Colin Clout might wager) the Jovian artist's desire to behold his muse and summon fugitive holiness into the Open.

While the self-conscious use of the word, Author, may arrest us in our tracks, confounded by the uneasy relation of compromised authority and aesthetic self-display, Mutability continues undeterred by the prospect of arraignment. She insists that her de facto primacy be acknowledged de jure by having Jove and his Olympian retinue relinquish their sovereignty and grant it to her. She demands a hearing in which she can air her claims. After confrontational encounters with the Moon and Mercury that leave these deities amazed and fearful, Mutability pursues her upward path: "So forth she rose, and through the purest sky / To *Ioves* high Palace straight cast to ascend" (VII.vi.23). This journey through the vast reaches of interplanetary space has been interpreted as a Neoplatonic allegory of the path to knowledge. Jove's grumbling about the uppitiness of "mortall thoughts" confirms this interpretation: "Will never mortall thoughts ceasse to aspire, / In this bold sort, to Heaven claime to make, / And touch celestiall seates with earthly mire?" (VII.vi.29). But although the representation of the desire for knowledge as a heavenly ascent may be a conventional trope – reprised, as we saw earlier, in The Song of Dido with its ecstatic climax – it is less common to find the celestial world figured as transitory and provisional.

Jove's world order is an historical accident, Mutability maintains, a usurpation with tenuous legitimacy. While its chanciness may owe much to Lucretius, the specter of *potentia ordinata* – as one among many possible worlds that God could have created – should not be dismissed.[71] Consider that when Mutability faces the Olympian cabal, Jove in effect admits that his sway over the lower world is conditional and might well have never been. He points out that "we by Conquest of our soveraine might, / And by eternall doome of Fates decree, / Have wonne the Empire of the heaven's bright" (VII.vi.33). While this 'might-makes-right' defense is

---

[71] For the complex synergies of Epicureanism and nominalism, see Blumenberg (1983), 148–173. For Taylor's disagreement with aspects of Blumenberg's argument, see 2007, 114.

problematic – not clinching Jove's authority in the way he imagines, but rather undermining it – it also suggests engagement with nominalist debates about the arbitrariness and contingency of the way divine powers have ordered the administration of the world. "Contingency," Oberman reminds us, "is perhaps the best one-word summary of the nominalist program" (1974, 13).

The heightened awareness of contingency in nominalism encourages meditation on history. Thanks to nominalism's prizing of experience and its enabling view of particulars as individuals, there is renewed appreciation of history's value as a cognitive pathway. Philosophy and history should therefore be viewed as complementary rather than as antithetical modes of knowing. Instead of seeing Mutability's genealogical claims to power pitted violently against Jove's metaphysical order of authoritative forms, as Teskey does, a nominalist approach to metaphysics solicits the vitality of historical bodies in all their genealogical particularity.[72] Mutability's adventures thus permit Spenser to explore issues of sovereignty, freedom, and justice in two registers: one with historical and political resonance, relating to the English plantations in Ireland and colonial imperialism, and another with theological and philosophical resonances relating to God's power. To be sure, Spenser deliberately aestheticizes history in *The Mutabilitie Cantos*, transmuting its pain and violence into the enchanting cadences of Ovidian epyllion. But more than Ovid, Spenser dwells on the desire for knowledge: its urgencies, limitations, and demands. Mutability's journey of protest represents the mind's need for accountability and understanding, even as her boisterousness enacts existential and epistemological dissatisfaction. Skeptical interrogation and disappointment suffuse the sublime interstellar spaces of a contrived mythology.

Finding Jove a partial judge and therefore unacceptable, Mutability appeals to Nature as a higher authority. Canto VII opens with a description of "great dame *Nature*" that is sublime. Not only is Nature larger and more majestic than other "gods or Powers," but her appearance confounds the cognitive powers of the narrator who resorts to a tissue of verbal figures in an attempt to capture the ineffable. For example, the fifth stanza ends:

---

[72] Teskey argues that the *Mutabilitie Cantos* stage "Spenser's defection from metaphysics" by enacting a conflict between metaphysics and genealogy: "an aesthetically legitimated order of forms" is subverted as "metaphysics, the study of things with independent being and freedom from change, is shown to have emerged from something other than itself which it subsequently tries to forget, or at least to contain" (1996, 173).

> Yet certes by her face and physnomy,
> Whether she man or woman inly were,
> That could not any creature well descry:
> For, with a veile that wimpled every where,
> Her head and face was hid, that mote to none appeare.

As Kenneth Gross has indicated, the image of the veiled countenance has so many associations and pulls in so many different directions that it is difficult to pin down how it is working here (1985, 247–248). But surely it is safe to say that Nature here represents something behind or beyond the veil of appearances, something more "real" perhaps but ultimately elusive.[73] Heidegger might identify Spenser's Nature with Being (*Dasein*) since it conceals itself and responds best to the Orphic powers of the poet if it is to be drawn forth. The truth of Nature's Being involves both veiling and unveiling for Heidegger. Spenser's "Orphic" description of Nature verges on the Heideggerian: "Unseene of any, yet of all beheld" (VII.13).[74] He shares with Heidegger an interest in Heraclitus' sense of mutability, in the dilemmas posed by nominalism, and in philosophical questions about art's relation to being. Spenser's Nature is hardly an allegory like Malbecco or Despair, her wimpled veil notwithstanding. Rather, she is a personified abstraction so sublime that the poet is at a loss for similes and metaphors, reduced to the topos of inexpressibility even as he shifts to a biblical register:

> Her garment was so bright and wondrous sheene,
> That my fraile wit cannot devize to what
> It to compare, nor finde like stuffe to that,
> As those three sacred *Saints*, though else most wise,
> Yet on mount *Thabor* quite their wits forgat,
> When they their glorious Lord in strange disguise
> Transfigur'd sawe; his garments so did daze their eyes.
>
> (VII.vii.7)

Since Nature herself cannot be fathomed, the poet can only describe the feelings of awe and rapt wonder experienced by those who behold

---

[73] Spenser's Nature belongs in Hadot's magisterial account of the "fortunes throughout the ages" of Heraclitus' phrase, "phusis kruptesthai philei," usually mistranslated as "nature loves to hide" (2006, 1). Glossing Heidegger, Hadot affirms the poet's Orphic role in enticing nature to disclose her secrets. "Heidegger," Hadot claims, "brings Heraclitus's aphorism up to date" (2006, 303).

[74] Nohrnberg (1976), 743.

her. The words garment and wit are each repeated in the stanza so as to link the dazzling apparition with the spectators' incoherence, even as the veil screens the terrors of the real. The shift to a biblical comparison attests to the inadequacies of the classical pantheon in supplying a simile elevated enough for so sublime an occasion.[75]

With his interpellation of the divine Word as a figure for the elusiveness of being, Spenser seems attuned here to Heidegger's intuition that "truth is the opposition of clearing and concealing" (59).[76] The poetic Word can only enter the Open in disguise. While Spenser may share Heidegger's nostalgia for the poet's Orphic power, he does not quarrel with traditional epistemological dichotomies, and therefore would surely disagree when Heidegger declares that "truth does not exist in itself beforehand, somewhere among the stars, only later to descend elsewhere among beings" (1971, 59). Although Spenser shies away from pronouncements on truth, preferring instead to chart her veiled appearances, he would agree that "poets who are of the more venturesome kind are under way on the track of the holy" (1971, 138).

Following Mutability's oration before Dame Nature, claiming that since the cosmos is all about change, it should therefore fall under her sway, Spenser pursues the holy by orchestrating a tableau at once sublime and *faux naïf* in its stately round. Personification, allegory, and circular motion come together in a remarkably serene and almost geometrical composition. Harry Berger, Jr. has noted "the foreground artifice" of these cantos: "the reduction to purely visual and spatial terms of a subject whose essential meaning is temporal" (1988, 156). Sporting quasi-medieval iconographic costumes, the months, hours and emblematic seasons of the year ride by, "marching softly" (VII.vii.32). On the one hand, this allegorical procession seems to instantiate the "rhythmical and seemly" swaying that Woolf describes as Spenser's "celestial rocking horse." The orderly cluster of mythological figures – as familiar as the dancing graces on Mount Acidale or the nymphs of the *Epithalamion* – seem like happy silhouettes projected against a vast, encroaching darkness. On the other hand, the unwieldy pageantry seems only to mask the anxiety provoked by transience and mortality. Owing to its vicinity to the sublime, the pageant's cosmic harmonies threaten to spin out, exposed as a terrifying illusion.

---

[75] Gross calls it a "dis-simile" (1985, 247).
[76] Bruns explains that for Heidegger "truth itself is inscribed by a rift that splits it, so to say, lengthwise, joining the familiar and the strange, openness and refusal, clearing and dissembling, unconcealedness and withdrawal, darkness and light. ... Truth is always historical; it is always an event" (1989, 34).

The nominalist abyss dividing God in his arbitrary majesty from the lower world elicits a sublime aesthetic tending toward skepticism. The gods that inhabit the *Mutabilitie Cantos* belong squarely to the lower world, although they convince themselves otherwise when they impersonate the inscrutability and caprice of the *deus absconditus*. Their claim to absolute power produces sublime ripples when they seek to overwhelm the cognitive capacities of their subjects, almost making them "reft of sense, / And voyd of speech" (VII.vi.25). Teskey notes the "anaesthetic" and "narcotic" effects of their pronouncements (1996, 180, 184). He argues that their Olympian delusion is premised on a massive forgetting of their own violent origins. They wish to repress not only the Hesiodic theogony evoked by Spenser when he makes Dame Mutability a Titaness, but also the possible worlds that could have come into being but for the *potentia ordinata*. Mutability, Teskey says, represents all the possible worlds struggling to emerge from non-being.[77] While he emphasizes their suppression and the erasures of history, I suggest that Spenser's aestheticizing of metaphysics issues from structures of feeling regarding freedom and power related to nominalist critiques of language and theology.[78] The realms of conceptual possibility opened up by God's *potentia absoluta* can be entertained alongside a reverent acknowledgment of the body's history in the political *agora*. Indeed, the Arlo Hill interlude, with its mythologizing of Irish places and intermittent humor, may form part of a structure of feeling that puts a puckish skeptical laughter about history in complex relation to the tragic tenor of the skeptical sublime.[79] After all, there is a terrifying beauty in the muted violence disturbing the glassy surface of Spenser's creations.

That said, Nature's riddling reply to Mutability's "plaintif Plea" (VII. vii.13) seems a piece of sophistry rather than a profound philosophical statement, in keeping with the poem's technical bravura and textual self-awareness.[80] Following a long "thinking moment,"[81] Nature uses the

---

[77] "Mutability ... contains every world that would struggle to displace this actual world were her genealogical power released, spawning worlds by the tens of thousands, like roe" (Teskey, 1996, 182).

[78] But see Kellie Robertson who argues that Spenser's philosophical poetics contends primarily with neo-Aristotelian views of nature (2017, 325–333).

[79] See Gross on "the founding skepticism" of Faunus's "transgressive laughter": "a brilliant trope for the troubling magic of Spenser's own poetic idiom, which seeks to disenchant even the dumb enchantment possible in the sounds of language itself" (1985, 243, 241, 244).

[80] Hadfield calls it "a neat trick," adding that "taking Nature at face value is to take the writing as witty but inconsequential metaphysical poetry" (1997, 190, 199).

[81] Teskey 2007, 122.

rhetorical figure of redescription (*paradiastole*) to deliver an aptly circular tautology:

> I well consider all that ye have sayd,
>   And find that all things stedfastness doe hate
> And changed be: yet being rightly wayd
>   They are not changed from their first estate;
> But by their change their being doe dilate:
>   And turning to themselves at length againe,
> Doe worke their owne perfection so by fate:
>   Then over them Change doth not rule and raigne;
> But they raigne over change, and doe their states maintaine.
>   (VII.vii.58)

That cyclical patterns "worke their own perfection," dilating the being of things, is hardly a refutation of Mutability's sway, let alone a consolation. Reminding her that the universe is in an eternal condition of flux seems unlikely to appease her demands. At best it may produce vertigo rather than outrage. As Ramachandran observes, "Nature's verdict deals in perceptions of the phenomenal world," illustrating "the limits of human knowing" even as it shuts down Mutability's "intellectual aspiration" (2010, 238). Being at the receiving end of gnomic intimidation has a long history going back to the Book of Job. Unfortunately we do not learn how Mutability responds to Nature's "doome" (VII.vii.57). We are told only that "the Titaness [was] put downe and whist," that is, silenced (VII.vii.59). But we do learn about the poet/narrator's response. Impressed by Mutability, convinced that "she beares the greatest sway," he chooses to "loath this state of life" and "to cast away" love of vain things (VII.viii.1). Before the immense metaphysical mysteries inspiring the sublime, he has few words, almost as silenced as Mutability.

Together with the sublime, nominalism's privileging of power, freedom and mental language may well characterize the aesthetic gestures of modernity. In the end Nature concedes that the lower world is a function of *potentia ordinata* when she foresees, "But time shall come that all shall changed bee, / And from thenceforth, none no more change shall see" (VII.vii.59). The apocalyptic future prophesied in these lines depends on a perspectival understanding of the difference between past and future; yet the changelessness foreseen seems ontological. The immutability imagined in these lines suggests that the categories and structures that organize our temporal experience here below are contingent and no match against the mystery of the cosmos. Consciousness itself is pictured like Mutability's pageant: a wheeling zodiac of temples and dancing chimeras, "Signes" projected against the nocturnal gloom of a cavernous mind (VII.vii.55). This consciousness is vulnerable, afflicted by its limitations, yet wide open to the unknown *eschaton*.

In the cantos' final line, the poet voices his desire to know changelessness and rest: "O that great Sabbaoth God, graunt me that Sabaoths sight." This scene is sober and quiet. No nymphs, no dancers, no woodland gods respond to the call. The poet's plea for access to a vision of eternal rest is no more than a whispered prayer, an austere ending to an epic phantasmagoria.[82] While Berger sees the poet attaining a "dynamic equilibrium at the end, still looking backward, still thrusting forward, still revolving doubts" (1968, 173), I see the weary poet crumpled in abject humility before the remoteness of his sublime, nominalist God.[83] As a wayfarer, he feels all too cut off from the beyond and free to improvise a life under "the dome." As Jane Grogan describes him, he is "certain only of his uncertainty, trudging into the future with wandering steps and slow" (2010, 12). Yet even at this stark moment, as we overhear the *viator* praying for eschatological immediacy, the language of Du Bellay's *Songe* resonates. "The pillours of Eternity" that the poet invokes as metonymy for the true and the real summon the mental image of a future monumental ruin. Like the young dreamer of those early sonnets for whom the heavens part to reveal a shining temple, the older poet prays that God will sustain that vision, keep it from crumbling, and grant him that Saboaths sight: "all things firmly stayd / Upon the pillours of Eternity." The presence of that elusive templework with its promise of rest would mean far more to him perhaps than the truth of the work of art.

---

[82] Of the final prayer, Greene notes "its terrible pathos" as "the slow, familiar, meditative voice breaks with unwonted poignance into a final cry for deliverance" (1986, 64). He adds, commenting on Douglas Bush's gloss, "If faith is indeed a refuge here, it is a lonely and bitter one" (64).

[83] This means muting the force of the etymological pun on "Elizabeth" in Hebrew, noted most recently by Christian (2016, 220–221) and earlier by Nohrnberg (1976, 83) and others. It also means muting the symmetry with the Faunus episode implied by the pun, suggesting "that the poet, in keeping with the theme of Diana's discovery, anticipates a sighting of his sovereign" (Maley 2001, 174).

CHAPTER 2

Fantasies of Private Language
Shakespeare's "The Phoenix and Turtle" and Donne's "The Ecstasy"

"Private language" is a vexed term seldom applied to the early modern period, mostly because it is anachronistic, having been coined by Ludwig Wittgenstein in the mid-twentieth century. Yet the idea of a private language would not have seemed far-fetched in the seventeenth century given the long history of sophisticated theorizing about language and semantics going back to the Scholastics. The nominalist idea of a mental language (*oratio mentalis*), discussed in Chapter 1, is part of this history. The formulation of "perfect" and "universal" languages takes many forms in the period – from abstract grammars of the sort favored by nominalist logicians to speculations about prelapsarian speech.[1] Notions of language as the privileged site of rationality derive in part from Adam's naming of the animals in Genesis 2:19. This biblical account of origins becomes the basis for divergent but related theories of language: the first involving a sovereign individual with the power to recognize essences and confer identity, the second involving a fantasy of fellowship and unitary language among speakers prior to Babel. The mental language of the nominalists participates in this fantasy inasmuch as its structure underlies and hence precedes all spoken languages. While the notion of a universal and therefore perfect language, common to all, may seem to be the antithesis of a private language, they share the same dream: an Edenic ideal of perfect communication. Both private and universal languages speak to a desire for perfect legibility. Private language is thus an instance, or sub-type, of a perfect language. While Wittgenstein's thought-experiments with private language occur in his later work (sections 243–315 of his *Philosophical Investigations*), they share concerns with the universal logic of his earlier

---

[1] Sixteenth- and seventeenth-century debates about biblical hermeneutics and prelapsarian languages provide a rich and germane context for a philosophical consideration of language in general, and poetic language in particular, as media with varying degrees of transparency and obscurity. See, among others, D. C. Allen (1949); Coudert (1999); Eco (1995); Hequembourg (2014); Ormsby-Lennon (1988); Poole (2008).

Tractatus. As a young man, Wittgenstein was attracted to mathematical logic as an instantiation of a universal language, going so far as to call it sublime.[2] He later repudiated it in favor of ordinary language, with its messy variations and ambiguities.

Private language, while apparently the opposite of the *Ursprache* or *lingua adamica* imagined by seventeenth-century thinkers, betrays a similar yearning for transparent communication. Both linguistic models aspire to clarity and complete understanding. In a fallen world both perfect and private languages are inaccessible, simultaneously inviting and resisting invention. Both are out of reach, the one in the paradisal past, the other as a figment or concept lodged inside one's head. Despite this temporal and spatial disparity, both perfect and private languages aim at a linguistic world without skepticism. They represent attempts to discover how theoretically possible ideal languages might work. This chapter argues that Shakespeare and Donne entertain the idea of an elusive tongue, not so as to probe the cosmological mysteries of the universe and the divine order of creation, but rather so as to investigate the possibilities of Edenic intimacy. They dream of a private language shared with an alter ego, but they represent it in opposed ways. Shakespeare's "Phoenix and Turtle" attests to the impossibility of accessing private language, insisting on our necessary reliance on linguistic practices like genre. By contrast, Donne's "Ecstasy" experiments with the thing itself, "inventing" a private language only to turn in the end to the body to find full expression.

As a preliminary to analysis of the poems, let me sketch how seventeenth-century philosophy at once anticipates and lays the groundwork for the private language argument. The connection hinges on notions of private experience and private sensation. Descartes, for example, frames the problem of the enclosed mind with his famous *cogito* and his thought-experiment about whether other people – those whom he sees from his window walking by – are mere automata. In his *Essay on Human Understanding*, Locke similarly operates with a model of an enclosed mind receiving impressions from the outside world and translating them into a private set of meanings. Although Descartes is often dubbed a rationalist and Locke an empiricist, they share a powerful vision of humans as isolated entities, cut off from one another, busily deciphering unreliable sense-data

---

[2] Wittgenstein asks, "In what way is logic something sublime? For logic seemed to have a peculiar depth – a universal significance. Logic lay, it seemed, at the foundation of all the sciences" (2009, § 89). This revised translation titles what was formerly known as part II of the *Investigations* as *Philosophy of Psychology: A Fragment*, abbreviating it as *PPF*.

in an effort to forge connections with the world. In certain moods Shakespeare and Donne also share this vision of individuals alone with their private experience. The idea of private experience held by empiricists and rationalists alike is one that Wittgenstein attacks. Although he avoids a historical approach, his targets are widely assumed to include Cartesian and Lockean views of enclosed minds finding words with which to label private sensations.[3] His objection to the idea of a private language is that language is by definition communal, such that it makes no sense to imagine inventing signs in isolation. When his fictional interlocutor asks, "But is it also conceivable that there be [sic] a language in which a person could write down or give voice to his inner experiences – his feelings, moods, and so on – for his own use?" (2009, § 243), the answer is ultimately no. Before arriving at the conclusion that private language is an oxymoron and nonsense, however, Wittgenstein entertains scenarios in which something resembling a private language emerges. Because these help illuminate the Shakespeare and Donne poems, let me mention two such scenarios of secret or hermetic language.

Wittgenstein concedes that occasions could arise when one might want to coin terms for one's private use.[4] He imagines a man keeping a journal about an intermittent pain he is feeling, proposing to jot down every experience of this mysterious twinge with the sign, "S." The diarist's process would involve an intensely focused inward gaze, a quality of strained attention, which would amount to an ostensive definition – an inward finger-pointing that would pick out the particular pain sensation and name it. This diarist is imagined as an Adam conferring names on his inward fauna in what Wittgenstein dubs a "ceremony" (2009, § 258). This diarist is different from a Donne or a Shakespeare trying to give voice to inner weather because he is trying to identify a feeling for which there are no known words. A related scenario involves Siamese twins. In this exceptional case, the question considers how the twins would verify their shared experience of the identical sensation. What words would they use? Presumably, ordinary, everyday words.

Speaking a language, Wittgenstein is at pains to point out, involves learning to negotiate a set of practices and conventions. Language is an inherited, rule-driven, social system emerging from different forms of life

---

[3] See, among others, Hacker (1986, 246); Kripke (1982, 62–69, 121–122); and Avrum Stroll (2002, 118).
[4] Commentators debate the relation of secret and private language. See, among others, Ayer and Rhees (1954); Cavell (1979, 344–350); Mulhall (2007); Saunders and Henze (1967, 6–30); Werhane (1992, 22–25).

(which Wittengenstein calls *Lebensformen*), as Shakespeare and Donne well knew. Neither the diarist nor the Siamese twins can generate a language from scratch. This is not to deny that cryptographers can invent secret codes or that ingenious people, in the seventeenth century no less than now, have developed a plethora of elite or esoteric languages. Wittgenstein's point is that each of these special languages is always already implicated in a social grammar. As he puts it, "Much must be prepared in the language for mere naming to make sense" (2009, § 257). Still, Wittgenstein concedes the longstanding appeal of a solipsistic model of mind, even while noting its distressing result in skepticism, understood as doubt about the outside world and other people. As he puts it, "The essential thing about private experience is really not that each person possesses his own specimen, but that nobody knows whether other people also have *this* or something else" (2009, § 272). The desire for assurance that another person shares seemingly private sensations runs deep. It can take the form of the question critical to Shakespeare and Donne's work: how can I know with certainty what my beloved is thinking? This curiosity about others' private experience should be seen as a vital response to the solitude associated with a skeptical consciousness.

The philosopher Stanley Cavell, a gifted interpreter of Wittgenstein and Shakespeare, among others, suggests that skepticism and the desire for intimacy go together when he contends that "with the birth of skepticism ... a new intimacy, or wish for it, enters the world; call it privacy shared" (2003, 21).[5] Because skepticism is experienced as a "withdrawal of the world" in Cavell's view (a formulation that construes the individual not as a mind so much as a body poised over the abyss), one who is in thrall to a skeptical crisis will act out the visceral need for attachment to the world by jealously demanding perfect knowledge of the beloved (2003, 19); think of Othello or Leontes. The skeptic in his lonely detachment craves intimacy, and the more it eludes him, the more he compensates with hyperbolic language and fantasies of ecstatic union. In other words, the Cartesian philosopher's hyperbolic doubt, whereby the world falls away and leaves only the assurance of the *cogito*, becomes transformed into a hyperbolic demand for the certainty and beauty of companionship. For Cavell, this means marriage – a union that

---

[5] For a fuller argument about the dialectical relays and rhythms characterizing the experience of skepticism, see Sherman (2007). Developing the Cavellian idea of skepticism's moods, Conant distinguishes "the Cartesian genre of scepticism" with its discoveries that end "in a mood of disappointment" from "the Kantian genre of scepticism" with its indifference, mystery, and attendant mood of despair (2004, 107, 111).

Shakespeare and Donne, as we shall see, also invite us to examine. In an uncanny echo of Wittgenstein's use of ceremony to describe the deictic inward gaze labeling a private sensation, Cavell describes marriage as a ceremony of single intimacy that arises as a form of defense against tragic consciousness. His phrase, "ceremony of single intimacy," captures the uneasy yoking of inherited practice with a model of relationality that seeks escape from the world (2003, 19). The problem, Cavell says, succumbing to a skepticism shared with Donne and Shakespeare, is that "no one knows from outside whether a marriage exists" (2003, 28). Marriage is thus an exemplary instance of the problem of other minds, eliciting doubt.

The difficulty of knowing from the outside whether a marriage exists is central to both "The Phoenix and Turtle" and "The Ecstasy." The lovers have to mythologize their love to fend off the threat of skepticism; in so doing, they resort to hyperbole.[6] As Cavell explains, "Since marriage ... is an image of the ordinary in human existence (the ordinary as what is under attack in philosophy's tendency to skepticism), the pair's problem, the response to their crisis, is to transfigure, or resurrect, their vision of their everyday lives" (2004, 422). Intimacy thus partakes both of everydayness (*Alltäglichkeit*) and of transcendence, understood as a desire for transfiguration. Cavell interprets Shakespeare's Cleopatra and her "reinvention of marriage" at the end of *Antony and Cleopatra* as a "quest for transcendence" involving multiple ceremonies ("coronation to religion to theater to marriage to revels to funeral") even as it invokes the ordinary (doing "the meanest chares") as its condition (2003, 28–29). That "a hallucinated marriage is an auto-erotic fantasy" does not preclude the presence and anticipation of an audience (2003, 34). Not only is Cleopatra surrounded by her attendants at her suicide, but Octavius is expected as well, Antony is imagined awaiting her with open arms in the afterlife, and we are there. The theatricality of this scene, the exhibitionism of its intimacy, its invitation to voyeurs – all this supports Cavell's view that skepticism,

---

[6] Hyperbole has a complex relationship to the sublime, but sometimes, as in the two poems discussed here, they operate in tandem. Longinus' treatise, *On the Sublime*, suggests that rhetors are able to transport their audiences and fill them with exalted feelings thanks partly to a judicious use of hyperbole (see 1985 ed., chapter 38). Porter deems that hyperbole "practically emblematizes sublimity in Longinus" (2016, 270). Yet in the seventeenth century Nicolas Boileau questions whether the sublime necessitates a hyperbolic style, preferring the *sermo humilis* of the Bible (Doran 2015, 110–123). That said, sublime effects are often conveyed with rhetorical figures while hyperbole itself can drive an aesthetic; as Christopher D. Johnson observes, hyperbole captures "the self-conscious indecorousness of excessive figuration" (2010, 329). Both terms concern the expressiveness of language: what can or cannot be said about the extraordinary and the exceptional. For more on hyperbole and the sublime, see, e.g., Porter (2016, 270–277, 562); Cheney (2018, 135, 219–220). For the sublime and skepticism, see my Chapters 1 and 5.

theatricality, and the desire for intimacy go together. Hyperbole allows Cleopatra to tap into the sublime and to stage a scene that purports to vanquish skeptical doubt.

Like the final tableau of *Antony and* Cleopatra, both "The Phoenix and Turtle" and "The Ecstasy" conjure up ceremonies of single intimacy that aim to disarm a skeptical consciousness.[7] Both poems present a sublime vision of ecstatic union. Both mythologize the lovers, and both invite passers-by to witness the unique relationship. Yet, their contrasting approaches to the problem of intimacy reveal a fundamental difference that can be imputed to neither genre nor rivalry nor premodern notions of intimacy. The heart of this difference involves the fantasy of a private language. For Shakespeare, the game is to show how genre can be as private and impervious to interpretation as another's secret thoughts. In "The Phoenix and Turtle," he memorializes the unique love of the central pair by orchestrating a chorale of voices united in communal grief. Through metaphysical conceits and theological paradox, he dramatizes the way genre can bar understanding. The poem's use of ceremonial genres – requiem, obsequy, anthem, threnody, prayer – masks more than it reveals. The elusiveness of the genres parallels the elusiveness of the noble pair's connection. For generations of readers, the result is a powerful, but "endlessly puzzling" poem.[8] In my view, its deliberate poetic obscurity instantiates the skeptical problematic at its center: the impossibility of knowing the marriage of true minds from the outside. In Donne's "Ecstasy," however, the lyric speaker gives us the inside track, letting us in on the intimacy shared by the two lovers. We are invited, if qualified, to

---

[7] Intimacy is a vexed term. Berlant calls it an enigma, naming a range of complex attachments (2000, 3). Nozick remarks that "in intimacy, we let another within the boundaries we normally maintain around ourselves, boundaries marked by clothing and by full self-control and monitoring" (1989, 64). Since these boundaries are informed by cultural codes, notions of intimacy vary across cultures, but many agree that the concept of intimacy emerges in response to modernity. Luhmann finds "the codes" of intimacy changing in the seventeenth century (1986, 45). Gil follows Luhmann's lead, arguing that "the historically specific early modern conflict between competing social imaginaries" informs sexual interactions and discourse (2006, 9). See, for example, Gil's analysis of Sir Philip Sidney in *Astrophil and Stella*: "Anticipating the eighteenth-century discourse of emotional intimacy, in which emotions are the sine qua non of intimacy precisely because they seem hidden and private, Sidney finally claims that he cannot represent his joy but only point to a reality that goes beyond the words that, unlike bodies, are available to all, indiscriminately" (2006, 39). Bromley historicizes intimacy, lamenting "the early modern contraction of the intimate sphere" and focusing on alternate forms of relationality in Renaissance texts (2012, 2). Eden takes a stylistic view of intimacy, relating it to the epistolary genre renewed by Petrarch and Erasmus and reinvented by Montaigne in his *Essais*. Eden observes that the "famous encounter between Petrarch and the epistolary Cicero sets the primal scene for the Renaissance rediscovery of intimacy" (2012, 50).
[8] Milward (1993), 60.

eavesdrop on their "dialogue of one" (74), a rarefied language uttered in an ecstatic state of mutuality and characterized by theological arcana and metaphysical paradox. It is as though Donne were answering the challenge of Shakespeare's lyric by selecting an ordinary pair of youths and demystifying their sublime love only to remystify it. He lets us hear shared "soul's language" (22), as though defying the unknowability at the heart of human relations. Thus, Donne offers a glimpse of interanimate legibility as a way of combating the "loneliness" (44) of skepticism, while Shakespeare gives us a chorus of voices witnessing as outsiders to a relationship so ineffable that language itself is stymied. This chapter, in other words, looks at these two metaphysical lyrics with their sublime flashes as instantiating problems of privacy and hyperbolic language central to skepticism.

Cavell points out that "the fantasy of the privacy of language" is one that "Austin, Wittgenstein and Derrida are all at pains to contest" (1994, 126). Nevertheless, it persists in part because it "covers a wish that underlies skepticism," namely the "unappeasable" wish for a perfectly transparent mode of communication that bypasses or obviates the need for speech.[9] This yearning for transparency suffuses both poems. However, the wish for perfect understanding, it bears noting, has an uneasy resemblance to a longing for omniscience on a par with God's alleged ability to read minds.[10] This suggests that the dream of reciprocity is uncomfortably close to a desire to possess the beloved rather than to melt in mystical dissolution. Regardless, the fantasy of transparency – whether construed as an ecstatic mutuality or a disguise of power – arises in response to skepticism, which Cavell describes as "a standing threat to, or temptation of, the human mind" (1996, 89). Skepticism can lead to solipsism and the seductive idea that there is an unbridgeable gap between people and that no one can know what goes on inside another. To allow oneself to think this way – a dangerous delusion Wittgenstein spent a career trying to preempt – is eventually to succumb to the fantasy of a private language that will provide certain knowledge and furnish insight into the mind's hidden life. The two "ecstasy" poems, to which I now turn, confront this

---

[9] Cavell states this as "a wish for the connection between my claims of knowledge and the objects upon which the claims are to fall to occur without my intervention, apart from my agreements" (1979, 351–352). Rorty puts this differently: "The idea of a private language ... stems from the hope that words might get meaning without relying on other words. This hope, in turns, stems from the larger hope, diagnosed by Sartre, of becoming a self-sufficient *être-en-soi*" (1989, 42).
[10] But see: "If God had looked into our minds, he would not have been able to see there whom we were speaking of" (2009, § 284).

fantasy, exploring the affective nexus of hyperbole, the sublime, and intimacy even as they dally with skepticism.

Both "The Phoenix and Turtle" and "The Ecstasy" are philosophical lyrics celebrating an exemplary couple whose perfect love is staged for our admiration. Shakespeare's lyric is impersonal, public, allegorical, and geared toward grief even as it memorializes a once glorious love. Donne's, by contrast, is intimate, private, seemingly autobiographical, and comic. "The Phoenix and Turtle" is a social poem about a community commemorating a famous couple in traditional genres or modes; yet the poem has a long history of thwarting interpretation partly because we assume that specific contexts (*Lebensformen*) will illuminate the text. The object of our critical desire and scholarly detective work becomes those largely unknowable contexts. Yet, although its context may elude us, the poem engages familiar language games (which Wittgenstein calls *Sprachspielen*) that readers recognize. The poem mobilizes the public resource of ancient ritual – mourning songs of various stripes – in order to create an aesthetic object that is hermetic, knowable at best only to a select few, the cognoscenti apprised of its secret meaning. Its diction is hyperbolic and sublime, soliciting us to stake our faith on the intimacy of the couple – a demand for belief bound to produce skepticism in some. This paradoxical result is Wittgensteinian inasmuch as it exemplifies the ineluctable mysteriousness of "grammar" (*der Grammatik der Sprache*).[11]

Three overlapping voices are orchestrated in honor of the Phoenix and Turtle. The first is the convener of the mourners. This magisterial persona speaks in the imperative voice, summoning and organizing the assembly of birds, which is not a parliament of fowls but a cortège. Even so, he requires a "Herald" (3) and dubs the occasion a "session" (9) from which "Every fowl of tyrant wing" (10) will be barred, "Save the eagle, feath'red king" (11).[12] He orders a "priest in surplice white" (13) to be the "death-divining swan" (15) and supply "defunctive music" (14). The convener also lets us know that the "troop" (8) is gathered in "obsequy" (12) and "requiem" (16) even as he announces the start of an "anthem" (21). A variety of public funeral rites are thus set in motion.

A choral anthem follows, sung it is not clear by whom but "perhaps best seen," according to William Matchett, "as expressing a general opinion held by 'chaste wings'" (1965, 41). Its central image is one of fiery

---

[11] Noting the poem's Wittgensteinian affinities, Zukofsky says of the *Tractatus*: "Wittgenstein appears to have traveled with the flame of *The Phoenix and the Turtle*" (1963, 45).
[12] See Cheney (2009).

immolation: the Phoenix and Turtle dying together in an ecstatic event described as "a mutual flame" (24). But rather than develop the erotic implications of this image, the anthem shifts to theology. Its second stanza descants on the couple's sublime mutuality in a vocabulary at once Scholastic and Trinitarian ("Had the essence but in one, / Two distincts, division none"). This witty view of their intimacy continues in a paradoxical vein:

> Hearts remote, yet not asunder;
> Distance and no space was seen
> 'Twixt this Turtle and his queen:
> But in them it were a wonder.
>
> (29–32)

This theological fantasy of mutual understanding and individual interpenetration returns now to the earlier image of ecstasy and fire: "So between them love did shine, / That the Turtle saw his right / Flaming in the Phoenix' sight" (33–35). The fire of love reflected in each other's eyes mingles with the flames of the pyre. Richard McCoy describes this connection as "a blend of death and sexual consummation taking the form of a perfect communion" (1997, 195). Their wordless connection is presented as something wondrous.

Then a third voice emerges, a personification of skeptical Reason, who is so "confounded" (41) by this love that he interrupts the anthem of praise so as to deliver his own separate song. Reason's "threne" (49) rehearses a fideistic leap of faith in the perfect couple, but regrets the absence of sex and lack of futurity resulting from their "married chastity" (61). Skeptical reason, in other words, ventriloquizes the voice of a community committed to "posterity" (59). Readers are excluded from these ceremonies until the very last stanza, when they are summoned: "To this urn let those repair / That are either true or faire" (65–66). Insofar as we feel alluded to, the illusion of connection is prolonged as we are invited into the grieving circle in the poem's final line: "For these dead birds sigh a prayer" (67). This line, as Barbara Everett comments, "may be brisk or tender or smiling or sad" (2001, 15). Its baffling tone notwithstanding, it is clear that the concluding appeal for "prayer" moves away from hyperbole into a more subdued register. Prayer, it seems, is among the most private of communal practices.

Wittgenstein, however, distinguishes prayer from other language games involving mourning. He observes: "When it is said in a funeral oration 'We mourn our ...,' this is surely supposed to be an expression of mourning; not to communicate anything to those who are present.

But in a prayer at the grave, these words would be a kind of communication" (2009, § 81). He contrasts – to use the terms of speech-act theory – two types of performatives, each with its own illocutionary "style": the communication conveyed in prayer to a dead or absent "someone" with the expressive force of communal mourning.[13] If I sigh a prayer for the Phoenix and Turtle, I may be communicating with the dead birds, transmitting a private message. The preceding funeral songs (e.g., anthem and threne), by this logic, eschew communication and enact mourning. "But here is the problem," Wittgenstein adds, "a cry, which cannot be called a description, which is more primitive than any description, for all that, does the service of a description of the psychological" (2009, § 82). While Shakespeare's elaborate verse can hardly be called a cry, let alone a primitive cry, his poem imagines an occasion of ritual grief, which neither describes nor communicates, but instead expresses a community's bereavement in a set of interlocking songs that attest to the challenges of apprehending the psychological intimacy of the central pair. Wittgenstein suggests "transitions" (*Übergänge*) are key for understanding the relationship of utterances to the psychological – words "may approximate" a cry more or less (2009, § 83).[14] Barbara Everett alludes to these verbal approximations of deep feeling when she locates "overtones of experience not merely inward but solitary" in the poem, "a tenderness, pain and pathos" belying its wit and "arcanely beautiful" conventions (2001, 15).

Yet, despite its melancholy, "The Phoenix and Turtle" resists intimacy. We have no access to the internal life of so "true a twain" (45), no purchase on their ecstatic love, no sense of their pain. The birds are silent. The best evidence we have of their connection is the anthem's insistence on the shining reflection in each other's flashing eyes. The overlapping set of embedded witnesses can only exclaim and mark the distance ("appalled," "confounded") between themselves and the unattainable pair, thus disclosing the problem of other minds. As a communal ritual of consolation full of shared meanings, the poem seems to illustrate the reverse of a private language. Yet, it verges on the unintelligible by offering us lyric fragments that elude reference and seem freighted with private meanings: in sum, the conundrum of a private language on a social scale. Saul Kripke believes that this dilemma is at the heart of the private language argument.

---

[13] See Austin on "performatives," especially 1962, 1–24 and 1961, 220–239; Searle on "differences in the style of performance of the illocutionary act" (1976, 7); Schalkwyk (2002) on Austin's performatives, Wittgenstein, and Shakespeare, 29–58, 117–124, and 238–242.
[14] For interpretations of Wittgenstein's fragmentary remarks on Shakespeare, see, among others, Hughes (1988), McDougall (2016), and Perloff (2014).

"Wittgenstein's main problem," he says, "is that it appears that he has shown *all* language, *all* concept formation, to be impossible, indeed unintelligible" (1982, 62). While this is a contrarian take on Wittgenstein's views, Kripke's idea that private language challenges the assumptions of language more generally is useful. It allows us, for example, to think about the phenomenological effects of Shakespeare's poem, especially the way the difference between private and public language has been effaced. The collectively voiced testimonial to love in "The Phoenix and Turtle" results in a paradoxical language game of overlapping speakers and well-worn tropes so hermetic that generations of readers have felt mystified.

Cavell might ask what wish this fantasy of hermeticism covers. Two impulses may be at work: on the one hand, an effort "to illuminate something about the publicness of language, something about the *depth* to which language is agreed in," and on the other, a fear of excessive intelligibility issuing in a desire to possess one's own words and make them inalienable (1979, 344). If Shakespeare is being Cavellian here and meditating on the problematic status of a public language engaged in praise, then the opacity of the poem would be more than an effect of riddling wit, Scholastic shibboleths, or the circumstantial genesis of *Love's Martyr*, the collection in which "The Phoenix and Turtle" first appeared.[15] It would be an effect of a larger meditation on language as a system.

In a sense, Shakespeare is having it both ways. On the one hand, "The Phoenix and Turtle" can be seen as a Wittgensteinian poem, showing, as Rupert Read would say, that "language itself binds us together, closer than close" and thus that "we do not *need* the absurd acquaintance with others' fantasized 'private objects'." As Read explains, "The Wittgenstein-style community is not defined over and against anything, not even nonhuman animals. It is a truly open field" (2010, 598, 601). We need only acknowledge one another and so resist our solipsistic tendencies. On the other hand, as a literary artifact "The Phoenix and Turtle" seems to operate like a private object, sufficient unto itself and repelling exegesis. Read might say that insofar as it remains an enigma, it "blunts the possibility – the necessity – the beauty – of genuine empathy" (2010, 600). Readers who find the poem cold and aloof might agree.

Cavell might suggest instead that Shakespeare is exercising his mastery here, showing that he can negotiate and overcome competing fears of

---

[15] For a persuasive account of reasons why Shakespeare contributed to Robert Chester's *Love's Martyr* (1601), a volume dedicated to Sir John Salusbury and including poems by Ben Jonson, George Chapman, and John Marston, see Bednarz (2007), especially chapter 3.

inexpressiveness and exposure. Cavell surmises that Wittgenstein's fantasy of private language conceals a fear of "inexpressiveness, one in which I am not merely unknown, but in which I am powerless to make myself known" and equally a fear "in which what I express is beyond my control" (1979, 351). He dubs this elsewhere "a fantasy of suffocation or of exposure," involving both a fear of unintelligibility and a fear that my words will escape me and be stolen so that we end up "too intelligible for our good" and "being torn apart."[16] Yet I would not go that far and project Cavell's surmise about Wittgenstein onto Shakespeare. After all, what would Shakespeare be trying to conceal? Some might attribute the gnomic quality of Shakespeare's voice in "The Phoenix and Turtle" to the political conditions of censorship and self-censorship operating at the time *Love's Martyr* was published in 1601. Indeed, proscribed religious sympathies and political affiliations have often been adduced as reasons for the poem's mystery. Nonetheless, I prefer to see the turn to allegory and mourning songs, not as a self-protective device, but as a way of exploring the relationship of private and public language. Rather than see them as antithetical systems, Shakespeare is experimenting with a metaphysical conceit whereby public and private become conflated. The inscrutability of the miraculous pair's marriage – "Two distinct, division none" – becomes displaced onto the poem itself, which thereby replicates, in a mitigated way, the opacity always already troubling language.

By contrast, "The Ecstasy" stages a fantasy of transparent intimacy whereby the man speaks for himself and his beloved in the first person plural. They are "one another's best" (4), he assures us in the first stanza, and have no need to talk because they share "soul's language" (22), in which "both meant, both spake the same" (26). He describes where they are in relation to the landscape and to each other: first sitting, then reclining side by side on a sloping bank with violets.[17] They are holding hands and staring into each other's eyes, lying as still as "sepulchral statues" (18) and as silent: "All day, the same our postures were, / And we said nothing, all the day" (19–20). Yet, in this parenthesis of dilated time, while their "souls negotiate" (17) in mid-air, having "gone out" (16) on a reconnaissance mission "to advance their state" (15), the speaker invites

---

[16] Cavell (1996), 157 and (1994), 126–127.
[17] Novarr asks, "Did they first sit, and then shift position so that they are on their backs, gazing at the heavens? Or have they been leaning, even reclining, on the bank, facing each other, their hands intergrafted? We cannot be sure, but we are sure that we have been projected into an unusual situation, and its strangeness is intensified when we are told that the lovers' souls have left their bodies, to hang in mid-air between the bodies" (1972, 231).

the passer-by to eavesdrop on their private language. The reader feels solicited and steps into the frame of the poem, happy to watch the recumbent lovers in their trance and to listen to their efforts to "unperplex" (29) the enigma of their perfect union. Using alchemical metaphors, Donne characterizes their intimate speech as a purifying agent, beneficial even to bystanders who "might thence a new concoction take" (27) if they come already initiated into the mysteries of "good love" (23). The speaker then launches into a translation, allowing us to hear the accents of their private language:

> This ecstasy doth unperplex
> (We said) and tell us what we love,
> We see by this, it was not sex,
> We see, we saw not what did move.
> (29–32)

The rhythms of the stanza with its iambic tetrameter and alternating rhymes enact the motions of a changing mind despite the earlier protestations of a lull and truce "'twixt her and me" (16). From a condition of perplexity, the couple arrive at discovery. Thanks to their ecstasy, they now understand what they love, sharing the surprising insight that "it was not sex." "We see . . . we see," the lovers repeat, transported by a quasi-mystical vision of their souls' bond. Yet even as they see, they fail to see "what did move." The terse sequence of assertion and denial, retracting the fullness of the insight just acquired, captures the irresolution of thought. The indeterminate reference of "what did move," seen and now unseen, suggests a speaker struggling to articulate what Wittgenstein might call "his immediate private sensations" (2009, § 243).

In thrall to the rush of insights and discoveries, the couple continues to disclose the secrets of their relation. Many literary critics have decoded Donne's specialized terminology in the last half of the poem. Catherine Gimelli Martin (2004), for example, discusses the "voluptuous rationalism" of Nicholas of Cusa and Marsilio Ficino. Ramie Targoff focuses on Donne's invention of the term "inanimation" and the verb "interinanimate" to dispute the poem's apparent Platonic dualism, acceding that "if we were forced to identify Donne within a single philosophical school, it would almost certainly be Aristotelian" (2008, 59). Julia Walker (1982) explores the alchemical imagery. But regardless of provenance, the poem's philosophical lexicon both represents and constitutes an esoteric tongue. We are hearing a translation of the elite dialect that souls (as united as Wittgenstein's Siamese twins) might speak in an ecstatic state of mutuality.

This private language indulges the fantasy of overcoming the problem of other minds, as skepticism dissolves in the wholeness of intimacy.

Despite its exaltation of souls in a state of perfect union, at stanza 13 the poem turns to bodies with this question, "But O alas, so long, so far / Our bodies why do we forbear?" (49–50). What follows is Wittgensteinian: now no longer a hypothetical translation of the soul's private language but instead an exhibit of the body as the site of the soul's expression. When Wittgenstein declares, "The human body is the best picture of the human soul" (2009, § 25) or "An 'inner process' stands in need of outward criteria" (2009, § 580), we get a secular, de-eroticized version of Donne's metaphysical conceit in his penultimate stanza:[18]

> To our bodies turn we then, that so
> Weak men on love revealed may look;
> Love's mysteries in souls do grow,
> But yet the body is his book.
> (69–72)

The lovers display themselves with theatrical self-consciousness, proffering their bodies as a text to be read: a book of revelation that will affirm the faith of the skeptical bystander.

The shift from the souls' private language to physical gesture is a concession at once to doubt and to doubters. The "lovers' souls" (65) must "descend / T'affections, and to faculties" (65–66) as a boon to the weak. Earlier, the souls' attitude to their bodies is explained disingenuously, not as a descent, but as an act of condescension, as if the desire for sexual congress were a matter of noblesse oblige:

> We owe them thanks, because they thus,
> Did us, to us, at first convey,
> Yielded their forces, sense, to us,[19]
> Nor are dross to us, but allay.
> (53–56)

The bodies surrender their forces to the conjoined soul in a continuation of the military metaphor broached in stanza 4, to musical accompaniment – the sibilant phoneme "us" drumming in martial beat five times. The alchemical metaphor returns with the image of an alloy as a fusion of

---

[18] Rorty puts this provocatively: "To be thoroughly Wittgensteinian in our approach to language, would be to de-divinize the world" (1989, 21).

[19] This line has variants, as A. J. Smith makes clear (1971, 370). It appears as "senses force" in seventeenth-century editions, shifting the emphasis toward the senses as primary drivers of the body. It also appears as "forces, since" and as "forces first" in various manuscripts.

substances, directly refuting Platonic notions of the body as dross. It is as though Donne agrees with Wittgenstein's dictum, "An inner experience cannot shew me that I *know* something."[20] To know something like ecstasy or love, the poem suggests, involves the body and all its sensory apparatus, along with the souls' shared private language. The two go together. Private experience is neither incoherent nor reprehensible for Donne, as it is for Wittgenstein. Rather, it improves, becoming more fully legible – especially to observers – thanks to corporeal translation.[21]

*

The representation of each ecstatic couple in these two poems seems a study in antithesis. In "The Phoenix and Turtle" the ecstatic event transpires in a flash and ends in "cinders" (55). By contrast, in the Donne poem, the ecstatic event involves stillness and duration. Although the lovers hold hands, the central simile describes them as "sepulchral statues" (18) – no annihilating heat here. While the recumbent lovers may be dead to the world, they stare at one another in companionable silence: "And pictures on our eyes to get / Was all our propagation" (11–12), an image boding well for future consummation. In the meantime, however, their bodies lie in suspended animation. Further, the philosophical disquisition on love in "The Ecstasy" replays the Shakespearean anthem's theme of two-in-one but in a different terminological register.[22] Instead of the neo-Trinitarian vocabulary used by Shakespeare to describe "Single nature's double name" (39), Donne gives a neo-Aristotelian account of "mixed souls" (35) and "atomies" (47).[23] Donne's lexicon, in this instance, is less sacred than Shakespeare's. It is as if, faced by Shakespeare's "opaque

---

[20] Wittgenstein (1972), § 569.
[21] Compare Wittgenstein: "How curious: we should like to explain our understanding of a gesture by means of a translation into words, and the understanding of words by translating them into a gesture. (Thus we are tossed to and fro when we try to find out where understanding properly resides.) And we really shall be explaining words by a gesture, and a gesture by words" (1967, § 227).
[22] Martin comments on the difference in tone between Donne and Shakespeare's metaphysical paradoxes, suggesting that Shakespeare's do not produce doubt in the way Donne's do: "Even the most disharmonious imagery (like for instance that found in such poems as Shakespeare's 'The Phoenix and the Turtle') may lack true metaphysical violence if its paradoxes are not 'contaminated' with a riddling logic that produces metaphysical doubt. So long as their allegorical mystery remains safely insoluble or transcendental, such poems produce complacent wonder instead of violent controversies over their missing or nonexistent keys. In contrast, Donne's *Songs and Sonets* provoke such controversies by playing with glaring inconsistencies. ... For all these works 'contaminate' spiritual and rational arguments with sensual analogies that continue to perplex, astonish, or even outrage their readers" (2004, 122).
[23] See Cunningham (1952), 273.

avian allegory" commemorating the death of a chaste and perfect pair, Donne felt compelled to respond with a poem about "married chastity" more hyperbolic than the bloodless love of the Phoenix and Turtle (Cheney 2009, 111). "The Ecstasy" thus ends not in cinders and wistful remembrance but in a celebration of embodied, human love.

Imagining Donne's "Ecstasy" as a response to Shakespeare's "Phoenix and Turtle" is not new. There is agreement that both belong to an "ecstasy" tradition beginning with the Eighth Song of Sir Philip Sidney's *Astrophil and Stella* and continuing through Lord Herbert of Cherbury's "Ode on a Question Moved."[24] There is also consensus that "The Ecstasy" postdates *Love's Martyr* (1601), the volume containing "The Phoenix and Turtle," whose title alone would have drawn Donne's eye even if the other contributors had not included friends like Ben Jonson. Indeed, the affinities of Donne's metaphysical poetry and "The Phoenix and Turtle" were noted long ago by Cleanth Brooks, who concluded his pages on Donne's "Canonization" by commenting on their shared language of paradox and the image of the well-wrought urn holding the ashes of the phoenix (1947, 18–21). Matchett also remarks on "Donne's (conscious or unconscious) memory of *Loves Martyr*" in "The Canonization" (1965, 158). More recently, James P. Bednarz has wondered "whether or not Shakespeare by 1601 had read John Donne's poetry in manuscript" and has observed that "it is Donne who seems to be echoing 'The Phoenix and Turtle' in 'The Canonization'" (2007, 121). With respect to "The Ecstasy," however, the received wisdom holds that the Donne poem debates the Neoplatonism advanced in Edward Herbert's "Ode." In her overview of the ecstasy tradition, Everett deems that "Shakespeare's poem is surely a kind of medium, a vital Missing Link, between Sidney and Donne-and-Lord-Herbert, transitional and strongly formative" (2001, 14).

Chronology aside, both poems explore the hyperbolical desire for a sublime intimacy, even while proclaiming its rarity. Both poems summon bystanders to admire and learn from the spectacle of "love revealed" ("The Ecstasy," 70), but the approach to audience is opposed. In "The Phoenix and Turtle," the implied audience is a community of grieving birds whose collective desire exalts the vanished pair. In "The Ecstasy," the audience is imagined as an individual who "by good love were grown all mind" (23) and who will "part far purer then he came" (28). This bystander is later pictured as "some lover, such as we" (73). Arthur Marotti argues that

---

[24] Critics who think each poem may owe a debt to the Eighth Song of Sidney's *Astrophel and Stella* include Everett (2001), Gardner (1965, 256), and Kay (1998, 82).

observer and reader are conflated, noting that the reader "is admitted into the inner sanctum of the love relationship so that his critical distance can be lost, then presented with his mirror image in the figure of the hypothetical observer, who is a docile convert by the end of the piece" (1974, 172). The poem's rhetoric is aimed at this embedded audience who need to be convinced of "the authenticity and goodness of their love" (1974, 171).

The presence of the embedded audience produces a theatricality that is different in each poem, but that in each case raises the question of skepticism since the audience's vantage point frames the action and limits knowledge. Shakespeare's poem trades in miniaturized genres and collective speech, offering us a theatricality that is ritualized and social, reminiscent as much of the playhouse as of the chancel or churchyard. Reason, after all, dubs the Phoenix and the Dove "Co-supremes and stars of love" (51) when it composes a "chorus to their tragic scene" (52). Yet this same "Reason, in itself confounded" (41), abdicates, resorting to fideism as grounds for belief in the incredible pair even while confirming the finality of their death. The theatricality of Donne's lyric is at once more intimate and exhibitionistic, challenging skepticism. We are invited to approach "within convenient distance" (24) so as to overhear the lovers and to "mark" them when they "are to bodies gone" (75–76). The teasing implication is that if we wait until they "are to bodies gone" – an ambiguous phrase suggesting both sex and death – we "shall see / Small change" (75–76), that is, little difference – as if, having "gone" to bodies, the lovers were as suspended in their ecstasy as before.[25] Regardless of what we may "see" in the poem's aftermath, however, the conceit is that we are right there, privy to the truth and beauty of this extraordinary relationship in an almost unmediated way. In the Shakespeare poem, by contrast, the embedded audiences can only sigh and sing and wonder over a relationship as foreign as it is absent. For all their efforts to know, knowledge recedes from their grasp.

Shakespeare's and Donne's contested engagements with skepticism and with deferred or incomplete knowledge inform the way these two poems parry the temptations of a private language. Both poets are masters at communicating a sense of interiority and private experience. Hamlet famously says, "I have that within which passes show" (I.ii.85). Yet the language with which they transmit their inwardness is perforce public: "public means which public manners breeds" (4), Shakespeare's Sonnet 111 notes bitterly. Hence, the fascination with a private language,

---

[25] For a reading of becalmed ecstasy as a sign of maturity, see Jorge Guillén's 1963 poem, "Al Margen de Donne" (58).

elite, apart, ideal, even sublime. As if recognizing with Wittgenstein the incoherence of such a concept, Shakespeare invents a compromise – a poetic game in resolutely public language that resists interpretation and comes across as a euphonious, stately, but slightly archaic enigma. He orchestrates the glorification of the Phoenix and the Dove, but withholds the stage-setting that would permit fuller comprehension. He presents a drama of inaccessible intimacy voiced through genre. If we believe in the love of the central pair, it is because we are swept up by the songs, enchanted by their magical music. Like the language of birds – a melodious, but indecipherable *lingua franca* – "The Phoenix and Turtle" is both public and private, intimating that genre can be the most abstruse of language games.[26]

If Shakespeare's vision of intimacy is diffident and always elsewhere, just out of reach, Donne's is defiant, vaunting his unsurpassable love as an ecstasy of mutual knowledge. Like Cavell's Cleopatra, Donne's poetic persona is bent on "transcendentalizing the domestic" and mythologizing the everyday.[27] The dream of a private language – when shared with a beloved – goes far in creating an ideal of intimacy. That ideal fostered and intensified by sublime, hyperbolical flights helps to offset the corrosive doubts attendant on skepticism. Christopher Johnson reminds us, "Hyperbole serves an essential psychological and narrative purpose – through it readers are urged to slake their own epistemological desire" (2010, 380). "The Ecstasy" may well satisfy our epistemological thirst, but "The Phoenix and Turtle," although engaging in hyperbole and broaching the sublime, serves not to slake our epistemological desire but to sharpen it.

This difference in the approach to the fantasy of perfect knowledge may be partly attributable to personality: Shakespeare is self-effacing in his work, while Donne's persona is ostentatiously present. But I would argue that, in the case of these two lyrics, this difference has less to do with ego than with discrepant stances toward language. Shakespeare crafts a lyric that gestures toward metaphysical paradox but actually entertains a Wittgensteinian puzzle, namely, that genre, the most consensual of linguistic conventions, can resist signification and obstruct interpretation. The resulting poem is hermetic and almost private. Donne's lyric, by contrast, pretends to be open, soliciting us to witness that impossibility: a private language in action.

---

[26] See Eco (1995, 184–185) and Ormsby-Lennon (1988, 322–323) for the language of birds as a residue of the *lingua adamica*.
[27] Cavell (1988), 27.

CHAPTER 3

Conformity / Neutrality in Lord Herbert of Cherbury

In the midst of the Civil War, as he looked back upon a long and eventful life from the retirement of Montgomery Castle, Lord Herbert of Cherbury harbored no doubts about his most lasting achievement: the writing of *De veritate* nearly thirty years before. His epitaph makes this clear. The only deed deemed worth recording is his authorship of that work: "auctoris libri, cui titulus est, 'De Veritate.'"[1] His memoirs written in the 1640s also attest to the high stock he placed in the book. They break off with a striking tableau: Herbert in the summer of 1623, while ambassador to Paris for King James, praying that God give him a sign whether to publish his manuscript. Since the passage in question is among the most controversial in Herbert's *oeuvre*, I quote it in full:

> ... yet as I knew it would meet with much opposition, I did consider whether it was not better for me a while to suppress it: being thus doubtfull in my Chamber one fair day in the Summer, my Casement being opened towards the South, the Sun shining clear and no wind stirring, I took my Book de Veritate in my hand, and kneeling on my knees devoutly said these words,
>
> O Thou Eternal God Author of that Light which now shines upon me, and Giver of all inward illuminations, I do beseech Thee of thy infinite Goodness to pardon a greater request than a Sinner ought to make; I am not satisfied enough whether I shall publish This Book De Veritate, if it be for thy Glory, I beseech thee give me some Signe from Heaven, if not, I shall suppress it.

---

[1] Herbert was buried in London at St. Giles-in-the-Fields. His epitaph reads: "Hic inhumator corpus Edvardi Herbert equitis Balnei, baronis de Cherbury et Castle-Island, auctoris libri, cui titulus est, 'De Veritate.' Reddor ut herbae; vicesimo die Augusti anno Domini 1648." *Reddor ut herbae* (I will return as grass, or I am redeemed as grass), with its whiff of theological heterodoxy, is Herbert's anagram for his own name. See "Epitaphium in Anagramma Nominis Suit, Reddor Ut Herbae" from his posthumously published *Poems* (1881 ed., 125). Sidney Lee doubts that he wrote his own epitaph, attributing it to Philip, Lord Stanhope, Earl of Chesterfield (1892, 299).

I had no sooner spoken these words, but a Loud though yet Gentle noise came from the Heavens (for it was like nothing on Earth) which did so comfort and cheer me, that I took my Petition as granted, and that I had the Signe I demanded, whereupon also I resolved to print my Book: This (how strange soever it may seem) I protest before the Eternal God is true, neither am I any way superstitiously deceived herein, since I did not only clearly hear the Noise, but in the Serenest Sky that ever I saw being without all cloud did to my thinking see the Place from whence it came. (*Life*, 120–121)[2]

This passage captures the complexity of Herbert's personality and the interpretive challenges posed by his philosophical theology. The tableau that he stages is an iconographic topos: an individual kneeling in prayer, holding a book near a window, and receiving a sign from heaven. The scene of devotion implies that Herbert believes in prayer and that God answers human prayers – beliefs stated and confirmed in *De veritate*.[3] Furthermore, by noting the fine weather, the stillness of the air and the absence of clouds, he both deflects and invites criticism: from doubters who might allege coincidence and charge him with mistaking dry thunder for the divine voice, and also from believers who take it as an article of faith that God speaks in thunder and lightning.[4] In keeping with the criteria set out in *De veritate* for evaluating the veracity of discrete sense perceptions, Herbert insists that on the day he prayed, optimal conditions were met for receiving a veridical sign and personal revelation. Moreover, the feeling of cheer and comfort that he experienced amounts to that "motion of assent" (*DV* 318 / 235), which he considers constitutive of probability. While it may be tempting to dismiss this passage as a parody of superstitious

---

[2] All citations of *The Life of Edward, First Lord Herbert of Cherbury* are to J. M. Shuttleworth's 1976 edition.

[3] "Every religion believes that the Deity can hear and answer prayers; and we are bound to assume a special Providence – to omit other sources of proof – from the universal testimony of the sense of divine assistance in times of distress" (*DV* 292 / 211) and "God does not suffer us to beseech him in vain, as the universal experience of divine assistance proves, to pass over all other arguments" (*DV* 294 / 213). All citations of *De veritate* (abbreviated to *DV*) are, first, to Meyrick H. Carré's edition and translation (University of Bristol, 1937), reissued by Routledge in 1992 and, second, to Günter Gawlick's 1966 facsimile edition of *De veritate*'s third edition (London, 1645). Aubrey confirms Herbert's belief in the efficacy of prayer, reporting that "Mr Fludd tells me that he [Herbert] had constantly prayers twice a day in his house, and Sundays would have his chaplain read one of Smyth's sermons" (1975, 141).

[4] See, for example, the following exchanges from a popular, Protestant, seventeenth-century catechism, *The way to true happiness* (1610). "How was the Law given. In thunder and lightning. Why was it given with such terror? That the people might more reverence him that gave it" (14). "What are the effects of his [the Father's] magnificence? Lightning, thunder, and voices, &c" (114).

thinking, it would be too easy.[5] In my view, its confounding mix of faith, empiricism, and phenomenological attentiveness is characteristic of Herbert's eclectic affiliations. But regardless of how one gauges Herbert's tone in this passage, his invocation of God's *imprimatur* shows his high estimation of the book.[6]

What was Herbert trying to accomplish in *De veritate*? Why was he most proud of this volume, his earliest, more than of the other eight eventually published? Herbert is usually recognized as a pioneer in the study of comparative religions and as a precursor of later deists, besides being a friend of John Donne, brother to George Herbert, and a metaphysical poet himself.[7] But he is seldom discussed as a thinker whose philosophical program exposes the political underside of skepticism: reaching beyond accommodation to neutrality. He did not see himself that way except perhaps in his last years. Instead, like Hobbes, Locke and other seventeenth-century thinkers appalled by the murderous violence of religious sectarians, Herbert saw himself as a peacemaker, offering a philosophical base for an ethics and a politics geared toward harmonious coexistence. As he declares in his preface "To the Candid Reader," he has "laid the foundations or ground-plan of the structure of truth" (*DV* 73). When Herbert asks, "Where, then, can an anxious and divided mind turn to find security and peace?," given "the multitude of sects, divisions, sub-divisions and cross-divisions," the answer is in his own pages (*DV* 75/1). *De veritate* operates as a guide and handbook for the perplexed, tutoring them in how to discriminate among classes of truth and how to distinguish certainty from probability, possibility, and error. In the process, it launches a salvo against the fashionable skeptical opinion that nothing can be known (*nihil scitur*). Like Descartes, Herbert wants to counter skeptical arguments that threaten the foundations of knowledge by offering a system that will defeat them once and for all. But unlike Descartes, he refuses to give skeptical doubt the floor. He rejects Descartes' narrative strategy of temporarily allowing doubt full sway before isolating the one experience whose veracity he cannot doubt, the *cogito*. Instead,

---

[5] Hill canvases the variety of reactions over the centuries (1987, 113–115), concluding that "the revelation shows the ironic force of Providence, teaching the true by parodying the false" (115). See the dry thunder of *Aeneid* VIII.523–536, a sign from Venus that Aeneas recognizes as "a covenant for wartime" against the Laurentians (trans. Ruden, 2008).

[6] Hartlib provides further proof, noting that Herbert wished "to speake with Aristotle et Plato to know of them what they would have judged of his De Veritate" (30/4/42B, *Ephemerides*, 1640) and that "Of the whole Booke hee said Hee had rather bee the Author of it if hee were put to his choice then to bee King of Poland" (30/4/31A, *Ephemerides*, 1639). See Sherman (2015), 56.

[7] See, among others, Ellrodt (2000), Fuller (1846), Pailin (2000), and Popkin (2003).

Herbert sidelines uncertainty, effectively silencing it, and presents his philosophical system as a set of irrefutable propositions. Adopting these propositions will produce a reformed consciousness that, in turn, will serve as the basis for an inclusive commonwealth. In laying out the criteria for truthful cognition, he exalts conformity and consent as epistemological ideals, not anticipating perhaps that these ideals – when tested by the perils of *praxis* – will underwrite a stance of political neutrality.

How did Herbert, a champion of truth and enemy of skeptics, end up embracing retreat, privacy, and neutrality, crossing over (unwittingly perhaps) to skepticism's quietist side? The answer is perforce historical and biographical. Herbert gradually changes in the face of personal setbacks and turbulent public circumstances as well as owing to his intellectual work of the 1630s, researching and writing his two histories: *Expedition to the Isle of Rhé* and *The Life and Reign of Henry VIII*. Yet the seeds for this change are already present in his philosophy, growing out of the appreciation for beauty implicit in his ideals of conformity and consent.

To support the claim that Herbert's philosophy of mind has unexpected political consequences for his life and reputation, let me juxtapose the sunlit scene of Herbert in prayer, seeking God's permission to publish *De veritate*, with a nocturnal scene of fear and danger that begins over twenty years later, on Wednesday, September 4, 1644, when Herbert's castle in the Welsh Marches is besieged. According to the report of James Till, Lieutenant Colonel of Horse under the Parliamentary commander, Sir Thomas Myddleton, Till arrived "suddainly to Mountgomery ... with about 800 foote and horse ... and sent Edward Lord Herbert a Summons to yield the Castle; whereupon the sayd Lord Herbert entred into a Parlee with him." Bringing his diplomatic skills to bear upon the situation, Herbert attempts to take charge and bargains for time. He offers "a large summe of money to free him and his Tennants and Neighbors from Plunder and his Castle from a Seige, desiring an answer thereof upon the next Friday morning at nine of the Clock" (Rossi 1947, 3.524). Till agrees on two conditions: that Herbert discharge some of his garrison and that he permit them "to place great store of Powder ... within the Bulwarks of the said Castle for that night." Herbert accepts. But instead of waiting till Friday morning to resume negotiations, as Herbert had requested, Till launches a night-time attack:

> Accompanied with strong Forces & having a Petard with him [he] came unto the Gates of the said Castle upon Thursday at night about Twelve of

the Clock, and causing a Trumpet to bee sounded required that the Castle might bee presently yielded to him, Whereupon the said Lord Herbert came in Person to the Gates; And finding that the said Leivetenant Collonell Till with others had entred betweene the Gate & the drawbridge desired the said Leivetenant Colonell with the rest to retreat since the business was deferred untill the next morning. But the Leivetenant Colonell requiring a present answer & affirming hee had a Petard at the Gate gave that Terror to divers of the said Lord Herberts Servants and Garrison that some desperately leaped over the walls of the Castle to save themselves. (Rossi 1947, 3.525)

Faced with the panicked behavior of his staff and Till's bravado, Herbert reiterates his demand that the Parliamentary troops retreat and wait until the morning for an answer, but Till refuses, whereupon negotiations ensue until "articles of agreement" are drawn up and witnessed. This document reveals Herbert in action, responding to a crisis. Resorting to pen and paper, he spells out the conditions of the troops' occupation. He tries to control the damage the soldiers might do by insisting that "noe violence shal bee offred to ... any p'son or p'sons within his castle," by limiting the size of the garrison stationed at the castle and by listing the property to be protected: "goods, bookes, and armes" as well as "money, silver, gould or plate." The articles promise that "noe trunkes or doores under locks and keyes shal bee broken open" and guarantee freedom of movement to Herbert and his family as well as "p'visions necessary for cloathing and diet." This document is "dated halfe an hour past twelve of the clocke at midnight on Thursday ye fifth day of September, Anno dni 1644" (Rossi 1947, 3.523). Sir Thomas Myddleton was apparently absent on this frightening night. Herbert must have appealed to him as James Till's superior, given that Myddleton appends a paragraph to the articles at a later time, stipulating the furnishings for his own lodgings in the castle as well as conceding "that there shall be noe person or persons enter into the library or study of the said Edward Lord Herbert, or the two next rooms or chambers adjoining to the said study or library, during the time of the absence of the said Edward Lord Herbert, or at any other time" (Rossi 1947, 3.524). These clauses betray Herbert's anxiety about safeguarding his books and manuscripts, even as he surrenders his castle and worries about violence. Herbert had renovated the castle in 1622–25, adding a new L-shaped building where the library had pride of place.[8]

---

[8] See Roberts (2015).

Herbert had left London two years earlier after a disastrous experience in Parliament. On May 20, 1642, he angered his colleagues in the House of Lords by "speaking moderately" (Shuttleworth 1976, xxvii). Moderation at this late date in the unraveling relations between King and Parliament was a difficult balancing act. Yet Herbert was not alone in hazarding compromise. In *The Moderator expecting Sudden Peace, or Certaine Ruine* (1642), Thomas Povey urged "that a peace warily concluded by an Accomodation must be the happiest issue that can be given to these Differences" (6).[9] On May 20, the fear was that the King, now in York, was recruiting supporters because he intended "to make War against Parliament." The Lords therefore resolved that those serving or assisting the King "in such Wars" were "traitors." Herbert stood up and said he "should agree" to the resolution against the King if he "could be satisfied that the King would make War upon the Parliament without Cause" (*Lords' Jour.* V.77). This evidently produced an uproar, whether owing to Herbert's finicky tone or to his attempt to have it both ways or to the implied suggestion that the King might well have cause to fight. "A real Neutral," Barthes says, "baffles the Yes/No, without withdrawing" (2005, 112). Perhaps that is what Herbert thought he was doing when he spoke up on May 20: baffling the yes/no without withdrawing. Rossi speculates that Herbert hoped to temper the mood of the gathered peers so as to narrow the breach they were opening between themselves and the King's supporters (1947, 3.77–78). If so, his comment backfired. Herbert was "commanded to withdraw" from the chamber, which he did. "Because it was now late," it was "Ordered" that he be "committed to the custody of the Gentleman Usher for the present, until this House take this business into further consideration" (*LJ* V.77). Rossi imagines a long night of meditation preceding "la scelta definitiva," the defining choice for a man who preferred to keep his options open (1947, 3.78–79). Call it a night of reckoning with occasion, his season for action, his *kairos*. Rossi deems it the final push into "the blind alley of neutrality."[10] The next day Herbert asked for pardon, professing "he meant no Ill, neither to the King nor to this House." He petitioned for release from detention and for "Leave to go into the Country for his Health; and, if he cannot have his Health in *England*, he desires Leave to go for a Time beyond the Sea, for the recovering of his Health" (*LJ* V.77–78). This was granted. Herbert then withdrew to Montgomery Castle. But before leaving London, he entrusted his two

---

[9] Aylmer calls *The Moderator* "undoubtedly one of the most eloquent neutralist tracts" (1989, 4).
[10] "Tutta la sua vita risorgeva ora a spingerlo nel vicolo cieco della neutralità" (Rossi 1947, 3.79).

prize possessions – a draft of his history of Henry VIII and a manuscript copy of John Donne's *Biathanatos* inscribed to him in April 1619 – to Thomas Masters, his erstwhile assistant, asking him to deposit the two works at the Bodleian Library in Oxford until further notice (Rossi 1947, 3.89).[11]

Herbert may have aspired to pursue his studies and stay out of trouble during his retirement, but he failed to remain above the fray. He refused to quarter royalist troops at Montgomery Castle, although Prince Rupert demanded it since it was a strategic location for his campaign. When Parliamentary forces surprised the castle in September 1644, Herbert tried delaying tactics, as we have seen, but his hand was forced. After surrendering the family seat to Sir Thomas Myddleton, he returned to London, where he petitioned Parliament for relief. He was granted an allowance of £20 per week (which he struggled to collect) and resumed his duties in the House of Lords. In 1648, shortly before dying, Herbert gave his history of Henry VIII to the printer, Thomas Whitaker. In 1649, Montgomery Castle was razed, reduced to rubble, which cleared Herbert's royalist son, Richard, of his debts.[12] In the end Herbert's decision to lie low and defy what Roland Barthes would call 'the paradigm' by taking a middle way produced only isolation.[13]

Why did Herbert of Cherbury adopt neutrality? After all, like so many aristocrats of his age, Herbert had grown up aspiring to model his comportment on the flower of chivalry. He held his honor in high esteem, jousting, duelling, and fighting in the Low Countries.[14] Like a good Renaissance humanist, he opted for the active life, advising on foreign policy and writing plays and poetry as well as histories. He served as ambassador to France. As late as 1639, during the first Bishops' War, Herbert heeded the King's summons to York, as he did again the following year. How, then, do we account for his change of course? After all, "neuters" were reviled in seventeenth-century England, likened to bats,

---

[11] Rossi quarrels with Gosse's dating, surmising that Donne's gift to Herbert occurred earlier (1947, 3.410).

[12] "The demolition lasted from 26 June to 27 October and included the new building, which had stood for less than a quarter of a century. The castle was, in the words of Sir Thomas Herbert of Tintern, 'metamorphosed into a horrid heape of Rubbish and Stones'" (Roberts 121, quoting from Cardiff Central Library, Phillipps MS. 5.7, p.129).

[13] "I define the Neutral as that which outplays {*déjoue*} the paradigm, or rather I call Neutral everything that baffles the paradigm" (Barthes 6).

[14] Horace Walpole ridicules Herbert's memoirs because in them Herbert tells a number of stories showing how quick he was as a young man to take umbrage in matters of honor. Herbert is looking back at the bluster of his swashbuckling adventures with bemusement and a self-deprecating irony that Walpole and others miss. A youth so easily slighted is attuned to power relations–hence his later, mature understanding of neutrality, consent, and conformity.

mongrels, two-sided Jacks, and half-way-men among other slurs. Citing Judges 5:23, a favorite text for condemning those opposed to war,[15] the preacher Thomas Adams inveighed, "Woe be to him that is a neuter. *Curse ye Meroz, because they tooke not the Lords part in the day of battell.* Here, even to stand and but looke on, is treason: to take part with neither is to be an enemy to both" (1633, 908). Margaret Cavendish could have been thinking of figures like Herbert and his neutrality when in her memoir she defends the conduct of her husband, the duke of Newcastle:

> He thought it his duty rather to hazard all, than to neglect the commands of his Sovereign; and resolved to show his fidelity, by nobly setting all at stake, as he did, though he well knew how to have secured himself, as too many others did, either by neutrality or adhering to the rebellious party; but his honour and loyalty was too great to be stained with such foul adherences. (1886, 19)

Neutrality is a foul adherence, in Cavendish's view, incompatible with honor, loyalty or duty. Merely a means for securing oneself, neutrality is no more than an opportunistic subterfuge. As Roland Barthes notes, in times of civil war there is an "obligation to choose, no matter what side: the Neutral is more enemy than the enemy" (2005, 183). Given the opprobrium cast upon neuters in 1640s England, how should we interpret Herbert's decision to withdraw from political engagement?[16]

I suggest that Herbert's philosophical ideals help explain his political trajectory from royal servant to "neuter" to parliamentary stipendiary. As a philosopher he had made it his goal to refute skepticism by isolating a set of criteria for identifying truthful cognition. These criteria – conformity and consent, developed in the second decade of the seventeenth century – were still playing out thirty years later as historical events and pressures forced Herbert to come to terms with the political corollaries of his philosophy, including (ironically) an appreciation for neutrality and political skepticism. The rest of this chapter will show how his aesthetic and epistemological understanding of truth as conformity contributed to his eventual stance of skeptical detachment.

At the start of *De veritate*, conformity is linked to consent, both criteria for truthful cognition. Together they form the basis for a radical intervention in the theory of *adiaphora* – the highly political, religious discourse negotiating the boundaries between the 'fundamentals' of doctrine and

---

[15] See Shami (2003), 69–70.
[16] Lee sets the tone for subsequent commentary: "After some parleying he determined to save his property at the expense of his honour" (1892, 284).

'indifferent' things. Herbert vastly expands the universe of indifferent things by narrowing the fundamentals of religious belief to five Common Notions. These are: (1) There is a supreme God (*Pontifex maximus*); (2) This deity ought to be worshipped; (3) This worship ought to be manifested in a life of virtue, piety and charity; (4) Penitence is the proper response to transgression; and (5) Expect reward or punishment in the afterlife. The last two notions are more controversial than the first three. Herbert associates penitence with a gospel of works, a belief in free will, and a merciful deity who has no truck with predestination. In *The Life and Reign of King Henry VIII*, it gets attention because Herbert believes penance to be more universal than either the Eucharist or baptism and so deplores its exclusion from the sacraments retained at the time of the King's reformation.[17] The fifth Notion gets discussed in *De veritate* when Herbert marshals arguments for the afterlife, most famously that God would not operate like a cozening tradesman.[18] Over the course of his career, this minimalist platform becomes Herbert's idée fixe, promoted in work after work with evangelical fervor. As his persona puts it in *A Dialogue Between a Tutor and his Pupil*, "For it is of great moment towards the making of an universal peace, if men can be brought to believe that their ancestors from all ages, and in all countries, have worshipped one and the same God" (153). Herbert is not alone in drafting a set of core beliefs designed to defuse religious conflict. As Ronald Bedford reminds us, Guillaume Postel, Jacob Acontius and many others had "a vision of concord" (1979, 215) that depended on reducing doctrine to a few key principles with which all peoples could agree. But Herbert is one of the earliest seventeenth-century thinkers to borrow the Stoic concept of universal consent (*consensus gentium*) and use it as an epistemological criterion for identifying common notions of religion (*notitiae communes* or *koinai ennoiai*, DV 125/47).[19]

---

[17] "But whatsoever any of the reformed might say for their only two sacraments, it was thought by some, that according to the king's instauration, penance might have been retained still upon some terms as a third: both as there is no other general way than aversion from sin, and conversion to God, known to all mankind for making their peace with him, and obtaining pardon" (*H8* 590).

[18] "Is it likely that eternal happiness should be offered to me as an article is offered for sale, and then, just as I am about to purchase it, that the contract should be broken in the manner of a dishonest tradesman? Am I to be defrauded of the immortality and eternal blessedness which I was on the point of enjoying?" (*DV* 329/246).

[19] The legacy of Stoicism is most evident in *De religione laici* (1645) when Herbert juxtaposes universal consent with right Reason (*Ratione recta*), exhorting the reader to "distinguish things brought to light by right Reason and universal consent from those rummaged out by hearsay" (*RL* 103).

1 Consensus Universalis

"Universal consent," Herbert declares, "will be found to be the final test of truth" (*DV* 117/39) and again, "Universal Consent must be taken to be the beginning and end of theology and philosophy" (*DV* 118/40).[20] But consent cannot be premised solely on something as external and contingent as a vote – the 'ayes' calling the truth. Consent, like assent, is an inward motion that occurs in response to – or, in conformation with – divinely implanted ideas. Herbert may be taking his cue from Cicero who attributed to Epicurus the view that "the gods exist, because nature herself has impressed a conception of them on the souls of everyone."[21] Thus Herbert explains: "I do not find this Universal Consent only in laws, religions, philosophies and written expositions; I hold that certain inner faculties are inscribed in our minds by which these truths are brought into conformity" (*DV* 118/40). This internal process of recognition or apprehension involves "Natural Instinct."[22] In his memoirs, Herbert elaborates on this, observing that the "morall vertues" have been "confirmed for the most part by the Platonique, Stoiques, and other Philosophers, and in generall by the Christian Church as well as all Nations in the World whatsoever, They being Doctrines imprinted in the soule in its first originall" (*Life* 24). Needless to say, Herbert was reproved for this logic.[23]

Readers as different as Gassendi and Locke argued that if consent were a criterion of truth, then all matter of nonsense would pass muster as veridical. Locke attacked Herbert head-on in his *Essay Concerning Human Understanding*, targeting the innateness of Common Notions and refuting the validity of consensus as a criterion, noting "that we are assured from history, of many men, nay whole nations, who doubt or disbelieve some or all of them" (1.3.15–19).[24] Gassendi was more circumspect, couching his objections in a letter that was never sent, but he too

---

[20] "*Consensus Universalis* & prima & summa Theologia & Philosophia habendus est" (40).
[21] *De natura deorum* 1.43–44 (cited in Reid 2015, 404).
[22] "I hold, therefore, that this universal consent is the teaching of Natural Instinct and is essentially due to Divine Providence" (*DV* 117/39). Bedford comments, "Herbert appears blandly to ignore Montaigne's devastating objections" to the belief that man has an innate capacity to grasp truth (1979, 53).
[23] For the early reception of *De veritate*, see Serjeantson who notes that before the 1670s, "readers were excited, influenced, and often confused by his writings and their purposes" (2001, 217).
[24] Aaron argues that Locke's real target is, not Herbert, but the Cartesians (1955, 84–88), cited in Bedford 1979, 78. See also Jonathan Barnes (1972), cited in Serjeantson 2001, 236.

wondered how Herbert could invoke universal consent when faced with "the great contrariety of judgments that one finds on almost every subject."[25] Richard Baxter likewise questioned "this consent of all mankind" (1672, 129), while Pierre Bayle had a slew of objections, including the prevalence of polytheism (Reid 2015, 408). Given this criticism, some of it leveled during his lifetime, why is Herbert so committed to the idea of consent?

For Herbert, consent in *De veritate* is not the political, ethical, and sexual conundrum that Shakespeare, for example, delights in anatomizing.[26] Instead, it has an incipiently aesthetic dimension associated with the idea of musical consent or harmony. In John Davies's *Orchestra* (1596), this usage is in evidence. "Yet with a certain aunswere and consent / To the quick music of the Instrument," the poem reads, and turning to dance, adds, "Dauncing the Art that all Arts doe approve: / The faire Caracter of the worlds consent, / The heav'ns true figure, and th'earths ornament," repeating later "uniforme consent doth dauncing praise" (stanzas 70, 96, 113). A similar aesthetic sensibility informs Herbert's view of how consent to the Common Notions operates. "The Common Notions which spring from natural instinct carry conviction with them," he explains (*DV* 135/56). "This feeling of conviction" characterized by "clear inner assent" corresponds to "Universal Consent" (*DV* 81/6). Arguing by analogy, he observes that the "Natural Instinct" triggering that consent "anticipates reason in perceiving the beauty of the proportions of a house built according to architectural principles. ... And the same point can be noticed in judging beautiful features, or graceful form, or harmony in music" (*DV* 139/60).[27] The instant appreciation of beauty or proportion is like the "gratitude" we experience upon encountering the innate idea of God (*DV* 296–297/215). As we shall see, the aesthetic dimension of consent relates to the symmetries and harmonies involved in the "conformation" of faculties with objects of perception.

Yet consent is not only an aesthetic feeling of concord and oneness with the world. For Herbert it is also a cosmopolitan principle with both spatial and temporal dimensions, even as he elides it with a sensation of internal approval.[28] The global reach of *consensus gentium* embraces indigenous

---

[25] "Quelle raison pourrait-on rendre de la grande contrariété des jugements qui se rencontrent presque sur chaque sujet?" (cited in Serjeantson 2001, 223). See "Ad Librum D. Edoardi Herberti Angli, De Veritate, Epistola" in *Opera omnia* (1964), 3.411–19.
[26] See, e.g., Lupton, "*All's Well That Ends Well* and the Futures of Consent" (2011, 97–129).
[27] "pulchrum symmetriae ... venustate faciei, formae elegantia, concentu harmoniae" (*DV* 60).
[28] For cosmopolitanism as a symptom of "loser romanticism," see Sloterdijk 2012, 45–46.

tribes in the present and the pagan peoples of the past. He is not thinking of social class or "the poorer sort," as he likes to say, when imagining the global community, but rather of his fascination with anthropology and comparative religion. In this he is not alone. Jasper Reid surmises that the "increase in international exploration probably was, indeed, a major driver of the upswing in interest in this type of argument in the early modern period" thanks to new data about native peoples (2015, 405). Herbert's *De religione gentilium*, published posthumously in 1663, is an erudite compilation of his own extensive readings in the field of comparative religion; major sources include *De theologia gentilium* (1642) by Gerard Vossius, *De diis Syris* (1617) by his friend and executor, John Selden, Roman authors such as Varro, as well as recent accounts of the New World.

But Herbert is not so invested in individuals that he is a nominalist – that is not his route to skepticism.[29] On the contrary, he is a realist – *universalia sunt realia* – although his faith in universals will be tested when he grapples with conformity. When dealing with consent, his curiosity about the variety of individual beliefs is only a means to an end, namely, his general claim that the Common Notions are ontological universals. Thus, he asserts,

> I take the chief criterion of Natural Instinct to be universal consent (putting aside persons who are out of their minds or mentally incapable). For I have always viewed particular principles with suspicion as savouring of deception, or at least mingled with error. In a word, pure Common Notions are universals, distilled as it were from the wisdom of Nature itself. (*DV* 139–140/60)

With his appreciation for the symmetries of microcosm and macrocosm, Herbert concludes that empirical evidence of global consent legitimizes a metaphysical armature in which the mind assents to universals.

Herbert's principle of consent is both aesthetic and cosmopolitan while wedded to innate ideas. His philosophy of mind tends toward realism and idealism rather than nominalism. Nevertheless, he arrives at skepticism through a circuitous route. His aesthetic appreciation for the relation of conformity will lead him to value an epistemological neutrality that shares features with skepticism's suspension of judgment (epoché).

---

[29] See Bedford (1979), 32–34.

2 Conformatio

Conformity is a complex word with a long and checkered history. Its most salient meaning for students of the seventeenth century is accommodation to the established church: going along to get along. Gregory Dodds (2009) has argued that the discourse of conformity was part of the Erasmian legacy in England and was coopted, not only by the establishment, but also by extremists as a way of rhetorically occupying the *via media*. In Dodds's view, conformity masquerades as a synonym for moderation when in fact it means uniformity.[30] More often, conformity bluntly evokes state power, as happened in the early 1660s when the Clarendon Code barred non-conforming ministers from preaching, depriving them of their livings. Conformity is also a term from diplomacy and international relations designating shared borders and the contiguity of nations (Elliott 2009, 7) – a usage in play for Herbert given his diplomatic background. Additionally, it has a distinguished philosophical genealogy, going back to Scholastic theologians and before them to Aristotle, and designates the metaphysical and epistemological agreement between different mental entities. For philosophers *conformitas* means congruence, correspondence, fit, or match. Thus, the connotations of conformity extend in two directions: first, toward the discourse of philosophy and theology in which the vocabulary of analogy, alignment, and metaphysical intimacy looms large; and second, toward the coercive practices of institutional power and individual maneuvers of self-preservation and dissimulation crafted in response, a usage touched on in *The Life and Reign of King Henry VIII*.[31] A metaphysics of unity melds with a political aesthetic of camouflage: perfect harmony in tension with forced assimilation. This can manifest itself in many ways.[32] What's important here is Herbert's exaltation of and allegiance to the term.

---

[30] Similarly, Shagan notes "what a dangerous chameleon the *via media* turned out to be," arguing that the discourse of moderation often masks violence (2010, 501). Shami, however, cautions that "evidence of 'moderation' or 'conformity,' of course, is difficult to gather and interpret" (2003, 17).

[31] See, e.g.: "For though (as *Sanders* saith) he would by the Bishop of *Rochester's* exemplary death have brought *More* to a conformity, yet finding that it was impossible..." (*H8* 392–393).

[32] For example, King James uses the term to describe the devil's wily pliancy: "For that olde and craftie Serpent, being a spirite, hee easilie spyes our affections, and so conformes himselfe thereto, to deceave us to our wracke" (1597, 8). Conformity here suggests mimicry, metaphysical intimacy, subjugation, and even complicity. But the term can also imply structural integrity and inner strength, as Justus Lipsius suggests when he says (in John Stradling's translation) that "our minds must be so confirmed and conformed that we may bee at rest in troubles, and have peace even in the midst of warre" (1594, 1.1.72). The Latin reads "& firmandus ita formandusque hic animus, ut quies nobis in turbis sit, & pax inter media arma."

2 Conformatio

In *De veritate* Herbert wants to reconfigure the semantic field of this contentious term so as to stake out a new approach to problems in the philosophy of mind. Herbert is searching for words to describe the operations of consciousness – fighting against Scholastic terminology, rejecting Calvinist anthropology with its notions of depravity, sin, and predestination, seeking answers in the works of medicine and botany that seem to represent the cutting edge of science, and testing all available European vocabulary against his own experience. Indeed, Herbert often inveighs against the inadequacy of words. "Ordinary language is very deficient in terms," he complains, adding "it is disgraceful that there are feelings that have no name" (*DV* 205/125). Elsewhere, he says:

> It is discreditable that there are plenty of terms appropriate to external factors while there is a lack of suitable terms for internal principles. For this reason I am led to refer to the Reader's internal modes of apprehension in ambiguous and devious ways, often employing periphrastic types of expression because of this deficiency of terms. (*DV* 114/36)

In coping with his frustration over a brittle vocabulary poor at evoking internal weather, Herbert develops a technical terminology of his own. At the start of his treatise he supplies a glossary of philosophical and theological terms, explaining that "it was necessary for me on account of the complete novelty of the subject, either to coin new terms, or to adapt those in common use, wherever possible, to my own meaning" (*DV* 73). Among the terms he adapts are Nature, Grace, Natural Instinct, Faculties, Revelation, and Possibility. Conformity and consent are absent from the list, but they too are pried loose from their conventional contexts. While consent remains recognizable to common usage, conformity acquires an odd elasticity, as if Herbert were trying out new ways to use the word.

Herbert defines conformity repeatedly, seeking to fix its identity once and for all; but no sooner has he asserted a definition with trenchant finality than his thinking seems to evolve so that he appends or inserts a subordinate clause lightly modifying the prior version. Insofar as Herbert seems to be experimenting with a "grammar" of conformity in *De veritate*, we can say (in a Wittgensteinian vein) that his usages bear a "family resemblance." But as Stanley Cavell reminds us, "All that the idea of 'family resemblances' is meant to do, or need do, is to make us dissatisfied with the idea of universals as explanations of language" (2000, 35). While Herbert is not prepared to disavow universals and become a nominalist, his dissatisfaction with conformity as a universal is palpable. In his work the polysemousness of conformity risks dissolving into an all-purpose semantic variable. It is as though Herbert were trying to conjure a new "form of life" for the word: a form of life that might solve the problems encountered by a wayward consciousness. As Cavell explains, "You cannot use words to do what we do with them until you are initiate of the forms of life which give those words the point and shape they have in our lives" (2000, 33). Herbert is trying to use the aesthetic connotations of the word to initiate – even jump-start – a form of life committed to ethical, political, and religious harmony.

How can an individual discriminate between truth and deception, if he or she depends on an inward feeling of consent as a criterion? The answer, according to Herbert, has to do with "the right conformation" of the faculties. Thus, he says that "whatever is believed by universal consent must be true and must have been brought into conformity in virtue of some internal faculty" (*DV* 116/38). Conformity becomes the chief criterion for gauging the truth of a belief or sensation, functioning as the measure of a successful act of cognition. If the faculties are in good working order – that is, in due conformity – then perceptions and thoughts are true. Resorting to simile, Herbert explains that "truth, like health, requires its special circumstances" (*DV* 88/12), and sets out the special circumstances for truthful cognition, all of which involve conformity.

Herbert lists ten conditions for producing the epistemological conformity necessary for the grasping of truth, declaring, "I hold that truth, being a matter of conformity between objects and faculties, is highly conditional" (*DV* 78/4). Herbert's ten conditions are designed to refute skepticism. Point by point they challenge the ten modes of Aenesidemus, a list of ten ways to produce uncertainty. As mentioned earlier, the modes of Aenesidemus were skeptical strategies devised in antiquity, relayed in the work of Sextus Empiricus in the second century, and circulated in the late sixteenth and early seventeenth centuries by Montaigne and his skeptical fellow travelers. These techniques for instilling radical doubt were remarkably effective, as Montaigne's "Apologie for Raymond Sebond" attests, and threatened the foundations of knowledge. Herbert's ten conditions address Aenesidemus' ten modes. Sometimes he uses the same examples: the case of the jaundiced eye that makes the world look yellow or that of the sick man to whom honey tastes bitter.[33] But usually he offers refinements, for example, Aenesidemus' Fifth Mode, which regards "positions and intervals

---

[33] "To the man with jaundice everything is yellow, and all things taste bitter to the fevered tongue" (*DV* 102/25).

2 Conformatio

and places," especially deceptions in appearance caused by the distance of objects (Annas & Barnes 1985, 99, 104) corresponds partly to Herbert's Second Condition "that the object should be of the right size" (*DV* 90/14), but also partly to his Third Condition "that the distance should be suitable" (*DV* 95/19) and to his Fourth Condition "that the object should occupy a fitting position" (*DV* 97/21). These refinements arise because Herbert wants his conditions to apply, not only to the external sensory problems favored by skeptics, but also to internal problems of apprehension having to do, for example, with beauty and memory. He wants to understand why "the idea of beauty excites us" (*DV* 152/72) and how memory can remain "reliable, fresh and steady" (*DV* 237/156).[34] So he introduces conditions not addressed by Aenesidemus, for example, tackling the question of how to neutralize temporality. "The object should remain for a sufficient time," Herbert declares, explaining that "when we pass from external to internal apprehension, time is so necessary that without it nothing can be adequately perceived. It is for this reason, due to insufficient examination of assertions, that rash and premature judgments and ludicrous beliefs gain ground" (*DV* 92–93/16). Ever the optimist, Herbert hopes to overwrite the ten skeptical modes by devising a set of conditions that will at once displace and supplement the skeptical analysis of perception by dealing with inward apprehensions.

Abraham Stoll comments on "the array of technical terms used to describe interiority" in Herbert's work (2002, 287). As Reid Barbour has observed, this attention to the mind's inner workings is typical of "the Caroline exploration of internal circumstance" prompted by the "critical legacy of skepticism" (2001, 16). Skepticism's obsession with misleading appearances inspires efforts to map the mind and pinpoint the junctures where thinking goes wrong. If faculties and objects are in conformity, so Herbert argues, then falsity and misprision are disabled and the veracity of a sense-impression or apprehension is guaranteed. Conformity thus offers all-purpose insurance against the myriad ways in which cognition can go awry.

Herbert may be reaching toward a notion of disinterestedness here – or perhaps impartiality or neutrality – but if so, he conceives of disinterestedness, not as detachment, but as a felicitous meeting of perceiver and

---

[34] "(*pulchri* enim Idea, ut de *turpi* taceam, nos afficit)" and "Maximè igitur interest, ut *Memoria* sit constans, integra, stabilis" (*DV* 72, 156).

perceived, a coming together that he will revisit as an ideal when writing history.[35] He exalts conformity as a perfect fit between knower and known, a relation marked by symmetry and balance as the mind and its objects face off and match up. "Truth is a harmony," he declares, "between objects and their analogous faculties. ... When we have grasped this we can see that a double movement takes place; objects affect us, and we affect them; but both activities occur at the same moment, so that the difference between them is almost unnoticeable" (*DV* 148/68). Double movement together with simultaneity produces a condition where difference is erased and harmony prevails. Truthful perception works like a dance: everything synchronized and in concert. To drive home this synergy, he repeats: "All truth according to this doctrine consists of conformity" (*DV* 88/13). What can this mean? Herbert offers an enthymeme and definitions in his effort to explain: "And since all conformity consists of a relation, it follows that all instances of truth will be relations, or aptitudes realized in act, that is in perception" (*DV* 88/13). Yet by speaking as if relations and aptitudes, perception and conformity were interchangeable synonyms, Herbert muddies his explanation.[36]

Seventeenth-century documents and letters testify to the difficulties that Herbert's contemporaries had with his prose. For example, Descartes thanks Mersenne for sending him a copy of his 1639 French translation of *De veritate*: "I can only say that I had much less difficulty in reading it in French than I had had with the Latin," adding "although I cannot be in complete agreement with this author's opinions I nevertheless consider that he is much above ordinary minds."[37] Similarly, Jacob Aretius, an

---

[35] See Murphy and Traninger's edited collection (2014) for historically nuanced distinctions among impartiality, neutrality, and disinterestedness, as well as for impartiality's skeptical origins. See also Dear who maps the shift from ontology to epistemology in the seventeenth century by tracking the way a concern with truth – which resides "in some kind of conformity between the thing itself and the idea of the thing" (1992, 620) – turns into a privileging of disinterestedness. For a polemical overview of the changing fortunes of "the neutral observer" in Western philosophy, see Sloterdijk (2012).

[36] In the following passage, for example, the curious phrase "obsolete conformities" (that is transient and fleeting versus eternal) makes sense if in this instance conformity means something like image (*eidolon*): "But the ideas which are imprinted by the mind or spirit appear to exist for ever; and this is true also of the faculty of recollection, which can recall obsolete conformities from associated objects, the constant features of things, and recover those which have fled. I conclude that everything which has been brought into right conformity in memory by means of the above laws attains immortality" (*DV* 238/156–157).

[37] Mersenne (1932–88), VIII, 551: "j'y ay trouvé beaucoup moins de difficulté en le lisant en françois, que je n'avois fait cy devant en le parcourant en latin ... encore que je ne puisse m'accorder en tout aux sentimens de cet autheur, je ne laisse pas de l'estimer beaucoup au dessus des esprits ordinaires." Descartes later gave Herbert a first edition of the *Meditations*. Herbert was interested enough that he started a translation of the *Discours de la méthode*; see Fordyce and Knox (1937), 53 ff. and Rossi (1947), 2.537.

2 Conformatio

Oxford theologian, writes Mersenne that "we all admire the most excellent Baron of Cherbury's treatise *De veritate,* and (as is just) adorn it with praise; but scarcely one in a thousand (even of the learned) understand it. Heroic intellects indeed are eagles (in the clouds)."[38] By the early eighteenth century Thomas Halyburton carps that Herbert's "use of vulgar words, in new and uncommon acceptations, and his obscure way of management of his notions, is scarce intelligible to any save metaphysical readers, nor to such, without greater application, than perhaps the matter is worth" (1798, 190).[39] The obscurity of *De veritate* can be largely ascribed to the denotational slippage in the key terms of its argumentation.[40]

The distinction between 'residual' and 'emergent' discourses, coined by Raymond Williams (1977), helps clarify Herbert's use of conformity. The residual connotations of conformity involve the language of philosophy and theology going back several centuries. Most familiar perhaps is the idea that the soul should conform itself to the will of God, yet Herbert specifically dismisses this locution when he reviews his own aims. He declares polemically:

> Much may be added to what I have said, but I leave this to the Schools. It is sufficient in this work to have laid the foundation of truth. If any doubt this let them consider the definitions of the Authors, such as that truth is the conformity with the Divine mind, truth is the form of true objects, truth is the property of each thing since it is founded on it. Such assertions are only morsels or fractions of definitions which it is tiresome to discuss. (*DV* 286/205)

Herbert is confident his account has displaced inferior definitions of truth, including those involving conformity to God's will. As his belligerent

---

[38] Mersenne (1932–88), VIII, 404 (cited in Serjeantson 2001, 220): "Excellentiss' Baronis de Cherbury tractatum *de Veritate* amamus omnes, atque (ut par est) elogijs ornamus, sed vix millesimus quisque (vel eruditiorum) intelligit. Heroica ingenia vere sunt Aquilae (In nubibus)."

[39] Cited in Pailin (2001), 123–124; Hill (1987), 34.

[40] Hill finds Herbert's "oddity of usage" to be most problematic with respect to the term, "faculty" (1987, 27). Other scholars attribute the difficulties of Herbert's writing to the "syncretism" of his thought, surveying his wide and eclectic reading in the tradition of *Quellenforschungen*. For example, Bedford writes, "The specific sources of Herbert's ideas are a matter for dispute – inevitably so since his mind, like that of many a Renaissance syncretist, does not sift its material and provide the sort of attributions that would make the task of defining those sources simple. Ideas and philosophies are absorbed in a kind of osmotic percolation" (1987, 88). Holmes believes that Herbert's obscurity derives from the way he "estranges" notions of selfhood, achieving a "denaturalization of perception and identity" (2001, 45–46). See also D. P. Walker (1972).

dismissal reveals, the phrase is important, figuring in debates over whether true knowledge requires divine illumination from God. Bonaventure (1217–1274) thought so, explaining in a sermon that "in creatures one finds three modes of conformity to God. For some are conformed to God as a vestige, some as an image, and some as a likeness" (Pasnau 2002, 87). This turns out to be an ascending hierarchy, pairing vestiges with "natural actions," images with "intellectual actions" and likenesses with "meritorious operations ... infused through grace," showing that God cooperates with the 'highest' conformity. Henry of Ghent (1217–1293), the so-called "last great defender of divine illumination" (Pasnau 2002, 109), uses conformity in locutions deceptively similar to those of Herbert, e.g. "The truth of a thing can be cognized only by cognizing the conformity of the cognized thing to its exemplar" (Pasnau 2002, 117). In support of this statement, he cites Anselm's *De veritate* (ch. 7) that "truth is the conformity of a thing to its most true exemplar" (Pasnau 2002, 117). The appeal to exemplars brings Henry of Ghent to Plato's divine archetypes and the challenge of recognizing the conformity, that is to say, the closeness in degree or relation between thing and exemplar. Peter Aureol (1280–1322) objects to Henry of Ghent's views, arguing that "it is impossible to cognize the conformity of two things unless one cognizes the quality in which they conform" (Pasnau 2002, 189). The issue for him is one of recognition – what features (or qualities) count when determining whether something is true and how God enables the act of apprehension, if at all. Like disjunctivist philosophers today, Aureol seeks to explain how objects can be present to the mind, even when absent. He avers that "the reality of the vision does not require the real presence of an existing object, although the truth of a vision requires this, since truth adds to the reality of a vision the relationship of conformity to the thing" (Pasnau 2002, 202). The distinction Aureol makes between reality and truth hinges on conformity – if the dagger I see before me is not only real, but true, this is because the relation between mind and dagger can be described as conformity. Closer in time to Herbert, the nominalist theologian, Gabriel Biel (d. 1495) uses the phrase *conformitas voluntatis* to suggest both an ethical and a mystical ideal, by contrast with Meister Eckhart's mystical sense of dissolution and essential union with God (Oberman 1963, 464). His protestations to the contrary, Herbert draws on this rich philosophical and theological tradition when he makes conformity a criterion of epistemological truth. Like Bonaventure, he also posits gradations of conformity, believing that in its highest manifestation the mind's apprehension of conformity comes from God.

2 Conformatio

Yet, Herbert's idiosyncratic understanding of conformity is Janus-faced – looking backward to the Schools in acknowledgment of his Oxford and Paduan teachers,[41] but also looking forward to emergent forms of philosophical writing and scientific investigation. As mentioned, he was in conversation with Descartes, Gassendi, and Mersenne, among others. He translated Hobbes's *De principiis*, an early draft of *De corpore* (Bedford 1979, 133; Rossi 1947, 1.281).[42] His library, numbering at least a thousand books, was furnished with scientific and medical treatises.[43] He also knew Francis Bacon. Bacon appointed Herbert, along with John Selden, the executor of his papers in an early draft of his will.[44] Critics may dispute the extent to which Bacon influenced Herbert, but it is clear they shared certain broad aims.[45] Like so many seventeenth-century thinkers, both were goaded by the challenge of skepticism to identify the mechanisms that produce cognitive error and thereby advance truth.

In *The New Organon* (1620) Bacon identifies four classes of cognitive error to which he gives the catchy names: idols of the tribe, idols of the cave, idols of the marketplace, and idols of the theater.[46] These idols of the mind are "false notions" that encompass a range of issues: from self-serving rationalizations to linguistic opacity and ideological mystifications. Like Herbert, Bacon targets physiological disorders as the chief source of

---

[41] In 1615 Herbert attended the lectures of Cesare Cremonini in Padua, himself a follower of Pomponazzi (Butler 1990, 103–104). See also Rossi (1947), 1.232–233.

[42] Tuck describes Herbert's version, not as a translation, but as "notes on a text of *De corpore*" (1993, 296).

[43] See National Library of Wales 5298E for Herbert's library catalogue, ca. 1630.

[44] Barbour 2003, 193, who in turn cites Mordechai Feingold, *John Selden* (Boston, 1991), 61.

[45] Butler follows Rossi in declaring that Bacon's philosophy "had little impact on Herbert, who never mentions his great predecessor" (1990, 126). Rossi opposes Armando Carlini's view that Bacon's influence was all-pervasive and extended to Herbert. See Carlini (1917) and Rossi (1947), 1.279–280. Sorley comments that "they cannot fail to have been known to one another by report, can hardly fail to have met personally. But each carried out his work in apparent unconsciousness of the investigations of the other" (1894, 492). Bedford concedes that "in Herbert's attitude to authority there are resemblances to Bacon's attitude toward 'cobwebs of learning' and the obfuscation of the mind through adherence to the idols" (1979, 138), but he concludes that "Herbert's total approach is peculiarly un-Baconian, in the sense that it lays itself wide open to the charge expressed in Bacon's diagnosis of the causes of learning's atrophy" (1979, 83). Christine Jackson says that in writing his history of Henry VIII, Herbert "drew upon recent studies such as Francis Bacon's *The History of the Reign of King Henry VII*," noting that he "endorses Bacon's Tacitean focus on human causation" (2012, 137–138).

[46] Might Herbert's four truths be seen as the reverse of Bacon's four idols? Herbert divides truth into four classes, only two of which are conditional in their conformity: the "truth of appearance," which "is not easily brought into conformity with things in themselves" (*DV* 84/9) and "truth of concept," which depends on a mind free of prejudice (*DV* 86/11). "Truth of thing" is not conditional because it comprises "the inherent conformity of the thing itself, or that ground in virtue of which everything remains constant with itself" (*DV* 88/12–13). By contrast, "truth of intellect consists of the right conformity between all the preceding conformities" (*DV* 88/13).

cognitive error, agreeing with skeptics that "sense by itself is a thing infirm and erring" (1965, 339). His philosophical mission is to expose these problems "so the access to truth may be made less difficult, and the human understanding may the more willingly submit to its purgation and dismiss its idols" (1965, 344). In keeping with Protestant discourses of iconoclasm and habits of bodily discipline, Bacon adopts religious and digestive metaphors to diagnose faulty cognition. Herbert prefers the discourse of purity, invoking "pure acts of conformity" to express the happy conjunctions of perfect cognition (*DV* 159/78). This matches the aesthetic minimalism of his five Common Notions – tenets pruned of superfluous clutter that he characterizes as strict, pure, and austere (*DV* 306/225).[47]

Although both men seek to reform ways of thinking through a prescribed method, Bacon uses the terms conformity and consent to record his observations about the world rather than the mind. In *The New Organon* he treats conformity as a principle of physical resemblance, noting, for example, that "the roots and branches of plants (which may seem strange) are Conformable Instances" (*Works*, ed. Spedding, IV.165), that "the scrotum in males and the matrix in females are Conformable Instances," and that it is not "an absurd similitude or conformity which has been remarked between man and a plant inverted" (IV.166). Bacon argues that these resemblances are stepping-stones to general axioms. At first, they "simply point out and mark a certain agreement in bodies," but thereafter they "are very serviceable in revealing the fabric of the parts of the universe, and anatomizing its members; from which they often lead us along to sublime and noble axioms, especially those which relate to the configuration of the world" (IV.164). Lest this seem too abstract, he offers "instances of Conformity; a looking-glass and the eye; and again, the construction of the ear and places returning an echo. From which conformity ... it is easy to gather and form this axiom, – that the organs of the senses, and bodies which produce reflexions to the senses, are of a like nature" (IV.164–165). Bacon uses the term consent to describe sympathy between bodies. Thus, he declares, "There is no difference between the consents or sympathies of bodies endowed with sensation and those of inanimate bodies without sensation" (IV.165). In a section titled, "On the Consent between Sensible and Insensible Bodies," consent

---

[47] Barbour comments on the austerity of Herbert's spiritual economy, identifying the common notions themselves as the enforcers of obedience: "For all the expansive freedom that Herbert bestows on human agency, his common notions are severe and demanding. After all, they internalize the conformity that Laudian divines would ritualize" (2001, 214).

means correspondence.[48] Although he uses neither term in his *Inquiry Respecting the Magnet*, preferring to speak of attraction, he does mention conformity when praising William Gilbert's work on the topic, saying, "The flight of iron from one pole of the magnet is well observed by Gilbert to be not a Flight strictly speaking, but a conformity and meeting in a more convenient situation" (IV.223). While he may approve of Gilbert's usage of the term, Bacon is keen to distinguish his understanding of conformity from "the superstitious or curious resemblances" and "similitudes" found by "frivolous persons" who dabble in "natural magic" (IV.167). Bacon may have his knives out here for Hermetic ways of thinking about uncanny correspondences of macrocosm and microcosm.[49] Moving on from nature, Bacon sometimes uses conformity to describe synergies in art. He notes, for example, that "the rhetorical trope of deceiving expectation is conformable with the musical trope of avoiding or sliding from the close or cadence" (IV.167). The relation of music and rhetoric, like that between mathematics and logic, shows "Conformity of Instances."

Herbert may be more indebted to scholastic models of mind for his understanding of conformity than he would like to admit.[50] Nevertheless, his aesthetic sensitivity to the relational processes of perception may well owe something to Bacon. This aestheticism manifests itself in a Baconian appreciation for nature's intricacies and in the emergent discourse of wonder associated with it.[51] "The larynx is a marvelous object," Herbert exclaims. "It is situated above the artery of the trachea and serves to provide the voice with its elementary material by means of its air-filled cavity" (*DV* 218/138). He puzzles over "those harsh and shrill noises which distress some people's teeth" (*DV* 176/96). He is amazed at the varieties of smell, reiterating his lament over the inadequacies of language: "There do not at present exist sufficient words to express the difference between types of smell; so that anyone whose delicacy of smell is challenged is obliged to betake himself to tasting, and savours a divided apple, mouth open, with nose and palate at the same time" (*DV* 212/132).

---

[48] Elsewhere in *The New Organon*, consent means an unthinking or reflexive reaction, e.g. "For a fetid odour is so rejected by the sense of smell as to induce by consent in the mouth of the stomach a motion of expulsion; a rough and bitter taste is so rejected by the palate or throat as to induce by consent a shaking of the head and a shudder" (IV.223).
[49] Herbert is thought to have had Hermetic leanings. See D. P. Walker (1972) and Bedford (1979).
[50] As Eggert notes of seventeenth-century thought, "Even theoretical systems that looked new often betrayed their reliance on the very ideas they were meant to replace" (2015, 210).
[51] See Daston and Park (1998).

Whether discussing opium or absinthe (222/142), the croaking of frogs (216/136) or the rose in winter (167/87), his precise descriptions are infused with wonder. In one puzzling instance, he conflates conformity and skin, asserting, "The external organ of conformity is nothing but the epidermis or extremity of the skin. When its condition is moderate and the other conditions which I have adduced at the beginning of the book are present, truth of sensation is produced" (230/149). Skin turns out to be a person's interface with the world, necessitating a homeostatic equilibrium of sorts that enables truth of perception. These examples suggest that Herbert fancies himself among those connoisseurs belonging to a "community of inquirers" united by a "sensibility" that Daston and Park characterize as "a state of painstaking attention trained on new, rare, or unusual things and events" (1988, 288, 218).

Both Herbert and Bacon aestheticize conformity when they discuss how and why sound works. Addressing the marvels of the ear, Bacon observes that "the organ of hearing has a conformity with an obstruction in a cave, from which the voice and sound is best re-echoed" (V.432). Herbert, by contrast, seems more empirical, even while embracing the metaphorical connotations of anatomical terms. "Let us consider the organ, or workshop of hearing," he begins, as if he were describing a blacksmith's forge. "In it I find that the labyrinth, the stirrup, the anvil and the mallet, etc., can be detected," adding more coolly, "It has been well pointed out that sound is produced by a compressed spiral impulse of air against a solid obstacle" (*DV* 217–218/137).[52] Yet, despite this appreciation for fluid dynamics, in Herbert truthful acoustics are achieved thanks to the proper conformation of the faculty of hearing together with the favorable conditions in the medium of transmission, such as no contrary wind. Bacon limits conformity's meaning to a physical resemblance aligning odd couples in the natural world, while Herbert expands its epistemological significance, elevating it by *fiat* into a criterion of truthful knowledge.

Herbert's fascination with the body and its interactions notwithstanding, in the end his thesis about conformity inhibits him from asking further questions. His descriptions often open or end in assertions of "conformity," effectively shutting down investigation rather than opening it up. "Flavour," for example, he defines as "the special object of the faculty of taste, and the correct medium is a kind of tasteless saliva, the presence of which, together with the conditions described at the beginning of the book, ensures that this faculty is in conformity" (*DV* 221/141). On

---

[52] Cf. the possible echo of Donne's "Satire 2": "the tender labyrinth of a soft maid's ear" (58).

occasions like this one, conformity functions rhetorically as a self-evident claim that precedes a disquisition on the great variety of flavors, but it tends not to promote further research, as it might do in Bacon. On other occasions, conformity operates as an excuse for Euphuistic bravura, as Herbert imagines a continuum between sensory stimuli and an appreciation for beauty that depends on shared conformity. Arguing by analogy with Euphuistic aphorisms, he says:

> The light of a flame is more quickly perceived by the eye than its heat by touch. In the same way the pleasant smell of agreeable food is more readily perceived than its taste. And so, too, the beauty of symmetry is more quickly apparent to our soul than its purpose. For the former is the object of natural instinct, the latter of discursive thought, and the further the kind of apprehension used is within us, the quicker the conformity results. (*DV* 96/19)

Here, conformity operates as a cognitive process that can be hastened or delayed. He goes on to draw "several very interesting corollaries from these facts," one of which is that "objects whose appearance can pass through several inlets can of course be brought much more quickly into conformity" (*DV* 96/20).[53] Whether the mind is engaged in smelling food or sizing up beauty, conformity is ultimately the goal because it is the measure of accurate perception.

While Bacon has utility in his sights and operates with the certainty that society will benefit from probing nature's secrets, Herbert is less confident about experimental science and more resigned to the limits of human reason. He says, "There are few features of nature which we can comprehend, and even they are obscure," adding, "No one ever has or will understand the real nature and movement of the pulse and the throbbing arteries" (*DV* 270/189). In this regard his skepticism is like Margaret Cavendish's, founded on respect for the unfathomable mysteries of nature and consciousness. Like her, Herbert is intrigued by the budding science of medicine, if we judge by the volumes he left to Jesus College;[54] but apart from the therapeutic hopes fostered by the recipe books of apothecaries, his sense of science is not instrumental in the Baconian sense. Nature may offer myriad activities that inspire aesthetic wonder, but rather than

---

[53] By "inlets," Herbert here seems to mean sense organs, which he is keen to distinguish from the senses. He declares, "I have computed the number of sense organs as five, with the Schools, but I have raised the number of senses to correspond with the number of differences, following the evidence of consciousness itself. It is absurd to suppose that there are only five senses" (*DV* 165/85).

[54] See Fordyce and Knox (1937).

leading to outer-directed experiments, Herbert's aesthetic sensibility compels him to look within and deepen his understanding of the human mind.

Herbert's interest in beauty is often ascribed to Neoplatonism thanks to poems that trade in Neoplatonic conceits.[55] Spenser's Neoplatonic "An Hymne in Honour of Beautie" is cited as inspiration (Butler 469). Sarah Hutton groups Herbert with the Cambridge Platonists even while acknowledging the "blend of Stoic, Neoplatonic and Aristotelian elements" in Herbert's thought (1996, 21). A scrap of paper relating to beauty found among Herbert's letters shows these eclectic affiliations. Under the title, "The new Philosophy of Beauty," Herbert has jotted some notes where Neoplatonism, scholasticism and traces of the new science mingle promiscuously (Rossi 1947, 3.442–443). Calling "Beauty the most visible part of knowledge," he begins with "the most visible part of beauty, which is Collour." After observing color's "calme light," he considers the "*Phaenomenon*" of the sky's color "in white and blew" as well as the relative beauty of diamonds and sapphires, supposing that "the white must have somewhat in it of the Orientall and ferne" if it is to be as beautiful as the blue sapphire. "The second part of beauty," he declares, "is Figure this consists in a 3fold proportion, according to the Genus, Species and Individuū." After a few examples, he takes up "The Beauty of Order" or "the 3d Beauty" before reverting to discussion of color. Praise of proportion unites this taxonomy of beauty.

Herbert praises proportion alongside symmetry and harmony throughout his poetry and prose,[56] criteria of beauty that also inform his concept of conformity. Objects and faculties "are not haphazardly brought into conformity with each other;" rather, "faculties are harmoniously directed

---

[55] See, e.g., his 1639 poem "The Idea" (1881, 109), which opens:

> "All Beauties vulgar eyes on earth do see,
> At best but some imperfect copies be
> Of those the Heavens did at first decree;
>
> For though th'Ideas of each sev'ral kind
> Conceiv'd above by the Eternal Mind
> Are such, as none can error in them find ..."

[56] In "To Mrs. Diana Cecyll," the third stanza reads:

> "Nor is that symmetry of parts and form divine
> Made of one vulgar line,
> Or such as any know how to define,
> But of proportions new, so well express
> That the perfections in each part confest
> Are beauties to themselves and to the rest" (52). See also *DV* 139/60.

2 Conformatio

toward objects" (*DV* 92/15). When it comes to "discovering" the Common Notions, Herbert assures "the Reader" that "he will be filled with extraordinary pleasure and experience an intimate harmony of the faculties through which the notions are brought into conformity" (*DV* 141–142/62). The happiness produced by the apprehension of the Common Notions borders on a type of aesthetic experience given its imbrication with the beauty of conformity as a relation. "A conforming faculty," he reiterates, "corresponds harmoniously with the object. . . . And from this mutual activity . . . apprehension springs as the outcome of the blending of forces" (*DV* 153–154/73). Conformity is an activity of coming together in joyous reciprocity. Furthermore, the experience of "right conformity" involves wonder at the system's beauty. As Herbert puts it, "The force and energy of the faculties when they are allied with their appropriate objects satisfy our spirits so completely that we must always marvel at the beauty of the system of truth" (*DV* 161/80).[57] Here the connection between conformity and the aesthetic experience of beauty is clearly stated. Later, he develops this insight, applying it not to the "system" but to the question of proportion and harmonic numbers when assessing particular objects of beauty:

> It is a pretty problem, and a hard one, to determine how much is due in the perception of a beautiful object to external activity and how much to the internal faculties. It requires a knowledge of the proportion of activity in things and anyone who grasps this grasps the entire scheme of the world: for the harmony of the world is composed of such proportions. (*DV* 176/96)

Herbert melds aesthetic evaluation, scholastic faculty psychology, and Pythagorean number theory in his explanation of conformity as a principle of cognition.

In sum, Herbert believes that truth is the result of cognitive and perceptual processes that are structurally aesthetic. This means that the experience of a properly ordered consciousness is also aesthetic. Wonder arises here, not only in response to the stimulus of aesthetic objects, but also as a manifestation of the aesthetic dimension of the mind's deep structures. Two aesthetic orders, then, coexist in Herbert's epistemology. The first envisions infinite iterations of 'neurological' conformity, as when Herbert declares that "every new object enters into conformity with a new faculty" (*DV* 110/33). This relation – if properly configured – is neutral, meaning unbiased, undistorted. If we think of this relation as a kind of

---

[57] ". . . ut *Veritatis* systema pulcherrimum nunquam satis mirari possimus" (*DV* 80).

discrete entity, it also approximates the sense of neutrality discussed by Dabney Townsend in adapting Edmund Husserl's phenomenological sense of *epoché* as a kind of mental bracketing (*Ideas* ¶ 32). "Objective neutrality," Townsend asserts, "is the fundamental aesthetic state" (1989, 94), explaining that "neutrality is a state of an object, not of the way that the subject regards the object" (1989, 97). But for Herbert both senses of neutrality are in play. Supervening on the objective neutrality of the conforming relation is the second aesthetic order, which does touch on the way the subject regards the object. This involves affect, in Herbert's case the wonder inspired by the beauties of nature. My point is that the conjunction of conformity and neutrality reveals Herbert's incipient exploration of aesthetics because it sets up an ideal premised on a spectator's distance and an attitude of aesthetic judgment toward inner as well as outer states and objects.

Herbert's interest in questions of judgment increases over the course of *De veritate*, but his metaphors lose their aestheticizing streak and become more legal and juridical. Midway through the text, he is not reaching toward the disinterestedness of aesthetic judgment so much as toward the impartiality of a disciplined and disciplining conscience – a topic, Herbert assures us as it too threatens to spiral out of control, to which he will someday devote a treatise (*DV* 186–187/106). Conscience and conformity become intertwined. Thus, he says, "The decrees of conscience are the laws of all good and evil action, made known in every circumstance examined by it. It is so widely diffused that no word or thought can escape its sway or be hidden from its gaze. ... It is so essential to us that there is no hope of inner peace except when it is brought into due conformity" (*DV* 184/104–105). Lest the juridical metaphor be missed, he adds, "I establish also a tribunal of divine Providence in conscience in order to unite in this way the higher with the lower realm, so that all that is holy and sacred may be here investigated as before a supreme court or parliament, beyond which there is no appeal. ... For conscience finds its only satisfaction in the right conformity of all the faculties" (*DV* 185/105). Herbert gets so carried away with the metaphorical possibilities of his phrase for conscience, *forum internum*, that he writes, "It is not then merely the court of the spirit and the body that is held in the hall of conscience, but the court of God, and before it all the causes of the inner faculties are pleaded, and particularly those which arrange and classify objects" (*DV* 185/106). The pleadings regarding arrangement and classification look to conformity as their outcome, as "conscience," he repeats "finds satisfaction only in the conformity of all the faculties" (*DV* 189/109). Somehow the aesthetic dimension of conformity with its prizing of harmony and consent in the musical sense has metamorphosed into a call for obedience and procedural rules. Despite his efforts to aestheticize the Scholastic rhetoric of conformity and to conjure up emancipatory meanings for the term, Herbert fails to expunge its disciplinary associations. It's not just that the free play of the signifier has gone too far – conformity having become so protean in Herbert's usage as to be nearly meaningless. Rather, it's that the magnitude of the task he has set for himself – the anatomy of consciousness – has become so overwhelming as to require law and order. Conformity helps tame a consciousness threatening to erupt in unruliness.

Were Herbert to have foregone the severities of conscience, his aesthetic of neutrality would more nearly approach that suspension of judgment privileged by skepticism. But Herbert cannot let go the prerogatives of authority. Thanks to the way conscience encroaches on his account of mind, his Pauline commitments emerge. Thus, Herbert remarks that "it is not surprising if all the inhabitants of the earth demand a law, since they are urged on by a secret impulse of nature; for thereby they lead us to perceive that what they desire is that their Common Notions should be clearly arranged, so that they might have a rule for conscience" (*DV* 188/108). The *consensus gentium* is expressed now as a universal demand for law understood as a rule for conscience. Herbert argues that all peoples desire the feeling of "repose" produced by "due conformity," since "there has never existed a nation so uncivilized that it has not desired to embrace virtue, though it may have been mistaken in its conception of it" (*DV* 202/122). Herbert echoes Paul's sense that even "the Nations" have rules of conscience inscribed in their hearts (Romans 2:14–15). Like Paul, Herbert speaks of "the witness of the inner consciousness, in proper conformity" (*DV* 198/118). The difference is that the Common Notions occupy the place of Paul's law. Furthermore, conscience not only witnesses but also regulates. Herbert captures this supervisory role when he sums up, saying, "All the internal forms of consciousness are subject to the faculty of conscience, which reduces to control the entire range of feelings, so that it constitutes the common consciousness of the interior forms of apprehension. Its object, then, is the conformity of all the other faculties, from which it follows that it is a state of conformity" (*DV* 205–206/125). Conscience and conformity control the multiplicity of faculties and objects, the many differences these generate, and the variability of media and conditions.

Herbert may also be recalling another verse from Romans: "And be not conformed to this world: but be ye transformed by the renewing of your mind" (12:2). Paul contrasts the worldly compliance entailed by conformity and the spiritual transformation of the mind. But for Herbert, conformity and mental renewal are not opposites; instead, they are mutually constitutive. A reformed mind will perceive truth and hence cease quarreling over indifferent matters. As he puts it, "There is no general agreement concerning rites, ceremonies, traditions, whether written or unwritten, or concerning Revelation; but there is the greatest possible consensus of opinion concerning the right conformation of the faculties" (*DV* 296/215).

Even if Herbert cannot suspend judgment in the skeptical sense and thereby sustain an aesthetic of neutrality, he nevertheless endorses a skeptical detachment from doctrinal details. He believes that if the mind is in right conformity experiencing inner motions of consent, a peaceful polity will follow. This position, formulated between 1618 and 1620, no doubt partly in response to the doctrinal strictures issued by the Synod of Dort, will undergo modifications over the next three decades even as it continues to color his thinking. In time Herbert will discover that his aestheticization of conformity has political implications to be reckoned with that he had not anticipated.

3   Conformity / Neutrality in *The Life and Reign of King Henry VIII* (1649)

While the political implications of Herbert's philosophy of mind are intimated in *De veritate*, they are more fully developed in his posthumously published *Life and Reign of King Henry VIII* (1649), one of Herbert's last works and arguably his masterpiece.[58] For example, conformity and consent, key philosophical terms in *De veritate*, become simplified and politicized – as if historical events and pressures had deflated the aesthetic and metaphysical aspirations that Herbert attaches to these words. In *The Life and Reign of King Henry VIII*, Herbert tends to use consent and conformity in conventional ways – consent usually extracted

---

[58] Locke praised Herbert's history of Henry VIII in "Some Thoughts Concerning Reading and Study for a Gentleman," saying "Those, who are accounted to have writ best particular parts of our English history, are Bacon, of Henry VII; and Herbert of Henry VIII. Daniel also is commended; and Burnet's history of the Reformation" (1823, 3.299). This compensates for his frontal attack on Herbert's Common Notions in the *Essay Concerning Human Understanding* (see footnote 24). For more recent praise of Herbert's history, see Merchant (1956), Rowse (1977), and Jackson (2012).

under duress and conformity represented as politic deference to arbitrary authority.[59] However, when Herbert discusses the Reformation or religion, he tends to hearken back to the Common Notions and thereby reclaim the moral high ground for conformity. He may be channeling the Erasmian usage of conformity as political moderation when he represents the Common Notions as offering a middle way in his history of the Reformation. Overall, his text shows appreciation for compromise in various manifestations: skills of negotiation and arbitration; respect for Parliament and law-making; support for rulers intent on eliciting consensus from quarreling factions, such as his idealized portrait of the Holy Roman Emperor Charles V working to convene the Council of Trent; and sympathy for neutrality as a political strategy.

Herbert surely did not foresee his own career as a historian when he delivered his disparaging view of historical writing at the conclusion of *De veritate*. "The entire body of history ... is best described as probability" (*DV* 316/234), he declares, adding that "the whole of ancient history rests upon conjecture, and therefore ... upon insecure foundations" (*DV* 322/239).[60] That is why "in reading histories it is important to distinguish between various roles assumed by the writer, such as historian, preacher, statesman, philosopher, theologian, or possibly jester" (*DV* 321–322/239). Thanks perhaps to his fear of becoming a jester, Herbert will have high standards when circumstances lead him to compose historical narratives. He will certainly take a skeptical view of historical sources and encourage readers to question authority and come to their own conclusions.

A fall from royal favor precipitated Herbert's turn to history. After five years as ambassador to France for King James, Herbert was recalled in 1624. Historians dispute the reasons.[61] In the event Herbert's career never

---

[59] For example, "The gallants of the court finding now the king's favour manifestly shining on Woolsey, apply'd themselves much to him: and especially Charles Brandon, who for his goodly person, courage, and **conformity** of disposition, was noted to be most acceptable to the king in all his exercises and pastimes" (*H8* 141–142). See also, "Adrian ... was (Jan. 9.) chosen pope, though not with such **an universal consent**; but that (as I find by our records) our cardinal had sometimes nine, and sometimes twelve, and sometimes nineteen voices. Guicciardine seems much to wonder at this election ..." (*H8* 216).

[60] Herbert's skepticism about history taps into a long-standing debate about the relative merits of historians, philosophers and poets. See, e.g., Sir Philip Sidney's *Defence of Poetrie* (1583) and Jean Bodin's *Methodus* (1566).

[61] Jackson follows Rossi, saying that Herbert "exceeded his brief by working to support James I's son-in-law, the Elector Palatine in the Bohemian crisis, and irritated the French king by his efforts to prevent persecution of the Huguenots" (2012, 135). Bedford thinks Herbert was too outspoken about Prince Charles's matrimonial prospects (1979, 4–5). Butler agrees, noting that Herbert relayed unfavorable reports to King James first about the Spanish match and then about the betrothal to Henrietta Maria (1990, 288–295).

recovered from what he himself called "so notable a Disgrace" (Rossi 1947, 3.467). Thereafter, his most successful attempts to leverage his experience as a diplomat and student of international relations were his forays into history writing: first, his *Expedition to the Isle of Rhé*, and second, his *Life and Reign of King Henry VIII*. Both were written with the encouragement of Charles I, who gave Herbert access to state papers and to Sir Robert Cotton's library; both were published posthumously. The *Expedition to the Isle of Rhé* is a thinly veiled apology for the Duke of Buckingham's failed leadership of that campaign. Relatively short, it debunks French accounts of the siege of the citadel of St. Martin near La Rochelle as well as explores the causes of the English defeat. The history of Henry VIII, by contrast, is a monumental work that consumed more than a decade of Herbert's life.[62] Not only did Herbert consult all the primary sources he could get hold of – letters, treaties, and statutes, many of which are faithfully transcribed – but also the widest possible range of historians, from Sleidan to Sandoval, Buchanan to Foxe, Guicciardini to Sarpi, Jacques-Auguste du Thou to Jean du Bellay, and many more.[63] His deep immersion in Reformation history seems to have shifted his understanding of conformity and consent in more political directions.

The Life and Reign's value is enhanced by the fact that King Charles is the intended audience.[64] Herbert's dedicatory epistle begins:

> I Present here in all humble manner unto Your Maiesty a Worke, the Authority whereof is solely Yours: not yet so much because it took its first beginning from Your Majestie's particular, and (I may say) unexpected commands; but that the parts thereof, as fast as I could finish them, were lustrated by Your gracious Eye, and consummated by your judicious Animadversions; besides, the substance thereof, in all home affairs hath been drawn chiefly out of your Majesties Records. So that by more then one Title it craves Your Majesties protection. (A2)

---

[62] For *The Life and Reign of King Henry VIII*, I have used the Folger Library's first edition (1649) and the 1870 Alexander Murray reprint of Kennet's 1719 Folio edition. Unless otherwise noted, all citations are to the latter (abbreviated to *H8*).

[63] One of the pleasures of reading the Folger's 1649 edition is that there are wide margins where some of the sources that Herbert and his assistants, Thomas Masters and Rowland Evans, consulted are listed. The first edition also includes the dedicatory epistle to King Charles.

[64] Sharpe observes, "In the recent Tudor past, perhaps especially in the reign of Henry VIII, Charles believed he saw what he sought for his own reign: uniformity, order, stability. The first adult Englishman to succeed to the throne since Henry VIII, he often consulted Henrician precedents" (1992, 196). Thomas Herbert, however, records that Charles had serious reservations about Henry VIII's conduct and policies (G. S. Stevenson 1927, 305).

Herbert reminds the king of his support and involvement in the writing of this history, despite disagreements ("judicious Animadversions"). If we take Herbert at his word and see Charles as the manuscript's immediate, implied reader, then it follows that Herbert – ever the ambassador and purveyor of humanist counsel – hoped his tome would influence the course of current affairs. For instance, Herbert's efforts to explain Henry VIII's remarkable mastery of his Parliaments seem keyed to his sense, not only that Charles will be interested in the topic, but also that he could use some pointers.[65]

Overall, the deteriorating political situation of the 1630s influences Herbert's presentation of events a century earlier, especially those policies pertaining to the management of religious conflict. Herbert seizes every opportunity to showcase talents for negotiating consensus. When King Henry makes conciliatory gestures of a similar sort, Herbert praises him. He remembers how, early in Henry's reign, the emperor "constituted our king arbiter of all emergent differences" (*H8* 196), and in his final portrait revisits this thwarted hope: "As for matter of state, I dare say, never prince went upon a truer maxim for this kingdom; which was, to make himself arbiter of Christendom; and had it not cost him so much, none had ever proceeded more wisely" (*H8* 744). But if Henry disappoints as an arbiter of religious differences, he is admirable as a manager of Parliaments. Before getting into the nitty-gritty of revenue-raising, Herbert explains the king's persuasive techniques in a passage written as late as 1638 and possibly later:

> At home it was his manner to treat much with his parliaments; where, if gentle means serv'd not, he came to some degree of the rough; though the more sparingly, in that he knew his people did but too much fear him. Besides, he understood well, that foul ways are not always passable, nor to be used (especially in suspected and dangerous times) but where others fail. However, it may be noted, that none of his predecessors understood the temper of parliaments better than himself, or that prevail'd more dexterously of them. Therefore, without being much troubled at the tumultuous beginnings of the rasher sort, he would give them that leave, which all new things must have, to settle. Which being done, his next care was to discover and prevent those privy combinations that were not for his service. (*H8* 745)

---

[65] E.g., "The king (whose masterpiece it was to make use of his parliaments) not only let foreign princes see the good intelligence betwixt him and his subjects, but kept them all at his devotion" (*H8* 656). As Jackson puts it, "Herbert's judicious presentation of Henry's kingship offered a timely reminder that a monarch who honoured his constitutional obligations to seek counsel from his nobility and secured the compliance of Parliament and the law courts could not be deemed a tyrant or be denied the obedience of his subjects" (2012, 147).

Herbert observes that effective leadership involves ignoring low-level dissent, deploying spies and twisting arms, but he draws the line at violence: "Neither should they [princes] inforce any thus violently, when business may be done in a calm and gentle manner: the harmony of government consisting in such a delicate proportion, that no one part can safely be strain'd higher, unless the rest may well be tun'd and accorded thereunto" (*H8* 267). Although the metaphorical turn to music as a way of understanding governance is a commonplace – the state as work of art – the musical orchestration of "emergent differences" should be seen as the pragmatic analogue of Herbert's prizing of conformity as a criterion of epistemological truth. Insofar as conformity is a mental relation characterized by harmony, proportion, and consent, its political counterpart is that "getting to yes" prized by arbitrators.

Yet, although Herbert documents domestic efforts to broker a peaceful reformation, he is equally interested in continental approaches to these problems, imperial diets and religious councils attracting his attention. Herbert focuses on the international arena for several reasons: to distinguish his project from those of his predecessors like William Camden; to show Henry as *primus inter pares* and hence as less anomalous in his behavior; and to display his own cosmopolitanism and shrewdness as a diplomat. As his autobiography puts it, "My Intention in Learning Languages being to make my selfe a Citizen of the world as farr as it were possible" (1976, 17). His partiality for global citizenship is one of the political corollaries of his philosophical investment in universal consent.

When Herbert ponders the causes of the Reformation, for example, he muses about the fractured unity of Christendom and the problems of managing dissent with an eye to his own utopian notions of universal consensus. In his comments on the astonishing success of Martin Luther, he considers why earlier manifestations of religious dissent went nowhere, noting that people kept their disagreements to themselves:

> All those, who for the present dissented inwardly from any opinion commonly taught, kept yet the unity of the Church. Of which kind though (I doubt not) there were many, yet by distinguishing in private only the good doctrines from the ill, they both conserv'd their consciences, avoided schism, and maintain'd towards God, and among themselves, an uniformity; being therein not unaptly compar'd to sheep, and other creatures, who in pastures, where both wholesom and hurtful herbs grow, choose yet only the better sort. While thus, they might not only reach to antiquity in all times, but universality in all places. ... And thus were all controversies (save those which the subtilties of the schoolmen brought forth) declin'd.

3 Conformity / Neutrality in King Henry VIII (1649)

> Neither did men think themselves bound to study the intricacies and sophisms of authors, in matters impertinent to salvation; but were contented with a single faith in God, the comfort of a good life, and hope of a better upon true repentance; taking the rest for the most part upon the faith of the Church. By which means as peace was generally conserv'd, so it was not doubted by those who search'd into the primitive times, but that together divers new doctrines (if not errors) were crept into the Church discipline. Among which some, yet, might have been more excusable, had they not been so severely commanded, that the common sort understood them for little less than necessary articles of faith. While thus they were held in much subjection, as being not able sufficiently to distinguish the true and essential parts from those that were added only for conveniency or ornament. But as learning now (the benefit of printing) became publick, so almost all men, either through reading or conversation, were literate. Insomuch, that they durst look into the principles of religion, and take upon them to discuss the parts thereof. Among these, none was more famous than one Martin Luther, an hermit fryer about thirty-two years old, living about this time at Wittenberg upon the Elbe ... (*H8* 175–176)

Much can be gleaned from this passage, not least a sense that Herbert is trying to adapt his universalist philosophy to realities on the ground pertaining to dissent, conscience, and the consequences of the printing press. He suggests that religious conflict could have been prevented had people been content to dissent inwardly and to distinguish good from ill doctrine privately. This would have permitted them to "conserve" their consciences. He regrets the loss of a united Christendom, not because he thinks "the common sort" should remain illiterate sheep, but because the public airing of religious controversy threatens "the comfort of a good life." Elsewhere Herbert speculates about the beginnings of the Reformation in England and how it might have been prevented. He identifies crucial turning points, but always excessive "rigour," insufficient "moderation," and paucity of "charity" are the culprits.

This nostalgia for the *consensus omnium* of the Middle Ages coexists with his relish for exposing ecclesiastical abuses and papal weakness. His glee at demystifying relics is palpable (*H8* 615). Nevertheless, his wistful longing for medieval unity complicates the violent anticlericalism of his later writings: *De causis errorum* and *De religione laici, Appendix ad sacerdotes* (1645), *De religione gentilium* (1663), and *A Dialogue between a Tutor and his Pupil* (1768). In this earlier text, composed for the eyes of a monarch sympathetic to an Anglo–Catholic compromise, Herbert counsels religious uniformity – let everyone consent to a few basic articles of faith such that they maintain "towards God, and among themselves, an uniformity" conducive to peace. He hints that this uniformity should not be "severely commanded," implying that a more relaxed approach to religious enforcement is advisable.

Although he finds Henry's imposition of uniformity through the Six Articles (1539) offensive, calling it "the bloody statute" (*H8* 628), Herbert attempts to recuperate uniformity as a wise approach to the management of religious conflict. His appeal to privacy, conscience, and Stoic reserve amounts to a "Don't ask, don't tell" policy intended to mitigate the indignities of dissimulation. He hopes thereby to dispel the punitive connotations of conformity, of which he is fully aware. (He himself uses it to denote surrender and obedience to authority.[66]) He wants to rehabilitate the term for the sake of his high-minded universalism, grounded in an *Ur*-monotheism. Universalism will sanitize conformity's repressive connotations.[67] In my view, Herbert's aestheticizing of uniformity in the history of Henry VIII has its origins in *De veritate* where conformity is not only a criterion of truth but also a relation of beauty premised on mutual accord and synchronicity.

One political consequence of this Erasmian effort to recuperate conformity is a fascination with church councils. Herbert delights in reporting the dysfunctional conduct of councils and the various ways that the goal of consensus is deferred or defeated by partisanship.[68] But he also recognizes that councils offer an ideal way to settle differences and arrive at compromise. He recounts, for example, the high hopes held for the Council of Trent:

> This [the Reformation] made the pope resolve at last on a council; and the rather, that all Christian princes desir'd upon any reasonable terms a peace of religion, as knowing how much it concern'd them to settle that affair:

---

[66] When Herbert gets wind that he will be recalled as ambassador, he writes to Buckingham, saying, "But I shall conforme myself evr, to my good L and mastrs will, onely could not chose but be troubled yf anyway – I should be thought unworthy to keepe that trust, wth that perpetuall faithfullnes and affection, I have inviolably mantained towards his M. or the exercise of my charge here might give me reason to expect" (Rossi 1947, 3.465).

[67] Today we might expect that an irenic agenda would celebrate dissent and difference rather than conformity. But, as Pailin notes, the intellectual shift from uniformity to tolerance occurs at the end of the seventeenth century when "fear of dire secular consequences" had abated such that "the intellectual pressure was not to find a common position on which all could agree (some religious lowest common denominator)" but was rather to spur "vigorous debates about the reasonableness of belief" (2000, 126). Toleration, according to Pailin, would have been too risky earlier.

[68] E.g. "Louis XII ... calls a synod of the French Church at Tours in France; where certain questions touching the pope's late actions and his authority were proposed, and resolved against him, and his excommunications pronounced void. It was also decreed, that an admonition should be sent to him, to imbrace peace and moderation; which if he refus'd, he should be summon'd to call a free and general council" (*H8* 121–122).

3 Conformity / Neutrality in King Henry VIII (1649) 127

> neither did they think there would be much difficulty, when all sides came prepared thereunto, most of the points in difference being to be reconcil'd in middle and indifferent terms, or to be rejected as doubtful, (upon the grounds taken on either side) or at least not tending to much edification. (*H8* 681)

Herbert adds that so far from "all sides" coming "prepared thereunto," only "some few prelates, (of the most affected to the pope)" showed up, despite this being a "universally desir'd council" (*H8* 681). These homogenous few "were all that could give name and reputation to this general council: so far was it from having other kingdom or religion concurrent therein" (*H8* 681). Herbert wishes the Lutherans and Protestant princes had participated at Trent, even as he chronicles the council's bumpy start "that it may appear, both what a slow and uncertain beginning this great council had, and what a different end it took, from that it now seem'd to promise" (*H8* 710). Herbert relies on a shared understanding with his implied reader (Charles Stuart) as regards the unexpected outcome of the council.

As his account of the council's proceedings develops, Herbert gradually takes on the Habsburg emperor Charles V's point of view.[69] This empathetic identification is not as surprising as it might seem. Reid Barbour has reminded us, for example, that the community gathered at Great Tew, whose "chief contribution" was "that skepticism itself might serve as the most godly form of Protestant heroism," is fascinated by Charles V's abdication, finding in the emperor's "vexed" combination of retirement and engagement a model for reflection (2001, 22, 40). They "admire the providence of God as it operates through Charles across the world" in his pursuit of "the unity of religion" (2001, 41). Herbert's admiration derives not from the abdication so much as from other factors: the sense that groups prone to faction will accomplish nothing without the oversight of a strong leader; and the predilection for grandiose thought-experiments involving world-rule (e.g., if I were emperor, how would I handle religious conflict?). He also projects his own appreciation for the beauties of Chantilly, the seat of the Duke of Montmorency – a highlight of his memoirs (*Life* 47) – onto the emperor when he stops at the same castle (*H8* 633). Usually, however, Herbert's identification with the emperor

---

[69] I disagree with Hill that "though neither a Protestant nor even a Christian, Herbert, like many of his countrymen, was fervently opposed to the papacy and to its close ally, the Spanish crown" (1987, 9). While it is true that Herbert opposed the Spanish match in the 1620s, in *The Life and Reign of Henry VIII*, where all the European leaders are first-order Machiavellians, the Spanish crown comes off arguably better than most.

confines itself to his frustrated efforts to reconcile conflicting religious interest groups, especially in the conciliar arena.

Herbert shows Charles V trying to manage the various constituencies under his mandate in preparation for the Council of Trent. In 1545, for example, he convenes a diet at Spire where "the emperor endeavoring to divide the Protestants" drives some hard bargains (among them, levying money for war against the Turks) that he then smooths over with promises of mediation:

> The emperor promis'd to commit the business of religion to certain good learned men, who should write some pious reformation, wishing the princes also to do the same: to the end, that upon comparison of them on all sides, some agreement might be made by common consent, which should be observ'd till a general council were held in Germany, or at least a national: and that peace should be kept in the mean while on all parts, and the rigorous edict of Augsburg suspended, and the anabaptists punish'd. (*H8* 691)

Similarly, some months earlier, "the emperor had commanded the divines at Lovain to reduce religion into some method and articles" (*H8* 698). The emperor is as impatient as Herbert with the polarizing details of doctrine. At the diet of Worms, however, the Protestants reveal their suspicion of and resistance to the Tridentine council. In reply, Charles says:

> he could not exempt them from the authority of the council (especially, being call'd for their sakes); yet if they had any just objections against it, that they should come and produce them openly in the council, and they should have an equal hearing. But the princes and confederate cities continuing to except against it, protested, ... The emperor finding thus no likelihood of peace, dissembled his displeasure. (*H8* 709)

Herbert shares the emperor's exasperation with his fractious charges and enters into his perplexity about what to do. Speaking of the diet at Ratisbonne, for example, Herbert says:

> The emperor knew not what well to resolve: he would have been glad of such a peace as might have conserv'd his authority, without caring much to hear of errors discover'd in either of the opposite parts; or that they had found out some witty and new distinction. But there is not anything more hard than to devise how a free and equal council may be held, or who should be a competent judge of the emergent differences. ... Nevertheless, it may be demonstrated, that a more even course may be kept herein than hath been hitherto practic'd, and a more indifferent for all mankind: which as it is deeply concern'd in all the rigid decrees of religion, so in some sort or

3 Conformity / Neutrality in King Henry VIII (1649)

other should intervene; in which case, certainly the Spirit of God would preside. (*H8* 728)

Herbert's vision of a "free and equal" council where people of diverse beliefs might speak openly and come to a consensus regarding doctrine is held out as a theoretical possibility, which coming to pass, God would surely sponsor. This optimistic vision may have its origins in *De veritate*'s coupling of universal consent (*consensus omnium*) and consent as an epistemic virtue experienced (when the conditions of truth are right) as an inward motion of spontaneous assent.

Herbert's ideas of properly exercised authority and wise leadership glimmer through the veil of his Tudor history. During the decade devoted to research and writing, Herbert becomes increasingly intrigued by neutrality as a political strategy even as he loses interest in the rituals of the honor code (tournaments, heraldry, ambassadorial decorum).[70] He comments, for example, on how Charles V plays the neutrality card, saying, "The emperor, who had now engag'd our king and Francis to a war, and therein reveng'd himself on both, thought it safer to be neuter, than to declare himself either way" (*H8* 705). Later, Herbert notes that King Henry would have done better sometimes had he remained more of a spectator than an actor: "But as he would be an actor (for the most part) where he needed only be a spectator, he both engaged himself beyond what was requisite, and by calling in the money he lent his confederates and allies, did often disoblige them when he had most need of their friendship" (*H8* 744). Herbert comes to value spectatorship and measured engagement as the war heats up around him. This belated discovery turns out to agree with his long-standing conviction that tendentious thinking and rash judgment result in destructive action. His philosophical preoccupation with unbiased perception legitimizes political impartiality,

---

[70] Probing the causes of both Buckingham and Henry's failed leadership, Herbert repeatedly confronts the shortcomings of the honor code. Of Buckingham's Isle of Rhé expedition, he says, "For while sometimes hee thought it a brave thing to conquer and subdue, and then againe it seem'd no lesse glorious to spare the prostrate and reduce them to better sense, hee was in no little perplexity how to behave himself, but how unseasonably, that I may not say carelessly, the event seemed to teach" (*Rhé* 1860, 139). Of Henry, he notes that the king "was ever most zealous of his honour and dignity" and attributes "his most branded actions" to this over-wrought sense of amour-propre. "Outward esteem and reputation," he explains, "being the same to great persons which the skin is to the fruit, which though it be but a slight and delicate cover, yet without it the fruit will presently discolour and rot" (*H8* 744). Herbert understands honor inside and out – its hold, its absurdities, its importance. Consider the flippant shift to Spanish with which Herbert sums up a lengthy dispute between Charles V and Francis I: "And this was the end of the Cartells and Pundonnores betwixt these two great Princes" (*H8* 205 in the first edition, 337 in Kennet, where "Pundonnores" is unfortunately transcribed as "*points d'honneur*").

inasmuch as both epistemological and political conformity share investment in neutrality.

Herbert's interest in neutrality does not prevent him from passing judgment on Henry VIII. In the dedicatory epistle to King Charles, Herbert describes Henry as one who was "subject to more obloquies, then any since the worst Roman Emperours times" and whose "*sanguine* humour came to be somewhat *sanguinary* and inclining to cruel." The volume closes with a body count: "two queens, one cardinal (*in procinctu*, at least) or two, (for Poole was condemn'd, tho' absent) dukes, marquisses, earls, and earls sons, twelve; barons and knights, eighteen; abbots, priors, monks and priests, seventy seven; of the more common sort, between one religion and another, huge multitudes" (*H8* 745–746). This unblinkered assessment of the damage Henry inflicted makes it difficult to accept Rossi's view that Herbert refuses to pass judgment because he is at heart a dilettante.[71] Herbert does not withhold criticism when appraising Henry's life; instead, in keeping with Jean Bodin's advice for historians, he aspires to a kind of equilibrium, noting of the king, for example, that "where he did ill, he made or found many complices" (*H8* 585).[72] Like the juxtaposed eulogies for Wolsey in Shakespeare's *Henry VIII* (4.2), Herbert presents the good and the bad of Henry's career, letting the reader decide for himself.[73] He frequently says, "I shall leave these things to the liberty of the indifferent reader" (*H8* 402).[74] Because he is profoundly sensitive to all forms of coercion, he will no more coerce his reader into passing facile judgments than he will concede authority to others. His insistence that readers come to their own conclusions is part and parcel of his investment in consent.

---

[71] "Discutere e criticare importa una decisione, e Herbert non vuol decidere – forse perché, anche como storiografo, era un dilettante, e il dilettante, cosciente della transitorietà dei suoi interessi, evita d'impegnarsi per restare libero di mutare opinione" (Rossi 1947, 2.506–507).

[72] Bodin thinks the historian should be even-handed toward his subjects. "If a reproach is due," he says, "it would be more suitable for a historian to make a mild criticism after the narrative has been given or to withhold his opinion altogether." He clarifies, "Any writer vituperates Nero more than enough when he recounts that he murdered the most honorable men, his tutor, two wives, his brother Britannicus, and finally his mother" (1966, 53).

[73] Jonathan Swift decided for himself, judging by his heavily annotated copy of the history. Of Herbert, he says, "This palliating Author, hath increased my Detestation of his Hellish Hero in every Article." Of Henry, he says, among other things, "I wish he had been Flead, his skin stuffed and hangd on a Gibbet, His bulky guts and flesh left to be devoured by Birds and Beasts, for a warning to his successors for ever. Amen" (Butler 1990, 397, 387).

[74] Sometimes his deferrals to the reader smack of defensiveness: "But as these things are set down by way of description, and not of apology, so I will leave them to come to my history, which for being free and impartial, will speak him better to the judicious reader than my annotations can" (*H8* 585). Note Herbert's aspiration to impartiality.

The studied neutrality of Herbert's narrative persona is consistent with his philosophy and his politics. He suspends judgment from time to time because he wants to remain dispassionate and detached – like the Emperor Charles summoning divines of each persuasion and asking them first to air and then to work out their differences, even as he arranges their diets, synods, and councils. Similarly, Herbert sees himself as orchestrating historical voices, silencing extremists with their salacious gossip, synthesizing at times, but generally giving his sources a free and equal hearing. Seldom does he relate this method to truth; he is no Milton in *Areopagitica*, although his text records the persecution of printers.[75] Instead, his approach to the documents is eclectic and impartial, as Jean Bodin recommends.[76] While this may strike some as "cold" (Rossi 1947, 2.509) and others as showing "witty distance" (Merchant 1956, 60) or a "secular mindset" (Jackson 2012, 148), I see Herbert's diffidence as evidence of several strands in his thought: his skepticism about historical memory; his sense that good leadership (as well as historiography) involves skill at arbitration; and his increasing appreciation for reserve call it intimations of the right to privacy – issuing from his philosophical investments in consent and conformity. Like a good Elizabethan, he sees no need to make windows into men's hearts, prying into their motives or beliefs.[77] It is enough to show how people influence events.

4 Doing Nothing

How does this survey of Herbert's commitments to conformity and consent help us understand his actions in the emergency of September 1644? As we saw earlier, care for his books and his library was a priority. A letter from Herbert to the Parliamentary commander, Sir Thomas Myddleton, opens with business matters: concern about the levying of his rents, the losses he has sustained and is "likely to sustaine upon the occasion of quitting my Castle," and his "goods in London" (Rossi 1947,

---

[75] Clauses about printers, censorship, and legislation constraining publication are often highlighted in italics, both in the 1649 and in the reprint of the 1719 edition – arguably evidence of political messaging among the typesetters.
[76] Bodin offers criteria for evaluating historians, among them "to be free from all emotion – a condition which we require in this author whom we seek" (1966, 44). He models this approach, saying, "I will bring forward the essential argument on each side and leave the matter to individual judgment" (1966, 51). Bodin may be adapting Tacitus' counsel in the *Annales* of writing "sine ira et studio."
[77] He dismisses Nicholas Sanders in *De schismate Anglicano* because "he pretends (in more than one place) to have known even so much as the king's thoughts (by revelation;)" (*H8* 402).

3.526). But the letter soon pivots away from financial demands and takes on an urgent personal tone: "I pray you at least love mee (as y^r father charged yo^u) and my Grandchildren for whom I hope you will take soe much care as that they may not want necessaries, As for the rest I shall not doubt but yo^u (for Iustice sake) will punctually performe what yo^u promised ..." (Rossi 1947, 3.526). The allusion to Myddleton's father, a powerful Welsh merchant, former MP and Lord Mayor of London who had died 14 years earlier, suggests a prior acquaintance in less troubled times (Rossi 1947, 3.209). Herbert's appeal to Myddleton's sense of justice and troth-plight is filled with pathos – a plea to their shared condition. He is not asking Myddleton to put aside his military responsibilities for auld lang syne – for the sake of old family ties that trump the nation's new alliances. Instead he suggests these loyalties coincide – allegiance to clan and party sharing the same honor code.

In response Myddleton tries to safeguard Herbert's person and estate. Reporting to Parliament, he attests to Herbert's disaffection from the royalist party in a long periodic sentence:

> Whereas I finde that Edward Lord Herbert of Cherbury did neither appeare at any time in the Commission of Array though appointed a Commissioner and was not at any of the severall Assemblyes or meetings of the Lords at Yorke or Oxford or any where els but hath contain himselfe at home for the space now of about two yeares and three moneths attending the recovery of his broken health, And whereas also hee hath furnished noe moneys for dragoneeres as was alledged in the house of Commons, and breifely (as hee protesteth or that I can learne) hee hath done nothing that might justly offend the houses of Parliament since the time of his departure thence, and that I beleive [sic] really hee hath beene ever carefull to observe due respect to both houses notwithstanding hee hath been many times pressed to divers things that might argue the Contrary I have thought fitt to certify the truth hereof to both houses to the intent hee may bee cleard in your good opinion and restored to his former place dignity and Reputation amongst yo^u as also to his goods in the former manner he enioyed them, And if his health serve him not for publique Businesses hee humbly desires that yo^u will give him leave to attend it by the Advise of Phisicians till hee bee fully enabled to performe those duties which may bee expected from him. (Rossi 1947, 3.525)

In this "certificate" Myddleton testifies that from 1642 to 1644 Herbert "hath done nothing that might justly offend the houses of Parliament." This is what Herbert's neutrality amounts to: doing nothing when war rages around him. How to interpret doing nothing? Herbert's situation is a far cry from Milton's "They also serve who only stand and wait"

(Sonnet 19). But what's clear is that doing nothing was as unlikely to help Herbert's dignity and reputation as to get him out of debt. It also shows him marching to his own philosophical drummer.

Nevertheless, if political neutrality is seen as corresponding to the impartial mind, then Herbert's disengagement from the Civil War can be interpreted as a principled stance showing that the order of knowledge produces social order. Consider the notion of mind that Herbert evokes in the closing tableau of his memoir, with which we began this chapter. It is characterized by conformity and consent understood as a kind of aesthetic epistemological composure. At once gathered in prayer and alert to God's signs, as he kneels by an open window, Herbert feels serene, neutral, poised to perceive truth. Twenty years later when he has retreated to his castle on the Welsh marches, he still seeks to arrive at truth through the promotion of conformity and consent. But, while it may have been enough in 1620s Paris for Herbert to preside over the competing apprehensions of his own interiority, now his mind seethes with heathen religions, as he seeks to reduce the Babel of doctrines to order. The bounded self notwithstanding, the war without invades the war within. In keeping with the iconoclasm of the war outside, Herbert strips pagan religions of their ornaments and in *De religione gentilium* works feverishly to reveal what Stoll calls "the radical implications of occult monotheism" (2009, 79). Herbert may not theorize about the social contract or sovereignty or toleration, let alone rights, as Locke was later to do. Nevertheless, thanks to the terms by which he defines truth, his project acquires political overtones of a utopian stripe. In Herbert's ideal commonwealth, peace prevails because everyone subscribes to the primacy of the "Common Notions and what has been universally accepted by every religion, age and country" (*DV* 302). The universalism of the Common Notions underwrites his controversial neutrality.

That said, there is precedent for political nonpartisanship in the stoic conduct advocated by Justus Lipsius in his bestselling dialogue, *De Constantia*. His interlocutor asks:

> Do you think it troubles Me, what the *French*, or *Spaniards* are plotting? who *keepes*, or who *loses* the Scepter of *Belgia*. . . . None of these. Guarded, and secur'd against anything *External*, I am *bounded* with *My Selfe*; Carelesse of all Things, but this *One*; That I may submit this my Mind, tam'd, and broken, to *Right Reason*, and *God*; and all other Humane Things to my *Mind*. (81–82)[78]

---

[78] Book 2, Chapter 2, p. 45 in George Bishop's 1586 Latin edition.

Like a stoic sage in times of persecution, Herbert submits his mind to right reason, even while presiding over learning ("Humane Things"). The stoic shares with the skeptic a search for wisdom that involves "the complete elimination from his mind" of beliefs, passions and desires "which cause harm ... which, if acted upon or expressed, would bring him into some kind of conflict with other men or with the world itself" (Tuck 1993, xiii). Richard Tuck groups Lipsius and Montaigne together as neo-stoic humanists whose skepticism leads them to value self-preservation. In the emergency of civil war Herbert may well be drawn to self-preservation through stoic *apatheia* and skeptical *ataraxia*. He may perhaps be modeling his conduct on that of Lipsius and Montaigne when he retreats to his library.

In my view, however, the allure of neutrality for Herbert in the 1640s should not be ascribed to a desire for security. Instead, Herbert's attitude of schooled detachment and political neutrality should be seen as stemming from his recalibrated understanding of conformity and consent in the aftermath of his historical research. Despite setbacks and the inescapable political connotations of ordinary language, his aspirations for these key words persist. He still wants these twin pillars of his philosophy to have aesthetic, metaphysical, rhetorical, empirical, and scientific meanings that will enable peoples around the globe to live in harmony. While he may recognize that this is far-fetched in a society where only political meanings matter, in Lord Herbert's optimistic imagination, teeming with heathen sects, cosmopolis is on the horizon, almost within reach.[79]

**

It is sometimes said that crossing over to skepticism's dark side begins with an appreciation for safety and privacy. Skeptics, it is said, dislike risk and avoid the public square, withdrawing to their gardens to cultivate them in peace. Richard Tuck, for example, believes that for neo-stoics like Lipsius and Montaigne, skepticism and self-interest go hand in hand, piety, patriotism and justice falling by the wayside (1993, 52–55).[80] "Starting from a position of scepticism about received moral theories," Tuck explains, "they recognized that the only secure basis for conduct was

---

[79] See Jacqueline Lagrée: "On peut noter combien cette théorie de la vérité est portée part un fort optimisme épistémologique lui même fondé sur un optimisme anthropologique à racines théologiques" (1989, 26).
[80] Compare Charles Taylor's sympathetic take on Lipsius. Lipsius "departs from Stoicism in his activism," Taylor argues, adding: "The firmness or perseverance doesn't just denote the strength passively to bear suffering; but it means the power to engage unrelentingly in the good fight" (2007, 116).

an acceptance of the force of *self-interest* or *self-preservation*" (1993, 62). This is part of Tuck's larger political argument that skepticism enables raison d'état theory. "This should not surprise us," he remarks, "for after all, a scepticism about the validity of moral principles is almost a necessary condition for a thoroughgoing confidence in the need to override the ethical and legal norms of a society" (1993, xiii). In this view, skepticism leads to an ethical relativism where anything goes because nothing can be known for certain.

Writing with more recent times in mind, Michael Oakeshott defends the politics of skepticism against the politics of faith, arguing that

> it is the comprehensive task of skepticism perpetually to be recalling political activity from the frontier of religion, to be always drawing attention to the values of civil order and *tranquillitas* whenever the vision of a total pattern of activity, imposed because it is believed to represent 'truth' or 'justice,' threatens to obliterate everything else. (1996, 81).

Rather than enabling states of emergency, as Tuck thinks, skepticism rejects "the call of emergency" thanks to a disposition for "understatement" (1996, 108). Oakeshott recognizes the shortcomings of the skeptical style in politics, conceding that it is often by default "the politics of the powerless" (1996, 69). It can "be overtaken by a nemesis of political quietism" and "self-defeat," its authority forfeited thanks to its moderation (1996, 108–109). For Oakeshott, the dark side of political skepticism is diffidence, not totalitarianism.[81]

Roland Barthes, by contrast, denies that skepticism issues in either feeble or autocratic conduct although admittedly he is more concerned with ethics than with governance. He associates skepticism with the Neutral, which he defends as "a guide to life," permitting a person to live "according to nuance" (2013, 11). Pyrrho "created the Neutral" out of weariness, Barthes declares; "he was worn out by all the words of the sophists and ... asked to be left in peace" (2013, 21). "Its essential form," he explains, "is a protestation ... a *No* so to speak suspended in front of the hardenings of both faith and certitude and incorruptible by either one" (2013, 14). He acknowledges that "the Neutral has a bad press" and lists the negative adjectives associated with it: ungrateful, shirking, muffled, limp, lazy, indifferent, individualistic, decadent, depoliticized, petit bourgeois, and vile, neither virile nor attractive (2013, 69 ff.). And yet, not

---

[81] "The [skeptical] style [of politics] in the early modern period drew upon a native diffidence in respect of human power which survived, not without some difficulty, the dazzling prospect of the Baconian enterprise" (Oakeshott 1996, 75).

unlike some Renaissance thinkers, Barthes offers the Neutral as a form of heroism: defiance in the face of social pressure – although he claims it is only a "lyrical, existential" stance, "good for nothing, and certainly not for advocating a position, an identity" (2013, 80). He observes that Montaigne in 1576 had a medal struck with a scale on one side and the motto, "I abstain," on the other. This illustrates "the relation of reciprocal temptation that ties Pyrrhonism and the Neutral" (2013, 181). But he cautions his audience "to spot from what or where he did not abstain," noting that Montaigne was very publicly engaged with his time. He also quarrels with the banality of balance and equilibrium as ideals, calling for a more nuanced "typology of balances" to which he would oppose the equally Montaignean image of drift (*la dérive*), an artful but free-form wandering (2013, 202–203). "The desire for the Neutral continually stages a paradox," Barthes reminds us. "As an object, the Neutral means suspension of violence; as a desire it means violence" (2013, 13). The violence of neutrality may be an oxymoron, he admits, "at the limit of language," but it designates a passion and desire that transcends the will-to-possess and exists as a will-to-live (2013, 206, 13–14). Interpreting the will-to-live as self-preservation can be misleading when it represents courage as cowardliness. The refusal to engage in polarized discourse can be a virtue, Barthes insists. Averse to violence and tormented by religious conflict, skeptics shun extremes and seek out spaces of neutrality. Far from ensuring safety, this conduct can be a form of recklessness, exposing one to notice and retribution. In this sense the neutrality available to skepticism can be a deed of strength.

The allure of neutrality for Herbert in the 1640s should therefore not be traced back to a desire for security. Rather, it should be traced to his aestheticization of the metaphysical principles of conformity and consent. Admittedly, Herbert does not address the topic of beauty systematically. In surveying the breadth of his oeuvre, it may seem like a minor concern, surfacing in his poetry in conventional ways and in his other writing at odd moments – when considering the merits of different colors or the intricacies of the ear canal or the beauty of an innkeeper's daughter, not to mention the "kindness" and "Charity" of a French "Hostes" who offers him a bowl of her own breast milk in the absence of heartier fare (*Life* 78–79). But if we broaden the definition of beauty to include wonder at harmony, proportion, and symmetry, then its relation to the concept of conformity becomes plausible. Ironically, Lord Herbert's reluctant crossover to skepticism's dark side begins with his appreciation of beauty.

CHAPTER 4

The Skeptical Fancies of Margaret Cavendish
Reoccupation

Margaret Cavendish, duchess of Newcastle, stands out in the panorama of seventeenth-century literature, for several reasons: first female natural philosopher, prolific author in every genre, and correspondent with the leading lights of the day, a few of whom took her seriously.[1] Cavendish becomes increasingly receptive to skepticism over the course of her life. Early on, she disavows it, regarding skepticism as the turf of a tribe of sophists spoiling for a fight.[2] Skeptics, she believes, are brawlers: "for all the Septicks [sic] were against the Mathematicians, the Natural Philosophers against the Divines, the severe Moralists against the Poets, and in the like opposition were all the rest" (*Nature's Pictures*, NP 106). Yet, despite her view that skeptics foment discord, she is fascinated by Lucretius and writes atom poems, evidence of her interest in Epicureanism (Clucas 1994). Later, however, Cavendish comes to embrace philosophical debate. She represents herself as participating in an international intellectual community, engaging in imaginary sets of objections and replies to her own work on natural philosophy. In her *Philosophical Letters* (*PL*, 1664), for example, she takes on the luminaries of the day: Descartes, Hobbes, Henry More, Van Helmont, and others.

Cavendish's desire to engage with her aspirational philosophical peers coincides with a more receptive attitude to skepticism. Indeed, after reading the first English translation of Sextus's work in Thomas Stanley's *History of Philosophy* (1655–1662), Cavendish openly subscribes to a

---

[1] Sir Walter Charlton, Joseph Glanvill, and Constantijn Huygens engaged in genuine intellectual exchanges with Cavendish, as did her brother-in-law, Charles Cavendish. Otherwise, her relations with scientific virtuosi and philosophers resemble those described in Mintz's account (1952) of the duchess's visit to the Royal Society.

[2] In the 1650s Cavendish dismisses skeptics, writing, e.g., "like hangmen as the Scepticks that strive to strangle, not onley all opinions, but all knowledge" (*The World's* Olio, *WO* 4). Suzuki, however (1999), detects the influence of Montaigne and Bacon on Cavendish's mini-essays in *Nature's Pictures* (1656).

mitigated epistemological skepticism (*Observations on Experimental Philosophy*, *OEP* 214).³ She harps on the limitations of knowledge, appealing to a skeptical epistemology in order to mock the pretensions of the new science. Skeptical doubt permits her to challenge male claims to knowledge. She insists, for example, that instruments like telescopes and microscopes distort "the truth of an object" and cannot reveal the inner workings of an observed entity (*OEP* 50). "The experimental philosophy has but a brittle, inconstant, and uncertain ground," she declares. "And these artificial instruments, as microscopes, telescopes, and the like, which are now so highly applauded, who knows but they may within a short time have the same fate [as weather glasses]; and upon a better and more rational enquiry, be found deluders, rather than true informers" (*OEP* 99). She does not take a Pyrrhonist position where nothing can be known (*nihil scitur*). She recommends instead an intermediate position where investigation relies on reason as much as on experimental art and where natural philosophers speak in terms of probability rather than certainty. We might say that she straddles first- and second-wave skepticism, if by first-wave skepticism we mean the Montaignean view, inspired partly by Sextus, that appearances are deceptive so it is futile to investigate them. Second-wave skepticism, by contrast, privileges investigation, insisting that through doubt and questioning, one can arrive at truth; call this a Baconian view.⁴

Cavendish's skepticism, however, is more thorough than the adjective, *mitigated*, suggests. Of all the figures discussed in this book, Cavendish is the most outspoken in imagining alternate worlds that overturn the status quo. That her possible worlds coincide with fantasies of female power has done her no favors. In her own time and even today, her refusal to obey the conventions of modesty has been cause for embarrassment. Even as self-aware a feminist as Virginia Woolf had her judgment of Cavendish clouded by her own fears. Woolf considered her "hare-brained" and "fantastical," a painful ancestress for female writers – inviting laughter

---

³ Popkin defines mitigated skepticism as "a theory which could accept the full force of the skeptical attack on the possibility of human knowledge, in the sense of necessary truths about the nature of reality, and yet allow for the possibility of knowledge in a lesser sense, as convincing or probable truths about appearances" (2003, 132). Several scholars have discussed Cavendish's skepticism. For example, Sarasohn notes that "the underlying methodological premise of Cavendish's natural philosophy is a form of extreme skepticism about the possibility of absolute knowledge of nature" (1984, 291), while Clucas explains that "what sets Cavendish's probabilism and limited skepticism apart from that of other mid-century philosophers ... is its derivation from her physical theories" ... specifically "her conception of nature as infinitely various" (2003, 205).

⁴ See Introduction on first- and second-wave skepticism. Similarly, Parageau distinguishes between "skeptical doubt" and "methodical doubt," understanding the latter as offering a "promise of truth" (2010, 166).

The Skeptical Fancies of Margaret Cavendish

for the discrepancy between her titanic desire for fame and what Woolf considered the mediocrity of her talent. "What a vision of loneliness and riot the thought of Margaret Cavendish brings to mind!" she wrote, "as if some giant cucumber had spread itself over all the roses and carnations in the garden and choked them to death" (2011, 64–65). In recent years, however, Cavendish has been vindicated. Although her ego still offends some, her work is not only recognized as philosophically important, but is also widely enjoyed, as the recent success of her science fiction novella, *The Blazing World* (*BW*) attests.

This chapter offers a new approach to Cavendish's skepticism by focusing on her performance of reoccupation as a skeptical strategy. I adapt Hans Blumenberg's notion of metaphorical reoccupation, treating it as a skeptical maneuver premised on uncertainty and doubt. Blumenberg believes that contested philosophical questions give rise to "conceptual vacancies" that are "occupied" by metaphors. When the meanings of those metaphors shift in response to changing times, the metaphors themselves acquire a double valence: on the one hand, becoming skeptical figures, conveying doubt about their own past usage as signs; on the other, ushering in new conceptual clusters to "reoccupy" the cultural blanks. Blumenberg's analytical framework has the advantage of allowing us to see Cavendish, not as a bizarre exception, but rather as an emblematic figure for the skepticism of "the modern age" (*Neuzeit*). By analyzing a few of Cavendish's favorite metaphors and *topoi* – seekers after truth, imaginary cityscapes, and the power of gemstones in texts such as *The Blazing World* – I show how reoccupation operates in her *oeuvre*. Blumenberg's notion of metaphorical reoccupation thus enables us to situate Cavendish's desire for fame and her drive for what Blumenberg calls self-assertion (*Selbstbehauptung*) within larger structural patterns at work in seventeenth-century thought, including the legacy of nominalism.[5]

Reoccupation is a complicated and contested concept in Blumenberg's *oeuvre*, emerging in response to a crisis of skeptical doubt.[6] Blumenberg uses it to identify key transitions in the use of metaphor that chart cultural change and intellectual innovation. How did we pass, he asks, from the mental world of Ockham to that of Descartes? Blumenberg points to dissatisfaction with old answers that in turn issues in "vacant answer positions" (*The Legitimacy of the Modern Age*, *LMA* 69). These vacant

---

[5] See Introduction.
[6] See the issue of *Telos* dedicated to Hans Blumenberg (vol. 158, Spring 2012); also see Rusch (2010).

positions cry out for reoccupation.[7] The emphasis on reoccupation stems from Blumenberg's determination to demolish and reconstitute the so-called secularization thesis with its presumption of a "break" between epochs masked by metaphorical continuities (*LMA* 463).[8] "What mainly occurred in the process that is interpreted as secularization," he declares, "should be described not as the *transposition* of authentically theological contents into secularized alienation from their origin but rather as the *reoccupation* of answer positions that had become vacant and whose corresponding questions could not be eliminated" (*LMA* 65). Old questions about mind, motion, causality, nature, knowledge, and power, etc., now demand genuinely new answers.

Blumenberg explains that seventeenth-century thinkers inherit problems bequeathed to them by the Middle Ages, but are dissatisfied with their medieval solutions, doubting them. As he puts it, "The continuity of history across the epochal threshold lies ... in the inheritance of problems, which obliges the heir, in his turn, to know again what was known before" (*LMA* 48). Cavendish is one such heir, grappling with old questions that she understands demand new answers.[9] The questions that haunt Cavendish's fictions are no mystery. Like so many of her contemporaries, her experiences of the Civil Wars and exile give her a keen appreciation for

---

[7] "When something that up until now had been thought to be unattainable is nevertheless attained, the vacancy in the systematics of consciousness results not in reassurance but reallocation. One can express this in a more topographical image: if the unattainable is lost in *one* direction, a substitute is sought in another direction" (*Care Crosses the River, CCR* 56).

[8] One of Blumenberg's aims is to challenge Carl Schmitt's notion of political theology. As Paul Fleming, Rüdiger Campe and Kirk Wetter put it in their introduction to the issue of *Telos* devoted to Blumenberg: "With it [reoccupation] he argues against the continuity of theology as the 'answer' to the question of the political in favor of the persistence of questions, including that of the political, that are constantly re-answered in original ways. Hence, the modern state for Blumenberg is not based on secularized theological concepts but on new answers to ongoing questions" (3). Also see my Introduction and footnote 22 below.

[9] In some ways Blumenberg's theory resembles Thomas Kuhn's notion of paradigm shifts whereby the steady accretion of "evidence" finally overturns and invalidates prior scientific explanations: "When the credibility and general acceptance of such answers dwindle away, perhaps because inconsistencies appear in the system, they leave behind them the corresponding questions, to which then new answers become due" (*LMA* 66). Only Blumenberg is thinking about the philosophy of history and the extent to which "the problematic of the carry-over of questions is above all a problematic of epochal thresholds" (*LMA* 66). He briefly discusses Kuhn, objecting that his "schema has no explanation whatever to offer" for the "preference given to the new 'paradigm'" or for "the process by which one system is replaced by another" (*LMA* 465–466). As Müller-Sievers puts it, "Blumenberg wants to counter the schematicism, the lack of cultural depth, and above all the neglect of the role of language and rhetoric in Kuhn's approach," especially his "obliviousness" to "paradigm" as "a rhetorical concept with far-reaching implications" (2012, 160). See Pippin for a useful précis of how Blumenberg and Kuhn diverge (1987, 553–554). Also see Haverkampf (2012, 45); Rusch (2010, 154).

problems of leadership and the dynamics of weakness and power. What is the best government? How should society be organized? How should religion be managed? The old answers have proved inadequate, and Cavendish (along with Hobbes and so many others) proposes her own.[10] Because she is dissatisfied with traditional approaches to political and metaphysical problems, she thrusts herself into the intellectual fray, identifying vacant positions and reoccupying them. While she chooses not to write a political treatise, reserving her expository efforts for natural philosophy, in her fiction she enacts the takeover of worn-out tropes. She uses inherited metaphors and *topoi*, but sensing their inadequacy and the way her turbulent times seem to have evacuated their traditional content, she steps in, ready to reoccupy contested intellectual positions with her sendups of political and philosophical authority. Her strategy is ludic, oblique, parodic, and skeptical.

The Intellectual Quest

Take, for example, Cavendish's predilection for staging intellectual quests, a metaphoric pattern constitutive of philosophy. She loves to stage seekers after Truth – *zetetics* in Sextus's parlance – those who are always investigating. These individuals embark on journeys in search of answers to profound questions. To allay their doubts, they consult experts. But Cavendish often varies this well-worn trope with changes relating to gender and authority. When the experts are men, they sometimes fall short and disappoint the seeker with their evasions. When the expert is a woman, she holds her own, and the seeker most often accepts her wisdom gratefully. These changes allow Cavendish to reoccupy the questing metaphor. The value of inquiry is reasserted such that the *function* of the metaphor persists. But the *content* changes, not only because of gender, but because the fantasy of expert authority clashes with recommended skepticism about truth claims.

Blumenberg's distinction between *function* and *content* comes from Ernst Cassirer's philosophy of symbolic forms (Adams 1991, 154, Pavesich 2008). Blumenberg believes overarching functional continuities in metaphor harbor different contents. As he remarks, "It is in fact possible for totally heterogeneous contents to take on identical functions in specific positions in the system of man's interpretation of the world and of

---

[10] As Blumenberg explains, "'Reoccupation' means that different statements can be understood as answers to identical questions" (*LMA* 466).

himself" (*LMA* 64). "Metaphorics" provide the deceptive appearance of functional continuity even as reoccupation means inserting new "content" into vacant "positions." Elsewhere he explains that certain metaphors "stand as if in the center of a horizon between a person and a situation" (*CCR* 76). Blumenberg adds:

> With every thinker one finds metaphors that seem to belong more to the epoch than to him. Occasionally, they expose the background of the thinker's technical questions and technical decisions. By moving him into a horizon of his contemporaries – perhaps by showing him as subjected to a Zeitgeist – metaphors, however, remain informative by displacements and disfigurations that can still be added to them and that let the force of a particular individual be grasped vis-à-vis the universal. (*CCR* 75–76)

Usually, Blumenberg argues, metaphors mediate the world, capturing the horizon of expectations and thereby operating as conduits of the Zeitgeist. Yet sometimes, in the hands of forceful individuals, metaphors can serve not only as a means of self-assertion, but as signs pointing to emerging cultural formations.[11]

For example, in the "The Travelling Spirit" from *Natures Pictures* (1656), Cavendish reconfigures the tale of the quest for knowledge. The zetetic pattern opens in a Faustian vein inasmuch as the seeker finds a witch "whom he intreated to aid his Desires; for, said he, I have a curiosity to travel, but I would go into those Countreyes, which, without your power to assist me, I cannot do" (*NP* 144). The witch dodges the man's requests to travel to the moon, to hell and to heaven, observing of the journey to heaven that "many Travellers go, some a quarter, and some half, and some three parts of the way, and then are forced to turn back again, and take another Guide; and so from Guide to Guide, until they have run them all over, or out of breath, and yet be as far to seek of their way as when they first set out" (*NP* 145). So much for "the Divines, who are the onely Guides." Disavowing her own role as guide (neither Sybil nor Virgil nor Divine), the witch consents to carry him to "the Center of the earth" if he eats "a Dish of *Opium*" (*NP* 145). Leaving his body behind, the man journeys to the underworld as a spirit, taking in sights such as "a very large Sea of Blood, which had issued from slain Bodyes" as well as "great Mines, Quarries and Pits," which the witch "being vers'd … did avoyd … so that

---

[11] Rusch stresses the high stakes of the project: "La 'métaphorologie', c'est-à-dire la constitution de séries analogiques, représente peut-être la tentative la plus avancée pour concilier l'oubli et la mémoire, le rationnel et l'irrationnel, le sens et le détour, dans la relation avec le passé" (2010, 153).

they were no hindrance in their Journey, which otherwise would have been" (*NP* 146). The witch knows the way and answers the seeker's questions with quiet authority. Close to their destination, the man sees "a Light like Moonshine: but when he came near, he saw the Circle about the Center was Glow-worms Tails, which gave that Light, and in the Center was an Old Man" (*NP* 146). The impression of moonshine turns out to be wrong and is corrected upon closer proximity; artfully arranged glow-worms supply the light. The skeptical trope of unreliable vision glimmers here, leaving traces of Aenesidemus's fifth mode. The witch apologizes for their intrusion and introduces her companion as "a Man [who] desired Knowledge, and would not spare any pains or industry thereunto" (*NP* 146).

A second set of questions now transpires, this time addressed to the Old Man who "hung as it were in the Air, nor never stirred out of his place, and had been there ever since the World was made" (*NP* 146). During their interview the seeker inquires about chemists, water-flow, and life underground. The old man gives long and detailed replies, describing himself as a brother of Adam and an alchemist, "for all the Gold that is digged out of the Mines was converted by me" (*NP* 147). He prophesies that "the World is not to continue long as it is," warning of its future vitrification: "for, said he, I by my Art intend to turn it all into Glass" (*NP* 147). This is not portrayed as an apocalyptic threat, but as a feat of alchemical skill, "the last act of Chymistry" (*NP* 147). After the travellers thank the old man "for his gentle entertainment" (*NP* 148), the story wraps up, and they voyage home without mishap.

Cavendish reoccupies the trope of the skeptic's intellectual quest by infusing her own concerns and scientific interests into the tale in ways that not only demythologize but also break with the long history of journeys to the underworld. This is not, after all, a classical epic about reuniting with the dead or glimpsing imperial futures. Nor is it a Dantesque allegory of sin and redemption, although there are Dantesque echoes, from the river of blood to the old Man of Crete. But even here, her modernizing bent is evident. Cavendish's "very rough" sea of blood is historical, the issue of violently slain bodies (*NP* 145), while Dante's Phlegethon is part of a moral topography. Dante's Old Man of Crete is an underground statue composed of gold, silver, bronze, iron, and clay, recalling the dream of Nebuchadnezzar (Dan. 2:31–33) and the Ages of Man as recounted by Ovid (*Met.* 1); but he also serves as a conduit for tears that drip through fissures and cracks, forming the infernal waterways (*Inf.* xiv.103–135). Cavendish evokes this figure even as her Old Man explains the mechanics of evaporation, rain, and water-flow: "for whatsoever Water the Sun drank from the Sea, and spued upon the Earth, run through the Veins into the Sea again by the Center, all little Pipe-veins meeting there" (*NP* 147). Water replaces tears, pipe-veins replace fissures. Overall, Cavendish minimizes the transcendental content of underworld encounters and reoccupies it, using the Old Man to poke fun at chemists and double down on questions of interest to her such as the source of the glow-worms' light. The Old Man's answers, with their gnomic mix of spirituality and science, evidently meet the seeker's needs. He comes away contented, his curiosity satisfied. No one is punished for crossing boundaries or aspiring to forbidden knowledge.[12] The tale, which starts out on a spooky note reminiscent of a Faustian bargain, sidelines the witch and ends up as a vehicle for the Old Man's pronouncements on geology.[13] He is an avatar of Cavendish, one of her many alter egos: an authority reigning over a parallel universe.

The reoccupation of the skeptical quest motif occurs in both early and late work. In a long story like "The Anchoret" and in *The Blazing World*, the new content pertains to gender. In "The Anchoret," the expert is an heiress who complies with her dying father's will in refusing marriage and living chastely. She does not join a convent, but instead mimics the life of an anchoret, encloistering herself and speaking through a grate. Her solitude notwithstanding, "she grew as famous as *Diogenes* in his tub, all sorts of people resorted to her, to hear her speak, and not only to hear her speak, but to get knowledge, and to learn wisdom" (*NP* 289). Over a dozen groups, representing different forms of social authority, come to her abode with questions. These include natural philosophers, physicians, moral philosophers, scholars of divinity, fathers of the church, judges, barristers, orators, statesmen, tradesmen, housekeepers and masters of families, married men and their wives, nurses and nurse-children, widowers and widows, virgins, lovers, poets, aged persons, soldiers, and finally,

---

[12] As Sarasohn observes, "What is surprising is that the witch is portrayed as an essentially benign figure, who, regardless of serving the Devil, is happy to help the traveler in any way she can. He is not required to sell his soul to the Devil. This portrayal may be meant as a dig at the witch-hunters and their philosophic supporters, including Cavendish's future correspondents Joseph Glanvill and Henry More, but it may also indicate her sympathy for all kinds of material being" (2010, 94).

[13] Critics have tended to be more interested in the witch than in the Old Man. See, e.g., Walters who notes that the witch "is someone who understands philosophy as she teaches her male companion about the mysteries of matter, rather than appearing as an emblem of female disorder" (2014, 108). She interprets the Old Man as an "explicitly prelapsarian" alchemist satirizing Henry More's Neoplatonic World Soul (2014, 111). In this tale Cavendish "redefines the concepts" of witchcraft and the occult, "situating them within a secular, material framework" (2014, 113).

historians. To each of these, she dispenses her wisdom "according to the severall studies, professions, grandeurs, ages, humors of her auditory" (*NP* 289). For example, when she holds forth on glow-worms, offering her solution to a scientific puzzle, it becomes apparent that the fascination derives from a desire for inter-cranial transparency:

> ... and certainly, said she, if we could see through the bodies of Animals, and likewise through their skull, as easy as the Glow-worms tail, we should see, said she, a much brighter flame in the heart and the brain, which flame is the light of knowledge; and the several Objects that the Senses bring in, are there visibly perceived. (*NP* 293)

This passage reveals the frustrations of the skeptical knower. Despite the stance of intellectual confidence, the mysterious universe of unknown things haunts Cavendish's reoccupations.

Nevertheless, Cavendish relishes ventriloquizing the subject-supposed-to-know, borrowing its forms. The anchoret is her spokeswoman. Yet the tone of the knowledge exchange wavers. Sometimes the conversation recalls, not a play, but the terse question-and-answer format of a catechism. For example, the natural philosophers ask her "what eternall was? She answered, an endless succesion [sic]. Then they asked her what infinite was? She said, a numberless succession; but said she, eternal is in respect to infinite, infinite to eternall" (*NP* 290). Cavendish appropriates the catechism as a pedagogical instrument for transmitting doctrine, except that the doctrine she purveys is her own. Yet sometimes, the burden of proof seems to shift, transforming the suppliants into skeptics testing the knowledge of the anchoret. When they object to her answers, it ostensibly provides an occasion for her to develop her points, but the resulting exchange can erode her authority; her pronouncements slip into the defensive tones of a student hoping to ace an oral exam and impress the judges. Consider the following dialogue:

> Then they asked what the Sun was?
> She answered, a body of Fire:
> Then they asked her, what Light was?
> She answered, Light was inflamed Ayre.
> They said, that if light was inflamed air, it would burn all things up, and so consume the world?
>
> She answered, that in thin bodies fire had but little power to burn, for the thinness of the matter weakens the power of the strength, which causeth flame, said she, to be of no great heat; for the hot flames doth rather singe than burn ... (*NP* 291)

This sounds more like a recital of knowledge under duress than inspired teaching. Yet at other moments, the anchoret reprimands her interlocutors, exposing their faulty assumptions and scolding them for lacking information (*NP* 292–293). This see-saw in power relations is further complicated by William Cavendish's insertions, in this tale a brief chapter on the night vision of cats, whose shining eyes he compares to the glowworms' light (*NP* 298–299).[14] His destabilizing incursions notwithstanding, the anchoret monopolizes knowledge, providing answers to the questions of all and sundry.

While others in Cavendish's oeuvre might be enjoined to adopt a posture of epistemological humility, in keeping with mitigated skepticism, the anchoret is exempt from this advice and retains her authority to the end. The story finishes on a conventional note when a lustful tyrant threatens to wage war on her country because she has spurned his advances. The anchoret delivers a heroic oration to his ambassadors, saying "I have sacrificed my life for my Countreys Peace and Safety" (*NP* 356). Then she dies, having poisoned herself. The country mourns and raises statues, altars, and pyramids in her honor. The church "deifie[s] her a Saint for her vertue and piety" (*NP* 356–357). "In golden letters" the historians record her life and death "in Fames brasen Tower" (*NP* 357).

Cavendish's pleasure in parodic theology depends on a notion of self-assertion that is key to reoccupation. Self-assertion is not only about self-promotion or a desire for fame of the sort she often invokes: "*If* Fortune *be my friend, then* Fame *will be my* Gaine, *which may build me a* Pyramid, *a* Praise *to my* Memory" ("To the reader," *Poems, and Fancies, PF*). Blumenberg argues that self-assertion also grounds the rise of theoretical curiosity and technological mastery.[15] As such, it is paradoxically bound up with skepticism. The renunciation of truth and the drive to explanation go together. As Blumenberg understands it, skeptical self-assertion is a function of "the new seriousness" imposed by "the constant and unrelieved pressure of confirming a relation to the world that is established within the

---

[14] See Hilda L. Smith for the view that "William and Margaret may have had more fundamental differences than has traditionally been recognized" (1997, 147).

[15] In Martin Jay's view, self-assertion "may be the most vulnerable element in the reoccupation thesis" precisely because it neglects individuals in favor of a transcendental subject: "For the self that is doing the asserting is essentially a transcendent one developing itself over time, engaging in what might be called a species *Bildung*" (1985, 194). Jay's criticism notwithstanding, Blumenberg's phenomenological sweep does not prevent him from focusing on individual thinkers with forceful egos, among them Giordano Bruno. Furthermore, the choice of the term, "self-assertion," Trierweiler points out, speaks to Blumenberg's supreme "irony" as he is appropriating the title of Heidegger's 1933 rectorial address and reoccupying it (2010, 21).

horizon of metaphysical conditions that leave no way out" (*LMA* 183). These metaphysical conditions "ambush" the human subject who reacts by consolidating her sense of self (*LMA* 196).[16] This "new sort of 'seriousness'," Blumenberg declares, "marks the modern will to knowledge" (*LMA* 182).[17] While Cavendish shares this will to knowledge, in her fiction (if not in her natural philosophy) her voice is playful, punchy in its mock solemnity.

In her late masterpiece, *The Blazing World*, the motif of the intellectual quest becomes more complicated, as it is embedded in a fantasy of sovereignty glorified by distributed networks of power and authority. Cavendish's chief avatar, the Empress, seeks answers to philosophical questions from societies of virtuosi that she herself has convened. Her stance is one of gracious patronage, reasserting the value of inquiry, even as she solicits information and exposes certain scholarly pursuits as bunk. The influence of Solomon's House in Francis Bacon's *New Atlantis* is evident in this text, as are her criticisms of the newly founded Royal Society and some of its experiments.[18] Whereas the anchoret provided the answers to questions posed mostly by groups of men, here the Empress asks the questions. While some of these experts espouse Cavendish's beliefs, others do not, and these the Empress ridicules. She dismisses those who dispute and wrangle, the logicians especially (*BW* 160–162). But she retains the upper hand by granting livelihoods to her far-flung network of virtuosi.

Taken together, these variations on the motif of the search for knowledge transmit a parodic sense of crisis in intellectual authority. Thanks to their self-assertion, Cavendish's avatars rise to the occasion, stepping in to occupy the vacancy in leadership. This also occurs in her 1662 *Orations of Divers Sorts*. Here, through her "shape-shifting experimentation with voice, identity and point of view," Cavendish represents herself as a nimble and articulate debater, now taking one side of a controversial issue, now taking the opposing side (Rees 2003, 170). Ashamed of her own stage-fright and "bashful" silence in 1651 when it was her cue to speak before the Committee for Compounding at Goldsmiths' Hall – she had traveled

---

[16] Note the metaphorical language and the Nietzschean overtones: "Under the enormous pressure of the demands made upon it by theology, the human subject begins to consolidate itself, to take on a new overall condition, which possesses, in relation to ambushes set by the hidden absolute will, something like the elementary attributes of the atom, that it cannot be split up or altered" (*LMA* 196).
[17] Later, Blumenberg deems seriousness a mark of epochal consciousness also true of earlier ages, which exhibit "this same basic pattern of contrasting one's 'new seriousness' with the past" (*LMA* 474).
[18] See Battigelli (1998), Lilley (1994), Price (1998), Sarasohn (2010), etc.

from exile in Antwerp to London in a bid to reclaim some of her husband's sequestered properties – she writes a book, one could argue, compensating for her failure of nerve on that earlier occasion.[19] But the book of orations is much more than a gesture of psychological compensation. It is a deliberate and self-conscious attempt to reoccupy the space of women's speech.[20] The story of Lady Fairfax's shouted protest from the upper gallery during Charles I's trial was already circulating by the time Cavendish penned her orations.[21] It is as if Cavendish wishes both to augment and supplant – at least in print – the barely articulate cries of women in public spaces. In short, the new concept adumbrated in her metaphorics of the skeptical quest is the role of female authority in the production of knowledge.

Cavendish's work thus instantiates the relation that Blumenberg seeks to establish between metaphorology and the history of concepts (*Begriffgeschichte*).[22] Blumenberg seeks to recuperate metaphors for philosophical analysis, arguing that they can be "*foundational elements* of philosophical language" that illuminate "the metakinetics of the historical horizons of meaning" (*PM* 3, 5).[23] Yet, the history of concepts cannot be reduced to tracking "terminological metastasis" (*PM* 63);[24] instead it requires testing that will produce "more secure insights" regarding the extent to which "background metaphorics" orient the process of concept formation (*PM* 63, 22). The relations between Blumenberg's ideas of "background metaphorics" and metaphorical "migrations" allow us to understand reoccupation as more than a symptom of an epochal threshold

---

[19] "I whisperingly spoke to my brother to conduct me out of that ungentlemanly place, so without speaking to them one word good or bad, I returned to my Lodgings, & as that Committee was the first, so was it the last, I ever was at as a Petitioner" (*Paper Bodies* 51).

[20] When she castigates the frivolousness of women's public speech under the Commonwealth, accusing "our Sex" of "Trafficking with idle words," she is presumably not only defending her silence before the Committee for Compounding, but also distinguishing her own published words as substantive speech (*PB* 52).

[21] See Geoffrey Robertson's account of how the story developed (2005, 374, 397, 409). It is unclear that Lady Fairfax was present at the trial; we may be assuming as fact what was rumored.

[22] Blumenberg defines "the relationship of metaphorology to the history of concepts ... as an ancillary one: metaphorology seeks to burrow down to the substructure of thought, the underground, the nutrient solution of systematic crystallizations; but it also aims to show with what 'courage' the mind preempts itself in its images, and how its history is projected in the courage of its conjectures" (*Paradigms for a Metaphorology, PM* 5). See Haverkamp's gloss on the "crystallization" metaphor (2012, 50).

[23] See Haverkamp for "the Heideggerian underpinnings" of the word, "metakinetics" (2012, 50).

[24] This may be a swipe against Carl Schmitt. Blumenberg attacks Schmitt on several fronts, among them his "decisionism," his "dualistic typology," his confusion of "structural analogies" with "transformations," and his settling for descriptive correlations rather than analyses of genealogical "derivation" (*LMA* 92–94).

(*PM* 23, 78). Reoccupation is a skeptical operation, manifesting itself in metaphorical language, that subtends the shift from a vision of history centered on transcendent intervention (*potentia absoluta* and miracles) to one centered on "immanent human processes" (*PM* 86).

Reoccupying Memory Palaces in *The Blazing World*

In a less obvious example of Cavendish's skeptical work of reoccupation, her agency rides the wave of the Zeitgeist. Cavendish's oeuvre abounds in architectural extravaganzas: ornate palaces, monumental tombs, broad courtyards, and luxurious convents. *The Blazing World* features glittering cityscapes entwined with rivers and dotted with islands. These imaginary cities, I argue, represent the era's growing skepticism toward the memory arts. Cavendish reoccupies the spatial system for ordering memory, using its armature as a staging ground for self-assertion. The arches, avenues, and gateways of her dream cities bear the iconographic marks of the art of memory, but do not help with the work of memorizing or memorializing. They do not remind anyone of the order of an oration, a legal plea or a religious meditation. Instead, they point only to themselves and to the Emperor and Empress. They function paradoxically like a House of Fame with no history.

Over half a century ago, Frances Yates acknowledged the decline of the memory arts in the seventeenth century, arguing that they do not die out so much as undergo a series of transformations that issue in scientific method (1966, 241, 369). More recently, Seth Long (2017) has refined Yates's narrative about the role of Protestant iconoclasm in the decline of visual mnemonics together with the rise of Ramism as a harbinger of method. John Shanahan (2002), writing about *Bell in Campo*, calls Cavendish's architectural ensembles "experimental spaces" where she is free to explore possibilities. If so, then Yates may well be right: the memory palace has morphed into the scientific laboratory. However, I see Cavendish's refitted palaces as evidence of Blumenberg's view that reoccupation underwrites the legitimacy of the modern age. Cavendish's ideal cities betray her ambivalence toward the cultural past – a gendered ambivalence issuing from her sense of exclusion from the intellectual heritage of her male counterparts. She reoccupies the urban space of the memory arts and uses it, not only to assert her own primacy, but also to express her desire for an unburdened approach to the future.

Yet, despite their empty content, *The Blazing World*'s urban tableaux suggest a functional continuity as regards old mnemonic forms. In the

Rhetorica ad Herennium, the foundational Roman treatise on the memory arts, advice is offered on how best to perfect the artificial memory. There are two components, the treatise says: figures and backgrounds. The best backgrounds are architectural involving streetscapes and palaces with intercolumnar spaces, niches, and arches. Lighting and spacing are always key. One must not overcrowd the memory palace nor dim the crisp silhouette of the figure because one wants each *imagine agente* to imprint itself on the receiving mind in all its strange and wacky vividness. The *ad Herennium* stipulates that

> we set up images that are ... doing something; if we assign to them exceptional beauty or singular ugliness; if we dress some of them with crowns or purple cloaks ... so that the likeness may be more distinct to us; or if we somehow disfigure them, as by introducing one stained with blood or smeared with red paint, so that its form is more striking ... that, too, will ensure our remembering more readily. (1953, 47)

Cavendish taps into this representational tradition in *The Blazing World*, reoccupying it through skeptical performance.

Take the Lady's arrival in the capital of the Blazing World. The city has arches, gates, cloisters, and passageways, producing an effect similar to those mental panoramas prescribed by the memory arts. Cavendish's description hews closely to the typical memory palace:

> Their architectures were noble, stately, magnificent, not like our modern, but like those in the Roman's time ... The highest of them did not exceed two storeys, besides those rooms that were under-ground, as cellars, and other offices. The Emperor's palace stood upon an indifferent ascent from the imperial city; at the top of which ascent was a broad arch, supported by several pillars, which went round the palace ... at every half mile was a gate to enter, and every gate was of a different fashion. ... The roof of [the palace] was all arched, and rested upon pillars, so artificially placed, that a stranger would lose himself therein without a guide. (*BW* 131)

Note the attention to problems of space, volume, and scale as well as "the stranger" Cavendish inserts into the scene. He has been dropped into the middle of the city. He is not perched on a hill to one side looking down at the urban vista, as in period engravings, nor is he staring head on at the Italianate piazza whose streets recede in vanishing point perspective, as in Renaissance paintings or even the set designs of Serlio or Jones.[25] This

---

[25] See Miranda Wilson who argues that Cavendish is drawing on Italian architectural theorists like Alberti, Palladio, and Serlio, who in turn were inspired by the Roman architect, Vitruvius (2004, 247).

observer is not distanced from, but fully engaged in the urban scene, as practitioners of artificial memory imagined themselves to be. Yet, unlike those practitioners, this *flâneur* has no agency. He is not returning in imagination to a familiar space that he then revisits in a certain order so as to call to mind the things he desires to remember. On the contrary, Cavendish's accidental tourist has no personal connection to the space and sees it with the eyes of a stranger – her word.

The stranger's disorientation should not be taken simply as a recurrent motif of travel literature; rather, it suggests alienation from the metaphorical edifices of knowledge. The memory palaces of old represent classical modes of learning – regimes of knowledge dominating pedagogy since ancient times. All the schooling that Cavendish missed out on – Greek, Latin, logic, law, not to mention oratory, something she craved to master – made use of the memory arts with its streetscapes and façades crammed with knowledge. The buildings of *The Blazing World*'s capital are new – not ruins like those of Nottinghamshire (*BW* 193). This Potemkin village approach to the memory arts appeals to Cavendish because it nullifies the demands of the past. Instead of cityscapes that prompt an observer to remember his book-learning or retrieve arcana, she invents a cityscape that is diverting and aesthetic, even utopian, precisely because it has effaced the past and looks to the future. That is one reason why she calls the capital Paradise: its innocence of history.

In her conversation with the immaterial spirits, the Empress imagines that they can see into the past and future without memory, a condition she envies. The Empress says, "I did believe . . . that spirits had no need of memory, or remembrance, and could not be subject to forgetfulness" (*BW* 166). When they correct her on this point, she is disappointed and insists, against their protestations, that "you know what is to come, without memory or remembrance, and therefore you may know what is past without memory and remembrance" (*BW* 167). For her, the ideal condition is to have "present knowledge and understanding" of all things without memory (*BW* 166). This would be like knowing everything in the library without ever having read it, surely an appealing fantasy: short-circuiting the learning process yet being in command of knowledge. In keeping with this dream of a world without memory, Cavendish waves her magic wand and wishes away the overwhelming demands of the old memory palaces so that only their elegant shells remain.

Consider the architectural scene in *The Blazing World* where the Empress, as part of her grand plan to reconfigure institutions, starts with the church and ends with a claim on posterity's memory. This occurs when she "resolve[s] to build churches, and make also up a congregation of women, whereof she intended to be the head herself" (*BW* 162). The Empress designs two superimposed chapels, each of which stands "upon pillars," and which she locates "in the middle of a round cloister which was dark as night." Whereas in the *ars memorativa*, the lighting has to be even and clear so as to prevent confusing shadows, Cavendish's edifice is all about extreme contrasts and chiaroscuro. One chapel features star-stones that "cast a splendorous and comfortable light," while the other blazes with diamonds and fire-stones that require, for their full effect, a plumbing system with sprinklers because "as long as the fire-stone was wet, the chapel seemed to be all in a flaming fire."[26] The engineering for the sake of dramatic lighting does not stop there. A stranger passing through the dark cloister can not only observe the two chapels glowing from within, but can also see right through them as they rotate on their axes. "Being everywhere open," the narrator explains, "allowed to all that were within the compass of the cloister, a free prospect into them; besides, they were so artificially contrived, that they did both move in a circle about their own centres, without intermission, contrary ways." The Empress has designed an extravagant architectural stage for her ministry. Lest we miss the iconographic significance of this double-decker structure, the text explains that "as that chapel was an emblem of Hell, so this was an emblem of Heaven" (*BW* 164). The Baroque emblem often operates as a rebus or visual riddle, its puzzling conceptual freight captured in an aesthetic snapshot.

Some view this architectural interlude in *The Blazing World*, not as an emblem repurposing the memory arts, but as a reworking of Henrietta Maria's extraordinary chapel in Somerset House, designed by Inigo Jones. Certainly the revolving contraption evokes the *machina versatilis* featuring in more than one of Jones's masques (Orgel and Strong 1973, 2.214). Other critics focus on Cavendish's abiding interest in spaces for female communities like convents.[27] Although I agree

---

[26] Radley finds a source for Cavendish's fire-stone in John Lyly's *Euphues, The Anatomy of Wit* where it "is said to have been quenched with milk" (2014, 162). Radley links the star-stone to the star-sapphire mentioned in *The Book of Secrets* by pseudo-Albertus Magnus.

[27] See Battigelli: "By organizing a congregation of women and building two magnificent churches, the sheer beauty of which is designed to draw converts, the Empress imitates Henrietta, whose household was organized by rules resembling those of a religious order and whose magnificent chapel at Somerset House had been built in 1636 precisely for the purpose of attracting converts" (1998, 81). Nelson and Aker see the elaborate stage sets of the Caroline court masque behind Cavendish's monumental vistas (2008, 17). Each of these interpretations of Cavendish's interest in

Reoccupying Memory Palaces in The Blazing World 153

these elements are in play, this peculiar scene strikes me as having ambitions that stake a claim on the future. The text explains that "thus the Empress, by art, and her own ingenuity, did not only convert the Blazing World to her own religion, but kept them in a constant belief, without enforcement or bloodshed." Somehow her performances in the pulpit produce religious uniformity, such that "both church and state was now in a well-ordered and settled condition" (*BW* 165). The architectural mise-en-scène enables the Empress's reforming impulses, as if the rhetorical force of her words would have no purchase in the world absent the gaudy spectacle. To get through to her audience and achieve her mission, she requires an awe-inspiring setting. It is as if the strangeness and singularity of the images designed for the memory arts were reinforced by the spectacular scene, as figure and background blend.

Together the Empress and her chapels constitute a powerful thought-image thanks to the display of precious stones. Cavendish literally builds a treasure-house for her striking protagonist. The building is co-extensive with the Empress, described not as a background locus so much as a continuation of her luminous presence. The Empress herself thinks of it as a garment, judging by the repeated use of the word "lined": "the one [chapel] she lined throughout with diamonds ... but the other she resolved to line with star-stone." The metaphor comes from sewing as much as from construction. When she adds, "the fire-stone she placed upon the diamond-lining" (*BW* 163), it shows that she imagines the chapels as if they were sculpted of mineral-encrusted fabric signifying her command and setting off her beauty like a cloak or clerical vestment. She is offering herself as an *imagine agente*, that is, as a statuesque and bizarre figure destined to imprint itself on the memory of her future readers. Several other scenes reinforce the Empress's efforts to impress her audience and their memories. While some do not involve buildings or architectural elements, all feature the Empress in outlandish costume and outrageous postures. Inasmuch as this mimicry of sovereignty functions as a skeptical reoccupation, it amounts to parody.

---

architecture is persuasive, and they need not be mutually exclusive. After all, the Cavendishes embarked on an "extravagant" building program at Bolsover Castle during the Restoration, reason enough for attention to architecture and a predilection for classical porticoes and statuary (Whitaker 2002, 325). Nevertheless, when these ornamental features and spatial forms surface in Cavendish's work, they bear the unmistakable whiff of the old memory arts.

Cavendish may mock sovereignty, but her fear of oblivion is real. She worried that she would be overlooked, if not entirely forgotten. She ends her brief autobiography, "A True Relation," on a poignant note, explaining that she has written this account "lest after-Ages should mistake in not knowing I was daughter to one Master Lucas of St. John's near Colchester in Essex, second Wife to the Lord Marquis of Newcastle, for my Lord having had two Wives, I might easily have been mistaken, especially if I should dye, and my Lord Marry again" (*PB* 63). Cavendish frets that she will be mixed up with wife number 1 or potentially wife number 3, recollected at best as one of the interchangeable spouses of the great William Cavendish. So while elsewhere she declares her ambition for fame, wishing that she could be revered in after-ages alongside Ovid and other illustrious men, here she discloses a more modest ambition: merely to be remembered as the second wife of the Duke and not to be lumped in with the other wives. Cavendish uses the verb mistake twice in this passage, revealing her fear that she will blur into the other wives and get lost in an indistinct grouping, mistaken for another woman. She is exercising her historical imagination here, looking back from the vantage point of the future at her own family history and predicting that she will survive at best as a foggy appendage to the memory of her noble husband. So her aim is to make her own legacy distinct and crisp. What better way to accomplish this than by fashioning herself as an *imagine agente*? Since she desires that future generations remember her in all her distinctive individuality, she crafts herself as a powerful mnemonic cue, doing this even in her frontispieces, like the one in her 1668 volume of *Playes* (Figure 3).[28] Draped in memory palaces that serve as an extension of her luminous presence, she fashions her avatars as lively objects of remembrance, hoping thereby to imprint herself on our minds.

Cavendish illustrates what Aleida Assman calls the secularization of memory (2011, 23–52). The old *ars memorativa* with its topological approach to knowledge, distributing what needs to be remembered in space, has been reoccupied by an approach that links memory and identity. Assman captures the difference in her phrase 'memory as art' versus 'memory as power': *ars* and *vis* (2011, 9, 17). Cavendish asserts the power of her identity over the memory of the future by adapting memorial loci and *imagines agentes*, using them to preserve her own legacy. In performing

---

[28] See Jane Stevenson for Cavendish's use of the image engraved by Pieter Louis van Schuppen after a design by Abraham van Diepenbeeck (2009, 211–212).

Figure 3   Frontispiece, Margaret Cavendish, *Playes*, 1668 (courtesy of the Folger Shakespeare Library)

this reoccupation, she heralds the demise of the memory arts and the advent of celebrity culture.[29]

Reoccupying Nominalism

Before returning to Cavendish, I need to say a little more about Blumenberg's work. The concept of "self-assertion" – so crucial to Cavendish no less than to Herbert of Cherbury – has a far more tangled philosophical derivation than, say, the Burckhardtian sense of Renaissance individualism might suggest.[30] Blumenberg anchors his abstract theorization of reoccupation and metaphorics with specific examples.[31] For my purposes, his most eloquent example demonstrates the way early modern mechanistic explanations reoccupy the vacancies inherited from nominalism. Blumenberg lays out the structural relations of nominalism and Epicurean materialism when he discusses the Leibniz–Clarke correspondence of 1715–1716. In this exchange of letters, Leibniz protests that exalting God's will and sovereign freedom – so important to voluntarism – amounts to endorsing chance and cosmic disorder. Leibniz's complaint "discloses," according to Blumenberg, "the structural connection between nominalism as a late-medieval phenomenon and atomism as an early modern one" (*LMA* 151). Reading Leibniz against the grain allows Blumenberg to show that reoccupation is at work in this structural connection. As he puts it, "the principle, employed in Leibniz's analysis, of the *equivalence* of nominalistic and mechanistic explanations of the world ... gives us the key to the *reoccupation* that was effected in the replacement of the late-medieval by the early-modern type of explanation

---

[29] A study of *The Blazing World*'s palaces suggests that reoccupation works something like Derrida's notion of a paleonomy. A paleonomy, according to Derrida, maintains "an *old name* in order to launch a new concept" (1972, 71). Richter elaborates: "The paleonomic gesture requires us to stand inside and outside a tradition at the same time, perpetuating the tradition while breaking with it, and breaking with the tradition while perpetuating it" (2007, 1). While Blumenberg might demur at the notion of standing outside a tradition, preferring the immersion of reoccupation, he agrees that old, absolute metaphors can launch new concepts and would add that reoccupation is the mechanism for it. See Haverkamp on "the paleonymic character of metaphor" in Blumenberg (2012, 54).
[30] For Blumenberg on Burckhardt, see his brief, approving remarks (*LMA* 468–469).
[31] Blumenberg distinguishes reoccupation from other ideas with which it shares a family resemblance. Hence, it is not to be confused with the process of secularization described by Karl Löwith or Carl Schmitt or with the *Begriffgeschichte* of Auguste Comte, Hans-Georg Gadamer, Nietszche or Hannah Arendt, among many others. This laborious process of negative definition permits increasingly nuanced refinements of his argument. Among the examples of reoccupation that he discusses, Blumenberg includes the concepts of progress, infinity, happiness, immortality, and curiosity.

of nature" (*LMA* 150). Epicurean mechanism, he argues, reoccupies positions left vacant by nominalism and in turn becomes "the tool of self-assertion" (*LMA* 151). In other words, self-assertion comes to reoccupy the "theological absolutism" of nominalism and before it of Gnostic dualism, which itself can be traced "back to the antithesis of atom and empty space in the philosophy of Democritus and Epicurus" (*LMA* 148).[32]

Blumenberg finds evidence for his claim – that Epicurean materialism had to 'pass through' voluntarism so as to rediscover the contingency of nature – in modern thought-experiments about multiform configurations and possible worlds (*LMA* 158–159). (*The Blazing World* constitutes Cavendish's major thought-experiment in that genre.) According to Blumenberg, nominalism, with its "intense consciousness of insecurity," radicalizes Epicurean atomism, in effect reoccupying "the atomistic plurality of *actual* worlds" with "the late-medieval doctrine of the plurality of *possible* worlds" (*LMA* 163). This situation, in turn, provokes self-assertion even as it encourages a skeptical attitude of restraint toward doctrinaire theoretical claims. Blumenberg implies that skepticism, which counsels doubt in the face of the world's baffling appearances, induces a contradictory mindset: theoretical self-restraint together with a compulsive need to write the self and create fictional worlds.

The notion of hypothesis, he argues, contains a similar contradiction: "*Hypothesis*, which from one point of view is the formal expression of the renunciation of the claim to truth in the traditional sense of adequacy [*adaequatio*], becomes from another point of view a means of self-assertion, the potential for human production of that which nature makes scarce or does not provide for man at all" (*LMA* 199). Skepticism about truth thus issues in serious investigation. Speaking of "the modern idea of science," Blumenberg writes, "In it too, knowledge of one's ignorance is an essential element, though admittedly less to know *that* one knows nothing than to know *what* one does not know, perhaps even what one *cannot* know, and, very important, what one does not *need* to know" (*LMA* 497). The many ways knowledge falls short carries over to Blumenberg's understanding of reoccupation as a symptom and strategy of skeptical doubt and skeptical inquiry.[33]

---

[32] "Viewed as an absolute metaphor, atomism is the antithesis of Stoicism's notion of providence" (*CCR* 12).

[33] Christopher Johnson says of *Care Crosses the River*, "The skepticism that informs Blumenberg's writing here is thoroughly humanist, won from a lifetime of finding concepts lacking in the face of historical contingency" (2012a, 291).

Descartes exemplifies the new seriousness of the modern age. "The *laboriosa vigilia* [laborious wakefulness] that Descartes recommends in the last paragraph of the first of his *Meditations* is," Blumenberg insists, "the tension of an extreme seriousness, which resolutely leaves behind it the past sleepiness and negligence" (*LMA* 474–475). By "his ability to withhold judgment" and reject the past's hasty and misguided ways of thinking, Descartes asserts his own sovereign freedom (*LMA* 183). Blumenberg describes Descartes' mode of self-assertion in various ways – "reserving assent, ... an act of decision in favor of indecision" (*LMA* 185) – but all hinge on his method of doubt. He shows "what it means to say that Descartes transformed the late medieval crisis of certainty into an experiment with certainty" (*LMA* 187), arguing that the experiment presupposes the crisis. "By radicalizing the nominalists' *potentia absoluta* into the hypothesis of the *genius malignus*," Blumenberg explains, "he sharpened the doubt surrounding certainty to such an extent" that nominalist answers were no longer adequate (*LMA* 194–195). He concedes that Descartes works hard to erase the tracks of this debt, consciously cultivating his image as a foundational figure, but insists that we recognize him as "a thinker who clarified the medieval concept of reality, all the way to its absurd consequences and thus made it ripe for destruction" (*LMA* 187).[34]

For all her scoffing at Descartes and their manifold differences, Cavendish is like him in this respect: she asserts herself by declaring herself free to doubt and reserve judgment. She also likes to minimize her intellectual debts and to cultivate her image as a novel personage and thinker: female natural philosopher, playwright, poet, author of essays and romances. A characteristic passage announces:

> Wherefore, I will neither follow the opinions of the ancient, nor of our moderns ... but search the truth of nature, by the light of regular reason: for, I perceive that most of our modern writings are not filled with new inventions of their own, but, like a lumber, stuffed with old commodities, botched and dressed up anew, contain nothing but what has been said in former ages. (*OEP* 239)[35]

While Cavendish does not reoccupy the positions left vacant by late Scholasticism as persuasively as Descartes does, she too aspires to fill her writings with "new inventions."

---

[34] "Descartes painstakingly effaced and disavowed the traces of his historical background in order to constitute the myth of the radical beginning of reason" (*LMA* 185).

[35] When describing why "scholars are never good poets" in *The World's Olio*, Cavendish uses the identical simile: "their head is nothing but a lumber stuft with old commodities" (*WO* 5).

Like Descartes and other mid-century thinkers, she too grapples with the crisis of certainty by thinking and writing about Epicurean atomism.[36] While Cavendish fails to appreciate the affinities between Epicureanism and skepticism, her own brand of skepticism emerges when she imagines the cosmos as entirely alive and occupied by sentient matter. She shares with Descartes a horror vacui, but cannot accept his or Hobbes's mechanistic view of the universe.[37] Her repudiation of atomism and her subsequent turn to vitalist materialism comes partly from her awakening ontological commitment to a plenum – a space that is entirely occupied instead of riddled with empty interstices (*OEP* 127–131, 261–262).[38] Her vitalist materialism corresponds, I suggest, to her predilection for reoccupation as a literary device and psychological stance. If the plenum proves obstinate and resists a body's will to occupy, one option is "to retreat to imaginary worlds of fancy" where the work of reoccupation can proceed unhindered (Cunning 2016, 243). In her fiction she can colonize traditional topoi and reshape them as she pleases.

At the level of language and syntax, her will to reoccupy often manifests itself in witty, if manic, games of substitution – one word or sign booting out another and taking its place. The "Allegories" section in *The World's Olio* illustrates Cavendish's penchant for "similizing." In an almost frantic exercise to fill-in-the-blank, the brain is compared to a government, a wilderness, a perspective glass, a flint, colleges, the hand, a pan, gamesters, God, nature, uncultivated ground and an island (*WO* 99–106). Lest this mode of reoccupation seem too literal given Blumenberg's high-flown criteria, let me counter that these individual acts of metaphorical substitution disclose problematic vacancies in normative questions – in this instance, what is mind? Cavendish's metaphors have an incremental effect

---

[36] Michaelian describes Cavendish "as a philosopher typical of her time but simultaneously as one whose views occupy a corner of logical space left vacant by other philosophers working then" (2009, 33).

[37] See, e.g., Ankers who argues that Cavendish proposes "to undermine the mechanical basis for Hobbes's analogies, especially those promoting a competitive 'state of nature'" by introducing a relational model of "willing compliance" that offsets "the danger of fully autonomous parts, such as atoms or human individuals" (2003, 245, 250). For more work comparing Cavendish and Hobbes, see Battigelli (1998), Hutton (1997), Sarasohn (2003), and others.

[38] There is an extensive literature on Cavendish's repudiation of atomism and adoption of vitalist materialism, aligning this philosophical change with developments in her political and social thought. See, for starters, Clucas (1994), Detlefsen (2006), James (1999), O'Neill (in *OPS* 2001), Rogers (1996), Sarasohn (1984, 297–298), Jay Stevenson (1996), and Catherine Wilson (2007). For Cavendish's "theory of material plenism, the view that the world is everywhere and only matter which is extended infinitely and which can be internally divided without end," see Detlefsen (2006, 200).

when seen in aggregate across her *oeuvre* and achieve a large-scale reoccupation: *per aspera ad astra*.

While literary *topos* research may not be as philosophical as the investigations into "absolute metaphor" that Blumenberg values, it also benefits from analysis that takes reoccupation as both enabling and dictating how humans imagine a better world.[39] For, "the crucial question," according to Blumenberg, is whether "a situation of paradisaic satisfaction … is to be brought about immanently or transcendently, whether man can achieve it by the exertion of his own powers or has to rely for it on the grace, which he cannot earn, of an event breaking in upon him" (*LMA* 86). In the context of Blumenberg's philosophy of history, Cavendish's boasts about the powers of her imagination no longer seem jejune, droll, plaintive or compensatory (depending on one's point of view), but rather symptomatic of a sea-change in European thought. She ends her preface to *The Blazing World*, boasting,

> … though I cannot be *Henry* the Fifth, or *Charles* the Second, yet I endeavor to be *Margaret* the *First*; and although I have neither power, time nor occasion to conquer the world as *Alexander* and *Caesar* did; yet rather than not to be mistress of one, since Fortune and the Fates would give me none, I have made a world of my own: for which no body, I hope, will blame me, since it is in every one's power to do the like. (*BW* 124)

Her decision to imagine possible worlds and alternate societies arises partly from impatience and indignation with the status quo – there is no hint of waiting for a transcendent event to improve matters – and ends with a democratic invitation and reminder that it is "in every one's power to do the like." Meanwhile, she proposes to step into the vacancy left by leadership, occupying it.

---

[39] Blumenberg contrasts "absolute" and "rudimentary" metaphors. "By providing a point of orientation," he explains, "the content of absolute metaphors determines a particular attitude or conduct [*Verhalten*]; they give structure to a world, representing the nonexperienceable, nonapprehensible totality of the real. To the historically trained eye, they therefore indicate the fundamental certainties, conjectures, and judgments in relation to which the attitudes and expectations, actions and inactions, longings and disappointments, interests and indifferences, of an epoch are regulated" (*PM* 14). They "resist" translation and are "conceptually irredeemable" (*PM* 3). Is Blumenberg suggesting that rudimentary metaphors (that practice "concealment" and invite "unmasking," activities with a suspiciously Heideggerian sound) often become the subject of *topos* research? This implies that absolute metaphors, because they are philosophically more "legitimate" (itself a favorite and problematic metaphor, as Robert Pippin 1987 observes), are the proper purview of *Begriffgeschichte*. Regardless, Blumenberg sees his task as "detecting the logical 'perplexity' for which metaphor steps in" (*PM* 3). Blumenberg's forays into detailed topos research are brilliant. See, e.g., *Shipwreck with Spectator*, *Care Crosses the River* or his analysis of the hunting metaphors in Nicholas of Cusa (*LMA*, 497 ff.).

Jewels and Gems

The Blazing World blazes with the light emitted by gemstones. What accounts for Cavendish's fascination with gems? To what extent is the cultural work performed by these minerals a form of reoccupation? Blumenberg explains that "the idea of 'reoccupation' says nothing about the derivation of the newly installed element, only about the dedication it receives at its installation" (*LMA* 49). His comment depends on the function / content distinction and implies what is obvious in someone like Cavendish (or Descartes) – that she can install herself as an utter original, obscuring her debts, even as she reoccupies old metaphors, traditional themes and classical genres.[40] The following pages investigate "the derivation" of the motif of jewels so as to better understand "the dedication it receives [from Cavendish] at its installation." I have already intimated that the jeweled chapel of Cavendish's Empress serves to enhance her power, awing believers who might otherwise be fractious into submission and imprinting her image on their memories. But how does the Empress's desire to wield power and appear powerful reoccupy the metaphorical positions usually taken by gems? A brief look at a few literary precursors shows how Cavendish configures reoccupation to put forth a parody of sovereignty.[41]

As Thomas Nicols reminds us in *Arcula Gemmea, or a Cabinet of Jewels* (1653), two biblical passages serve as the foundational texts for allusions to precious stones: Exodus 28:15–30 and Revelation 21:10–27. In the first passage God is speaking to Moses, instructing him on how he wishes to be worshipped, specifically as regards the priestly garments and the

---

[40] See Rees and Lara Dodds for different understandings of Cavendish's stance toward her literary debts. Rees argues that "it is through careful choices of genre that Cavendish succeeds in formulating controversial arguments. Repeatedly she lulls the reader into believing that he or she is reading a generically familiar text. When that genre's antecedents are examined, however, Cavendish's unique take on it emerges in all its tantalising and subversive force" (2003, 5). Dodds claims that "by casting her writing as independent of all predecessors, Cavendish offers originality as compensation for the authorial attributes she so conspicuously lacks. Denying influence and insisting upon singularity, Cavendish draws upon conventions of aristocratic exemplarity as well as print culture's demand for novelty in her portrait of herself as an autonomous author" (2013, 11).

[41] Blumenberg distances himself from the philological methods of a scholar like Ernst Robert Curtius who studied the derivations and genealogies of particular literary images. As Michael Spitzer observes, "Blumenberg rejects the 'historical substantialism' of Curtius, with its 'substantialist conception of historical identity' (2015, 29)," offering instead a "functionalism [that] approaches intellectual history as a system of 'positions' that are 'occupied' and 'reoccupied' by ideas" (2015, 134). That said, Johnson is surely right that "Curtius may be said to provide the material out of which a Blumenbergian problem or 'paradigm' emerges" (2012b, 152).

breastpiece that Aaron will wear. The breastpiece of judgment has four rows of three precious stones each, including some that feature in Cavendish's work: diamonds, sapphires, rubies, agates, and carbuncles. Each of the "ouches" (Nicols 1653, 58) is inscribed with the name of one of the twelve tribes of Israel so that when Aaron officiates in the sanctuary, he bears their names "upon his heart ... for a memorial before the Lord continually" (1653, 28:29). This account of the priest's ceremonial dress imagines the life of worship with its ritual occasions extending far into the future. Earlier in Exodus, when the elders experience a theophany on Mount Sinai, it says of God: "and there was under his feet as it were a paved work of a sapphire stone" (1653, 24:10). Metaphor and simile combine to communicate awe and grandeur. Similarly, the passage from the Book of Revelation uses figural language to conjure its apocalyptic vision of the New Jerusalem, understood as a sign of the last days. The passage begins with a simile about the holy city: "her light *was* like unto a stone most precious, even like a jasper stone, clear as crystal" (1653, 21:11). Then the simile collapses into metaphor and offers itself as reality: "And the building of the wall of it was *of* jasper: and the city *was* pure gold" (1653, 21:18). The city has twelve foundations and twelve gates. Each foundation is "garnished" with a precious stone, including some that adorn *The Blazing World*: carnelian, topaz, and again sapphire. Each of the twelve gates is comprised of a single pearl (1653, 21:21). Augustine says of Revelation that "the prophetic style of speech is apt to mingle metaphorical with literal expressions and so, as it were, to veil the meaning" (1984, 927–928). According to Augustine, the precious stones of the foundations signify the twelve Apostles, and the pearls of the gates signify Christ (Nicols 1653, 80). Access to the splendor of this shining city is vouchsafed only to the saved, for "there shall in no wise enter into it any thing that defileth, neither *whatsoever* worketh abomination, or *maketh* a lie: but they which are written in the Lamb's book of life" (1653, 21:27). If the New Jerusalem represents the hope of another, better world, waiting for those who have lived devoutly, Aaron's breastpiece signifies the responsibility of leadership in this world with its decisions, judgments, and duties. These scriptural passages glimmer in the background of *The Blazing World*.

Needless to say, these passages have influenced many works in many periods in many countries, including, among others, the dream vision of the New Jerusalem recounted in the Gawain poet's *Pearl* or in John Bunyan's *Pilgrim's Progress*. But since I am pursuing the migration of this biblical motif in order to show how Cavendish's parody of sovereignty depends on reoccupation, I want to pause over texts in which worldly concerns overtake the religious meanings imparted to jewels (Blumenberg, *LMA* 78). John Skelton's *Book of the Laurel*, for example, opens with a vision in which the poet sees "a pavylioune wonderly disgisyd, / Garnnysshid freshe, after my fantasy, / Enhachid with perle and stonys preciowsly, / The grounde engrosid and bet with burne gold" (1990, 38–41). Lest we imagine that this "traunce" or "extasy" (1990, 37) concerns the New Jerusalem, the poet explains that this pavilion belongs to Dame Pallas – "Madame Regent of the Scyence Sevene" (1990, 54) – who is listening to the Queen of Fame's complaint that "Skelton is wonder slak" and therefore should be denied access to her court (1990, 69). After they debate the merits of Skelton's work, consider his productivity, and hear the testimonies of learned witnesses like Gower, Chaucer, and Lydgate, Skelton eventually arrives at "the riche palace of the Queene of Fame" (1990, 450). Its magnificence dazzles him, filling more than three stanzas:

> With turkis and grossolitis empavyd was the grownde,
> Of birralle embosid were the pyllars rownde,
> Of oliphauntis tethe were the palace gatis,
> Enlosengyd with many goodely platis
>
> Of golde enhachid with many a preciows stone:
> An hundred steppis mountynge to the halle,
> Oon of jasper, another of whalis bone:
> Of dyamauntis poyntid was the rokky walle:
> The carpettis with in / and tappettis of palle,
> The chaumbers hangid with clothis of Arace:
> Envawtid with rubis the vawte was of this place.
>
> Thus passed we for the, walkynge unto the pretory,
> Where the postis were enbulyond with saphiris indy blu,
> Englasid, glittrynge / with many a clere story:
> Jacinctis and smaragdis owte of the florthe they grew:
> (1990, 466–480)

Skelton's description recalls Chaucer's *House of Fame* with its beryl and gold walls, but it is far more ornate: decorated not only with diamonds, sapphires, emeralds, turquoise and jasper, but also ivory ("oliphauntis tethe"), whalebone, and tapestries. When "Skelton" finally encounters the Queen of Fame, she sits "under a gloriows clothe of astate, / Fret alle with orient perlys of garnate, / Enkrownde as empress / of alle this worldly fate" (1990, 484–486). Might Skelton's empress in her refulgent palace glimmer in the background of *The Blazing World*? Because the Cavendishes were playwrights and well versed in English drama, it is likely they knew Skelton as the author of *Magnificence*, a Henrician interlude, in addition to other works. They likely knew that Skelton is a character in Ben Jonson's masque, *The Fortunate Isles*.[42]

Could Cavendish be thinking of these treasure houses when she composes her aphoristic emblem, "Natures House"? "The whole Globe is Natures House," it begins.

> The Earth is her Bed-Chamber; the Floor is Gold and Silver; and the Walls Marble and Purfry; the Portals and Doors are *Lape-Lazarus* [sic] ... her Bed is of several Pretious Stones; the Bedposts are of Rocks of Diamonds; the Beads-head of Rubyes, Saphires, Topus, and Emeralds ... her Table is of Agats ... (*NP* 156)

The conceit includes, not only minerals, but plants, flowers, and earth. The effect is playful as the allegorical equivalences pick up speed and social hierarchies intrude. The prose-poem ends: "Life is her Gentleman-usher. / Time is her Steward. / And Death is her Treasurer." Dame Nature and her staff live in a cosmic palace where even the planets have a designated function, e.g., "Venus is her Dressing Room." It is tempting to conclude that secularization is manifest in this instance of metaphysical wit. God's role as creator of the cosmos has dropped out, while the jewel motif, having lost its biblical resonance, seems a marker of wealth. But I think reoccupation is a better description than secularization of the skepticism at work here. The degree of intentionality in Nature's pantheistic dwelling reveals Cavendish's skeptical impatience with normative discourses (religious or astrological) and her desire to occupy the conceptual vacancies of the planetary universe.

If Cavendish's built worlds evoke the New Jerusalem, houses of Fame, and Quintilian's memory palaces, they also overwhelm the reader with abundance of treasure. Diamonds proliferate in colors like the rainbow and invented minerals like the fire-stone start out as decoration only to end up as a weapon of war. While the Blazing World is given no political history and seems to exist in an eternal condition of angelic bliss, cognizant sans memory, its minerals, by contrast, have a geological history. The formation of gold puzzles the Empress. She summons the worm-men, "her natural philosophers" (*BW* 134), to ask them a series of questions, among them

---

[42] Ben Jonson called William Cavendish his "best patron." Cavendish commissioned from him entertainments for the court, performed at Welbeck and Bolsover Castle in 1633 and 1634 (Donaldson 2011, 423–424; Whitaker 2002, 65).

"whether minerals and vegetables were generated by the same heat that is within the bowels of the earth" (*BW* 149). The worm-men have "no positive answer" so they digress, holding forth on geography:

> Neither do we observe, that the torrid zone does contain so much gold and silver as the temperate; nor is there great store of iron and lead wheresoever there is gold; for these metals are most found in colder climates towards either of the Poles. (*BW* 149)

The Empress seizes on this answer because it meets her agenda: to confute the claims of the alchemists. Glad to learn that violent heat does not produce gold, she asks, just like the seeker in "The Travelling Spirit," "whether gold could not be made by art" (*BW* 149). The worm-men fudge the question, mumbling something about other metals, so the Empress follows up, asking "whether art could produce iron, tin, lead or silver" (*BW* 150). Their inadequate replies prompt the Empress to rebuke them and point out contradictions. After the worm-men excuse themselves, saying "they were ignorant in that art," the questions resume, this time regarding "sensitive perception" under ground and whether "there is light in the bowels of the earth" (*BW* 150–151). This discussion of mineral properties and life underground offers more than philosophical instruction on Cavendish's beliefs about sentient matter. It suggests a fascination with the environments where minerals form and possibly with mines as sites of mineral extraction and labor.

Allusions to gold and diamonds abound in early modern texts, inspired not only by literary precedents, but also by the spoils of colonialism, as Cavendish well knew. Christopher Marlowe's Barabbas invokes "the merchants of the Indian mines, / that trade in metal of the purest mould" (1.1.19–20). John Donne rhapsodizes about "both the Indias of spice and mine" ("The Sun Rising" 17). "O my America, my new found land," Donne exclaims to his mistress, adding, "My mine of precious stones, my empery, / How blest am I in this discovering thee!" (Elegy 8, 27–30). Ben Jonson's Sir Epicure Mammon, soaring on his own eloquence, rolls together the New World and the Bible. "Here's the rich Peru," he cries, "And there within, sir, are the golden mines, / Great Solomon's Ophir" (*The Alchemist* 2.1.2–4). Samuel Chappuzeau in his *History of Jewels, and of the Principal riches of the East and West taken from the relation of divers of the most famous travellers of our age* (englished in 1671, originally published in Geneva in 1665) traces gemstones to their places of origin, stressing the challenges of excavating and buying them. Chappuzeau boasts that his work "shews the ways to those precious mines of *Asia* which hitherto have not been well known, and of those fertile Regions into which our most

Powerful King hath a desire to establish commerce, for the benefit and glory of his subjects" (Preface, np). Without doubt, the voyages of exploration and trade with their accounts of strange peoples, new flora and fauna, and fabulous mines promising infinite wealth fired Cavendish's imagination in *The Blazing World* and elsewhere.[43] We have noted that she modeled her utopian novella on Francis Bacon's *New Atlantis*.[44] Like Bacon, Cavendish not only imagines a society of scientific virtuosi in a remote land, some of whom conduct their research below the earth's surface, but she also plays on the tropes of colonial domination, including ceremonies, chariots, and palaces involving precious stones. Nevertheless, in addition to her participation in the Zeitgeist with its excitement over stolen treasure, I suggest that one source of Cavendish's interest in the underground life of stones may lie closer to home.

Mining was a source of revenue for the Cavendishes. Lead and coal were mined on the Welbeck estates (Whitaker 2002, 323). In the 1660s and 1670s, gunpowder was used to extract tin and copper from mines in nearby Ecton. Later, blue john crystals, a rare form of calcium fluoride known for its eerie glow, were harvested from underground caverns near Castleton (Worsley 2007, 25). On the eve of the Restoration, when extolling the riches of his native land to the King, William Cavendish enumerates "the staple Comodaties of the kingdome, as Lead, Iron, Tin, Cloth, & many More Comodeties of Great valewe," mentioning ores his own family owned and traded (Slaughter 1984, 36). The Peak Country of northwest Derbyshire, made famous by Daniel Defoe, became the locus of mining disputes. As Andy Wood explains, "After the 1570s ... the vague customary laws by which free mining had hitherto been allowed to dominate the lead industry were challenged by wealthy gentlemen and nobles, anxious both to exert control over the industrial workforce and to gain possession of the lead mining industry" (1999, 8). The Cavendishes were among those nobles. As early as 1598, the leadworks of the first earl of Devonshire, William's half-uncle, are mentioned in the accounts of Henry Travice (Folger X.d.428).

---

[43] "But the Spanish Queen, being then wiser than the rest, imployed him [Columbus], and adventured a great Sum of Money to set him forth in his Voyage, which when the Success was according to the Mans Ingenious Brain, and when he had brought the Queen the discovery of Golden and Silver Mines, for the Spanish Pistols, Then other Nations envyed the King of *Spain*, and like a Company of Dogs, which fought for a Bone, went together by the Ears to share with him" (*WO* Y2 v.).

[44] See, e.g., Marina Leslie who notes, "In her utopia, Cavendish will naturalize Bacon's artificial wonders by assimilating both rainbows and precious stones to the charismatic bounty of the Empress herself" (1996, 17).

William himself had conflicts with the miners. In 1634 the king ordered him in his capacity as lord lieutenant to suppress "a multitude" of miners who organized to intercept the king's progress through Derbyshire to Nottingham, hoping to present him with a petition detailing their grievances over the lead tithe; apparently Cavendish failed to disband them (Wood 1999, 236–237). In 1643 he "ignored miners' complaints and began a blockade of the movement of lead ore to Hull, arguing that the trade benefited the parliament" (Wood 1999, 274). In 1649 the miners published a petition in the Leveller newspaper, *The Moderate*, protesting the erosion of their customary rights at the hands of "Great Men" (Wood 1999, xiii). Wood's book describes the political maneuverings by which miners sought to hold their own against the nobles whose lands they mined. Legal records from 1616–1620 show that in the lordship of Ashford, for example, the Cavendishes and their mining tenants were able to forge a "very political, social alliance" (Wood 1999, 245). Similarly, in 1659 the third earl of Devonshire, one of William's relations, reached a compromise with the Youlgreave miners over their rights to work in Meadowplecke Grange (Wood 1999, 21). I suggest that, given her increasing interest in estate management (Whitaker 2002, 322–327), Margaret was aware of mining issues and the genealogies of labor involved in the extraction and production of metals and precious stones.

Is it possible that she would have known about the 'T'Owd man'? This is how miners spoke when they stumbled across evidence of human remains and toil in old mine shafts and caverns. References to him start in 1625, "and as the miners delved deeper, so they encountered him with greater frequency" (Wood 1999, 198). As a figure for the ancestors, 'T'Owd man' acquired supernatural associations, a subterranean spirit alive with the collective memory of generations of prior workers. To what extent might the old man and the worm-men Margaret positions in the center of the earth in tales like "The Travelling Spirit" and *The Blazing World* have a folk origin, in addition to a basis in literary epic? Speculation aside, it is reasonable to surmise that Cavendish's fascination with the subterranean formation of precious metals is grounded partly in the lives of her tenants and not only in fashionable debates about alchemy and the corpuscularian theories of Robert Boyle.[45]

---

[45] See, e.g., Robert Boyle's *An essay about the origine & virtues of gems* (1672) when he tests the properties of "*Tinn-Glass*" by crushing and melting it in iron molds so as to make a "Bullet" (1672, 66). Could the Empress on her naval campaigns in *The Blazing World* be satirizing the way Boyle "weaponizes" gems (*BW* 211)?

This rough overview of some of the literary and historical contexts informing Cavendish's interest in jewels supports Blumenberg's distinction between function and content. The metaphorics of gemstones provide a deceptive appearance of functional continuity: diamonds on Aaron's breastpiece, diamonds on the Empress's buckler. But their content, or meaning, is worlds apart. Aaron's vestments, ordained by God, symbolize his religious authority over the twelve tribes of Israel and depend on a vision of history centered on transcendent intervention. The Empress's "accoutrement," by contrast, results from the sumptuary privileges of the ruling caste and depends on a Machiavellian vision of history (*BW* 132). As the narrator explains, echoing the advice William Cavendish gave to the king upon his restoration: "None was allowed to use or wear gold but those of the imperial race, which were the only nobles of the state; nor durst anyone wear jewels but the Emperor, the Empress, and their eldest son, notwithstanding that they had an infinite quantity both of gold and precious stones in that world" (*BW* 133).[46] The value of the gems derives, neither from scarcity nor religion, but rather from the pragmatics of procuring obedience – dressing for success through intimidation. The text says as much:

> In her left hand she held a buckler, to signify the defence of her dominions; which buckler was made of that sort of diamond as has several different colours; and being cut and made in the form of an arch, showed like a rainbow; in her right hand she carried a spear made of a white diamond, cut like the tail of a blazing star, which signified that she was ready to assault those that proved her enemies. (*BW* 133)

The profusion of bejeweled regalia contributes to the parody of sovereignty performed in *The Blazing World*. The parodic aspects of the novella attest not only to its skeptical questioning of modes of governance but also to the ways that reoccupation works. As Blumenberg observes, "it is possible ... to use historical mimicry in the service of innovation" (*LMA* 93). New answers to old questions can insinuate themselves through parody as well as mimicry. Take, for example, the scene touched on earlier when the Empress declares herself the head of "a congregation of women" and by dint of her "excellent gift of preaching" gains "the extraordinary love of all her subjects" (*BW* 162–163). She worries that "her labours and pains" to keep them on the right path will not prove long-lasting, so she studies "all manners of ways to prevent it" (*BW* 163). After consulting with

---

[46] In his letter to Prince Charles, Newcastle warns that "degrees of Aparell, to Severall Conditions, & callings, is of Great Consequence, to the peace of the kingdome" (Slaughter 1984, 46).

her worm-men, she devises her solution to the problem of defective religion: overwhelming her audiences with manifestations of power. Perhaps she is still wearing her earlier ensemble: a headpiece, coat, and sandals, studded with pearls, carbuncles, gold, and diamonds (*BW* 133). The Empress dazzles, even as the exaggerated opulence of her chapels sparkle with fantasy jewels. Some critics take this moment seriously.[47] They suggest Cavendish is betraying her overweening ambitions and delusions of grandeur, an interpretation they would never extend to Andrew Marvell in "Upon Appleton House" when his fictional double says, "Under this antic cope I move / Like some Great Prelate of the Grove" (591–592). Admittedly, Marvell's speaker is bedecked with leaves and vines, camouflaged in greenery, as he surrenders to nature in a paroxysm of self-effacement. By comparison with Marvell's sophisticated simile, Cavendish's may seem brash and merely vain, but we should not assume that she wears her heart on her sleeve. Both similes mock prelatical finery.

It is possible to interpret the Empress's monopoly on diamonds in terms of Roland Barthes' analysis of the secularization of gemstones. In one of his essays on the semiotics of fashion, Barthes describes the gemstone at its origin as "an infernal object that had come through arduous, often bloody journeys, to leave behind those subterranean caverns where humanity's mythic imagination stored its dead, its damned and its treasures" (2013, 54).[48] Lapidaries in the Middle Ages and well into the sixteenth century described the "virtues" of gems, including their prophylactic powers, drawn not only from subterranean regions (*pace* Barthes) but also from the stars (Evans 1922, 149). Still, Barthes' point stands. He traces the gradual transformation of gems into mere jewelry, trinkets that add style to an ensemble, but also emit "great energy," traces perhaps of their forgotten history (2013, 58). In his words, "Just as the gemstone basically expressed the essentially theological nature of ancient society, so jewellery today … has in one word become *secularized*" (2013, 57). *The Blazing World* has moments that lend themselves to a Barthesian interpretation. For example, when the Empress asks the Duchess (Cavendish's fictional double) "why she did take such delight … in being singular both in accoutrements, behaviour and discourse," the Duchess confesses that it is "extravagant …

---

[47] Prakas interprets *The Blazing World* as "a fictive space of intellectual coercion" (2016, 125). See also Gallagher (1988) and Trubowitz (1992).
[48] Hopkins may be following Barthes' hint here when she argues that in English Renaissance drama jewels "feature on the body not only as adornments but also as scars, marking sites of disruption and trauma and figuring the skin as an eerie site of two-way traffic" (2014, 136).

but yet her ambition being such, that she would not be like others in any thing if it were possible; I endeavour, said she, to be as singular as I can" (*BW* 218). The Duchess fashions her outfits so as to draw notice, affecting a singular style. She tells the Empress she would "rather appear worse in singularity, then better in the mode" (*BW* 218). But while it is tempting to analyze the flaunting of dazzling accessories in terms of Barthesian secularization and even bad taste, I prefer Blumenberg's concept of reoccupation because its emphasis on self-assertion rather than style offers a more comprehensive insight into the ways Cavendish expresses her skepticism, including her parodies of sovereignty.

How, then, is Cavendish's parodic sovereignty a form of reoccupation? What old question is her self-assertion answering?[49] The questions are quite obvious, as I intimated earlier, and occupied many seventeenth-century thinkers: how to govern; how to lead; how to advance a country and inspire loyalty. Her texts, I suggest, betray a disappointment with monarchy and the leadership of the Stewarts in particular. Her sense that the church could use some revamping is also clear. Take, for example, her early poem, "The Ruin of this Island," where the onus for reoccupation is neither gender nor political leadership so much as the vacuum in theological authority. The poem, published alongside her much-discussed atom poems in *Natures Pictures*, is part of a diptych and follows "A Description of an Island," about a happy land before war ravaged it. The poem reveals the disorientation and insecurity that Cavendish experiences as a result of the Civil Wars and asks skeptical questions about God's purposes. It does this by entertaining a set of hypotheses about causes that scramble incompatible forms of providentialism: Homeric, Virgilian, and Christian.

The poem's eclecticism – sampling different theories – fits in with a skeptical approach to the variety of opinions.[50] In the poem's first scenario,

---

[49] Wayne Hudson claims that the identification of key questions is a stumbling block for Blumenberg. Hudson observes that "Blumenberg offers quasi-historical narratives which suggest that something valuable can be learnt if we understand what made the contingent cultural formations we have possible" (2013, 30). He adds, "this is plausible if what we learn is *to change the questions we ask*" (2013, 30). The problem, as he sees it, is isolating a methodology for identifying the questions that signal a structural shift. Hudson concedes that this "structural problem remains unsolved after Blumenberg, as it does after Foucault and after Rorty" (2013, 30). While Hudson may aspire to invent a better methodology that "reformulate[s] transitivity without transcendentalism" (2013, 30), I think Blumenberg's framework captures the skeptical dynamism of Margaret Cavendish's work.

[50] Parageau discusses the affinities of eclecticism and skepticism, citing Diderot, noting that both share an attitude of "prudence" toward the multiplicity of philosophical opinions (2010, 152–153). She argues that "eclectic doubt" like "methodical doubt" forms the first stage of skeptical inquiry (2010, 153).

England suffers thanks to the whims of the gods who turn against the mortals they previously favored. In the second scenario, the Fates – taking a Calvinist line – wonder at this retribution, surprised at the divine ignorance of human doings, "as if the gods did not poor men foreknow" (14):

> For why, said they, if men do evil grow,
> The gods, foreseeing all, men's hearts did know
> Long, long before they did man first create?
> (15–17)

Having expressed their doubts about divine foreknowledge, the Fates now entertain a Manichean theodicy, saying, "If evil power hath gods to oppose, / Two equal deities it plainly shows" (23–24). Then, in a classic Augustinian move, the poem veers towards a free will theology, saying in a rhyming couplet, "It is the mind of man that's apt to range, / The minds of gods are not subject to change" (33–34). But it quickly sidesteps this Arminian danger zone and leaves us with astrological conspiracy:

> Then did the Fates unto the planets go,
> And told them they malignity must throw
> Into this island, for the gods would take
> Revenge on them, who did their laws forsake;
> (35–38)

The gods buck the punishment to the Fates who buck it to the planets who do the dirty work by siphoning off "bad vapors from the earth" (40) and infusing this poison into people's veins.[51] There are Virgilian echoes here as Junonian madness overwhelms the land. Providentialism is under pressure in this poem, tasked with compassing the enormity of historical change. While the poem concludes on a conventional note, that man's disobedience has caused England's troubles, its witty seriousness – treating Christianity as equivalent to pagan religion – undermines its overt moral, exposing the inadequacy of transcendent causes in explaining the situation on the ground. In grappling with old questions about why sudden and seemingly incomprehensible events happen, Cavendish takes an eclectic approach and canvases both old and revived answers, such as the atomism of nearby poems.

The poem is also unusual because in it Cavendish effaces her persona. There are neither self-accusatory nor self-promoting locutions. This helps

---

[51] As *Sociable Letters* 135 and 138 show, Cavendish was intrigued by notions of astrological influence, but disowned them in the end.

us understand Blumenberg's idea of self-assertion as subtle, something more than tooting your own horn. He sees self-assertion as a vital response to the philosophical struggle to understand existence.[52] If Cavendish makes a cameo appearance at all, it is as an allegory of compassion: "Compassion wept, and virtue wrung her hands, / To see that right was banished from their lands" (61–62). Compassion here is a witness and bystander reduced to hand-wringing. She can do nothing but mourn, keening on the sidelines as England goes to hell. If this poem was written during Cavendish's exile in Antwerp or Paris, then the Lucretian trope – an instance perhaps of what Blumenberg calls "the metaphorics of shipwreck" (10) – may have some purchase and may even be overlaid with Shakespearean overtones. Like Shakespeare's Miranda anguished at the distant sight of the foundering ship at the start of *The Tempest*, Compassion in Cavendish's poem may possibly be construed as standing on dry land gazing across the Channel at an England in flames. If so, skeptical impotence has supplanted – reoccupied – Epicurean tranquility. If "The Ruin of this Island" offers no answers to the questions it poses, it nevertheless reveals dissatisfaction with explanations of historical change premised on transcendent interventions. The inadequacies of conventional knowledge expose the need for reoccupation.

In sum, Cavendish's recurrent use of certain image clusters and thematic patterns – for example, the quest for knowledge, neoclassical architecture, the superabundance of jewels – accomplishes the double task of reoccupation: namely, exposing the inadequacy of traditional motifs to the demands of the times while clearing the ground for innovation. This double movement comes about, in Cavendish's case, thanks to her gentle parodic skepticism. She makes fun of philosophers who imagine that perfect knowledge is available if only they have the right instruments: telescopes or microscopes. A close-up look or an anatomy will take you only so far, she insists, and never all the way. As she likes to repeat, "I do not believe, that the subtillest, learnedst, and most practiced Anatomist, can exactly tell all the Interior Government or motions, or can find out all obscure and invisible passages in a man's body" (*PL* 406). Similarly, her fantastical cities mock the aspirations to knowledge exemplified in the old art of memory. Despite the profusion of arches, pillars, and gates, her built environment is surprisingly empty. Hardly anyone navigates its streets and plazas except for the Lady, later turned Empress. She literally reoccupies

---

[52] "Self-assertion is made necessary precisely because of 'finitude'" or "consciousness of contingency," Pavesich explains (2008, 434, 437).

the urban fabric of the Blazing World, inserting herself into the vacant spaces of its pristine memory palaces. As for the gemstones that encrust the robes and dwellings of "the imperial race," these too have a double function: both satirizing the trappings of power and boosting the Empress's fame. Her sparkling aura, alight with diamonds, compounds the mnemonic effects of the architecture, enhancing the Empress's sway over the memory of future readers. Thanks to her skepticism, Cavendish's deft metaphorics capture the epochal changes of her times, including its thrust toward self-assertion.

**

Like Herbert of Cherbury, Cavendish hopes to reform the political world through constant, compulsive writing. The French philosopher, Jacques Rancière, discusses "the political and theoretical space opened by the English Revolution and the political philosophy of Hobbes" (1994, 21), observing that it makes room for the hitherto unheard voices of the poor, the so-called children of the Book. Hobbes, Rancière tells us, is horrified by "the revolution of the children of the Book ... the proliferation of speakers who are outside their place and outside the truth, gathering the properties of the two great bodies of writing lingering within their reach, prophetic epilepsy and mimetic hydrophobia" (1994, 20). Hobbes deplores "the literary and antiquating *hydrophobia* that joins religious *epilepsy* to ruin, through words and phrases, the body of the sovereignty" (1994, 20). Quentin Skinner would presumably agree with Rancière's sense that for Hobbes, "the peril comes from all these floating names, from the multiplicity of homonyms and figures that don't name any real property but find, in their very motion, the means to incorporate themselves anywhere at all" (1994, 21). For Hobbes, the problem with metaphysics is that it produces "words to which no determined idea is attached," a copiousness in the order of knowledge that fuels "the disorder of politics" (1994, 21). As admirers of Hobbes, Herbert and Cavendish would most likely agree with the analysis that "the disorder of politics is strictly identical to a disorder of knowledge" (1994, 21). Like Hobbes, they see their own philosophical and literary productions as efforts to recompose the order of thought, language, and politics. But judging by the reception of their contemporaries, it is arguable that their labors backfire, contributing to the morass of confusing metaphysical discourse rather than clarifying it. Like "the children of the Book," they too struggle with "prophetic epilepsy and mimetic hydrophobia." They too aspire to a "fantastical legitimacy" prompted by a glut of historical reading and religious writing (1994, 20). Despite their aspirations to frame an order of knowledge that will produce political order, they fail to hew to what Rancière calls Hobbes's regime of "royal-empiricism" (1994, 21).[53]

Furthermore, Herbert and Cavendish share the ambition of having their voices heard as literature. Rancière defines "the historic distinctiveness of literature" as "due to a new balance of the powers of language, to a new way language can act by causing something to be seen and heard" (2011, 7). Literature, Rancière observes, has the power to make certain practices visible and intelligible, thereby intervening politically "in the sharing of the perceptible" or in its "distribution," depending on how one translates "le partage du sensible" (2011, 7). For Rancière it follows that literature is not about aesthetic autonomy, but is democratic in its impulse (coinciding here with Wai Chee Dimock). He wants to recuperate aestheticism (predicated on the "indifference" of literature) for a radical egalitarian politics. Taking Flaubert as his example, he defends Flaubert's "sublime elevation" of style as the "dissolution of all order." Contrasting "the classical order of representation" to "literary democracy," he explains that "raising style to an absolute meant firstly pulling down all the hierarchies that had governed the invention of subjects, the composition of action and the appropriateness of expression" (2011, 10–11). Rancière would probably consider Herbert and Cavendish proponents of the classical order of representation, as fully committed to literary hierarchies as to socio-political ones. But I argue first, that the privileging of wit raises style to an absolute that also dissolves order, and second, that as disgruntled outliers in the Stuart regime of the visible, their unedited torrent of words aspires to flood the political landscape, disrupting, if not leveling, it. Rancière might counter that their "will to signify" reveals their ideological allegiance to the "classical representative universe" wedded to rhetorical eloquence and "speech-in-action" (2011, 14). Yet no doubt because they lived through the Civil Wars and the Licensing Act that lifted much censorship, Herbert and Cavendish were swept up in the outpouring of texts that accompanied their country's political turmoil. When Rancière writes of the democracy of literature as "the regime of the world-at-large that anyone can grab hold of ... any reader whatsoever," it is tempting to think, not only of the French nineteenth-century realist novel, but also of

---

[53] Rancière contrasts Hobbes's royal-empiricism – "a theoretical tradition" founded on "an alliance between the point of view of science and that of the royal place" – with Jules Michelet's republican romanticism (1994, 21).

the range of English voices that entered the public fray in the 1640s and later (2011, 13). Rather than treating Herbert and Cavendish as Cavaliers set apart from these events and commenting on them from their exiled *otium*, we should consider their skeptical work in its phantasmagoric abundance as part of the literature of revolution. Although it has taken Cavendish more than three centuries to reach the democratic world of readers she imagined, her words are now redistributing what Rancière calls the regime of the visible as people grab hold of them.

CHAPTER 5

The Enchantments of Andrew Marvell
Skepticism and Taste

What is enchantment? Jane Bennett defines it as a state of wonder marked by an "odd combination of somatic effects" that includes conditions of "exhilaration or acute sensory activity." It involves surprise, disruption, and "a mood of fullness, plenitude, or liveliness, a sense of having had one's nerves or circulation or concentration powers tuned up or recharged" (2001, 5). Overall, it produces "a strange combination of delight and disturbance" (2010, xi). Etymologically, Bennett points out, the word derives from the French, *chanter*, to sing, and hence means "to cast a spell with sounds ... to carry away on a sonorous stream" (2001, 6). Rita Felski develops this definition, associating "the erotic undertow of aesthetic enchantment" with *jouissance* (2008, 53, 60).[1] Felski sees enchantment as the antithesis of skepticism, arguing that the discourse of disenchantment sinks us "ever deeper into the void of a dispiriting, self-corroding skepticism" (2008, 58).[2] Yet, if skepticism is understood as a stance or *mentalité* inviting all manner of compensatory responses, then it follows that skepticism may have enchanting powers: moments when the attention trained on unreliable appearances becomes enamored of their numinous aura, their metamorphic beauties displacing worries about truth.

Marvell's lyric poetry invites us to experience enchantment, understood as a consensual seduction driven by an aesthetic appreciation for the world's surprises: its appearances, sonorities, and entanglements. Inasmuch as Marvell asks readers to join him in falling in love with the world, his lyric poetry confutes Stanley Cavell's views. Falling in love with the world to Cavell means blindness, something that happens, if at all, with one's eyes shut. Cavell is thinking of Wittgenstein's question: "But, if

---

[1] Michael Saler, who champions "the ironic imagination," downplays eroticism, describing enchantment as meaning "both 'delight' in wonderful things and the potential to be placed under their spell, to be beguiled" (2012, 138).
[2] See my Introduction for skepticism's problematic associations with Max Weber's term, disenchantment (*Die Entzauberung*).

you are *certain*, isn't it that you are shutting your eyes in the face of doubt?" Certainty means closing your eyes to doubt. The philosopher, Cavell believes, "pries the lids up with instruments of doubt." In that unblinkered state, the philosopher feels disappointed with the world and dissatisfied with finitude. This leads Cavell to imagine an alternative: blinkered, unphilosophical, but happy. "To live in the face of doubt, eyes happily shut," he declares, shifting into the conditional mood, "would be to fall in love with the world" (1979, 431). Andrew Marvell, however, opens his arms to the world with his eyes wide open and his philosophical mind attuned to skeptical doubt.

Critics have long remarked on the skeptical tone of Marvell's work. Barbara Everett notes "a surprising absence of insistence, rare in an age of dogmatism" (1979, 70). Balachandra Rajan identifies "controlled uncertainty" as the objective (1978, 160), while L. E. Semler finds Sextus Empiricus behind Marvell's lyric, "Mourning," noting the poem's closing move: "I yet my silent judgement keep, / Disputing not what they believe" (1995, 33–34). Takashi Yoshinaka agrees that Marvell's suspension of judgment derives from Pyrrhonist *epoché*; he groups Marvell with John Hales and Joseph Glanvill, both of whom recommended skepticism as a salutary antidote to religious dogmatism (2011, 56).[3] Virtually all critics recognize Marvell's elegant sense of irony and ambiguity, traits often linked to skepticism. Louis Martz, for example, dubs Marvell's style Mannerist because it combines performance and disguise – masques and masks – to create works that are "skeptical, guarded, constrained, ambiguous" (1989, 211).[4] But no one, to my knowledge, has argued that Marvell's philosophical skepticism contributes to the enchanting effects of his poetry.

Philosophical skepticism is never seen as producing enchantment. It is therefore all the more important to recognize that the way skepticism manifests itself in literature is not commensurate with the way it manifests itself in other forms of discourse. It does not express itself as "a subtraction story," demystifying language and stripping it of ornament and figure.[5] Nor does it operate as an instrument of reform, purging idolatrous superstition from language with iconoclastic fervor. Nor does it necessarily

---

[3] Yoshinaka quotes John Hales: "It shall well befit our Christian modesty to participate somewhat of the sceptic" (2011, 65); see *The Works of the Ever Memorable Mr. John Hales of Eaton*, 3 vols (Glasgow: Robert and Andrew Foulis, 1765), ii.42.

[4] In line with Martz, Lobsien links Marvell's skepticism with dissimulation, noting "this is not a quietist's skepticism." Instead, "the final suspense achieved' in "A Drop of Dew," for example, works "as a potential matrix for ways of thinking as yet unexplored" (2010, 254).

[5] See Bennett (2001) and Taylor (2007) on "subtraction stories." See also, e.g., Stark (2001).

engage in mimesis of the new mechanized world picture with its view of matter as *res extensa* governed by mathematical laws. Neither am I suggesting that literature emerges at this time of spiritual and political crisis as a way to reenchant the world, offering its own brand of white magic in order to compensate for or mitigate feelings of loss. The notion that art replaces religion, substituting its own forms of consolation, transcendence, praxis, and sublimation develops much later in the nineteenth century.[6] Similarly, the notion that aesthetic pleasure has depoliticizing effects (as Brecht, for example, thinks) has no purchase in Marvell's case, as the abiding fascination with his shifting political allegiances proves. Instead, I propose that literary engagements with skepticism shift their philosophical focus over the course of a century (1569 to 1681), engaging different theological, linguistic, political, and aesthetic problems, even as they become increasingly secular and enchanting.

Marvell has the distinction of aestheticizing his engagements with skepticism. By aestheticizing, I mean an impulse to transform the object of his contemplation into a work of art characterized by beauty and occasioning aesthetic pleasure. In this Marvell may approximate the man of taste, a novel figure that Giorgio Agamben describes as making its appearance around the middle of the seventeenth century. Agamben describes him as one "who is endowed with a particular faculty, almost with a *sixth sense* – as they started to say then – which allows him to grasp the *point de perfection* that is characteristic of every work of art" (1999, 13). Agamben lifts the phrase from La Bruyère's *Characters,* noting that it implies a portrait of the man of bad taste: "the person who loves what is 'short of the right point or beyond it'" (17). The man of taste, Agamben elaborates, suffers from a split subjectivity even as he cultivates his aesthetic judgment. He distinguishes this figure, essentially a spectator with a refined sensibility, from the artist who is increasingly represented as an eccentric and unbalanced genius. Marvell, of course, occupies both positions, being both artist and spectating arbiter of taste. Yet, Marvell's work is also marked by the struggle to discern his role in the divine plan and his duties as a historical actor. Wittily echoing the closing verses of Marvell's "Upon Appleton House," Marshall Grossman describes this struggle as "the temporal predicament of amphibious humankind, resident in timely and eternal media," thereby indicating that the Marvellian subject suffers from a hybrid theological subjectivity (1998, 201). These forms of divided subjectivity come together in Marvell. The man of taste emerges from,

---

[6] See, e.g., Daniel Bell (1982), Graham (2007), and Saler (2012).

even as he overtakes, the godly amphibian preoccupied with the opacity of providential design. The resulting "temporal predicament" manifests itself in an enchanting skeptical epistemology. Agamben reminds us that aestheticization has a secularizing bent in that it frames experience in terms of private sensations and elite culture. His emphasis on split subjectivity also helps us understand the cultural transition from decorum to taste – a shift from a neoclassical concern with rhetoric, norms, and questions of appropriate style to an interest in aesthetic consciousness and the cultivation of an aesthetic sensibility.[7]

Repurposing Agamben's analysis, this chapter argues that Marvell's aestheticizing skepticism has secularizing effects that engage the sublime and questions of taste even as these paradoxically work to reenchant us. The chapter has four sections: (1) an interpretation of "The Garden," showing how Marvell transmutes the nominalist preoccupation with language and skeptical epistemology into an experience of aesthetic pleasure; (2) an exploration of how the skeptical sublime manifests itself in "On Mr. Milton's *Paradise Lost*" only to flourish in "Upon Appleton House"; (3) a view of Marvell's skeptical, but sublime understanding of history primarily through a reading of his "Horatian Ode"; (4) an analysis of several "spectator" poems, illustrating how Marvell's skeptical persona interrogates his own desire by experimenting with lapses of taste. Overall, the sequence of readings demonstrates the aesthetic pleasures afforded by a skeptical sensibility, even as it tracks the emergence of the aesthete from the godly individual struggling to understand radical historical change.

Enchanting Nominalism

"The Garden," arguably Marvell's most famous lyric after "To His Coy Mistress," has long been singled out for its mysticism and transcendental moves, as well as for its hermetic echoes. Rationality is annihilated, critics tell us, as mind and world blend into an undifferentiated consciousness. Noel Sugimura and Robert N. Watson think skepticism provides the most helpful philosophical context for understanding the cognitive exaltation represented in "The Garden." Sugimura sees the collapse of subject and object into "an unspeakable phenomenological singularity" as evidence of "an extreme scepticism's attack on reason" while coming down "in favour of mind" (2010, 258). Watson sees the speaker as trapped in the mind's "insurmountable dualism," unable to achieve "real intercourse with

---

[7] On the emergence of aesthetic consciousness, see, e.g., Cassirer (1955); Ferry (1993).

nature" such that his "alienation" from the garden "is complete" (2006, 112, 110, 118). Watson goes further, identifying nominalist moments in the poem as "ironic" gestures showing the futility of attempts "to recuperate referentiality itself" (2006, 109). As support, he quotes Herbert of Cherbury on the non-conformity, or incommensurability, of sense-data and perceptions. Marvell may hunger for erotic union with nature, but in the end, he cannot "twist free" from his mind's skepticism (Watson 2006, 111). While I agree that skepticism is central to "The Garden," I find that the tragic view of skepticism – resulting in disconnection from nature, in Watson's case, and nihilistic solipsism in Sugimura's – violates the spirit of the poem.

"The Garden" radiates serenity and contentment. Its dominant emotion is aesthetic pleasure.[8] Insofar as a skeptical epistemology is in play, the overall effect is one of enchantment. Marvell lets the experiential language of perception – taste, touch, color, and sound – guide his journey to the heady pleasures of poetic inspiration. If one accepts the later dating of the poem to 1668 rather than the early 1650s, one can even interpret this account of creative ecstasy as a gentle riposte to Milton's grandiose claims of divine inspiration in *Paradise Lost*. The poem opens by playing on the pastoral trope of retirement, not from the favoritism of the court, but from the world of competition: military, civic, and literary. The detached speaker wonders at the "uncessant labours" of men (3), admitting that he once belonged to their ranks, naively seeking Quiet and Innocence among them: "Mistaken long, I sought you then / In busy companies of men" (11–12). He recounts a change of heart from mistaken seeking to "delicious" experience: "Society is all but rude, / To this delicious solitude" (15–16). The contrast between the rude coarseness of society with its competitive elbowing and the exquisite gustatory pleasures implied in "delicious" isolation support Denise Gigante's claim that the languages of "appetite and aesthetic discernment" converge "in the literary history of taste" (2005, 20). The speaker extolls his love affair with his Edenic garden, praising its "lovely green" and the surpassing "beauties" of its trees: "Fair trees! Wheres'e'er your barks I wound, / No name shall but your own be found" (23–24). The suggestion is that the speaker has access to Adam's perfect language, delving into the essence of each tree and finding the name that corresponds to that essence: the *signatura rerum*, be it of "the palm, the oak or bays" (2). In defense of his arboreal

---

[8] See Lobsien who discusses "the confidence with which it ["The Garden"] points to the power of the aesthetic." She understands the poem's "aesthetic exuberance" and "attention to ... the conditions of its own beauty" as evidence of Neoplatonic structures and motifs (2010, 154).

investigations the speaker observes that the gods in their pursuit of "mortal beauty" (27), Daphne and Syrinx, "Still in a tree did end their race" (28).

Both Joanna Picciotto and Robert Watson interpret these verses as rebukes of Petrarchism and celebrations of immersion in nature, but each takes their analysis in a different philosophical direction. Picciotto emphasizes the innocent pleasures of empiricism:

> By making metamorphosis the goal of the chase, [and] literalizing the laurel as an object of erotic desire, [Marvell] treats the Petrarchan tradition as a lengthy gloss on a vulgar error: a misconstrual of "vegetable Love" as it originally flourished and is now revived in the famous vines, fruits, and grass in which the solitary Adamic wanderer can become ensnared and fall without sin or danger. (2010, 371)

Watson, by contrast, emphasizes the alienation produced by nominalism. He rejects the Adamic interpretation and insists the passage be read ironically. Recalling Orlando's mutilation of the Forest of Arden's trees with Rosalind's name in Shakespeare's *As You Like It*, Watson points out that Petrarchism yields to nominalism in Marvell's verses. What the trees want is to be left alone, their bark unmarked with human names and classifications. He explains,

> Marvell may even be pushing the nominalist mistrust of the categorical functions of language toward post-structuralism, by suggesting that many words presumed to refer legitimately to things rather than delusively to abstractions are still false impositions of the human mind on the material universe. (2006, 109)[9]

Nominalism, in Watson's tragic view, gets in the way of the real, which keeps receding. But language-games in Marvell are neither instruments of empirical insight nor arbitrary webs of signification. They are a source of intellectual and visceral delight because they bring into being a world of uncertainty and possibility whose multiplicity occasions pleasures that are an end in themselves.

The fifth stanza of "The Garden" is a paean to enchantment, as eloquent an expression of falling in love with the world as one is likely to find:

> What wondrous life is this I lead!
> Ripe apples drop about my head;
> The luscious clusters of the vine

---

[9] Watson adds, "The garden begins to look like Lewis Carroll's 'dark wood where things have no names'; Alice stammers, "'I mean to get under the ... under the ... Well, *this*, you know!' putting her hand on the trunk of the tree. 'What does it call itself, I wonder?'" (2006, 109).

> Upon my mouth do crush their wine;
> The nectarine, and curious peach,
> Into my hands themselves do reach;
> Stumbling on melons, as I pass,
> Insnared with flow'rs, I fall on grass.
>
> (33–40)

The sensuality, eroticism, and self-abandonment of the speaker are striking, as are the vitality and agency of the garden's fruits. The grape clusters thrust themselves upon the speaker's palate; the peach and nectarine stretch toward his hands; the melons cross his path, while the flowers ensnare him, bringing him down. Jane Bennett might perceive these gestures of vegetative action as anti-Cartesian in their implications. Bennett's political ecology of "vibrant matter" with its Lucretian and Spinozist antecedents depends on a notion of vitality that she sees as "absolving matter from its long history of attachment to automatism or mechanism" (2010, 3).[10] Yet Marvell's vibrant fruits clearly share more with the beckoning apricots of Sydney's estate in Jonson's "To Penshurst" than with Descartes' *res extensa*. Moreover, his plants are "innocent of their potential theological import," Robert Watson declares, although he concedes that "Marvell tempts readers to pack [fallen meanings] back in" (2006, 111). Watson must count himself among those tempted readers when he says of the falling speaker, "the good life starts looking a lot like death" (2006, 111). On the contrary, blissful union with nature is achieved in a comical because clumsy embrace. Philip Larkin notes "a touch of the ludicrous in the Hulot-like figure of the speaker" when he imagines a stumbling Jacques Tati in the starring role (1979, 152).

If the fifth stanza sings the full consciousness of a "wondrous life" entwined with vibrant matter, the sixth extolls more cerebral pleasures in language that invites philosophical analysis:

> Meanwhile the mind, from pleasures less,
> Withdraws into its happiness:
> The mind, that ocean where each kind
> Does straight its own resemblance find;
> Yet it creates, transcending these,
> Far other worlds, and other seas;
> Annihilating all that's made
> To a green thought in a green shade.
>
> (41–48)

---

[10] Bennett defines vitality as "the capacity of things – edibles, commodities, storms, metals – not only to impede or block the will and designs of humans but also to act as quasi agents or forces with trajectories, propensities, or tendencies of their own" (2010, viii).

The opening adverb, "Meanwhile," alerts us that it is during "the tussle with the melons and grass" that the ecstatic withdrawal transpires (Picciotto 2010, 372). The speaker's experience of nirvana occurs while entangled in vibrant matter. The philosophical difficulties arise in the second and last couplets of the stanza because they evoke a model of cognition that, in typical Marvellian fashion, is both richly allusive and elusive. The metaphor comparing the mind to an ocean is straightforward enough, but the puzzle lies in imagining that mental ocean not as tempest-tossed but rather as a calm and orderly meeting-place of "kinds" and "resemblances" – a medium, furthermore, where free-floating kinds immediately "find" their own resemblances. This enigmatic language has been interpreted in many ways. Daniel Stempel, for example, claims that "Marvell's sharp distinction between that Ocean, the mind, and the solid continental mass of the physical world is Cartesian, not Platonic" (1967, 108). Drawing on Descartes' *Dioptrics*, Stempel sees greenness as an innate idea, rather than a datum furnished by the senses, and so understands "annihilating" as part of Descartes' "method of doubt" (1967, 110). The Platonic view, which Stempel disputes, takes "kinds" to be archetypal Forms that have inferior copies or "resemblances" in the lower world. Yet, it seems odd to think of Plato's forms on the look-out for their mirror images; that sounds more like the myth relayed in the *Symposium* with divided beings looking for their better half – only here there's no delay. Kinds find their resemblances straightaway.

I propose instead that we interpret "kinds" as universals, that is, as general nouns that locate individual instances of themselves, particular "resemblances," in a joyful epistemological encounter. This has the advantage of connecting to the previous act of textual finding in the poem, at the end of stanza 3, when the speaker imagines his arboreal wounding in terms of name-finding, his graffiti confirming the identity of individual trees – a nominalist exercise, as Watson points out. The reunion of kinds and resemblances has a similarly neo-Scholastic flavor for me: grammatical categories creating order out of proliferation. Stephen Hequembourg (2014) prefers to contextualize Marvell's views of language in more contemporary terms: pitting the poet's flaunting of metaphor against Hobbes's fears of ambiguity and John Wilkins's scheme for a universal language prizing univocal meanings. But the sense in stanza 6 that this semantic ordering is occurring inside the speaker's head – the universals meeting and subsuming local versions of themselves – strikes me as the residual traces of late medieval metaphysics. I prefer putting Marvell into play with the neo-Scholasticism in transition of Herbert of Cherbury, anthropomorphizing conformity and consent; resemblances conform to kinds, and kinds consent to union with resemblances.

The third couplet takes this process of intellectual abstraction further, as the mind withdraws into an even more removed happiness. Transcending the marine domain of matching kinds and resemblances, "it creates . . . / Far other worlds, and other seas." The couplet describes the happiness of creativity when the mind is like a little god inventing worlds for its own delectation. Yet this creating mind is also a destroyer, "annihilating all that's made." This seems violent, even dark, but the impression is momentary, heightened only if we ignore the continuation of the line. This continuation – "To a green thought in a green shade" – is at once so luxuriant and ordinary that we understand annihilation as a kind of everyday ecstasy, available to anyone attuned to the life of contemplation. The overall effect is to figure the mind as a decentered cosmos with multiple worlds and oceans, each continually staging encounters of kinds and resemblances, even as the inner creator can silence this cognitive activity and achieve the blissful tranquility of "a green thought in a green shade." Marvell's cosmic imagery broaches the sublime, but then the poet retreats from it; no sooner has he conjured the unknown vastnesses of the human mind, filling us with awe and fear, than he follows it with the homey consolations of pastoral imagery.

The pastoral–philosophical mood continues in stanza 7 when the speaker represents himself as lounging in the garden, "casting the body's vest aside" while his "soul into the boughs does glide" (51–52). He likens himself to a singing bird preening its feathers "till prepared for longer flight" (55). Perhaps this portrait of the artist as a pretty bird gearing up for longer flight is a playful response to Milton's invocation of the muse at the start of *Paradise Lost*. There Milton compares his "advent'rous Song" (13) to a soaring flight, even as he channels the Holy Spirit that "with mighty wings outspread / Dove-like satst brooding on the vast Abyss" (20–21). The 1668 dating of Marvell's poem has the advantage of allowing us to imagine Marvell's silly songbird, vainly occupied in combing "its silver wings" and waving "its plumes" to catch "the various light" (54, 56) as a counterpoint to the sublime seriousness of Milton's brooding spirit. Marvell's prefatory poem to the second edition of *Paradise Lost* also addresses Milton's opening bird imagery:

> At once delight and horror on us seize,
> Thou sing'st with so much gravity and ease;
> And above human flight dost soar aloft
> With plume so strong, so equal, and so soft.

> The bird named from that Paradise you sing
> So never flags, but always keeps on wing.
>
> (35–40)

I hear echoes of "The Garden" in these verses, especially in the word "plumes" and in the contrast between Marvell's sitting bird distracted by his own lovely appearance and the majestic bird "from that Paradise you sing" whose flight "never flags."[11]

The paradise that Marvell describes in the last stanzas of "The Garden" is very different from Milton's: a "happy garden-state / While man there walked without a mate" (57–58). The speaker continues singing the pleasures of delicious solitude, exclaiming, "Two Paradises 'twere in one / To live in Paradise alone" (63–64). For Marvell, paradise is the ecstasy of artistic creation. His garden celebrates the solipsistic delights and temporal aporias of traffic in language – figuration, names, grammar, musicality. It is as if the poet were coming down from a poetic high when he closes the poem in a more conventional garden, admiring "th'industrious bee" that "Computes its time as well as we" (69–70). This last portrait of the artist as a hard-working and humble time-keeper brings the poem to earth, deflating its heady raptures with ordinary delights. Overall, "The Garden" draws a portrait of the meditating artist at one with vibrant matter and enchanted by his own oceanic mind presiding over a teeming dance of kinds and resemblances until he arrives at an even better paradisal place: the nirvana of "a green thought in a green shade."

Sublime Skepticism

Might the sublime qualify as a mode of reenchantment? Bennett would presumably resist this idea since she sees enchantment as premised on wonder, a gentler affect more attuned to observation and contemplation than to the transitory ruptures and raptures of the sublime. Conversely, Felski prizes the shock value of the sublime, its violence and power to disturb rather than enchant (2008, 130). However, I suggest that the sublime has enticing charms when shadowed by skepticism.

As mentioned in the first chapter, the odd synergies of skepticism and the sublime have been theorized. David Sedley, for example, notes that thinkers as diverse as Kant, Paul de Man, Jean-François Lyotard, and

---

[11] Joseph Wittreich, crediting Lawrence Hyman, notes the echo, observing "that to enter into the imaginative world of *Paradise Lost* Marvell reverts to an image he had used in 'The Garden'" (1978, 299).

Stephen Greenblatt have wrestled with this relationship, disagreeing about how it works. Sedley sees skepticism as interfering with the Renaissance economy of historical recovery and empirical discovery premised on wonder, draining its power. The uncertainties of knowledge, exposed by methodical doubt, leave ignorance in their wake – a nescience that incites the sublime. As Sedley puts it, "Whereas the wonderful reaches the frontier of understanding, the sublime plunges the mind into confusion. Knowledge inspires wonder; sublimity thrives on ignorance, the only inspiration available in the modern age of skepticism" (2005, 11). In his view, the threat of skepticism enables the sublime, which he understands as a set of aesthetic responses involving grandeur, intensity, explosiveness, and self-forgetting together with rapt attention. James Noggle agrees that there is "a deep homology" between skepticism and the sublime (2001, viii). For Noggle, the nexus of sublimity and skepticism consists in the desire to escape human finitude and hence in a straining against the limits of language and knowledge. He understands this in terms of a motion of epistemological reversal fraught with power relations. The grandeur of a sublime experience may initially be overwhelming, but then the mind recovers in Kantian fashion, absorbing some of that sublimity, only to use its powers to doubt and ironize the experience. What Noggle calls the sublime economy consists of the sublime's skeptical "erosion of grounded purposive thought in its very effort to secure for thought a transcendent status" (2001, 6).[12] Rhetorical reversals from height to depth and *hypsos* to *bathous* capture this economy in the Augustan satirists that Noggle studies. But they also shed light on Marvell's method and tone, especially the way he initiates a motion toward the sublime only to retreat from any sustained encounter with overwhelming force, instead displacing and disowning it with self-deprecating skepticism. The ending of "The Garden" illustrates this rhetorical reversal and enacts Noggle's sense of the skeptical sublime when it downshifts from nirvana to a flowered sundial.

Noggle argues further that the mitigated skepticism favored by Glanvill and other Restoration thinkers as a way of mediating conflict in fact disguises the threat of a radical skepticism affiliated with the sublime. He notes "skepticism's duplicity" (2001, 19) especially in "the disproportion between the destructive power of its critique of dogmatism and the

---

[12] Elsewhere Noggle defines the sublime aesthetic effect in terms more Lucretian than Kantian as "the proximity that it establishes between absolute precariousness and absolute security – the aesthetic unification of our terror of the ocean storm with our safety on shore" (1996, 612).

modest, constructive method it puts in dogmatism's place" (2001, 17). Noggle thus emphasizes the tentative intellectual consensus built around notions of epistemological probability and the radical doubts this consensus suppresses. "The skeptical sublime," he claims, "appears at moments when upholders of the moderate epistemological order find themselves willing to recognize and articulate the ironies of its operation" (2001, 17). Marvell is attracted to the skeptical sublime. From a skeptical vantage point, he makes intermittent forays into sublime regions.

In his prefatory poem to the second edition of Milton's *Paradise Lost*, Marvell inaugurates the tradition identifying Milton as the originator of the sublime in English literature.[13] In the poem, Marvell has doubts about the sublime and distinguishes his own more modest poetic practice from Milton's. The poem opens with these doubts although they are later allayed. Yet, although he does not aspire to the Miltonic sublime, in poems like "Upon Appleton House" and perhaps even "The Garden," he offers his own version of sublime skepticism. The aesthetic responses inspired by Marvell's lyrics usually feature words like beauty, wonder, and enchantment – terms often contrasted with the fear, horror, and ecstasy associated with the sublime. In Marvell's case, however, beauty and sublimity are not antithetical, *pace* Burke and Kant, but rather come together under pressure from his skepticism.

Marvell's skeptical appraisal of the world can be viciously satirical, as we find in his prose polemics and some of his poems. It can lead to detachment – a word often attached to his tone – or to activism, as his work in Parliament to promote toleration shows. In most of the poems examined in this chapter, Marvell's skeptical investigations test the sublime, broaching aesthetic criteria. Filtered through the prism of doubt, intuitions of beauty and feelings of wonder, enchantment, and ecstasy shift color and mood. Pastoral and Petrarchan conventions buckle. Marvell represents himself as a bystander who aestheticizes what he sees. He adopts the personae of the discriminating critic, the voyeuristic spectator, and the historical witness to explore the confluence of ethics and aesthetics. These skeptical personae engage in hallucinatory games with size, shape, and perspective that owe as much to Sextus's skeptical modes as to political upheaval, literary models or proto-scientific developments.

---

[13] For establishing Milton as the great poet of the sublime, see Edmund Burke, *A Philosophical Enquiry into the Origin of our Ideas of the Sublime and the Beautiful* (1757), Part 2, sections 3, 4, 14 and the treatise's concluding pages in Part 5, section 7.

"On Mr. Milton's Paradise Lost"

Marvell takes up the persona of discriminating critic and aesthete most clearly in "On Mr. Milton's *Paradise Lost*," the poem he wrote for the second edition of Milton's epic in 1674. In it he represents himself as a skeptical reader gingerly weighing the sublimity of Milton's epic. He mobilizes "the 'sublime' as most nearly resolving the uncertainties explored in this tribute" (Von Maltzahn 2001, 167). The poem begins with his fears on Milton's behalf that *Paradise Lost* will not live up to its author's hopes and ambitions. Midway, however, the poem pivots as Marvell realizes that he was wrong to be worried; the epic surpasses his highest expectations, as he finds it awe-inspiring and sublime.[14] In the course of his praise, Marvell defends Milton's "Biblical poetics," as Joseph Wittreich puts it, thereby identifying "the aesthetic system that points the way to Milton's achievement" (1978, 291–292).[15] His defense addresses issues of poetic style and its components – tone, rhyme, decorum – going so far as to thematize problems of style given the choices of the poem at hand.

Critics have discussed this poem from various angles, but most agree with Judith Scherer Herz that it is "as odd a commendatory poem as ever accompanied its master from press to bookstall" (1978, 244). While Andrew Shifflet may be right that there is both Jonsonian and Senecan precedent for praise poems that open in a mood of skeptical doubt but then shift to a more conventional encomiastic mode, it strikes me that Marvell's pose as a man of taste evaluating the aesthetics of style, while not unprecedented, is nevertheless "odd," to echo Herz. Shifflet thinks that treating the poem "as a document in the history of poetic taste" is merely "interesting," absent its association with a Stoic tradition of political resistance. Yet aesthetics cannot be isolated from politics. Marvell's critical stance is as informed by notions of poetic beauty and literary enchantment as it is by political commitments and circumstances.[16]

The poem opens with the verb "beheld," signaling Marvell's position as spectator of a panoptic view of *Paradise Lost*. In what Kenneth Gross

---

[14] "Although at first skepticism threatens to erode rather than uphold grandeur, as 'On *Paradise Lost*' grows in length skepticism grows in value. Marvell invests in skepticism as a cognitive property and develops it in order to vitalize the sublimity he celebrates" (Sedley 2005, 125).

[15] Wittreich contrasts "Biblical poetics" with "the emerging neoclassical aesthetic," observing that Marvell's poem sets the parameters of much future Milton criticism (1978, 297).

[16] Nicholas von Maltzahn distinguishes between the "rational" and the "pathetic" sublime, associating the latter with the Restoration's aestheticization of heroism (2001, 160). He sees Marvell invoking "the rational sublime" in "On Mr. Milton's *Paradise Lost*" (2001, 170).

describes as a "dramatic and visionary scene of reading" (1989, 170), Marvell sees arrayed before him the poet, the book itself and an epitome of its contents before introducing his misgivings:

> When I beheld the poet blind, yet bold,
> In slender book his vast design unfold,
> Messiah crowned, God's reconciled decree,
> Rebelling angels, the forbidden tree,
> Heaven, hell, earth, chaos, all; the argument
> Held me a while misdoubting his intent,
> That he would ruin (for I saw him strong)
> The sacred truths to fable and old song
> (So Sampson groped the Temple's post in spite)
> The world o'erwhelming to revenge his sight.
>
> (1–10)

Marvell misdoubts Milton's intent, a word Nigel Smith glosses as "suspicious of; fearing" (2007, 183). He is afraid that Milton will "ruin" Christian truth for two reasons that Marvell renders as one. The first is aesthetic; including "fable and old song" may be a problem, presumably of decorum. The second is psychological; the poet may not be detached enough to do justice to his theme. Bent on "revenge" like Samson, his "spite" may be too "strong" and bring the whole artistic edifice crashing down. Smith points out that this is "the first instance in the tradition of comment associating Samson with Milton himself" (2007, 183). Marvell worries that rage and bitterness will spoil the *ataraxia* – the serenity of mind and skeptical detachment – that he deems indispensable to a poetic project of this kind.

Yet he soon finds his misgivings unwarranted, although now new worries intrude regarding audience reception:[17]

> Yet as I read, soon growing less severe,
> I liked his project, the success did fear;
> Through that wide field how he his way should find
> O'er which lame Faith leads Understanding blind;
> Lest he perplexed the things he would explain,
> And what was easy he should render vain.
>
> (11–16)

---

[17] Speaking of Restoration audiences, Von Maltzahn notes that Marvell's "larger strategy" in this poem "is to intimate Milton's evocations of transcendence to a sceptical audience, while reserving his own judgement and proclaiming instead the success of Milton's sublime style" (2001, 167).

Marvell portrays himself in the act of reading. "Severe" and skeptical at first, he gradually warms up, liking Milton's project, though "the success did fear," a fraught phrase, thanks largely to the ambiguity of the word success, which can mean consequences (as in succession), aesthetic felicity, and applause. Could Marvell be admitting to jealousy? Is he masking his envy under the guise of an impartial judge? In an elegant imitation of Milton's own way of playing off the end-stopped line against its enjambment, it turns out, no, that's not what he means. We breathe a sigh of relief, glad that Marvell is redirecting, if not preempting, an ungenerous response. Instead, he voices a concern both aesthetic and theological. Echoing the last lines of *Paradise Lost* in which Adam and Eve "with wand'ring steps and slow" have to make "their solitary way" across the "World ... before them," Marvell pictures Milton from a similar vantage point as a fallen man finding his way "through the wide field" where faith and understanding stumble. This theological misgiving – that Milton has bitten off more than he can chew – translates into a worry about Milton's stylistic choices. What if he has "perplexed" and made more difficult "the things he would explain"? That would show a tin ear, an inability to calibrate his rhetorical mode to the demands of the situation. What if he renders easy things vain, thereby trivializing important, albeit obvious, truths? Marvell is conscious here of what could go wrong in Milton's poem. These hypothetical failures of decorum would be unfortunate lapses of taste.

The next stanza confirms Marvell's intense interest in questions of taste and in the delicate policing they involve. He takes a swipe at hack poets in general, but also at John Dryden who turned *Paradise Lost* into an opera, *The State of Innocence and the Fall of Man* (with Milton's permission, according to John Aubrey):

> Jealous I was that some less skilful hand
> (Such as disquiet always what is well,
> And by ill imitating would excel)
> Might hence presume the whole creation's day
> To change in scenes, and show it in a play.
>   (18–22)

Marvell feels proprietary about Milton's poem, fearing poor imitations and presumptuous adaptations. He deems it in bad taste to take an infinite work of art of "vast design" and reduce it to an entertainment, a play with scenes – high culture traduced by popular culture.

At this point, the poem pivots, as Marvell addresses Milton directly, *volta* and apostrophe converging:

> Pardon me, mighty poet, nor despise
> My causeless, yet not impious, surmise.
> But I am now convinced, and none will dare
> Within thy labours to pretend a share.
> Thou hast not missed one thought that could be fit,
> And all that was improper dost omit:
> So that no room is here for writers left,
> But to detect their ignorance or theft.
>
> (23–30)

Marvell apologizes for having mistrusted Milton's capacities and taste, ascribing his doubts to an excess of piety. "I am now convinced," he declares, implying that he lacked conviction earlier. He then tries to sum up the qualities that distinguish *Paradise Lost*, as if he were deducing criteria of excellence from it. He starts with fitness and propriety, conventional standards, but goes on to majesty, gravity and ease:

> That majesty which through thy work doth reign
> Draws the devout, deterring the profane.
> And things divine thou treats of in such state
> As them preserves, and thee, inviolate.
> At once delight and horror on us seize,
> Thou sing'st with so much gravity and ease;
>
> (31–36)

The criteria of excellence include sublimity – "delight and horror" – gauged by reader response.[18] But they also include a kind of purity. The notion that Milton "preserves" things divine and keeps himself "inviolate" in the course of treating them suggests magisterial distance.[19] "Inviolate" connotes isolation and an absence of contamination – perhaps from the

---

[18] See Von Maltzahn: "This recalls a passage from Lucretius – *'divina voluptas / percipit atque horror'* – where that author had praised Epicurus, and the testimonial is the more striking if returned to its original context, where Lucretius had celebrated Epicurus as a writer who brings light out of darkness. When Marvell responds readily to the 'gravity and ease' of Milton's song it is not therefore as a technique alone but as a way of evoking 'delight and horrour' as a means to an end, the sublime of the epic's revelation" (2001, 168). With this phrase, then, Marvell evokes the Lucretian sublime (Porter 2016, 466). Norbrook discusses the paradoxical synergies of Longinus and Lucretius for Puritans at mid-century and later, showing how these classical texts underwrite a radical and "anticourtly sublime." He explains that "Marvell's poem ... points to an engagement with a specifically English and politicized reception of Longinus" even as it is "responding to Lucretian elements in the Miltonic sublime" (2010).

[19] Wittreich accuses Marvell of trying to normalize Milton's poem, stripping it of "its political and religious radicalism" (1978, 298). Insofar as Wittreich's charge hits home, might this not be partly

Samson-like emotions that Marvell feared might ruin the poem's bold design. If so, this implies that ataraxia – the detached tranquility prized by epicureans and skeptics alike – has enabled the poem's sublime grandeur.[20] Marvell's awe expresses itself in questions: "Where couldst thou words of such a compass find? / Whence furnish such a vast expense of mind?" (41–42) He repeats the adjective "vast," as if at a loss for words, even as he praises the cosmic register of "words of such a compass."

After comparing Milton's prophetic powers to those of Tiresias, he returns to the bad taste of "town-Bayes" and other "tinkling" rhymers. Marvell seems to be continuing his role as a literary arbiter, laying down norms of taste when suddenly, in a twist of self-recognition, he turns his judicious eye upon himself and includes himself among the rhymers he has castigated:

> Well mightst thou scorn thy readers to allure
> With tinkling rhyme, of thine own sense secure;
> While the town-Bayes writes all the while and spells,
> And like a pack-horse tires without his bells:
> Their fancies like our bushy points appear,
> The poets tag them, we for fashion wear.
> I too transported by the mode offend,
> And while I meant to praise thee must commend.
> Thy verse created like thy theme sublime,
> In number, weight, and measure, needs not rhyme.
>
> (45–54)

Although a consummate writer of rhyming couplets, as the poem shows, Marvell disparages rhyme as if it were a debased way to "allure" readers. Compared to a "pack-horse" whose pace would flag without his "bells," the town poet follows "fashion," adopting prevailing "fancies." "Transported by the mode," Marvell follows suit, a dupe to trends. Milton stands apart thanks to his "theme sublime," which ordered like God's creation "in number, weight, and measure, needs not rhyme." Marvell posits two orders of poetry here: a sublime prophetic labor that makes its own rules versus entertainment attuned to commercial tastes and easy listening. Having opened the poem in a skeptical and arguably haughty frame of mind, he closes it with the modesty topos, counting himself among the insecure and offending poetasters.

---

due to the speaker's transcendent vantage point, itself perhaps developed in homage to Milton's prophetic voice?

[20] See Porter on "the ataraxic sublime" (2016, 55).

"Upon Appleton House"

"Upon Appleton House" is described as "one of the most sophisticated works of the most sophisticated poet of the English Baroque" (Warnke 1978, 243). It is often acknowledged as sublime. Derek Hirst and Steven Zwicker, for example, say the poem "makes sublime ... the imperfection, the incompleteness, and the contingency of this world," in effect agreeing with Sedley's sense that uncertainty inspires sublimity (2012, 40). I argue that Marvell's imaginative play with skeptical modes in "Upon Appleton House" contributes to the atmosphere of contingency that permits the achievement of sublime poetic heights. Marvell works through uncertain appearances, discrepant proportions, and paradox to destabilize perception and stage fugitive moments of ecstatic melding with the natural world. These hallucinatory effects depend on the power of the mind to take aesthetic pleasure in doubt-inducing experiences.

The poem opens with praise of Appleton House's architectural proportions by ringing the changes on disproportions physical and ethical. Even as it compliments Lord Fairfax for the sobriety and modesty of his dwelling, the poem, like Donne's "The Relic," flashes forward to a hypothetical "after age" when admirers will visit the site "in pilgrimage." The poem predicts they will marvel at the disproportion between the monumental stature of the heroic owners and the "dwarfish confines" of their house. A series of hyperbolical figures underscores the contrast between the Master's grandeur and his humble home, culminating in one of the poem's characteristic gestures: a fluidity of shape and animation of matter that together make the contours of things both uncertain and erotically charged in their possibilities: "But where he comes the swelling hall / Stirs, and the square grows spherical" (51–52). The personification of the servile hall accommodating itself to the rotund "magnitude" of its Master is far more playful than Sextus in his wildest dreams.[21] Yet Sextus's dry dicta – "Objects appear dissimilar depending on moving or being at rest. Things which we see as still when we are stationary seem to us to move when we sail past them" (1994, 29) – contain the potential for Einsteinian adventures in relativity and other perceptual illusions.

The games with proportion continue throughout the poem resulting in hallucinatory images that gesture at, but often fall short of the sublime. "And now to the abyss I pass," the speaker announces in stanza 47, signaling a transition from the focus on Fairfax's career and history to his own tour of the sights in the estate's garden. The word, "abyss," has

---

[21] T. S. Eliot called the image "absurd" and "unintentionally ridiculous" (1975, 165).

sublime connotations, but these are quickly dispelled by the playfulness of the disproportionate similes that ensue:

> And now to the abyss I pass
> Of that unfathomable grass,
> Where men like grasshoppers appear,
> But grasshoppers are giants there:
> They, in their squeaking laugh, contemn
> Us as we walk more low than them:
> And, from the precipices tall
> Of the green spires, to us do call.

The squeaking laughter of the giant grasshoppers subverts the sublime vista of "the precipices tall / Of the green spires." Grasshoppers were a favorite allegorical topos of Cavalier poets, but critics agree that Marvell subverts Cavalier practice here by making the insect menacing and contemptuous. Either way, the grasshopper is interpreted as a political hieroglyph (Marcus 1986, 247). I suggest instead that the teasing grasshoppers are like Montaigne's cat, whose viewpoint Montaigne may speculate about, but never presume to inhabit. "When I play with my cat, who knows if I am not a pastime to her more than she is to me?" Montaigne asks in his skeptical essay, the "Apology for Raymond Sebond" (II.12.331). Cats and men may trade places like grasshoppers and men in a disorienting world.

Yet Marvell does not dwell on the vantage point of the grasshoppers on their vertiginous perch. Instead he revels in perceptual uncertainty, pursuing the sublime conceit of deep, oceanic grass with its biblical echoes rippling from Exodus to Isaiah and beyond:

> To see men through this meadow dive,
> We wonder how they rise alive.
> As, under water, none does know
> Whether he fall through it or go.
>   (377–380)

Rapt in wonder, "we" (perhaps speaker and reader) watch the men's fluid movements and fusion with nature. Their emergence resurrected and reborn recalls the disorientation of immersion in deep water. This wondrous sensation converges with what Rosalie Colie calls "the unknowing which is the poem's principal condition" (1970, 101).[22]

---

[22] Glenn Most understands wonder as a precursor of the sublime (2002, 105). See Most for a historical account of the sublime as an emotion and for its increasing identification "with the subject who responds to it rather than with the object that seems to cause it" (2002, 113).

This skeptical unknowing – "none does know" – gives way to "the tawny mowers" who tower over the fields in the foreshortened vision of the speaker who sympathetically identifies with the small birds nesting hidden in the tall grass. The mowers "seem like Israelites to be, / Walking on foot through a green sea" (389–390), but not for long, as they mow down the birds and turn the meadows into a red sea "quilted o'er with bodies slain" (422). The slaughter is not planned, however, and comes about thanks to an uncanny conjunction of contingent forces:

> With whistling scythe, and elbow strong,
> These massacre the grass along:
> While one, unknowing, carves the rail,
> Whose yet unfeathered quills her fail.
> The edge all bloody from its breast
> He draws, and does his stroke detest;
> Fearing the flesh untimely mowed
> To him a fate as black forbode.
> (393–400)

An "unknowing" mower initiates the causal chain of events, even as he tries to undo it: pulling out the blade from the unfledged bird's breast, detesting his own stroke, fearing the fateful consequences.

In enters Thestylis, a minor character from Virgil's second eclogue. She breaks the poem's narrative frame and jolts us into the present of our reading experience by calling out the poet/narrator (the "he" has an indexical purchase on Marvell's poetic persona) and exploiting his simile, even as she seizes the dead bird like a Machiavellian occasion:

> When on another [rail] quick she lights,
> And cries, 'He called us Israelites;
> But now, to make his saying true,
> Rails rain for quails, for manna, dew.' (405–408)

Virgilian and biblical imagery conjoin with a double time scheme uneasily layering the temporality of the estate tour with an embedded character's meta-commentary on the literary device in which she figures so as to interrupt the reader's lived present. This aesthetic sleight of hand passes as a quasi-historical explanation, suturing the gap between an accident committed by an unwitting mower with a conscience and an intentional political massacre of innocents. It is hard not to hear political overtones in these stanzas juxtaposing a reluctant agent and a bloodthirsty opportunist, as if contrasting Fairfax with those who swept in in his wake. Yet the sanguinary opportunist who glibly musters biblical sayings in post-facto justification of her deeds is aestheticized – triply distanced thanks to gender, allegory, and literary allusion. Marshall Grossman observes that "the poem first presents the death of the rails as contingent, but Thestylis's comic apology re-presents it as destined." The stanza thus shows "the struggle for authority between author and poetic creation," dramatizing "the tension between individual choice and providential destiny" (1998, 215). The Thestylis episode, in other words, offers secular and providential interpretations of a historical event mediated through an aestheticized irony that savors of skepticism.

The narration moves on to the pastoral pleasures of the mowers and their female mates, even as it monumentalizes the hay bales in terms at once sublime and skeptical:

> We wond'ring in the river near
> How boats among them safely steer.
> Or, like the desert Memphis sand,
> Short pyramids of hay do stand.
> And such the Roman camps do rise
> In hills for soldiers' obsequies.
>
> (435–440)

In thrall to the tricks of the eye detailed by Sextus, the narrator confuses field and stream, imagining boats steering among the hay bales, as susceptible to his own poetic turns of phrase as to the fluid sights before him. The hay bales acquire a nearly sublime resonance with the comparison to Egyptian pyramids, but the adjective "short" undercuts the simile's grandeur. Still, the poet persists in seeing the hay bales as sublime commemorations for the dead like Roman "obsequies."

These games with size and disproportion develop into metaphysical conceits in stanza 58 and become paradoxes by stanza 60, poetic figures often associated with skepticism and later frowned on by the likes of Samuel Johnson and Joseph Addison as lapses in taste.[23] In stanza 58, the aestheticizing is so extravagant – a quicksilver succession of four

---

[23] See Rosalie Colie, "The Skeptic ... naturally expresses himself in paradox" (*Paradoxia Epidemica* 1966, 117). Coining the phrase "metaphysical poets," Johnson describes their wit "as a kind of *discordia concors*; a combination of dissimilar images, or discovery of occult resemblances in things apparently unlike.... The most heterogeneous ideas are yoked by violence together; nature and art are ransacked for illustrations, comparisons, and allusions ... though he [the reader] sometimes admires, is seldom pleased" (Rumrich 2006, 740). Addison condemns "the Taste of most of our *English* Poets, as well as Readers" as "extremely *Gothick*," decrying the fondness for ornament and "the Extravagances of an irregular Fancy" (Robert Allen 1970, 193–194).

similes – that the reader's memory is tested, as the object of comparison is nearly lost:

> They seem within the polished grass
> A landskip drawn in looking-glass.
> And shrunk in the huge pasture show
> As spots, so shaped, on faces do.
> Such fleas, ere they approach the eye,
> In multiplying glasses lie.
> They feed so wide, so slowly move,
> As constellations do above.
>
> (457–464)

Who can remember the cows when dazzled with a mirrored painting, a spotted face, fleas under magnification, and the wheeling constellations? The mind struggles to forge analogical links, the exercise of yoking microcosm and macrocosm verging on failure. David Sedley might argue that the nexus of skepticism and sublimity consists in precisely this tension between fragmentation and infinity. The mind's inability to compass the object of contemplation together with its demand for comprehension produces a sublime event predicated on disproportion (2005, 151). Yet here, the homeliness of the tenor, the grazing cows, restrains the sublime tremor of the stanza.

Stanza 59 signals a shift as sluicegates upriver are opened, flooding Nun Appleton's fields. The speaker reiterates the transition in stanza 60, resorting to paraleipsis – "let others tell the paradox" – to distance himself from the string of paradoxes that follow, which describe a topsy-turvy world where fish travel on land and "boats can over bridges sail" (477). "Retiring from the flood," Marvell's persona takes "sanctuary in the wood," a hallucinatory experience of intoxicating sensuality that dominates the last third of the poem and is relayed in a dizzying array of vocal tones: often glossed as empiricist, historical, allegorical, apocalyptic, and erotic, but seldom as comical, skeptical, and sublime (481–482). Not least among its surprises is that this poetry – which vies with Rimbaud's and Whitman's in its unleashed imagery and unabashed confessionalism – consists of tidy eight-line stanzas in rhyming couplets of iambic tetrameter, a comical incongruity.[24]

Consider, for example, the liminal *jouissance* of the sequence that begins: "Thus I, easy philosopher, / Among the birds and trees confer"

---

[24] For a different sense of how the stanzaic "little squares" work thematically, see Grossman 1998, 206.

(561–562). Ensconced in the shrubbery in a puckish mood,[25] he imitates bird calls, channeling the remnants of the perfect language spoken in Eden:

> Already I begin to call
> In their most learned original:
> And where I language want, my signs
> The bird upon the bough divines.
> (569–572)

This oneness with nature continues as a kind of ecstatic surrender full of erotic provocations: "oak leaves me embroider all" and "ivy, with familiar trails, / Me licks, and clasps, and curls, and hales" (587, 589–590). Likening himself to "some great prelate of the grove," wearing a leafy "antic cope" (591–592), he finds himself "languishing with ease" and thanks the breezes for cooling his "panting brows" (593, 596), apostrophizing them:

> And unto you cool zephyrs thanks,
> Who, as my hair, my thoughts too shed,
> And winnow from the chaff my head.
> (598–600)

As if the winds were threshing his mind, letting superfluous thoughts fly away, our easy philosopher arrives at a higher state of consciousness, freed from mundane cares, even as he bids the "woodbines" to bind him, the "brambles" to "chain" him, and the "courteous briars" to "nail" him through (609, 615–616).

This masochistic fantasy of vegetal ravishment turns out to be a ruse of safety, protecting our speaker from the aggressions of Beauty:

> How safe, methinks, and strong, behind
> These trees have I encamped my mind;
> Where Beauty, aiming at the heart,
> Bends in some trees its useless dart.
> (601–604)

The image of the speaker crouched in the forest ducking Beauty's shafts has proved irresistible to critics. Could Marvell be repurposing Milton's fulminations in the Anti-Prelatical tracts? After all, he has just likened himself to a "Prelate of the grove" camouflaged with an "antic cope" of oak leaves and ivy. If so, he may be remembering Milton's attacks on the

---

[25] See *A Midsummer Night's Dream* 3.1.107–111.

Bishops' excesses in language and ceremonial trappings as manifestations of inward deformity.[26] In accusing them of stylistic abominations like "pamper'd metaphors" and "fantastic ... flashes," Milton thunders: "They seek the dark, the bushie, the tangled Forrest, they would imbosk" (*YP* 1, 568–569). Could Marvell's alter ego be playfully embracing these violations of decorum, happily hiding out from the strictures of the world of Beauty? If so, Milton's condemnation of excess as indecorum is transmuted here into a concern with taste. As Ernst Cassirer might see it, Marvell's persona is dodging the neoclassical aesthetic associated with Descartes' clear and distinct ideas and opting instead for a new way of understanding aesthetic consciousness associated with inexactness, ambiguity, and problems of delicacy associated with taste.[27]

By shielding himself from Beauty (in the neoclassical sense), the speaker betrays his attraction to the "pleasures" of bosky excesses in dubious taste (652). Imploring the vines and thorns to "stake" him down, he shuns Beauty and seeks capture by nature (624). Indeed, the easy philosopher finds Beauty's dart "useless" compared to the joys afforded by camouflage (604). The entangling world enables concealment, blurring the shapes of bodies. Even the receding waters in the flooded fields partake of perceptual ambiguity, described in visual terms that Sextus would have appreciated: "Where all things gaze themselves, and doubt / If they be in it or without" (637–638). Fluid conditions, uncertain contours, and retreats from decorum incite skepticism.

The speaker's indulgence in sensory doubts and flights from Beauty abruptly end when he descries a real beauty, "the young Maria" walking in the gardens in the twilit evening (651). He describes her in hyperbolical terms as "the law ... her age's awe" who causes the sun "in blushing clouds" to conceal himself (655–656, 664). Piling on sublime similes, he ascribes to her a quasi-apocalyptic power: "by her flames, in heaven tried, / Nature is wholly vitrified" (687–688). The prophesied vitrification of the world's last days (Rev. 4:6 and 15:2) may be sublime, but it is a far cry from the hospitable greenery and "velvet moss" that our poet reveled in moments prior (594). Maria's presence brings the poem back full circle to

---

[26] See Kranidas 2005.
[27] See his chapter 7, especially the section on "Taste and the trend toward subjectivism," in which Cassirer compares the neoclassical aesthetic of Boileau's *L'Art Poétique* (1674) with Bouhours' *La manière de bien penser dans les ouvrages de l'esprit* (1687), understood as a precursor of Hume's skeptical account of taste. Bouhours champions an "ideal of *inexactness*" and an "art of indirection," defending "the ambiguous" so as to evoke "the region of aesthetic illusion" requiring "a contrast, a distribution of light and shade" (1955, 301–302).

the Fairfax family, its history and future in a series of stanzas much glossed by critics and whose occasional lapses of taste we will later address.

When the meditation on the Fairfax estate ceases, we are suddenly returned to the present – after sunset at a place near the river:

> But now the salmon-fishers moist
> Their leathern boats begin to hoist;
> And, like Antipodes in shoes,
> Have shod their heads in their canoes.
> How tortoise-like, but not so slow,
> These rational amphibii go!
> Let's in: for the dark hemisphere
> Does now like one of them appear.
> (769–776)

The speaker seems to be accompanied, sharing the disconcerting experience with another. "Let's in," he says, addressing us, his complicit readers, or perhaps Maria standing silently beside him.[28] This intimate moment is tinged with protective affection. The companionable gesture, caught in two small words, offsets the skeptical and sublime grandeur of the poem's concluding stanza. Our perceptions are destabilized and our certainties fractured, as we try to visualize the fishermen and the inhabitants of the earth's underside half hidden in convex vessels like tortoises or "rational amphibii." As Stephen Hequembourg observes, the closing of the poem reveals "the free play of radical metaphor ... as the foundational mode of orienting ourselves in the world," as even its last word is equivocal (2014, 110). *Appears* "means both *to come into being* and also *to seem like*" (2014, 109), thereby merging "seeing and *seeing as*, in the language of Martin Heidegger or the late Ludwig Wittgenstein ... into a single, hazy act" (2014, 110). The ambiguity of "appear" together with the triple comparison may make the mind stagger, but it neither deflates nor subverts the sublimity of the cosmic spaces intimated in "the dark hemisphere." This sublime phrase with its planetary view of the gathering dusk is allowed to resonate as the poem's final note, closing the long day at Nun Appleton with a sense of mortality and cyclical time in an immense universe.

---

[28] The question arises: is it legitimate to elide the sound of the *s* so that one hears "Let's sin" as a "harmonic" undertone (to borrow Theodore Leinwand's term, 2016) to the more innocent, typographical meaning? If so, then perhaps Maria is more clearly the addressee. Consider Hirst and Zwicker's "harmonic" reading of "The young *Maria* walks tonight" (651). "Could the poet have been unaware of the shocking pun?" they ask, adding "the figure of night-walking, a seventeenth-century synonym for prostitution, concentrates the sexual tensions of the entire scene" (2012, 53).

Aestheticizing Kairotic Time

If Marvell broaches the sublime at discrete moments in "Upon Appleton House," he also exploits the perceptual uncertainties that incite skeptical doubt, recreating the instability of the observer's sensory experience (Hirst and Zwicker 2012, 47). This dialectical relay I'm calling sublime skepticism bears upon Marvell's investigations into the intersections of secular and kairotic time. I borrow these terms from Charles Taylor's *A Secular Age* (2007). Secular time, in Taylor's definition, is ordinary time when one damn thing happens after another; he equates it to Walter Benjamin's "empty, homogeneous time." Taylor contrasts this with "higher times" that "introduce 'warps' and seeming inconsistencies in profane time-ordering" (2007, 55). One subset of these higher times is kairotic time, which manifests itself in "knots" or "moments whose nature and placing call for reversal." Taylor points out that revolutions "are understood by their heirs and supporters as such kairotic moments" (2007, 54). In much of his work, Marvell is inquiring (in a zetetic way) whether he is living through some such knot or warp. These inquiries require him to think and observe from the sidelines.

Marvell's exploration of the phenomenology of impartial witness is often neglected in favor of psychoanalysis.[29] The way Marvell positions his persona at the margins of a scene to gaze at a central object, person or tableau has been described as voyeurism, the stance of a neurotic or peeping Tom or worse, a flasher hiding in the bushes only to pop out in a spasm of "self-display" (Hirst and Zwicker 2012, 50, 112). At the risk of sanitizing this entertaining portrait of Marvell's poetic persona, I interpret the figure of the spectator as usually engaged in exercises of skeptical judgment and aesthetic discrimination. Assailed by doubt and conflicting emotions, he copes by standing back and assessing a fluid situation by rational means. Kenneth Gross understands this stance as "more likely derived from prophetic and apocalyptic literature, where the alienated reader and speaker are set to watch the conflict between the false visions of history and the true, providential design of God" (1989, 174). In writing about Marvell's prefatory poem to Milton's epic, Gross refers to the speaker as "a witness." Similarly, Grossman understands Marvell's acts of witness as interrogations of providential design, "for the poet on the

---

[29] See, for example, Victoria Silver on "the real ambivalence of the Marvellian green world, where after the fashion of psychoanalytic parapraxis, errant incongruities are actual and meaningful but apparent oppositions merely specious" (2001, 51).

borderline is at once a historical subject and the subject of history" (1989, 207). Marvell's historical spectator, however, is also a skeptic and an aesthete. He looks at both sides of the question (*in utramque partem*) and weighs the pros and cons in an effort to assess the moral beauties of each side. To better understand his dilemma, he adopts an impartial viewpoint. But Marvell is nothing if not an ironist, virtually all critics agree, so he is aware of the extent to which impartiality is a ruse – an aspirational ideal perhaps but hardly within reach of ordinary mortals. His skepticism about impartiality notwithstanding, he likes to try out various poses in that vein – riffs on the detached observer sifting through confusing data in search of a coherent hypothesis. This posture, which David Carroll Simon (2015) describes as a kind of nonchalance or carelessness, is not as visible in the satires or in Marvell's prose polemics where his commitments are brandished with passionate intensity even when he purports to speak from the sidelines. But in the lyric poetry, one might say, borrowing Peter Sloterdijk's terms, that Marvell's "observing ego" struggles with his "position-taking ego," its ascendance fluctuating in response to literary and historical circumstance (2012, 18). So while the guise of impartial spectator may be intermittent and occasional, it is important because it brings Marvell's phenomenological acuity to bear on his ethics and aesthetics of history.

Marvell's "Horatian Ode," for example, features a spectator observing the inauguration of an unprecedented political era. He is astonished at first, blindsided by the tumultuous change, but then gradually swept up in the historical tide such that he feels compelled to testify about events and account for his actions and inaction. The therapeutic goal of skepticism's suspended judgment is ataraxia or tranquility. While this might be appealing in theory, given the political reality of civil war, it is not an option. He cannot stand back like the Lucretian spectator watching the shipwreck of history from the distance of dry land and philosophical wisdom.[30] Instead, he tries to understand what is happening to his country, even as political events test the limits of his beliefs and allegiances.

Consider the spectator's attempt at objectivity as he comes to terms with Cromwell's seizure of power. The Ode opens by calling a youth to arms, urging him to abandon his poetic pursuits and pastoral retirement for a life of military valor. One could be forgiven for imagining that Marvell was ordering himself to come out of the shadows and to take a stand lest he be charged with a kind of Montaignean *mollitia* or *mollesse*. But this

---

[30] See the opening of Book 2, *De rerum natura*.

identification of Marvell's persona with the Ode's "forward youth" is quickly deflected when the third stanza opens with the explanatory "so" of epic similes: "So restless Cromwell could not cease / In the inglorious arts of peace" (9–10). This clarifies the forward youth as Cromwell, even as it slyly suggests the poet's identification with the general – both cultivating their gardens quietly prior to the historical summons.[31] But if Cromwell jumps into the fray, eager for action, the youth seems reluctant to "forsake his Muses dear" (2) and slow "to oil the unused armor's rust" (6). If the Ode was written in June or July of 1650, after the Irish campaign but before Cromwell's Scottish campaign, then this was a time of shifting loyalties. Former royalists had to decide the extent to which they were prepared to accommodate themselves to the new regime. The Ode captures this moment of both hesitation and anticipation, as if the speaker were trying to persuade himself to stop hanging back and to see the new order as promise-filled. In the meantime, he feels compelled to review and appraise extraordinary events as impartially as possible.

The problem is Cromwell's power – the forcefulness and suddenness of his takeover. Marvell rehearses the extreme violence of recent events, as a traumatized witness might, in an effort to understand how his country has arrived at this moment. Marvell admires Cromwell's single-handed ability to change the course of history, even as he recoils from the bloodshed. He writes:

> ' Tis madness to resist or blame
> The face of angry heaven's flame;
>   And if we would speak true,
>   Much to the man is due.
> Who, from his private gardens, where
> He lived reservèd and austere,
>   As if his highest plot
>   To plant the bergamot,
> Could by industrious valor climb
> To ruin the great work of Time,
>   And cast the kingdoms old
>   Into another mould.
>   (25–36)

Marvell may be invoking here the great man theory of history in all its secularity. He may see Cromwell as a Machiavellian prince or Napoleon

---

[31] Hirst and Zwicker also note the moment when "the poet *manqué*," namely "the 'forward Youth,' metamorphoses into 'restless *Cromwel*' through that similitudinous 'So,' a conjunction that marks sequence but urges identification" (2012, 141, 146).

avant la lettre, an unstoppable historical force, sweeping all before him.[32] This secularity cannot simply be attributed to genre, that is, to the Pindaric–Horatian genealogy of the Ode with its celebration of epic heroes returning from the wars. Its secular mood conjures up a bleak vision about the will to power of super-men. As in Cavendish's poem, "The Ruin of This Island," providentialism is under pressure here, exposed as inadequate to the task of explaining events.

Whether Marvell is interrogating Providence in this poem or endorsing a Machiavellian view of history, which would be one way to interpret his skepticism, it is clear that he is investigating the intersections of secular and kairotic time. Taylor's philosophical terms help to capture long-recognized tensions in the Ode, which is famous for the tricky tone of its act of historical witness.[33] Is the summer of 1650 a higher time when events are gathered and reordered in significant ways, or is this just a bizarre, secular time when one unaccountable thing happens after another? What must the individual do in these circumstances, besides gape from the margins? According to David Norbrook, the tradition of Horatian counsel dictates that the poet model a political voice here, giving advice, in this instance a recommendation of restraint, moderation, even obedience: "How fit he is to sway / That can so well obey" (83–84). The extended falcon simile toward the poem's end, Norbrook points out, conveys this message; after the killing spree, the falcon – that is, Cromwell – should return to its handler, the Republic. The falcon represents power held in abeyance, poised for action, waiting for a signal (1990, 157). Thus, two thirds of the way through the poem, the poet renounces his impartial stance – the luxury of a private man taking stock – and surrenders to the political tide by assuming the mantle of humanist counsel. On this reading, it is tempting to suggest that this early poem proleptically maps out the arc of Marvell's career: from skeptical detachment to political engagement. However, I want to resist these polarities and argue that the relationship of skepticism and activism is tangled. A skeptical outlook can inform political action as easily as the converse: political events can incite doubt.

---

[32] See, e.g., Mazzeo (1964).

[33] Robert Ellrodt describes the poet as "a detached spectator of history in the making who makes a dispassionate evaluation of character and destiny" (2000, 75), while Blair Worden, by contrast, sees the Ode as a passionate poem that "rather than taking neither side, takes both" (2007, 86), creating "a bi-polar language, at once direct and deceptive" (2007, 100). Donald M. Friedman identifies "the transition we witness in reading the 'Ode'" as "something like the shift from Newtonian physics to quantum theory, from one way of perceiving the structure of reality to another" (1999, 129).

For the bulk of the Horatian Ode, political events incite a judicious and ironic distance in the poem's speaker. While the poem seems to endorse Oliver Cromwell's success, it also shows signs of reserve and dismay. Insofar as the Ode's skepticism about Cromwell is audible, it is thanks to the convergence of several factors, both stylistic and thematic, that it produces effects of uncertainty and doubt. These include what Nigel Smith calls "grammatical openness," whereby individual words may have plural syntactic functions – both subject and object, both active and passive, both transitive and intransitive. It also includes the "antiphonal" character of the stanzas, as if two voices were speaking (2007, 270). Barbara Everett notes the "remarkable thinking metre" of the Ode, whereby the monosyllables of the short three-beat line undercut the longer four-beat lines (1979, 74). Similarly, on a structural level, the poem exhibits some undercutting; call it even-handedness, as if Marvell were engaged rhetorically in presenting an argument from each side. The evidence here is the 12-line section occupying the poem's center, which can be said to undercut or balance the praise of Cromwell by describing the execution of King Charles in sympathetic terms. Annabel Patterson, however, disavows the ascription of "evenhandedness," calling it "effete" – a charge redolent of bad taste with overtones of class and gender – preferring instead to say that the Ode "goes beyond ambivalence to a disciplined acclimatization" (1994, 39). Patterson's vocabulary reveals the relative standing of skepticism and stoicism, the latter associated with masculine pragmatism.

Whether seen as stoical or skeptical, the Ode's balancing act raises issues of taste. The speaker's zetetic inquiry into the metaphysics of historical time is filtered through a sensibility that responds to taste as a criterion of aesthetic and moral judgment. The bystander who speaks this poem – at once "the forward youth" and not – stands back and contemplates the rough-and-tumble sequence of political events like a set of artistic tableaux in freeze frames. He stages the beheading of King Charles as a play, describing the "royal actor" as one who "nothing common did or mean / Upon that memorable Scene" (57–58). In this scene, he does not position himself as an impartial observer, but rather as a member of the audience, offended by "the armèd bands" who "Did clap their bloody hands" (55–56). Earlier, when Cromwell is described as emerging from his private gardens "As if his highest plot / To plant the bergamot" (30–31), the punning ambiguity of plot (garden plot / political plot) together with the fragrance evoked by bergamot compounds the aestheticizing effect.

Giorgio Agamben argues that the exercise of good taste – "enabling those who have it to perceive the *point de perfection* of the artwork"

(1999, 18) – exists in a dialectical relation to bad taste. Citing a 1671 letter from Madame de Sevigné where she wonders at her own attraction to second-rate novels, Agamben observes that we moderns are no longer surprised at the "inexplicable inclination of good taste towards its opposite," taking it for granted that "good taste carrie[s] within itself a tendency to pervert itself" (1999, 19, 18). But it is more than a tendency, Agamben argues. Good taste "is, in some way, the very principle of any perversion, and its appearance in consciousness seems to coincide with the beginning of a process of reversal of all values and all contents" (1999, 22). While Agamben may be overstating the importance of taste to the history of consciousness, his analysis allows us to see that Marvell wrestles with the burgeoning problematics of taste. I suggest that the Ode presents Charles as an artwork at its historical *point de perfection* and further, that Charles exemplifies good taste in the *ars moriendi*, given the anomalous and macabre circumstances. Cromwell, by contrast, exhibits something like bad taste with his garish forcefulness. When Marvell likens Cromwell to "the three-forked lightning" (13) – "burning through the air he went, / And palaces and temples rent: / And Caesar's head at last / Did through his laurels blast" (21–24) – the simile with its sublime imagery may strike the reader as over-blown, perhaps verging on the grotesque.[34] That the lightning breaks the clouds, dividing its fiery way "thorough his own side," also raises questions of taste. The image does Cromwell no favors especially if we fixate on "side" as meaning not the Parliamentarian or Independent party so much as his rib cage alight with electrified stigmata (15); the word allows for both meanings. The point is that Marvell's explorations of taste aestheticize the contact zone between secular and kairotic time. The split subjectivity of Agamben's man of taste compounds the predicament of Grossman's Marvellian subject "suspended between his own moment of moral choice" and his doomed intellectual efforts to perceive the contours of the divine plan (1998, 212). Taste thus enters into the impartial spectator's efforts to understand his own obligations vis-à-vis history.

Agamben sees taste as a sign of self-alienation typical of modernity, agreeing with Hegel that skepticism is a form of tragic consciousness. In

---

[34] Donald M. Friedman comments: "To reify the meaning of a Caesarian birth by picturing the hero as giving birth to himself by bursting 'thorough his own Side' (15) is to introduce a mode of metaphorics that we have come to recognize as peculiarly Marvellian" (1999, 127). Thanks perhaps to his sense that the Ode is evoking Lucan's *Pharsalia*, Norbrook acknowledges the grotesque aspect of this poetic moment, noting the "refusal to shrink from such grotesque but sublime images" (1999, 268). Overall, however, Norbrook sees Marvell's Cromwell as instantiating "the republican sublime" while "Charles is the courtly beautiful" (1990, 156).

Marvell's case, however, taste can have a comic dimension associated with pleasure.[35] Thanks to the split in subjectivity, taste offers Marvell a kind of liminal *jouissance*, heightening the tension of clashing temporalities. The friction between secular and providential experiences of time, for example, sharpens his aesthetic sensibilities, honing his appreciation for uncertainty. When he aestheticizes warps and knots in time, the diffidence of his skeptical sensibility is seductive. His delight in perceptual instability carries over to delight in skepticism. Marvell's exquisite attunement to the phenomenology of his states of mind – a stance characteristic of skepticism – transforms his meditations on history and historical violence into a beguiling aesthetic experience.

In at least one of his meditations on history, however, Marvell abandons kairotic time – and then his skepticism acquires an accent of resignation. In a controversial and much-glossed passage toward the end of *The Rehearsal Transpros'd*, Marvell looks back from a distance of more than twenty years on the regicide and Cromwell's rise to power:

> Whether it were a War of Religion, or of Liberty, is not worth the labour to enquire.
> Which-soever was at the top, the other was at the bottom; but upon considering all, I think the Cause was too good to have been fought for. Men ought to have trusted God; they ought and might have trusted the King with that whole matter. The *Arms of the church are Prayers and Tears*, the Arms of the Subjects are Patience and Petitions. The King himself being of so accurate and piercing a judgement, would soon have felt where it stuck. For men may spare their pains where Nature is at work, and the world will not go faster for our driving. Even as his present Majesty's happy Restauration did it self; so all things else happen in their best and proper time, without any need of our officiousness. (2003, 1.192)

Marvell dissociates himself not from the good old Cause so much as from activists who wish to speed historical progress. He argues that they should leave well enough alone "as the world will not go faster for our driving." Margarita Stocker believes that he is alluding to Fifth Monarchists and other radicals, claiming that Marvell was allied to "moderate chiliasts" who supported a "gradualist political philosophy" (1986, 10, 12). Nigel Smith, by contrast, thinks Marvell is being facetious, "looking at us with a big grin on his face" (1992, 151). Smith cites Jennifer Chibnall's analysis of the passage where she observes that Marvell was well aware that "the

---

[35] Although critics recognize Marvell's playfulness, his sense of humor often gets lost in critical analyses.

Restoration demanded some considerable officiousness for its accomplishment" and that he himself, through his writing, was trying "to drive things a little faster in the direction he believe[d] they should go" (1986, 100). But this overlooks the complicated predestinarian theology of secondary causes and perhaps more importantly, Marvell's fluctuating moods. That he was intermittently discouraged about the effectiveness of his own activism is attested in a letter to his nephew where after expressing his disgust at the political situation, he asks poignantly, "In such a Conjuncture, dear *Will*, what Probability is there of my doing any Thing to the Purpose?" (1952, II.302).[36] However one interprets the passage from *The Rehearsal Transpros'd*, it is ironic that Marvell alludes to *kairos* to designate what Taylor would call secular time. Marvell evokes that most skeptical of biblical books, *Ecclesiastes*, when he defers to seasons when "all things else happen in their best and proper time." Given providential design, Marvell suggests, it is best to let the seasons of secular time have their way rather than trying to jump-start and collaborate with the time-knots and time-warps Taylor calls kairotic. The passivity always *in potentia* with skepticism surfaces here: resignation about one's abilities to penetrate the divine plan together with an acceptance of those intellectual limitations. The feeling of futility – it's "not worth the labour to enquire" – dissolves the pleasure of the aesthetic mood.

Spectator Ethics and Taste

If at one moment Marvell's imagination delights in exuberant metamorphoses, so that the ground beneath our feet falls away, at other moments he longs to stop motion and freeze time. In "The Gallery" and elsewhere, Marvell's speaker uses the rhetoric of the visual arts, and especially of the framed painting, to contain the danger of a world in spatial and temporal flux. The threat of skeptical doubt with its elusive objects – Stanley Cavell lists Descartes' melting wax, Price's tomato, "Moore's raised moving hands," and "Heidegger's blooming tree" (2003, 8) – is met, in Marvell's case, with a controlling gaze determined to fix and hold still the object of its attention. Critics have long noted that the rhetoric of the visual arts helps Marvell immobilize the ephemeral. The Ode, for example, features

---

[36] For further evidence of Marvell's moods, see the letter to Sir Henry Thompson where he uses his "listlessness" as the excuse for not having attended to a business favor and where he advises Thompson in another matter "not to presse or apply to him much but give him line and expect *what things of themselves will work to*" (1952, II.314) (italics mine).

one of Marvell's favorite literary techniques: capturing lives of action at a dramatic moment as if in a historical tableau or framed portrait. As Michael Schoenfeldt explains, "the practices of painting offer the fantasy that the fetching visual tableau of this fleeting moment might be captured and preserved" (2012, 96).

As a literary device, however, framing does far more than stop the clock. As I have argued elsewhere, framing is a skeptical strategy. Frames are conducive to skeptical doubt because they "presume a viewer with perspective" and oftentimes "enclose a locus of epistemological uncertainty" (Sherman 2007, 16). When frames are multiplied, this can serve "to neutralize the persuasiveness of any given position or perceptual schema." Frames thus "contribute to the suspension of judgment" as the observer weighs competing viewpoints (2007, 17). Framing also provides the occasion for practice in aesthetic discrimination. As David Marshall explains, framing helps define aesthetics as "a way of looking" so that the focus is not on an autonomous, free-floating object of art but rather on the aesthetic experience of the spectator (2005, 8). Often, the result is "a representation compulsion" whereby these spectators experience the world "as if it were a work of art," blurring the boundaries between art and life (2005, 13). At the same time, Marshall adds, "the act of framing represented by an aesthetic perspective inserts aesthetic distance into everyday life" (2005, 8). Framing thus enables exercises in taste even as it produces ethical quandaries regarding agency and objectification.

In "The Gallery," for example, the sequence of framed portraits incites the reader's skepticism, even as the poem's speaker displays the split subjectivity that Agamben believes defines the man of taste. The speaker represents himself less as an impartial judge than as a discriminating aesthete with a hint of vindictiveness. He invites Clora to visit the art gallery in his mind where portraits of her in various guises are exhibited. He invites her, as Colie puts it, "to appraise his taste" (1970, 109). Life and art blur, even as he distances himself through aestheticization. The conceit begins as a joint stroll through a hallway hung with paintings – an echo of those mnemonic exercises promoted by Quintilian and other adepts in the art of memory that involve streetscapes and palaces furnished with objects designed to prompt recall. But instead of evoking reminiscences, the imagined portraits elicit a sequence of mini-lectures engaged in ekphrasis. Each stanza describes a painting showing Clora in action. She is literally framed so as to give rise to an aesthetic disquisition. Yet, she is neither commodified nor fully objectified because she is also present as the viewer of the paintings and silent partner of the speaker – a *flâneur* like him in the imagined gallery. Although we never hear from Clora, we are conscious of her presence (the speaker refers to her throughout as "thou") and understand that she might see the pictures differently. The perspectives of the two embedded viewers diverge, even as the pictures proliferate and Clora recedes as a knowable being. The framing device helps expose the limits of our knowledge.

Schoenfeldt (2011) observes that "the invitation to aesthetic judgement quickly becomes a referendum on the ethics of her behavior," as the speaker's ekphrastic pedagogy becomes a form of passive-aggressive reproach:

> Here art thou painted in the dress
> Of an inhuman murderess;
> Examining upon our hearts
> Thy fertile shop of cruel arts:
> (9–12)

Depicted on the canvas as a cruel artist anatomizing the hearts of her lovers, Clora becomes momentarily indistinguishable from the speaker, as if the split between subject and object were threatened with collapse. The verses offer a painted version of the speaker's own activity in the poem, a mise-en-abyme of the cruel artist/lover. The overall effect is of a hall of mirrors where images both splinter and reflect. This sense of Clora as an artist engaged in activity identical to that of the poet–speaker recurs in the penultimate stanza. There the speaker assures Clora that his gallery stores over a thousand pictures of her "in all the forms thou can'st invent, / Either to please me, or torment" (43–44). Clora, he implies, is a creative artist using techniques of invention to keep him fascinated.

The pictures, it transpires, are two-sided, the witch-like Clora balanced by the goddess-like Clora: "But, on the other side, th'art drawn / Like to Aurora in the dawn" (17–18). Similarly, in the next pair of stanzas, an evil "enchantress" is opposed to Venus. The first is a nocturnal scene in a cave where "by a light obscure" she vexes "her restless lover's ghost," attempting to divine the future.[37] The second features "Venus in her pearly boat," a tranquil ocean scene with flying halcyons. For Schoenfeldt, "the genre of the two-sided picture expresses the contradictions and ambivalences of eros" (2011, 88). Yet surely it also expresses the see-saw rhythms of skeptical disputation with its ethical investment in argumentation *in utramque partem*. The effect for the reader, if not for the embedded

---

[37] I hear echoes of Donne's "The Apparition" in these stanzas. In "The Apparition" the speaker imagines a future when his "ghost" will enter a dark room where a "taper will begin to wink," as he restlessly vexes the bed of a love whom he calls "murderess" because she scorns him.

viewers, is suspended judgment. For us, the jury is still out on Clora's character as the vilifying and idealizing portraits of Clora cancel each other out and produce a cipher. Clora remains unknown, an enigma, and a placeholder for the artist-lover's obsessions. She is arguably also his self-projection as he wavers between self-hate and his ego-ideal in search of a standard of taste that will help him negotiate extremes and adjudicate the *point de perfection* of the artwork.

Faced with a plethora of pictures, the speaker does not suspend judgment. In the end, he picks his favorite: "A tender shepherdess, whose hair / Hangs loosely playing in the air" (53–54). He also explains why he has made that aesthetic choice:

> But, of these pictures and the rest,
> That at the entrance likes me best:
> Where the same posture, and the look
> Remains, with which I first was took.
> (49–52)

His preference rests on chronology – when he first laid eyes on Clora, at "the entrance" of their relationship, before getting to know her. As a man of taste, he discriminates among the artworks in his gallery, considering which one has achieved the *point de perfection* lauded by La Bruyère. He reflects on the criteria of beauty and plumps for pastoral convention, his first love.

As a spectator, Marvell usually hangs back. Sometimes, however, he abandons his bystander role and walks into the picture he has framed. Hirst and Zwicker have commented on his fascination with "the moment of entry, the point of becoming," arguing that the instabilities of liminality constitute one of his ongoing concerns (2012, 142). Marvell stands poised at the threshold of participation, tempted by aesthetic detachment, but drawn in by ethical concern. The result is a split subjectivity in which he watches himself watching, assessing the *point de perfection* of the artwork, even as he considers entering the scene. This happens in the first stanza of the Horatian Ode when "the forward youth," whom we take to be the poet, forsakes the muses. It happens more overtly in "A Poem upon the Death of his Late Highness the Lord Protector" when the self-effacing speaker suddenly materializes after 246 lines and announces, "I saw him dead" (247). Standing over the bier, he peers at Cromwell's corpse, inches from his face: "All withered, all discoloured, pale and wan" (253). This physical proximity with its intimacy reminds us of Marvell's closeness to Cromwell and his political activism. But the interlude is brief, and soon

Marvell has resumed his pose outside the frame as a disembodied commentator and witness.

Understanding the spectator poems as skeptical investigations into aesthetic taste has at least two benefits, one relating to intellectual history, another to Marvell's poetic practice. First, it shows how skepticism's attention to the problematics of vision gradually becomes secularized. If the deceptions of the eye in earlier decades elicited the corrections of both religious reformers and the budding scientific establishment, here the wayward gaze is no longer a stumbling block in the way of truth, but rather a feature of aesthetic taste, a secular concern.[38] Second, the focus on taste allows us to discuss the distinctive tonalities of Marvell's poetic voice in terms of aesthetic philosophy rather than of neuroses or source-criticism. When does Marvell's exquisite voice become precious? When does his nostalgia veer into sentimentality? When does his coyness – "coy" is a favorite adjective – become cloying? When does proffered exemplarity incite doubt? Why does beauty turn ugly? These are questions his poems raise.

Critics have noticed in passing problems of tone and taste, dismissing these as unfortunate lapses or the result of notions of decorum and accommodation that now seem awkward; occasionally these lapses are attributed to Marvell's psychosexual neuroses.[39] However, I think they are deliberate, neither aberrations nor accidents. Marvell is choosing to explore problems of tone and diction because he is deeply interested in the poetic space where good blurs into bad taste. This is a consequence of his fascination with the faculty of deliberative judgment necessary for navigating the world of uncertain appearances. His skepticism, in other words, with its privileging of impartial adjudication, encourages him to question and test notions of decorum. In his public work, this interest manifests itself in self-conscious disquisitions about different registers of style and decorum, terms he repeatedly uses. Marvell's avowed concern with decorum in the polemical tracts is the public face of the private impulse to experiment with dubious taste in the poems. While taste is a term that Marvell uses only in the gustatory sense, it is well known that this

---

[38] See Picciotto who argues that Marvell's gaze is oriented toward the future with Baconian purpose. She describes his gaze as "millennial," bent on "insight" geared to the "restoration" of a paradisal world (2010, 364, 366). While it is true that Marvell strives to discern providential meanings through the mist of his own ignorance (a skeptical predicament), his preoccupation with historical time's opacity coexists with a voluptuous pleasure in the possibilities of the present moment in all its perceptual waywardness.

[39] For example, the "Epigramma in Duos montes" is, Patterson says, "an unsuccessful experiment" showing "errors of tact and procedure" (1978, 98).

gustatory sense precedes and underlies its later philosophical and aesthetic connotations. While the split subjectivity that Agamben deems characteristic of the man of taste is evident throughout Marvell's oeuvre – even in some of his personal letters – it is more pronounced in the poetry than in the prose. This split subjectivity contributes to the cultural shift from decorum with its "universal" rules to taste with its private pleasures. In response to the bewildering variety of tastes, philosophers like David Hume sought to develop a "universal" standard of taste. But in the late seventeenth and early eighteenth century, the discourse of taste eluded regulation, flourishing in tandem with libertinism. One might have a taste for godly sobriety, for masculine strength and plainness; or one might be tempted by effeminate, foreign "sucreries dévotes" like those "baits for curious tastes" with which "the subtle nuns" at Nun Appleton lure Isabel Thwaites (94, 182).[40]

To probe the tricky linguistic, social, and aesthetic zone differentiating registers of taste, Marvell exploits gender and at times religion, playing with cultural stereotypes to provoke doubt. Consider, for example, the bizarre digression in stanza 92 of "Upon Appleton House" when the poet interrupts his panegyric on the beauties of Maria Fairfax, his adolescent tutee and heiress of the Nun Appleton estate, to excoriate the vanities of dissolute women. Sounding like Henry Higgins or Hamlet on a misogynist rant about women's misplaced priorities, Marvell scolds "the fond sex that on your face / Do all your useless study place" (729–730). With cruel glee he warns:

> Yet your own face shall at you grin,
> Thorough the black bag of your skin;
> When knowledge only could have filled
> And virtue all those furrows tilled.
>   (733–736)

What is this ugly, teasing memento mori doing here? Pointing to similarly abrupt changes of diction in other poems, such as Donne's *Anniversaries* exalting Elizabeth Drury, is not an adequate explanation. Nor is it adequate to point to his general "love of anti-climax" (Everett 1979, 70) or even to the rhetorical reversal from *hypsous* to *bathous* that Noggle identifies as characteristic of the skeptical sublime. The outburst might more plausibly be attributed to "the rhetoric of disharmony, illness, excess" from which "a pervading concept of harmony, radiant unity, *decorum* ... takes

---

[40] See Patterson (1978), 103.

life" (Kranidas 2005, 484). This would imply that in order to set off Maria's perfections, we require as a foil railing at womankind. If so, then Marvell would be hewing to the conventions of classical decorum. But the split subjectivity of the speaker – at once artist and spectator, omniscient narrator and eccentric character in his own poem – suggests that Agamben's analysis of the man of taste applies here. It is as if Marvell has become cloyed with his own sublime rhapsodies about the divine Maria and feels compelled to violate them. For one brief eight-line stanza he destroys the transcendent beauty of the twilit evening and indulges in what Addison might call a "gross" and "indecent" sally (#411, #160) or Hume "want of delicacy" and "prejudice" – all markers of bad taste.

This foray into bad taste is not unique. In the lyric poems about young girls Marvell's liminal stance can be troubling because his leering gaze is prurient. Critics have noted this over the years, often ascribing Marvell's attraction to nubile pre-adolescents to problems with his sexuality. Nabokov's Lolita and Lewis Carroll's Alice often lurk behind these discussions.[41] Alternatively, critics invoke literary precedents, e.g. epigrams from the Greek anthology praising "infant charms" and other classical or contemporary poems dealing with similar themes (Smith 2007, 112–113). I argue instead that Marvell wishes to test the boundaries of good taste and even occasionally to step over them. Although Marvell precedes by a generation the first English philosophers of aesthetics (e.g., Frances Hutcheson, Anthony Ashley Cooper, third earl of Shaftesbury, Joseph Addison), he is contemporary with intellectual movements in France and Italy that aspired to refine taste as part of a larger project of religious, cultural, and national renewal.[42] He would have been aware of these theorists not only thanks to his own curiosity and breathtaking range of reading, but also thanks to Dryden who was instrumental in circulating some of this work and bringing it to the attention of his compatriots.[43] That said, it is important to remember that most of Marvell's poems were never shared and seem to have been written for his eyes alone. As Hirst and

---

[41] See, e.g., Matthew Augustine (2008), DiSanto (2008), Hammond (1996), Hirst and Zwicker (2012), Michael Long (1984), Silver (2001).

[42] See, e.g., Minor (2006), Moriarty (1988). Minor observes that attacks on the Baroque "were caught up in complex ways with debates on free will and religious experience." The Baroque's association with Jesuit poetics led to criticisms that "emotive images" displayed "*cattivo gusto*" (2006, 5).

[43] See, e.g., Dryden's *Essay on Dramatick Poesie*, his 1683 revisions to Sir William Soames's 1680 translation of Boileu's *Art of Poetry*, and his "Preface" to and translation of Charles du Fresnoy's *De arte graphica* (1695). Hobbes's notions of art and decorum (influenced by his time in France) also circulated widely and so offended Anthony Ashley Cooper that they motivated him to write.

Zwicker put it, "What kinds of performances are such acts of privacy?" (2012, 162).[44] In these private poems, Marvell documents his inner weather, exploring the conditions of desire, pleasure, beauty, and happiness by testing them, in the skeptical sense, and bringing their dark sides to light.[45] In them, he "is deeply interested in the ethics of aesthetics" and pursues questions of taste (Schoenfeldt 2011, 99).

In "Young Love," the speaker's physical and moral attractiveness is in question. Rosalie L. Colie calls him "an honest sensualist" but also "predatory" (1970, 52–54). Victoria Silver calls his attempts "perverse" (2001, 36), while Hirst and Zwicker note that the lyric "goes far to indulge the paedophilic imagination" (2019, 400). Is the poem's speaker a peer of the infant's "agèd father"? He compares himself to "old Time beguiled" by "young Love," suggesting that he is no longer a young man. The age of the charming child is vague, as is the gender. The "little infant" of the opening line, wordless and mute in keeping with its Latin etymology, seems to grow in leaps and bounds thanks to apt similes and metaphor. The second stanza refers to "our sportings ... free / As the nurse's with the child." By the third stanza, the child has developed into an uncommon beauty of about fifteen:

> Common beauties stay fifteen;
>   Such as yours should swifter move;
> Whose fair blossoms are too green
>   Yet for Lust, but not for Love.

The speaker entices the child, flattering him or her with confusing talk about lust and love, casuistry that fails to disguise his desire. In today's parlance, he might be described as "grooming" the lovely child. The speaker's seductive maneuvers confine themselves to a pastoral register with a glance at a nursery in a domestic setting, but the fourth stanza takes a violent turn. Its central image of animal sacrifice features innocent babies, "the snowy lamb" and "the wanton kid," attracting the bloodthirsty god of Love as much as more mature specimens, "the lusty bull or ram":

---

[44] Hirst and Zwicker "wonder what happens to illocutionary effect when a text has no published status, no public bearing, no reader, no auditors. Can we turn questions of illocutionary force inwards, can we ask after the internal bearing of words and forms?" (2012, 162). But see McDowell who questions the assumption of Marvell's literary solitude, arguing that he was affiliated with Thomas Stanley's poetic circle in the late 1640s (2008, 4 ff). Thanks to Ben LaBreche for suggesting that we might see Stanley's circle as a group cultivating a certain kind of aesthetic taste in poetry.

[45] Stephen Bardle argues that the literary underground during the Restoration associated pleasure with the Stuart court's debauchery (2012, 147–151). While it is clear that opponents of the regime, including poets like Cowley and Milton, took a dim view of courtly pleasures, it is unconvincing to extrapolate that courtly contexts may have limited and tainted Marvell's imagination of pleasure.

> Love as much the snowy lamb
> > Or the wanton kid does prize,
> As the lusty bull or ram,
> > For his morning sacrifice.

If we identify the speaker with personified Love, then it follows he requires appeasement and demands "his morning sacrifice," a daily affair like breakfast. The stanza seems to anticipate the child's objection that he or she is not old enough to be slaughtered. The riposte suggests that Love is an omnivore with ecumenical appetites, his more conventional tastes abiding alongside more rarefied fancies. The fifth stanza is both wheedling and imperative, frightening the silent child with yet another specter of death, although this time more decorously phrased in the conventional accents of carpe diem:

> Now then love me. Time may take
> > Thee before thy time away:
> Of this need we'll virtue make,
> > And learn love before we may.

The implied sense of prohibition in "before we may" and the plasticity of "virtue" reveal the speaker's efforts to dismiss his own uneasiness.

The last three stanzas resume the theme of "cold jealousy and fears" mentioned at the poem's start in that the speaker wants first dibs on the child, reserving him or her to himself before "foreign claims" and "rivals" interpose themselves. With talk of Fate, kingdoms, and crowns, the poem ends on a note of reciprocity, as the speaker invites the child to an act of mutual coronation:

> Thus as kingdoms, frustrating
> > Other titles to their crown,
> In the cradle crown their king,
> > So all foreign claims to drown,
> So, to make all rivals vain,
> > Now I crown thee with my love:
> Crown me with thy love again,
> > And we both shall monarchs prove.

Nevertheless, the simile of the infant monarch in the crib leaves us with the queasy sense of the speaker as a cradle-robber. The closing image of the two lovers as crowned monarchs and equal sovereigns cannot erase the impression that the poem's persuasions are manipulative and coercive.

The speaker insists on his innocent intentions to the youngster, and yet the poem is aware of his bad faith. Doubt shadows the second stanza's opening line, "Pretty, surely, 'twere to see / By young Love old Time beguiled," owing to the subjunctive tense displaying the speaker's qualm that the situation might be unpretty. Indeed, the "fears" clouding the "agèd father's brow" meld with the beguiling of old Time, and together betray the speaker's knowledge that his infatuation is misplaced and inappropriate. It is as if the speaker were trying to reassure himself of the decorum of the situation, evoking a wealth of literary precedents so as to assuage his own conscience. Too honest to repress his desires, he anatomizes them in the open, testing the extent to which classical conventions can accommodate his erotic longings. When I say he worries the line between good and bad taste, I mean in this instance that he explores the flexibility of classical decorum – how far the tropes will bend before the speaker's self-presentation as a wily seducer produces recoil. Insofar as the poem is beautiful but alarming, Marvell can be seen as conducting aesthetic investigations into the limits of permissible desire, skirting the libertine excesses of the earl of Rochester while risking charges of hypocrisy and artistic sublimation.

Although "The Picture of Little T. C. in a Prospect of Flowers" is far more restrained than "Young Love" in its approach to the child at its center, the poems share several features: a fear of the child's maturity; a wish to arrest time; a metaphorical vision of love as a bloody, war-like enterprise with sacrificial victims; a play on pastoral conventions, including the carpe diem trope; and a problematic gaze, at once tender, protective, and prurient. Unlike the child in "Young Love," there is no sense that little T. C. hears the speaker's words and responds to them in the spaces between the stanzas; even when she is directly addressed, she seems to be out of earshot. Instead, the speaker invites the reader to "see" with him. The poem begins, "See with what simplicity / This nymph begins her golden days!" As Nigel Smith explains, "the addresses are all made in the intimate space between speaker and reader" (2007, 113). Thanks to this intimate space, a complicity ensues whereby readers share the speaker's aesthetic appreciation of the child as a delicate and endangered creation.

The title together with the opening stanza renders little T. C. pictorially, the flowers operating as a framing device. This has Roman Catholic iconographic resonances as the Virgin Mary was often represented in a floral surround.[46] It also evokes poems like "The Gallery" in which

---

[46] See, e.g., paintings by Jan Brueghel the Elder and the Younger, Andries Daniels, Jacob Jordaens, Peter Paul Rubens, Daniël Seghers, Gerard Seghers, Nicolaes van Verendael, and many others across Europe and the Americas (e.g. the Cuzco school).

Marvell uses the visual arts to produce emblematic effects. We see little T. C. sprawled on the grass, talking to the roses, even as she "tames / The wilder flowers, and gives them names" (4–5). She is playing at Adam and Eve in her paradisal garden, naming the flora in a childish simulation of the originary language. By the second stanza, the specter of her adult sexuality begins to haunt the poem. The speaker fantasizes about her future as a femme fatale, intimidating Cupid:

> Yet this is she whose chaster laws
> The wanton Love shall one day fear,
> And, under her command severe,
> See his bow broke and ensigns torn.

Insisting on her invulnerability to the assaults of love, he calls her "this virtuous enemy of Man," using oxymoron both to trigger and deny her association with the serpent in the garden.

The complicity between speaker and reader reaches a breaking point in the third stanza when the speaker inserts himself into the framed picture, representing himself as a supine voyeur. Like the moment in "Upon Appleton House" when the speaker ecstatically describes the young Maria from his covert position in the wood, here too the speaker lies hidden while imagining the "glories" of little T. C. But instead of an apocalyptic Maria vitrifying the world with her supernatural powers, here little T. C. is envisioned as a merciless dominatrix trampling the adoring hearts of her lovers with her triumphal chariot. Note the enjambment after "drive," disallowing any pause for breath as the "glancing wheels" rush by, wreaking destruction:

> O then let me in time compound,
> And parley with those conq'ring eyes;
> Ere they have tried their force to wound,
> Ere, with their glancing wheels, they drive
> In triumph over hearts that strive,
> And them that yield but more despise.
>   Let me be laid,
> Where I may see thy glories from some shade.

The stanza opens with the speaker's desire to "parley," but this wish for face-to-face encounter never happens. He wants to "compound" with little T. C. before she grows up and it is too late to negotiate. The repetition of "ere" emphasizes the temporality of his foreboding and dread. As in "Young Love," the speaker wants first dibs – to interpose himself before the throngs of rival suitors aspire to her attention. The verb, "compound," suggesting compensation for an offense or injury (Nigel Smith 2007, 114), intimates an awareness of guilt, reminiscent of the speaker's guilty conscience in "Young Love." Certainly, the speaker seems to take an abject pleasure in identifying with "them that yield" and whom she therefore "more despise[s]." Our complicity with the speaker's masochistic fantasies is most strained in the couplet when the shady spot from which he gazes up turns out to be the grave. One is reminded of the couplet in "To His Coy Mistress:" "The grave's a fine and private place, / But none I think do there embrace" (31–32). From the fine privacy of the grave, at once protected and laid low, he can luxuriate in little T. C.'s wounding and conquering eyes. Presumably the likes of Addison would have found this conceit "Gothick" (#62), insufficiently "manly" (#61), devoid of heroism (#70), altogether impolite (#411), and hence of dubious taste.

Yet, the odd spectacle of the upright, guilty speaker picturing himself in abject, buried ecstasy – surely a figure of suppression, if not repression – does not last. The fourth stanza returns to a pastoral register and describes a pleasant flowered vale. But even this benign scene has a sting. The speaker at last addresses little T. C., using three imperative verbs that call for change, yet have no hope of affecting anything, let alone reaching her ears. "Reform the errors of the spring," the speaker commands, "make" the tulips be fragrant and "procure / That violets may a longer age endure." The illocutionary futility of these commands lends an aura of defeat to the stanza. The speaker wants little T. C. to wave a magic wand and improve nature, harnessing her own "beauty" to make spring more lastingly beautiful. He is, in essence, uttering a prayer for eternal youth.

This wistful plea appears to take a conventional turn in the final stanza with its carpe diem trope and the speaker's retreat to a magisterial "we." Yet Marvell again breaks the enchanted mood of his pastoral idyll. He wittily describes the "young beauty" as unknowingly committing a "crime," killing Flora's "infants in their prime." The scene recalls that of the baby rails in "Upon Appleton House," nesting in the tall grass and mowed down before their time:

> But O young beauty of the woods,
> Whom Nature courts with fruits and flowers,
> Gather the flowers, but spare the buds;
> Lest Flora angry at thy crime,
> To kill her infants in their prime,
> Do quickly make th'example yours;
>   And, ere we see,
> Nip in the blossom all our hopes and thee.

The jarring effect of the infanticide metaphor is heightened once we recall the circumstances of the poem. Little T. C. was in fact Theophila Cornewell, aged between six and eight, whose mother was a Skinner, a family Marvell knew (Nigel Smith 2007, 112). An older sister, also baptized Theophila, had died in infancy. There is something cruel about taunting the little girl playing in the meadow with the fate of her sibling and invoking the rhetoric of exemplarity in the process. Evoking the perils of mortality in a general way hews to convention, enhancing the pleasures of melancholy; but evoking a particular death and brandishing it as a bogeyman seems too personal, a stroke of dubious taste. *In cauda venenum*, they say of the scorpion's sting. This aggressive sally – no longer directed at little T. C.'s imagined future triumph as a punitive Diana, but at the present eight year old in her oblivious innocence – twists the knife in the wound of the family's loss. Taken to its extreme, Marvell's stylistic criterion of seasonableness (as enunciated later, for example, in *The Rehearsal Transpros'd*) threatens to turn into tactlessness.

Were this a public poem about a public figure, one might claim that the conventions of *soteria* are in play, as Annabel Patterson does with the portion of Marvell's "First Anniversary" thanking God for sparing Cromwell in a coaching accident. "The purpose of *soteria*, to define value by exploring its near loss, requires or at least justifies the use of hyperbole," Patterson explains (1978, 80). As a panegyric motif, it celebrates deliverance from danger or sickness. But since the poem was a private production, initiated perhaps with the idea (possibly later scuttled) of giving it to the Cornewells, it is arguable that Marvell is not adhering to, so much as violating, recognizable forms of aesthetic decorum.[47] I take seriously Hirst and Zwicker's salutary reminder that Marvell's creativity was often inspired by conditions of patronage and service. As they put it, "the ghost in the machine is always idealization – a structure of feeling that encompasses not only instrumentality but admiration, affection, even desire, and always with Marvell, the shadows of subversion" (2012, 153). I also accept their view that the vulnerability of children was one of Marvell's abiding obsessions (2012, 159). But I disagree that "The Picture of Little T. C." is preoccupied with "lineage, estate, and authority" (2012, 154). The Cornewells may have helped Marvell's father in the 1620s, but they were not among the families

---

[47] Nigel Smith describes it as "a presentation piece for the Cornewell family" (2010, 100), but acknowledges that the only surviving manuscript copy (possibly in the hand of Edmund Waller's daughter) post-dates the 1681 publication of Marvell's poems (2007, 112).

Marvell served. While idealization may well be evident in the poem, it needs in this instance to be divorced from socio-economic conditions of dependence and instead attached to the skeptical problematic, as Stanley Cavell understands it, whereby idealization both compensates for and appeases doubt. Cavell describes the "endless specific succumbings to the conditions of skepticism and endless specific recoveries from it, endless as a circle" (2003, 30). Idealization may contribute to recoveries from skepticism, returning cyclically as part of an existential praxis, but it also falls away, exposing disappointment or hostility.[48]

While Marvell never explicitly addresses the category of aesthetic taste in either his private or public work, he seems to have felt freer to explore it in his private poems. Yet, as we have seen, his public work engages in literary criticism and evaluation. His polemical tracts and satires also address questions of decorum. Sometimes, Marvell protests mightily that his style falls within the bounds of acceptable speech, not sinking to the "immodest and deformed manner of writing lately entertained" by his opponents (2003, 1:433). Sometimes, he demands license for giving as good as he gets, noting that if the Animadverter's style is "Enthusiastick and Fanatical, it is the first crime of which I should be glad to be guilty" (2003, 2:44). But even in these public screeds (and quite apart from issues of anonymity and censorship), Marvell's split subjectivity is in evidence: framing scenes, giving advice to the painter, now descending into the fray, pointing an accusing finger, now standing back and with aesthetic distance giving us a panoramic view. This split subjectivity complicates the problem of decorum, serving as a symptom of the cultural shift toward taste.

Rather than feeling bewildered at the contrast between Marvell's idealizing lyric sensibility and his muckraking political satires, we should be receptive to the intimations of violence and perversion in the poems, understood in Agamben's sense as the dark side of good taste. We know that Marvell had bouts of explosive anger. In a German village, on the return from a long and unsuccessful diplomatic mission to Russia as the earl of Carlisle's secretary, he menaced a carter with a pistol and was

---

[48] Annabel Patterson observes that in "The Unfortunate Lover" Marvell borrows words and images from John Cleveland's satire, "The mixt Assembly" – a poem that lambasts a "strange Grottesco" to convey scorn – and transforms them into an "elegant icon" showing "the power of art to confer dignity" (1978, 23–24). Marvell's refinement of Cleveland's grotesque image illustrates his interest in the plasticities of taste and the way idealization works on refractory material.

roughed up by the peasantry (Nigel Smith 2010, 180).[49] He was twice forced to apologize in the House of Commons for provoking a scuffle (Nigel Smith 2010, 169, 317). He was devious and dubbed a Machiavel, which seems borne out by the suspicion that Marvell's election as MP for Hull, when he beat the experienced statesman and distinguished republican, Sir Henry Vane the Younger, was not squeaky clean.[50] He was probably a spy, possibly a double-agent (Nigel Smith 2010, 172; Bardle 2012, 68). Given his potential for angry outbursts together with his abundant wit and gifts for irony, understatement, and suavity, it is not surprising that Marvell should be deeply interested in transgressions of decorum. *The Rehearsal Transpros'd*, for example, obsesses over faults of style (Patterson 1978, 205). In it, vulgar thrusts are a point of honor. Manic hilarity takes over as Marvell boisterously goes into attack mode, mimicking and overgoing the dubious rhetoric and style of his opponents, even while castigating himself for so doing.[51] Both his poetry and polemical work show that Marvell takes pleasure in exploring the borderlands of decorum and testing the malleability of its conventions.

This does not detract from Marvell's important defense of Nonconformity, toleration, and liberty of conscience, political positions long associated with skepticism. On the contrary, the mix of vituperation and thoughtful argument strengthens Marvell's plea for doubt. "What will become at this rate of the poor simple Doubter?" he asks (2003, 1:349). Marvell's sympathy for the poor simple doubter comes from his rich complex forms of skeptical doubting. I have isolated some of the poetic strategies characterizing his skeptical imagination: fantasies of intellection

---

[49] Bardle writes: "On the way back from Russia Marvell almost started a riot and had to be rescued from a mob of angry peasants after he had tried to pistol-whip an uncooperative wagon owner in Bremen" (2012, 71–72).

[50] The election "was thought to be a close-run affair. ... Marvell appears to have been seen by his electors as a Protectorate man, ... The Protectorate court had certainly used its influence on his behalf against Vane, who was said to have had the majority in the Hull vote" (Nigel Smith 2010, 154–155). Bardle elaborates: "Marvell had been elected to Richard Cromwell's Parliament in early 1659 in the place of the radical Henry Vane through what looks to have been some underhand election rigging by the Hull Corporation: Vane had probably secured more votes than Marvell, but Hull wanted to disassociate itself from Vane as his presence was a constant reminder of the town's uncompromising parliamentary past" (2012, 62).

[51] The consensus is that Marvell hews to decorum in his prose polemics because he is imitating the style of the Marprelate tracts a century earlier that reveled in exuberant flyting. Alex Garganigo (2019) invokes Menippean satire. But Anthony Collins in 1729 thought they evinced an "Excesse of Burlesque" in his *Discourse Concerning Ridicule and Irony* (quoted in Chibnall 1986, 85). Burlesque exemplifies bad taste in Boileau's *Art of Poetry* (see footnote 43).

and naming that interrogate universals and impart vibrancy to matter; jarring shifts of tone that create a skeptical sublime; fraught intersections of kairotic and secular time; competing frames, and other techniques for destabilizing perception such as the compacted sequence of dissimilar analogies in "Upon Appleton House." Together, these strategies amount to far more than a witty set of metaphysical conceits. I share Matthew Augustine's impatience with the view that singles out harmony in dissonance, *discordia concors*, as Marvell's master trope. But rather than speaking of a poetics of indeterminacy or contingency as Augustine does (2008), I prefer to describe Marvell's metaphysical play with disproportion, tone, and judgment as producing an aesthetics of skeptical doubt. That is, it creates an epistemological ambiance so fluid that our phenomenological purchase on the world is put in jeopardy. By seeing through the speaker's eyes, our certainties about perception are fractured. We encounter a world in analogical flux. This flux need not be seen as an aspect of Baconian experimentalism: the "torsions of perspective" accompanying "a lifting – and, ultimately, a tearing – of the veil," as Simon (2015) or Picciotto (2010) might argue (554, 337). On the contrary, the kaleidoscopic metamorphoses of Marvell's imagined worlds produce the perversions of the secular man of taste. What starts out as a way to fall in the love with the world, as Marvell reenchants it through hallucinatory ecstasies, transforms into poetic essays in connoisseurship. In sum, Marvell's exploration of aesthetic taste is a salient feature of his skepticism and a symptom of skepticism's secularization.

Sometimes the skeptic's anxiety about the limitations of knowledge issues in dissatisfactions with finitude and yearnings for certainty that have religious and existential dimensions. At times it issues in attitudes of epistemological modesty and resignation – that suspended judgment (*epoché*) recommended by Sextus. At other times it calls for renewed discernment and attention to acts of interpretive procedure. This in turn exalts the subject as an observer summoned to arbitrate on doubtful questions, including aesthetic matters. As impartiality becomes privileged in many domains (a response in part to raging polemic), the exercise of taste becomes an increasingly important discourse. Acknowledging the turn to taste as part of skepticism's history means contesting Enlightenment views of skepticism as a wholly emancipatory force. Taste helps us understand the vulnerabilities of skepticism in the face of fanaticism: the risks of solipsism, the ruses of autonomy, the susceptibility to fashion, and the weakness born of flexibility. Historians of taste attribute its centrality in the eighteenth century to many factors, among them the rise of consumer culture, the democratic rumblings threatening the *anciens régimes*, and the concomitant desire to police social boundaries.[52] But they seldom factor skepticism into their histories, even though the philosophical identification of the aesthetic sense derives from the practice of the inward gaze encouraged, among others, by skeptical philosophers and poets.

---

[52] See Introduction.

Afterword
Experience in Crisis: Milton's Samson Agonistes

At the end of *Samson Agonistes*, the Chorus claims that Samson's great action – the destruction of the Philistians' temple – has taught them the meaning of "true experience" (1756). What is "true experience" for Milton?[1] Due partly to the defeat of the English republic but also partly to the philosophical and intellectual turmoil of the seventeenth century both inside and outside England, the whole concept of experience is in crisis in *Samson Agonistes*. Thanks to this crisis, Milton's closet drama endorses a salutary skepticism about internal urges and introspection more generally. It shows skepticism retreating to an inward forum, even as it portrays Samson's furious desire to bridge the fissures between private and public spheres and to achieve an ethical and epistemological alignment between his clouded perceptions and his political deeds.

Milton is not often discussed alongside skepticism, and with good reason.[2] As a man of passionate convictions and political action, he can hardly be mustered under the aegis of suspended judgment, apathy, neutrality or detached spectatorship.[3] Nevertheless, I argue that *Samson Agonistes* is a skeptical poem because, in keeping with its tragic genre, it

---

[1] The question has attracted many. See, e.g., Lewalski, 1988 and 1992; also Loewenstein who sets the "intimate impulses" and "rousing motions" that prompt Samson to political action in the context of Quaker theology and "radical religion" (2001).

[2] But see, e.g., Rushdy (1990), Sedley (2005), Stoll (2002) and, most recently, Ayesha Ramachandran who says of *Paradise Lost*: "While the poem explains cosmic order and relation at length, it simultaneously doubts this knowledge by disclosing its human origins, thus producing a deep-seated thread of skepticism in the poem" (2015, 197). She observes that competing creation accounts "produce a strong skeptical undertow" (2015, 205), concluding that "*Paradise Lost* suggests how poetry ... could ... produce a new kind of skeptically grounded faith, one which acknowledged uncertainty but triumphantly asserted its own creative potential" (2015, 208).

[3] See Milton's *Eikonoklastes* on those who "slide back into neutrality" (1957, 815). Also see Netzley: "The poem dramatizes the [political] inaction that results from Manoa's and the Chorus's focus on Samson's internal salvational state" (2006, 518).

shows the existential anguish caused by the uncertainties of interpretation.[4] It serves as a fitting *envoi* for this book because it brings together several of its themes: the loneliness of the *viator* in a nominalist cosmos (Chapter 1); fantasies of perfect intimacy (Chapter 2); frustration over the indecipherability of inner weather (Chapter 3); postures of self-assertion in compensation for weakness and perceived vacancies (Chapter 4); an emerging aesthetic of the skeptical sublime in response to the opacity of providence (Chapter 5). While the closet drama can by no stretch be seen as exemplifying the aestheticization of skepticism that can be glimpsed in Andrew Marvell's lyric poetry, Samson's repeated postures of self-assertion amount to what Cavell calls a skeptical recital – that is, statements of identity proffered in response to a dread of meaninglessness.[5] In addition, Samson's destruction of Dagon's temple reprises this book's beginnings with the apocalyptic crumbling of pagan temples in Spenser's dream-sonnets, materializing Spenser's visions. Finally, Milton's decision to make the Philistian temple a theater (1957, 1605), thus stressing the site's association with art, attests to the secularization of the temple motif and, more broadly, to the secularization of Philistian society, a fitting close.

Certainly the Chorus's phrase, "with new acquist / Of true experience," suggests two things: first, a learning process that takes place over time and culminates in hard-won wisdom, and second, the evocation (by implied contrast) of false, misleading or deceptive experience. The poem is notorious for offering examples of experience that are difficult to decipher. Samson himself is defensive about his interpretations. When the Chorus asks him early on why he chose to wed Philistian women, he explains that he "knew from intimate impulse" that what he "motion'd was of God" (221–224). Although the woman of Timna soon proved false, thus confirming his parents' reservations about marrying an infidel, Samson repeats the same mistake by marrying Dalila. While he does not claim that this second fatal marriage was prompted by intimate impulses motioned by God, saying rather that he "thought it lawful from my former act," it

---

[4] While I agree that Milton has created "a disenchanted story world" in *Samson Agonistes*, Stoll's conclusion seems extreme: "Following exactly the trail blazed by Cherbury, Milton expands a skepticism toward the specific revelation of supernatural beings to a skepticism toward the total Judeo-Christian revelation." Stoll concedes, however, that "this skepticism will finally be rejected" (2002, 281, 300, 284).

[5] "Horror is the title I am giving to the perception of the precariousness of human identity, to the perception that it may be lost or invaded, that we may be, or may become, something other than we are, or take ourselves for" (Cavell 1979, 418–419). The skeptical recital of identity is one response to this horror.

nevertheless appears that Samson has failed to learn from his mistakes and to doubt the basis of his judgments.

Samson seems to be in thrall to *Erlebnis*, that German word for experience connoting a subjective immediacy, a jolt of sensation, an almost mystical quickening. Associated with a vital rupture in the continuum of history, *Erlebnis* approaches the sublime in its ecstatic intensity. Samson may subscribe to the *Lebensphilosophie* of Wilhelm Dilthey with its privileging of plenitude and encounter as the criteria of true experience. Milton's contemporaries might have dubbed this experiential confidence enthusiasm.[6] Nevertheless, Manoa, like the Chorus, takes a dim view of the stock Samson places in these surges of heightened feeling, saying, "I cannot praise thy marriage choices, Son, / Rather approve them not; but thou didst plead / Divine impulsion prompting" (420–422). As his use of the phrase, "marriage choices" indicates, Manoa objects to Samson's understanding of these discrete moments of ostensibly transcendent connection because they result in bad choices. Manoa would like Samson to be more skeptical regarding his inner weather.[7] When Samson reaches the nadir of his despair, saying "All otherwise to me my thoughts portend / That these dark orbs no more shall treat with light (590–591), Manoa dismisses his foreboding as the intuitions of a fevered consciousness, replying, "Believe not these suggestions which proceed / From anguish of the mind and humors black, / That mingle with thy fancy" (599–601). This time, however, Samson's portentous thoughts speak to him, not of divine impulsions, but of "Heav'n's desertion" (632), so that the Chorus encourages him to have a Gestalt shift, as it were, about his "faintings" and "swoonings of despair," urging him to "feel within / Some source of consolation from above; Secret refreshings" (663–665). From Manoa's point of view, Samson's inner flutterings are a form of deceptive experience. The Chorus is less skeptical than Manoa, less prone to distrust Samson's exercises in introspection, and at the same time more practical, their pep talk designed to harness Samson's remaining energy. Nevertheless, Manoa has a point: *Erlebnis* has been too much with Samson, laying waste his powers.

---

[6] See Grossman: "Milton's 1671 volume confronts the politically pressing inaccessibility of inward revelation by depicting Samson as a case study of enthusiasm under the Law in contrast with Jesus, who is rendered as reason's martyr" (2013, 384). But see Stoll who suggests that Milton's language of impulses, instincts, and motions evokes not enthusiasm but the "technical jargon" and "scientific specificity" present in Lord Herbert of Cherbury's epistemology (2002, 286, 290).

[7] Stoll deems Manoa an "exemplary skeptic" (2002, 289).

Yet it is not only Manoa who is skeptical. The poem itself questions the legitimacy of Samson's inner promptings, as is shown through the sexually charged language used to describe them. Not unlike the cruel fun Shakespeare has at Othello's expense when the cornered Moor boasts about his "sword" even as he is twice disarmed (5.2), bawdiness shadows Samson's transient "rousing motions." Compare in this regard Samson's swift decoding of *Erlebnis* – which seems so often conveniently to dovetail with what he wants to do anyway – with the thoughtful diffidence of Jesus in *Paradise Regained* when he experiences the push of "strong motion."[8] Samson arrives at the knowledge of what God wants for him with ease – he says, "I knew / From intimate impulse" (222–223). Jesus, by contrast, places a premium on ignorance and a trusting openness to what might befall. Jesus says, "And now by some strong motion I am led / Into this Wilderness, to what intent / I learn not yet; perhaps I need not know; / For what concerns my knowledge God reveals" (1.290–294). Not only is God's "motion" desexualized in *Paradise Regained*, but it also does not dictate a particular action. Instead, it prompts a general attentiveness amid a serene faith. Samson longs for a revelation from God and keeps hoping it might be happening, but the poem belies this hope by showing that Samson has things figured out too neatly – God's plan for him already anticipated and thereby foreclosed. It is only at the end, when Samson does not know what will happen – when he says, "I know not" (1418) – but is open to whatever God might send his way, that he begins to acquire that condition of poised receptivity that characterizes Jesus. The poem wants Samson (and us) to step back and question the supposition that his "rousing motions" are a sign of divine favor. They may not be a reliable sign. They may function like the modes of Aenesidemus and be no more trustworthy than the bent stick or the dove's neck regarding the actual situation at hand.

True experience, by contrast, involves trial and error, that is, learning from mistakes.[9] Milton uses the word throughout his *oeuvre* in a manner that is generally faithful to its Latin etymological root. As Martin Jay explains, "to try ('experiri') contains the same root as 'periculum' or danger," while the "ex-, meaning a coming forth from" suggests "having

---

[8] See Grossman's comparison between the "motions" impelling Samson and Jesus: "The non-representation of Samson's thoughts in the one poem and the dialectical representation of Jesus's thought-process in the other divide the old and new covenants according to whether or not divine motions are first mimetically articulated and submitted to reason" (2013, 384).

[9] See Russ Leo who argues that passions "are mobilized across the poem to this end: the acquisition of experience" (2019, 238).

survived ... risks and learned from the encounter" (2005, 3). When Eve, having bitten into the forbidden fruit, says, "Experience, next to thee I owe, / Best guide" (IX. 807–808) and afterward, when she entices Adam with the apple, adding, "On my experience, Adam, freely taste" (IX. 988), the ironies of her hymn to experience are rife. Indeed, in a proto-Baconian fashion, she later describes her experience as a "sad experiment" (X. 967). But if experience is a feature of fallen consciousness, as it certainly is in the Divorce tracts, where Milton invokes "lamented experience" which "daily teaches," it can also have positive connotations. In *Of Education*, it means broadening the traditional curriculum through practical, hands-on learning involving technical training and grand tours. Like Satan in *Paradise Regained* lamenting the provinciality of Jesus' upbringing and tempting him with panoramas of the larger world, "Best school of best experience" (III.238), Milton in *Of Education* describes "those vernal seasons of the year, when the air is calm and pleasant," saying "there is another opportunity of gaining experience to be won from pleasure it self abroad." Here again, experience has Baconian overtones with its notions of observation and exploration.[10] It corresponds to that other German word for experience, *Erfahrung*, with its root in the word, *fahrt*, meaning journey with its connotation of wisdom "acquist" over the course of peripatetic travel in space and time. *Erfahrung*, as Walter Benjamin understands it (1969), offers an integrated, holistic account of experience that builds on public memory and acknowledges the collective past. *Erlebnis*, by contrast, is private, brief, intense, disruptive, and divorced from the all the sticky cobwebs clinging to the lessons of history. In *Samson Agonistes*, the Chorus and Manoa are proponents of *Erfahrung* with its more measured rhythms and appeal to temporality, while Samson himself responds to the summons of *Erlebnis*, ascribing it to divine inspiration.

"At issue," as Barbara Lewalski has written, "is the right interpretation of past experience: how to validate and evaluate the external and internal signs that apparently testified to Samson's mission" (1988, 236). This dilemma is never solved. It never becomes clear how Samson's past bunglings fit into God's providential schemes. What is clear, however, is that the epistemological uncertainty produced by the split between *Erfahrung* and *Erlebnis* opens up a space for ethical choice in the here and now. The opacity of experience, the poem suggests, leads to opportunities for political action. Might Milton be remembering Marvell's

---

[10] "Milton's Baconianism, and the skeptical influence that accompanies it, stretches far into his careers in prose and poetry" (Sedley 2005, 85).

Cromwell in the "Horatian Ode"? Samson is hardly an untested and "forward youth," yet as a warrior he too feels compelled by heaven to seize the martial occasion. Might Milton also be remembering "the extraordinary equivocation" shown in Calvin's *Institutes* regarding feelings of "certainty [as] the basis of political action" (Walzer 1974, 59)?[11]

Consider the final scene when Samson's reasoning is anatomized as he struggles to understand what God wants him to do – hence, what is the right thing. Samson debates with himself and the Chorus about how to respond to the Officer's command that he perform feats of strength for the Philistians at the Temple of Dagon. When the Officer first bids Samson to the solemn feast, Samson refuses, giving as his reason the Hebrew Law, which forbids his presence at Philistian religious rites. When the Officer persists, Samson replies, "I will not come," objecting that his "conscience and internal peace" will not allow it – thereby taking ownership of his refusal, as numerous critics have pointed out. After the Officer leaves, the Chorus and Samson discuss how to take ethical action in circumstances of political constraint. The Chorus opines that "Where the heart joins not, outward acts defile not" (1368). This verse is often cited together with the Lady's famous lines in *Comus*: "Thou canst not touch the freedom of my mind / With all thy charms, although this corporal rind / Thou hast immanacl'd" (663–665). But the import of these verses is quite different. The Lady's words defy Comus, challenging him, while the Chorus's counsel equivocation and conformity. Samson replies that if he complies – and he is still in the hypothetical "if" mode – his act of compliance will be his own choice. "Commands are no constraints" (1372), he says, distinguishing "commands" from "outward force." "If I obey them, / I do it freely" (1372–1373), he says, even as he admits that God could never forgive him for that paradoxical act of free obedience since it implies "venturing to displease / God for the fear of Man, and Man prefer, / Set God behind" (1373–1375).

Then, the direction of Samson's reasoning shifts, illustrating the tortuousness of ascertaining the ethical path in the absence of divine guidance. All along he has been hewing to ideas of inner peace and freedom such that, up until this moment, he has said no to the command performance. Suddenly he changes his mind. First, he backtracks and observes that even a jealous God can make exceptions when expedient. He says, "Yet that he

---

[11] Calvin warned that "experience shows, that the reprobate are sometimes affected with emotions very similar to those of the elect, so that, in their own opinion, they in no respect differ from the elect" (1921, III.ii.11); cited in Walzer 1974, 59.

may dispense with me or thee / Present in Temples at Idolatrous Rites / For some important cause, thou needst not doubt" (1377–1379). In keeping with nominalist thought-experiments, Samson suggests that God has the power and freedom to break his own laws, "thou needst not doubt." The double negative translates to 'is pretty sure' or 'well-nigh certain,' meaning a degree of certainty just short of the real thing and closer to probability. The Chorus senses the reversal in Samson's thinking, saying, "How thou wilt here come off surmounts my reach" (1380). And now Samson is caught once more in the full grip of *Erlebnis*, revived by what he hopes is the return of his internal vitality and strength: "Be of good courage, I begin to feel / Some rousing motions in me which dispose / To something extraordinary my thoughts" (1381–1383). Samson's reasoning takes him from refusal to compliance, and yet Samson goes – he assures the Chorus – as a free man ready to channel the power of God.

Numerous critics have observed that Samson becomes ironic as the Officer leads him away, engaging in coded speech that has different meanings for different audiences. In the pursuit of covert policy, he becomes adept at equivocation and double-speak. So when he asks rhetorically, "And for a life who will not change his purpose? / (So mutable are the ways of men)" (406–407), to the Officer it may mean that thanks to coercion, Samson is reduced to quips about self-preservation. The Chorus may suspect a renewed attempt to discern the direction of his vocation with that reference to "life" and "purpose." To those readers for whom ideas of liberty accompany the word "life," Samson is revealing his paradoxical desire to be a free agent conformed to God's will. By taking the purpose of his life into his own hands, Samson hopes to breach the distance between himself and God and thereby redeem himself.

As a wayfarer, Samson experiences God as a *deus absconditus*, hidden and enigmatic.[12] He imagines God in a nominalist vein: a sublime Being with the power to abrogate his own laws if he chooses. Yet God has a covenant with him. Samson's sense of himself and his vocation depends on this covenant. Nevertheless, as a creature "under the dome" of heaven (to echo Oberman), Samson is radically free to forge his own path. His autonomy is a responsibility and a burden, issuing in dreams of intimacy (with Dalila) and terrible loneliness. Nominalist structures of feeling (described in Chapter 1) are on full display in *Samson Agonistes*: from the implicit possibility that God might exercise his power to induce false

---

[12] "The divine absence is all the more glaring given that *Samson* is Milton's only major poem without any divine beings present or directing the action" (Herman 2005, 172).

beliefs in his creatures to eschatological openness and a readiness to seize on divine signs. At the same time the unbridgeable distance to God makes Samson feel bereft. The sense of abandonment in turn induces a "quest for immediacy" and a desire "to transcend the dome" (Oberman 1960, 62–63). Samson embodies the struggles and emotions of the *viator* in a nominalist cosmos. As he weighs his limited options, struggling to determine which action or inaction might best restore his sense of dignity and purpose, one might say that Samson seeks to reoccupy "the vacancy in [his] systematics of consciousness" (Blumenberg 1987, 56). His self-assertion fills the ambient emptiness, his performances of identity in effect a skeptical recital uttered to assure himself as much as others that Samson still is Samson. Although he may well be an avatar of Spenser's dreamer in the translations from Du Bellay, he has traveled a long way from the sleepy piping of Colin Clout. The temple he envisions crumbling with apocalyptic finality is no chimera in his mind but hewn stone under his palms. No longer dreaming, Samson blindly experiments.

What passes though Samson's mind as he pauses in meditative silence between the massy pillars of Dagon's temple? We will never truly know as befits a world marked by the inaccessibility of other minds. Yet, the Messenger reports that "with head a while inclin'd, / And eyes fast fixt he stood, as one who pray'd, / Or some great matter in his mind revolv'd" (1636–1638). Samson is perhaps praying, perhaps revolving some great matter, the Messenger speculates, using the "or" that Peter Herman argues characterizes Milton's poetics of incertitude (2005, 173).[13] In his last words to the Chorus, Samson approaches the Temple, anticipating that "This day will be remarkable in my life / By some great act, or of my days the last" (1388–1389). Here the Miltonic "or" signifies Samson's own uncertainty about what is to transpire. But he goes, open, ready, receptive, harboring the almost naïve hope that this time will be different, this time his rousing motions will redound to the glory of God. In *Paradise Regained*, Satan tempts Jesus with the old saw that God helps only those who help themselves, saying, "Zeal and Duty are not slow, / But on

---

[13] See Lewalski: "Like the reader, Manoa and the Chorus have no direct access to this event: they experience it only at a distance, through several filters, and the resulting ambiguities elicit from them most of the interpretative possibilities offered by the exegetical tradition" (1988, 245). Fish affirms that "the moment is presented as radically indeterminate" (1989, 567), suggesting that this indeterminacy is characteristic of Milton's "strategy" in the poem: "Everything that serves in the sources and analogues to produce interpretive certainty is also to be found in *Samson Agonistes*, but it is found in the wrong place, that is, in a place where it multiplies rather than reduces interpretive crisis" (1989, 570).

Occasion's forelock watchful wait. / They themselves rather are occasion best, / Zeal of thy Father's house, Duty to free / Thy country from her Heathen servitude" (III.172–176). He continues in this vein, reminding Jesus that "the perfect season" for delivering the world "is nowhere told": "each act is rightliest done, / Not when it must, but when it may be best" (IV.475–476). In the silence of his meditation between the massy pillars, Samson may fall prey to this form of Satanic thinking – seize occasion's forelock! If not now, when? Yet the poem also entertains the possibility that this is Samson's perfect season, his *kairós*. He has served by standing and waiting, even suffering, and now his time has come.[14] This ambiguity is structural and cannot be resolved.[15] Yet, Samson's own uncertainty about the final meaning of his action and his willingness to risk all in the face of that uncertainty discloses not only nominalist structures of feeling, the challenges of providentialism, and the quandaries of ethical choice. It also shows how skepticism is intertwined with the sublime as the blind seeker pits himself against the vast unknown.[16] More broadly, the poem attests that experience is in crisis in the seventeenth century, portending its impoverishment in aftertimes.[17]

In *Infancy and History: The Destruction of Experience*, Giorgio Agamben has argued that the mid-seventeenth century sees a fundamental shift in the concept of experience. Traditionally it was possible for a person not only to "undergo," but also to "have" experience such that as the individual gained in maturity and approached death, he arrived at "an achieved totality of experience" (2007, 26), at once having and undergoing it.

---

[14] See Norbrook: "Within the constraints of the situation he faces, Samson has the options only of seizing or refusing the occasion" (2003, 144).
[15] See Wittreich: "If Milton leaves indefinite what actually happens in *Samson Agonistes*, he does so because there are finally no means of knowing the answers to the questions that his retelling of the Samson story poses" (2002, 11). See Kahn: "In obscuring the grounds of Samson's decision, Milton puts the reader in Samson's position of deciding the meaning of his act. It is this interpretive reticence on Milton's part which helps to make reading *Samson Agonistes* such an ambivalent experience" (1996, 1088). But see Shore: "Milton conceals the source of Samson's motions to take advantage of Royalist anxiety while ministering to Dissenter hopes. This concealment should be understood as a means of persuasion expertly fitted to the practical circumstances, what Annabel Patterson has called a 'functional ambiguity'" (2012, 160).
[16] See Budick who argues that *Samson Agonistes* influenced Kant's philosophy of the sublime (2010, 216–253).
[17] Loewenstein situates the uncertainties experienced by Samson in terms of Puritan providentialism, citing the Commonwealth preacher John Owen: "[God] holds the minds of men in uncertainty, and suspence, for his own glorious ends, ... When God is doing great things, he delights ... to keep the minds of men in uncertainties, that he may ... try them to the utmost" (2001, 278). Surveying Milton's *oeuvre*, Lewalski argues that "Milton's concern, early to late, with the uses and the problematics of experience owes something to this pervasive Puritan emphasis, but in his usage the term draws upon the full range of seventeenth-century meanings" (1992, 8).

The prototype here is Montaigne in his concluding essay, "Of Experience." By contrast, Agamben contends, the modern subject can only "undergo" experience. As an example of the way the subject of experience splits in two in the seventeenth century, he cites *Don Quixote*: "Don Quijote, the old subject of knowledge, has been befuddled by a spell and can only undergo experience without ever having it. By his side, Sancho Panza, the old subject of experience, can only have it, without ever undergoing it" (2007, 27). Sancho, after all, is a fount of maxims and proverbs, "which were the guise in which experience stood as authority" (2007, 17). Insofar as this dichotomy maps onto the distinction between *Erfahrung* and *Erlebnis*, it offers a window into Samson's crisis of experience.

Might we say that while Manoa and the Chorus have experience, Samson can only undergo it?[18] If so, *Samson Agonistes* mourns the passing of "true experience" from history, the Chorus's consoling remarks notwithstanding. Certainly, the poem dramatizes the pathos of the individual striving to understand the will of God when all he has to go on are the obscure promptings of his inner light. By focusing on Samson's changes of heart and what passes for reasoning as he interprets the presages of his mind, the poem asks us to ponder the withdrawal of *Erfahrung*, the dubiety of *Erlebnis*, the desire for ethical knowledge, and the rebuffs to understanding. Perhaps this analysis brings Milton's poem too close to Walter Benjamin's nostalgic sense that the modern world has seen "the increasing atrophy of experience" (1969, 159) as men retire to their forts of silence, unwittingly "grown ... poorer in communicable experience" (1969, 84). Yet, independently of Benjamin's apocalyptic and melancholy view, I think Samson's desire to exercise strenuous liberty in the face of indecipherable experience captures the modern condition inaugurated by the nominalist sense of God's distance and inscrutable power. Samson's yearning for clarity together with his rage at his clouded awareness results in a tragic consciousness made tolerable for him – and sublime for us – by his compulsion to experiment and blindly hazard all.

---

[18] Lewalski observes that the Chorus "tend to privilege the maxims, proverbs, and exemplary histories that codify the common cultural experience of the nation or of humankind, and to resist indications that something truly extraordinary is now happening to them," while "Samson's primary reference point is always his inward, subjective experience" (1988, 237–238). This contrast corresponds, mutatis mutandis, to that between Sancho and Don Quixote, supporting Agamben's views on the seventeenth-century crisis of experience.

Bibliography

Aaron, R. I. *John Locke*, 2nd ed. Oxford: Oxford University Press, 1955.
Adams, David. "Metaphors for Mankind: The Development of Hans Blumenberg's Anthropological Metaphorology." *Journal of the History of Ideas* 52.1 (1991): 152–166.
Adams, Marilyn McCord. "Intuitive Cognition, Certainty, and Scepticism in William Ockham." *Traditio* 26 (1970): 389–398.
"Ockham's Nominalism and Unreal Entities." *The Philosophical Review* 86.2 (1977): 144–176.
Adams, Thomas. *A Commentary or, exposition upon the divine second epistle generall, written by the blessed apostle St. Peter*. London: Richard Badger [and Felix Kyngston] for Iacob Bloome, 1633.
Adorno, Theodor W. *Aesthetic Theory*. Trans. Robert Hullot-Kentor. Minneapolis: University of Minnesota Press, 1997.
Adrichem, Christiaan van. *Briefe description of Hierusalem and of the suburbs thereof, as it flourished in the time of Christ*. Trans. Thomas Tymme. London: Thomas Wright, 1595.
Agamben, Giorgio. *Infancy and History: The Destruction of Experience*. Trans. Liz Heron. London and New York: Verso, 2007.
The Man without Content. Trans. Georgia Albert. Stanford, CA: Stanford University Press, 1999.
Taste. Trans. Cooper Francis. London, New York, Calcutta: Seagull Books, 2017.
Aggeler, Geoffrey. *Nobler in the Mind: The Stoic–Skeptic Dialectic in English Renaissance Tragedy*. Newark: University of Delaware Press, 1988.
Allen, D. C. *Doubt's Boundless Sea: Skepticism and Faith in the Renaissance*. Baltimore, MD: Johns Hopkins University Press, 1964.
"Some Theories of the Growth and Origin of Language in Milton's Age." *Philological Quarterly* 28 (1949): 5–16.
Allen, Robert J., ed. *Addison and Steele: Selections from The Tatler and The Spectator*. 2nd ed. New York: Holt, Rinehart and Winston, 1970.
Altman, Joel. *The Tudor Play of Mind: Rhetorical Inquiry and the Development of Elizabethan Drama*. Berkeley: University of California Press, 1978.
Anderson, Judith H. "Mutability and Mortality," in *Celebrating Mutabilitie*. Ed. Jane Grogan. Manchester: Manchester University Press, 2010. 246–274.

Ankers, Neil. "Paradigms and Politics: Hobbes and Cavendish Contrasted," in *A Princely Brave Woman*. Ed. Stephen Clucas. Aldershot: Ashgate, 2003. 242–254.
Annas, Julia, and Jonathan Barnes. *The Modes of Scepticism: Ancient Texts and Modern Interpretations*. Cambridge: Cambridge University Press, 1985.
Asad, Talal. *Formations of the Secular: Christianity, Islam, Modernity*. Stanford, CA: Stanford University Press, 2003.
Assman, Aleida. *Cultural Memory and Western Civilization*. Cambridge: Cambridge University Press, 2011.
Aubrey, John. *Brief Lives*. Ed. Richard Barber. London: The Folio Society, 1975.
Augustine. *City of God*. Trans. Henry Bettenson. London: Penguin, 1984.
Augustine, Matthew. "'Lillies without, roses within': Marvell's Poetics of Indeterminacy and 'The Nymph Complaining.'" *Criticism* 50.2 (2008): 255–278.
Austin, J. L. *How To Do Things With Words*. Cambridge, MA: Harvard University Press, 1962.
Philosophical Papers. Ed. J. O. Urmson and G. J. Warnock. Oxford: Oxford University Press, 1961.
Ayer, A. J., and R. Rhees, "Symposium: Can There Be a Private Language?," Proceedings of the Aristotelian Society, Supplementary Volumes 28 (1954): 63–94.
Aylmer, G. E. "Collective Mentalities in Mid Seventeenth-Century England: IV. Cross Currents: Neutrals, Trimmers and Others." *Transactions of the Royal Historical Society* 39 (1989): 1–22.
Bacon, Francis. *A Selection of His Works*. Ed. Sidney Warhaft. New York: Odyssey Press, 1965.
The Works of Francis Bacon. Ed. James Spedding et al. 14 vols. London: Longman, 1857–74.
Barbour, Reid. *Literature and Religious Culture in Seventeenth-Century England*. Cambridge: Cambridge University Press, 2001.
John Selden: Measures of the Holy Commonwealth in Seventeenth-Century England. Toronto: University of Toronto Press, 2003.
Bardle, Stephen. *The Literary Underground in the 1660s*. Oxford: Oxford University Press, 2012.
Barkan, Leonard. "Ruins and Visions: Spenser, Pictures, Rome," in *Edmund Spenser: Essays on Culture and Allegory*. Ed. Jennifer Klein Morrison and Matthew Greenfield. Burlington, VT: Ashgate, 2000. 9–36.
Barnes, Jonathan. "Mr. Locke's Darling Notion." *Philosophical Quarterly* 22 (1972): 193–214.
Barthes, Roland. *The Language of Fashion*. Trans. Andy Stafford. London: Bloomsbury, 2013.
The Neutral. Trans. Rosalind E. Krauss and Denis Hollier. New York: Columbia University Press, 2005.
Battigelli, Anna. *Margaret Cavendish and the Exiles of the Mind*. Lexington: The University Press of Kentucky, 1998.

Baxter, Richard. *More Reasons for the Christian Religion, and no reason against it . . . being. . . II. Some Animadversions on a tractate De veritate.* London, 1672.
Bedford, R. D. *The Defence of Truth: Herbert of Cherbury and the Seventeenth Century.* Manchester: Manchester University Press, 1979.
Bednarz, James P. "*The Passionate Pilgrim* and 'The Phoenix and Turtle,'" in *The Cambridge Companion to Shakespeare's Poetry.* Ed. Patrick Cheney. Cambridge: Cambridge University Press, 2007. 108–124.
  Shakespeare and the Truth of Love: The Mystery of "The Phoenix and Turtle." New York: Palgrave Macmillan, 2012.
Bell, Daniel. "Return of the Sacred: The Argument about the Future of Religion," in *Progress and Its Discontents.* Ed. G. A. Almond, M. Chodorow, and R. H. Pearce. Berkeley: University of California Press, 1982. 501–523.
Bell, Millicent. *Shakespeare's Tragic Skepticism.* New Haven, CT: Yale University Press, 2002.
Benjamin, Walter. *Illuminations.* Ed. Hannah Arendt. Trans. Harry Zohn. New York: Schocken, 1969.
Bennett, Jane. *The Enchantment of Modern Life: Attachments, Crossings, and Ethics.* Princeton, NJ: Princeton University Press, 2001.
  Vibrant Matter: A Political Ecology of Things. Durham, NC: Duke University Press, 2010.
Bennett, Joan S. *Reviving Liberty: Radical Christian Humanism in Milton's Great Poems.* Cambridge, MA: Harvard University Press, 1989.
Berger, Jr., Harry. *Revisionary Play: Studies in the Spenserian Dynamics.* Intro. Louis Adrian Montrose. Berkeley: University of California Press, 1988.
  "The *Mutabilitie Cantos*: Archaism and Evolution in Retrospect," in *Spenser.* Ed. Harry Berger, Jr. Englewood Cliffs, NJ: Prentice-Hall, 1968. 146–176.
Berlant, Lauren, ed. *Intimacy.* Chicago: The University of Chicago Press, 2000.
Biard, Joël. "Nominalism in the Later Middle Ages," in *The Cambridge History of Medieval Philosophy.* Ed. Robert Pasnau and Christina Van Dyke. Cambridge: Cambridge University Press, 2014. II: 661–673.
Bieman, Elizabeth. *Plato Baptized: Towards the Interpretation of Spenser's Mimetic Fictions.* Toronto: University of Toronto Press, 1988.
Bilgrami, Akeel. *Secularism, Identity, and Enchantment.* Cambridge, MA: Harvard University Press, 2014.
Bloom, Harold, ed. *Andrew Marvell: Modern Critical Views.* New York and Philadelphia: Chelsea House, 1989.
Blumenberg, Hans. *Care Crosses the River.* 1987. Trans. Paul Fleming. Stanford, CA: Stanford University Press, 2010.
  The Legitimacy of the Modern Age. 1966. Trans. Robert M. Wallace. Cambridge, MA: The MIT Press, 1983.
  Paradigms for a Metaphorology. Trans. Robert Savage. Ithaca, NY: Cornell University Press, 2010.
  Shipwreck with Spectator: Paradigm of a Metaphor for Existence. Trans. Steven Rendall. Cambridge, MA: The MIT Press, 1997.

Bodin, Jean. *Method for the Easy Comprehension of History*. Trans. Beatrice Reynolds. New York: Octagon Books, 1966.
Bourdieu, Pierre. *Distinction: A Social Critique of the Judgement of Taste*. 1979. Trans. Richard Nice. London: Routledge & Kegan Paul, 1989.
Boyle, Robert. *An essay on the origine & virtue of gems*. London, 1672.
Bradshaw, Graham. *Shakespeare's Scepticism*. Brighton: Harvester Press, 1987.
Bredvold, Louis I. *The Intellectual Milieu of John Dryden*. Ann Arbor: University of Michigan Press, 1934.
Broad, Jacqueline. "Margaret Cavendish and Joseph Glanvill: Science, Religion, and Witchcraft." *Studies in History and Philosophy of Science* 38.3 (2007): 493–505.
Bromley, James M. *Intimacy and Sexuality in the Age of Shakespeare*. Cambridge: Cambridge University Press, 2012.
Brooks, Christopher W. *Law, Politics and Society in Early Modern England*. Cambridge: Cambridge University Press, 2008.
Brooks, Cleanth. *The Well Wrought Urn*. New York: Harcourt Brace, 1947.
Brown, Richard Danson. "'I would abate the sternenesse of my stile': Diction and Poetic Subversion in *Two Cantos of Mutabilitie*," in *Celebrating Mutabilitie*. Ed. Jane Grogan. Manchester: Manchester University Press, 2010. 275–294.
Bruce, Steve. *Secularization*. Oxford: Oxford University Press, 2011.
Bruns, Gerald L. *Heidegger's Estrangements: Language, Truth, and Poetry in the Later Writings*. New Haven, CT: Yale University Press, 1989.
Bryskett, Leonard. *A Discourse of Civill Life* in *Literary Works*. Ed. J. H. P. Pafford. Farnborough: Gregg International Publishers, 1972.
Budick, Sanford. *Kant and Milton*. Cambridge, MA: Harvard University Press, 2010.
Burke, Edmund. *A Philosophical Enquiry into the Origin of our Ideas of the Sublime and the Beautiful*. 1757. Ed. Adam Phillips. Oxford: Oxford University Press, 1990.
Burke, Peter. "Religion and Secularization," in *New Cambridge Modern History*. Cambridge: Cambridge University Press, 1979. XIII: 293–317.
"Tacitism, Scepticism, and Reason of State," in *The Cambridge History of Political Thought 1450–1700*. Ed. J. H. Burns and Mark Goldie. Cambridge: Cambridge University Press, 1990. 479–498.
Burrow, Colin. "Spenser and Classical Traditions," in *The Cambridge Companion to Spenser*. Ed. Andrew D. Hadfield. Cambridge: Cambridge University Press, 2001. 217–236.
Butler, John. *Lord Herbert of Cherbury (1582–1648): An Intellectual Biography*. Lewiston, NY: The Edwin Mellen Press, 1990.
Caldwell, Melissa M. *Skepticism and Belief in Early Modern England: The Reformation of Moral Value*. London: Routledge, 2016.
Calhoun, Craig, Mark Juergensmeyer, and Jonathan Van Antwerpen, eds. *Rethinking Secularism*. Oxford: Oxford University Press, 2011.
Calvin, John. *The Institutes of Christian Religion*. Ed. and trans. John Allen. Philadelphia, PA: Presbyterian Board of Publications, 1921.

Carlini, Armando. *Classe di scienzi morali, storiche, e filologiche.* Firenze: Reale Accademia dei Lincei, 1917.
Cassirer, Ernst. *The Philosophy of the Enlightenment.* 1932. Trans. Fritz C. A. Koelln and James P. Pettegrove. Boston, MA: Beacon Press, 1955.
Castro, Américo. *El pensamiento de Cervantes.* Madrid: Hernando, 1925.
Cave, Terence. *Retrospectives.* Ed. Neil Kenny and Wes Williams. London: Legenda, 2009.
Cavell, Stanley. *Cities of Words.* Cambridge, MA: Harvard University Press, 2004.
  The Claim of Reason: Wittgenstein, Skepticism, Morality, and Tragedy. Oxford: Oxford University Press, 1979.
  Contesting Tears: The Hollywood Melodrama of the Unknown Woman. Chicago: The University of Chicago Press, 1996.
  Disowning Knowledge in Seven Plays of Shakespeare. Cambridge: Cambridge University Press, 2003.
  "Excursus on Wittgenstein's Vision of Language," in *The New Wittgenstein.* Ed. Alice Crary and Rupert Read. London: Routledge, 2000. 21–37.
  In Quest of the Ordinary: Lines of Skepticism and Romanticism. Chicago: The University of Chicago Press, 1988.
  Must We Mean What We Say? Cambridge: Cambridge University Press, 2002.
  Philosophy the Day After Tomorrow. Cambridge, MA: The Belknap Press of Harvard University Press, 2005.
  A Pitch of Philosophy. Cambridge, MA: Harvard University Press, 1994.
Cavendish, Margaret. *The Blazing World and Other Writings.* Ed. Kate Lilley. London: Penguin, 1994.
  Life of William Cavendish, duke of Newcastle. Ed. C. H. Firth. London: Routledge, 1886.
  Natures Pictures. London: J. Martin & J. Allestrye, 1656.
  Observations on Experimental Philosophy. Ed. Eileen O'Neill. Cambridge: Cambridge University Press, 2001.
  Orations of Divers Sorts. London, 1662.
  Paper Bodies: A Margaret Cavendish Reader. Ed. Sylvia Bowerbank and Sara Mendelson. Peterborough, ON: Broadview Press, 2000.
  Philosophical Letters. London, 1664.
  Playes. London, 1662.
  Poems, and Fancies. London, 1653.
  Sociable Letters. Ed. James Fitzmaurice. New York and London: Garland, 1997.
  The World's Olio. London: J. Martin & J. Allestrye, 1655.
Chappuzeau, Samuel. *The History of Jewels, and of the principal riches of the East and West taken from the relation of divers of the most famous travellers of our age: attended with fair discoveries conducing to the knowledge of the universe and trade.* London: Hobart Kemp, 1671.
Chaucer, Geoffrey. *The Riverside Chaucer.* Ed. Larry D. Benson. Boston, MA: Houghton Mifflin, 1987.
Cheney, Patrick. *English Authorship and the Early Modern Sublime: Spenser, Marlowe, Shakespeare, Jonson.* Cambridge: Cambridge University Press, 2018.

"The Voice of the Author in 'The Phoenix and Turtle': Chaucer, Shakespeare, Spenser," in *Shakespeare and the Middle Ages*. Ed. Curtis Perry and John Watkins. Oxford: Oxford University Press, 2009. 103–125.

Chernaik, Warren L., and Martin Dzelzainis, eds. *Marvell and Liberty*. New York: St. Martin's Press, 1999.

Chibnall, Jennifer. "Something to the Purpose: Marvell's Rhetorical Strategy in *The Rehearsal Transpros'd* (1672)." *Prose Studies* 9 (1986): 80–104.

Christian, Margaret. *Spenserian Allegory and Elizabethan Biblical Exegesis*. Manchester: Manchester University Press, 2016.

Clark, Stuart. *Vanities of the Eye: Vision in Early Modern Culture*. Oxford: Oxford University Press, 2007.

Clucas, Stephen. "The Atomism of the Cavendish Circle: A Reappraisal." *The Seventeenth Century* 9 (1994): 247–273.

"Variation, Irregularity and Probabilism," in *A Princely Brave Woman: Essays on Margaret Cavendish, Duchess of Newcastle*. Ed. Stephen Clucas. Aldershot: Ashgate, 2003. 109–209.

Coldiron, A. E. B. "How Spenser Excavates Du Bellay's *Antiquitez*." *JEGP* 101.1 (2002): 41–67.

Coleridge, Samuel Taylor. "Spenser's Art" (1818), in *Edmund Spenser's Poetry: A Norton Critical Edition*. Ed. Anne Lake Prescott and Andrew D. Hadfield. New York: Norton, 2014.

Colie, Rosalie. *"My echoing song:" Andrew Marvell's Poetry of Criticism*. Princeton, NJ: Princeton University Press, 1970.

Paradoxia Epidemica. Princeton, NJ: Princeton University Press, 1966.

Compagnon, Antoine. *Nous, Michel de Montaigne*. Paris: Seuil, 1980.

Conant, James. "Varieties of Scepticism," in *Wittgenstein and Scepticism*. Ed. Denis MacManus. London: Routledge, 2004. 97–136.

Conway, Anne. *The Principles of the Most Ancient and Modern Philosophy*. Ed. Allison P. Coudert and Taylor Corse. Cambridge: Cambridge University Press, 1996.

Coudert, Allison P. ed. *The Language of Adam / Die Sprache Adams*. Wolfenbütteler Forschungen, *Bd*. 84. Wiesbaden: Harrassowitz, 1999.

Courtenay, William J. *Covenant and Causality in Medieval Thought*. London: Variorum Reprints, 1984.

"In Search of Nominalism: Two Centuries of Historical Debate," in *Ockham and Ockhamism: Studies in the Dissemination and Impact of His Thought*. Boston: Brill, 2008. 1–20.

Cox, Harvey. *The Secular City: Secularization and Urbanization in Theological Perspective*. New York: Macmillan, 1965.

Cox, John D. *Seeming Knowledge: Shakespeare and Skeptical Faith*. Waco, TX: Baylor University Press, 2007.

Croce, Benedetto. *Aesthetic: As Science of Expression and General Linguistic*. Trans. Douglas Ainslie. New York: Noonday Press, 1956.

Cummings, Brian. *Mortal Thoughts: Religion, Secularity and Identity in Shakespeare and Early Modern Culture*. Oxford: Oxford University Press, 2013.

Cunning, David. *Cavendish*. London: Routledge, 2016.
Cunningham, J. V. "'Essence' and the Phoenix and Turtle." *ELH* 19.4 (1952): 265–276.
Curley, Edwin M. "Skepticism and Toleration: The Case of Montaigne," in *Oxford Studies in Early Modern Philosophy*, Vol. 2. Ed. Daniel Garber and Steven Nadler. Oxford: Oxford University Press, 2005. 1–34.
Darmon, Jean-Charles. "Questionnements sceptiques et politiques de la fable: les 'autres mondes' du libertinage érudit," in *Skepticism and Political Thought in the Seventeenth and Eighteenth Centuries*. Ed. John Christian and Gianni Paganini. Toronto: University of Toronto Press, 2015. 83–112.
Daston, Lorraine, and Katherine Park. *Wonders and the Order of Nature, 1150–1750*. New York: Zone Books, 1998.
Davies, John. *Orchestra or A poeme of dauncing*. London: N. Ling, 1596.
Davis, Kathleen. *Periodization and Sovereignty: How Ideas of Feudalism and Secularization Govern the Politics of Time*. Philadelphia: University of Pennsylvania Press, 2008.
Dear, Peter. "From Truth to Disinterestedness in the Seventeenth Century." *Social Studies of Science* 22.4 (1992): 619–631.
Demonet, Marie-Luce, and Alain Legros, eds. *L'Écriture du scepticisme chez Montaigne*. Geneva: Droz, 2004.
Derrida, Jacques. *Positions*. Trans. Alan Bass. Chicago: The University of Chicago Press, 1972.
Detlefsen, Karen. "Atomism, Monism, and Causation in the Natural Philosophy of Margaret Cavendish." In *Oxford Studies in Early Modern Philosophy*, Vol. 3. Ed. Daniel Garber and Steven Nadler. Oxford: Clarendon Press, 2006. 199–240.
Dimock, Wai Chee. "A Theory of Resonance." *PMLA* 112.5 (1997): 1060–1071.
DiSanto, Michael. "Andrew Marvell's Ambivalence Toward Adult Sexuality." *SEL* 48 (2008): 165–182.
Dodds, Gregory D. *Exploiting Erasmus: The Erasmian Legacy and Religious Change in Early Modern England*. Toronto: University of Toronto Press, 2009.
Dodds, Lara. *The Literary Invention of Margaret Cavendish*. Pittsburgh, PA: Duquesne University Press, 2013.
Dollimore, Jonathan. *Radical Tragedy*. Chicago: The University of Chicago Press, 1984.
Donaldson, Ian. *Ben Jonson: A Life*. Oxford: Oxford University Press, 2011.
Donne, John. *The Complete English Poems*, Ed. A. J. Smith. London: Penguin, 1971.
Doran, Robert. *The Theory of the Sublime from Longinus to Kant*. Cambridge: Cambridge University Press, 2015.
Doyle, John P. "Another God, Chimerae, Goat-Stags and Man-Lions: A Seventeenth-Century Debate about Impossible Objects." *The Review of Metaphysics* 48.4 (1995): 771–808.
Du Bellay, Joachim. *Les regrets, Les antiquités de Rome*, Ed. S. de Sacy. Paris: Gallimard, 1967.

Dupré, Louis. *Passage to Modernity*. New Haven, CT: Yale University Press, 1993.
Dykstal, Timothy. *The Luxury of Skepticism: Politics, Philosophy, and Dialogue in the English Public Sphere, 1660–1740*. Charlottesville: University of Virginia Press, 2001.
Eco, Umberto. *The Search for the Perfect Language*. Trans. James Fentress. Oxford: Blackwell, 1995.
Eden, Kathy. *The Renaissance Rediscovery of Intimacy*. Chicago: The University of Chicago Press, 2012.
Eggert, Katherine. *Disknowledge: Literature, Alchemy, and the End of Humanism in Renaissance England*. Philadelphia: University of Pennsylvania Press, 2015.
Eliot, T. S. *Selected Prose of T. S. Eliot*. Ed. Frank Kermode. New York: Farrar, Strauss and Giroux, 1975.
Elliott, J. H. *Spain, Europe and the Wider World 1500–1800*. New Haven, CT: Yale University Press, 2009.
Ellrodt, Robert. *Seven Metaphysical Poets*. Oxford: Oxford University Press, 2000.
Engle, Lars. "*Measure for Measure* and Modernity: The Problem of the Skeptic's Authority," in *Shakespeare and Modernity*. Ed. Hugh Grady. London: Routledge, 2000. 85–104.
Evans, Joan. *Magical Jewels of the Middle-Ages and the Renaissance, particularly in England*. Oxford: Clarendon Press, 1922.
Everett, Barbara. "Set upon a golden bough to sing: Shakespeare's Debt to Sidney in 'The Phoenix and Turtle,'" *Times Literary Supplement*, 16 Feb. 2001, 13–15.
"The Shooting of the Bears," in *Andrew Marvell: Essays on the Tercentenary of His Death*. Ed. R. L. Brett. Hull and Oxford: Oxford University Press, 1979. 62–103.
Fallon, Stephen M. *Milton among the Philosophers*. Ithaca, NY: Cornell University Press, 1991.
Felski, Rita. *Uses of Literature*. Oxford: Blackwell, 2008.
Ferry, Luc. *Homo Aestheticus: The Invention of Taste in the Democratic Age*. Trans. Robert de Loaiza. Chicago: The University of Chicago Press, 1993.
Fish, Stanley. "Question and Answer in *Samson Agonistes*." *Critical Quarterly* 11 (1969): 237–264.
"Spectacle and Evidence in *Samson Agonistes*." *Critical Inquiry* 15.3 (1989): 556–586.
Fleming, Paul, Rüdiger Campe, and Kirk Wetters. "Introduction." *Telos* 158 (2012): 3–7.
Fletcher, Angus. *Allegory: The Theory of a Symbolic Mode*. Ithaca, NY: Cornell University Press, 1964.
Colors of the Mind: Conjectures on Thinking in Literature. Cambridge, MA: Harvard University Press, 1991.
Floridi, Luciano. *Sextus Empiricus: The Transmission and Recovery of Pyrrhonism*. Oxford: Oxford University Press, 2002.
Fordyce, C. J., and T. M. Knox, "The Library of Jesus College, Oxford: With an Appendix on the Books Bequeathed thereto by Lord Herbert of Cherbury," *Oxford Bibliographical Society, Proceedings and Papers* 5 (1937): 49–115.

Formigari, Lia. *A History of Language Philosophies*. Trans. Gabriel Poole. Amsterdam / Philadelphia: John Benjamins, 2004.
Fowler, Alastair. "Neoplatonic Order in *The Faerie Queen*," in *Spenser: The Faerie Queene, A Casebook*. Ed. Peter Bayley. London: Macmillan, 1977. 224–239.
Friedman, Donald M. "Rude Heaps and Decent Order," in *Marvell and Liberty*. Ed. Warren Chernaik and Martin Dzelzainis. London: Macmillan, 1999. 123–144.
Fuller, Margaret. "The Two Herberts." *Papers on Literature and Art*. New York: Wiley and Putnam, 1846.
Funkenstein, Amos. "Scholasticism, Scepticism and Secular Theology," in *Scepticism from the Renaissance to the Enlightenment*. Ed. Richard H. Popkin and Charles B. Schmitt. Wolfenbütteler Forschungen. Wiesbaden: Otto Harrassowitz, 1987. 45–54.
  Theology and Scientific Imagination from the Middle Ages to the Seventeenth Century. Princeton, NJ: Princeton University Press, 1986.
Gadamer, Hans-Georg. *Truth and Method*. 1960. London: Continuum, 1975.
Gallagher, Catherine. "Embracing the Absolute: The Politics of the Female Subject in Seventeenth-Century England." *Genders* 1 (1988): 24–39.
Gardner, Helen, ed. *John Donne: The Elegies and The Songs and Sonnets*. Oxford: Oxford University Press, 1965.
Garganigo, Alex. *"The Rehearsal Transpros'd* and *The Rehearsal Transpros'd: The Second Part"* in *The Oxford Handbook of Andrew Marvell*. Ed. Martin Dzelzainis and Edward Holberton. Oxford: Oxford University Press, 2019, 517–542.
Gassendi, Pierre. *Opera omnia: Faksimile-Neudruck der Ausgabe von Lyons 1658...* 6 vols. Stuttgart-Bad Cannstatt: F. Frommann, 1964.
Gerson, Lloyd P. "Neoplatonic Epistemology: Knowledge, Truth and Intellection," in *The Routledge Handbook of Neoplatonism*. Ed. Pauliina Remes and Svetla Slaveva-Griffin. London and New York: Routledge, 2014. 266–279.
Gigante, Denise. *Taste: A Literary History*. New Haven, CT: Yale University Press, 2005.
Gikandi, Simon. *Slavery and the Culture of Taste*. Princeton, NJ: Princeton University Press, 2011.
Gil, Daniel Juan. *Before Intimacy: Asocial Sexuality in Early Modern England*. Minneapolis: University of Minnesota Press, 2006.
Gillespie, Michael Allen. *The Theological Origins of Modernity*. Chicago: The University of Chicago Press, 2008.
Giocanti, Silvia. *Penser l'irrésolution: Montaigne, Pascal, La Mothe Le Vayer: trois itinéraires sceptiques*. Paris: Honoré Champion, 2001.
Glanvill, Joseph. *Scepsis Scientifica: or, Confest Ignorance, the way to Science; in an Essay of The Vanity of Dogmatizing, and Confident Opinion*. London, 1665.
Gorski, Philip S. "Historicizing the Secularization Debate: Church, State, and Society in Late Medieval and Early Modern Europe, ca. 1300 to 1700." *American Sociological Review* 65.1 (2000): 138–167.
Graham, Gordon. *The Re-enchantment of the World: Art Versus Religion*. Oxford: Oxford University Press, 2007.

Greenblatt, Stephen. *The Swerve*. New York: Norton, 2011.
Greene, Thomas. "*Mutability and the Theme of Process*," in *Edmund Spenser: Modern Critical Views*. Ed. Harold Bloom. New York: Chelsea House, 1986. 57–71.
Greenlaw, Edwin. "Spenser and Lucretius." *Studies in Philology* 17.4 (1920): 439–464.
Gregory, Brad S. *The Unintended Reformation: How a Religious Revolution Secularized Society*. Cambridge, MA: Harvard University Press, 2012.
Griffioen, Sjoerd. "Modernity and the Problem of Its Christian Past: The *Geistesgeschichten of* Blumenberg, Berger, and Gauchet." *History and Theory* 55 (2016): 185–209.
Grogan, Jane, ed. *Celebrating Mutabilitie*. Manchester: Manchester University Press, 2010.
  "Introduction," in *Celebrating Mutabilitie*. Ed. Grogan. 1–23.
  Exemplary Spenser: Visual and Poetic Pedagogy in The Faerie Queene. Farnham, Surrey: Ashgate, 2009.
Gross, Kenneth. "'Pardon me, mighty poet': Versions of the Bard in Marvell's 'On Mr. Milton's *Paradise Lost*'," in *Andrew Marvell: Modern Critical Views*. Ed. Harold Bloom. New York and Philadelphia: Chelsea House, 1989. 169–185.
  Spenserian Poetics: Idolatry, Iconoclasm, and Magic. Ithaca, NY: Cornell University Press, 1985.
Grossman, Marshall. "Poetry and Belief in *Paradise Regained, to which is added, Samson Agonistes*." *Studies in Philology* 110.2 (2013): 382–401.
  The Story of All Things: Writing the Self in English Renaissance Narrative Poetry. Durham, NC: Duke University Press, 1998.
Guignon, Charles B. *Heidegger and the Problem of Knowledge*. Indianapolis, IN: Hackett, 1983.
Guillén, Jorge. *Aire Nuestro*. Ed. Óscar Barrero Pérez. Barcelona: Tusquets, 2008.
Hacker, P. M. S. *Insight and Illusion: Themes in the Philosophy of Wittgenstein*, rev. ed. Oxford: Clarendon Press, 1986.
Hacking, Ian. "Five Parables," in *Philosophy in History*. Ed. Richard Rorty, J. B. Schneewind, and Quentin Skinner. Cambridge: Cambridge University Press, 1984. 103–124.
Hadfield, Andrew D. *Spenser's Irish Experience: Wilde Fruit and Salvage Soyl*. Oxford: Clarendon Press, 1997.
Hadot, Pierre. *The Veil of Isis*. Trans. Michael Chase. Cambridge, MA: Harvard University Press, 2006.
Halyburton, T. H. *Natural Religion Insufficient: and Revealed Necessary to Man's Happiness in his present State*. 1714. Edinburgh and Leith, 1798.
Hamlin, William M. "A Lost Translation Found? An Edition of *The Sceptick* (c. 1590) Based on Extant Manuscripts [With Text]." *ELR* 31.1 (2001): 34–51.
  Montaigne's English Journey. Oxford: Oxford University Press, 2014.

Tragedy and Scepticism in Shakespeare's England. Basingstoke: Palgrave Macmillan, 2005.
Hammill, Graham, and Julia Reinhard Lupton, eds. *Political Theology and Early Modernity.* Chicago: The University of Chicago Press, 2012.
Hammond, Paul. "Marvell's Sexuality." *The Seventeenth Century* 11.1 (1996): 87–123.
Hartlib, Samuel. *The Hartlib Papers.* Ed. Leslie M. Greengrass and M. Hannon. HRI On-line Publications, 2013. Web. August 28, 2014.
Hashhozheva, Galena. "The Christian Defense Against Classical Skepticism in Spenser's Legend of Holiness." *ELR* (2014): 193–220.
Haskins, Charles Homer. 1927. *The Renaissance of the Twelfth Century.* Cleveland, OH: Meridian, 1957.
Haverkamp, Anselm. "The Scandal of Metaphorology." *Telos* 158 (2012): 37–58.
Hegel, G. W. F. *The Phenomenology of Mind.* Trans. J. B. Baillie. New York: Harper Torchbooks, 1967.
Heidegger, Martin. *Poetry, Language, Thought.* Trans. Albert Hofstadter. New York: HarperCollins, 1971.
Helfer, Rebeca. *Spenser's Ruins and The Art of Recollection.* Toronto: University of Toronto Press, 2012.
Hequembourg, Stephen. "The Dream of a Literal World: Wilkins, Hobbes, Marvell." *ELH* 81.1 (2014): 83–113.
Herbert of Cherbury, Edward. *De Religione Laici.* Trans. Harold R. Hutcheson. New Haven, CT: Yale University Press, 1944.
  De veritate. Trans. Meyrick H. Carré. 1937. London: Routledge/Thoemmes, 1992.
  A Dialogue between a Tutor and his Pupil. New York: Garland, 1979.
  Expedition to the Isle of Rhé. London: Whittingham, 1860.
  The Life and Reign of King Henry VIII. London, 1649.
  The Life and Reign of King Henry VIII. London: Alexander Murray, 1870.
  The Life of Edward, First Lord Herbert of Cherbury written by himself. Ed. J. M. Shuttleworth. Oxford: Oxford University Press, 1976.
  The Poems of Lord Herbert of Cherbury. 1665. Ed. John Churton Collins. London: Chatto & Windus, 1881.
  Works. Ed. Günter Gawlick. Stuttgart-Bad Cannstatt: F. Frommann / Günther Holzboog, 1966–71.
Herman, Peter C. *Destabilizing Milton: "Paradise Lost" and the Poetics of Incertitude.* New York: Palgrave Macmillan, 2005.
Herz, Judith Scherer. "Milton and Marvell: The Poet as Fit Reader." *MLQ* 39.3 (1978): 239–263.
Hiley, David R. "The Politics of Skepticism: Reading Montaigne." *History of Philosophy Quarterly* 9.4 (1992): 379–399.
Hill, Eugene D. *Edward, Lord Herbert of Cherbury.* Twayne's English Authors Series. Boston, MA: G. K. Hall, 1987.
Hillman, David. *Shakespeare's Entrails: Belief, Scepticism and the Interior of the Body.* New York: Palgrave / St. Martin's Press, 2007.

Hirst, Derek and Steven Zwicker. *Andrew Marvell, Orphan of the Hurricane.* Oxford: Oxford University Press, 2012.
  "Marvell and the Lyrics of Undifference," in *The Oxford Handbook of Andrew Marvell.* Oxford: Oxford University Press, 2019. 387–405.
  The Cambridge Companion to Andrew Marvell. Cambridge: Cambridge University Press, 2011.
Holmes, Michael Morgan. *Early Modern Metaphysical Literature: Nature, Custom, and Strange Desires.* New York: Palgrave, 2001.
Hopkins, Lisa. *Renaissance Drama on the Edge.* Farnham: Ashgate, 2014.
Horkheimer, Max. "Montaigne and the Function of Skepticism," in *Between Philosophy and Social Science: Selected Early Writings.* Cambridge, MA: The MIT Press, 1993. 265–311.
Houston, Alan, and Steve Pincus, eds. *A Nation Transformed.* Cambridge: Cambridge University Press, 2001.
Hudson, Nicholas. "John Locke and the Tradition of Nominalism," in *Nominalism and Literary Discourse: New Perspectives.* Ed. Hugo Keiper, Christoph Bode, and Richard Utz. Amsterdam: Rodopi, 1997. 283–299.
Hudson, Wayne. "Theology and Historicism." *Thesis Eleven* 116.1 (2013): 19–39.
Hughes, Peter. "Painting the Ghost: Wittgenstein, Shakespeare, and Textual Representation." *New Literary History* 19.2 (1988): 371–384.
Hutton, Sarah. *Anne Conway: A Woman Philosopher.* Cambridge: Cambridge University Press, 2004.
  "In Dialogue with Thomas Hobbes: Margaret Cavendish's Natural Philosophy." *Women's Writing* 4 (1997): 421–432.
  "Lord Herbert of Cherbury and the Cambridge Platonists," in *British Philosophy and the Age of Enlightenment.* Ed. Stuart Brown. Routledge History of Philosophy, Vol. 5. London: Routledge, 1996. 20–42.
Jackson, Christine. "'It is unpossible to draw his Picture well who hath severall countenances': Lord Herbert of Cherbury and *The Life and Reign of King Henry VIII*," in *Henry VIII and History.* Ed. Thomas Betteridge and Thomas S. Freeman. Farnham: Ashgate, 2012. 135–149.
James I. *Daemonologie.* Edinburgh, 1597.
James, Susan. "The Philosophical Innovations of Margaret Cavendish." *British Journal for the History of Philosophy* 7.2 (1999): 219–244.
Jay, Martin. "Rev. of *The Legitimacy of the Modern Age* by Hans Blumenberg." *History and Theory* 24.2 (1985): 183–196.
  Songs of Experience. Berkeley: University of California Press, 2005.
Johnson, Christopher D. "Blumenberg's 'huge field': Metaphorology and Intellectual History." *Intellectual History Review* 22.2 (2012): 289–292.
  Hyperboles: The Rhetoric of Excess in Baroque Literature and Thought. Cambridge, MA: Harvard University Press, 2010.
  Memory, Metaphor, and Aby Warburg's Atlas of Images. Ithaca, NY: Cornell University Press, 2012.

Jordan, W. K. *The Development of Religious Toleration in England.* Cambridge, MA: Harvard University Press, 1932–40.
Journal of the House of Lords. British History On-Line. www.british-history.ac.uk/lords-jrnl/vol5 (accessed October 12, 2016).
Kahn, Victoria. "Aesthetics as Critique: Tragedy and *Trauerspiel* in *Samson Agonistes*," in *Reading Renaissance Ethics.* Ed. Marshall Grossman. New York: Routledge, 2007. 104–127.
  The Future of Illusion: Political Theology and Early Modern Texts. Chicago: The University of Chicago Press, 2014.
  "Political Theology and Reason of State in *Samson Agonistes.*" *SAQ* 95.4 (1996): 1065–1097.
  Rhetoric, Prudence, and Skepticism. Ithaca, NY: Cornell University Press, 1985.
Kantorowicz, Ernst H. *The King's Two Bodies.* Princeton, NJ: Princeton University Press, 1957.
Karger, Elizabeth. "Ockham's Misunderstood Theory of Intuitive and Abstractive Cognition," in *The Cambridge Companion to Ockham.* Ed. Paul Spade. Cambridge: Cambridge University Press, 1999. 204–226.
Kaske, Carol V. *Spenser and Biblical Poetics.* Ithaca, NY: Cornell University Press, 1999.
Kay, Dennis. *William Shakespeare: Sonnets and Poems.* New York: Twayne, 1998.
Keiper, Hugo, Christoph Bode, and Richard Utz, eds. *Nominalism and Literary Discourse: New Perspectives.* Amsterdam: Rodopi, 1997.
Kellogg, Amanda. "Pyrrhonist Uncertainty in Shakespeare's Sonnets." *Shakespeare* 11.4 (2015): 408–424.
Klima, Gyula, and Alexander Hall, eds. *The Demonic Temptations of Medieval Nominalism.* Proceedings of the Society for Medieval Logic and Metaphysics, Vol. 9. Newcastle: Cambridge Scholars, 2011.
Knapp, James A. *Image Ethics in Shakespeare and Spenser.* New York: Palgrave Macmillan, 2011.
Knight, Stephen. "Chaucer – A Modern Writer?" *Balcony: The Sydney Review* 2 (1965): 37–43.
Korab-Karpowicz, W. J. "Martin Heidegger." *Internet Encyclopedia of Philosophy.* www.iep.utm.edu/heidegge/#H5 (accessed September 27, 2019).
Kranidas, Thomas. *Milton and the Rhetoric of Zeal.* Pittsburgh, PA: Duquesne University Press, 2005.
Krier, Theresa M. *Gazing on Secret Sights: Spenser, Classical Imitation, and the Decorums of Vision.* Ithaca, NY: Cornell University Press, 1990.
Kripke, Saul A. *Wittgenstein on Rules and Private Language.* Cambridge, MA: Harvard University Press, 1982.
Kuzner, James. *Shakespeare as a Way of Life: Skeptical Practice and the Politics of Weakness.* New York: Fordham University Press, 2016.
LaBreche, Ben, and Jason A. Kerr, eds. "The Varieties of Political Theology." *Journal of Early Modern Cultural Studies* 18.2 (2018).
Lagerlund, Henrik. "A History of Skepticism in the Middle Ages," in *Rethinking the History of Skepticism.* Ed. Lagerlund. 1–28.

ed. *Representation and Objects of Thought in Medieval Philosophy*. Aldershot: Ashgate, 2006.
ed. *Rethinking the History of Skepticism: The Missing Medieval Background*. Leiden: Brill, 2009.
Lagrée, Jacqueline. *Le Salut du Laïc: Edward Herbert de Cherbury*. Paris: Vrin, 1989.
Langer, Ullrich. *Divine and Poetic Freedom in the Renaissance: Nominalist Theology and Literature in France and Italy*. Princeton, NJ: Princeton University Press, 1990.
Largier, Niklaus. "Mysticism, Modernity, and the Invention of Aesthetic Experience." *Representations* 105 (2009): 37–60.
Larkin, Philip. "The Changing Face of Andrew Marvell." *ELR* 9.1 (1979): 149–157.
Larmore, Charles. "Scepticism," in *The Cambridge History of Seventeenth-Century Philosophy*. Eds. Daniel Garber, Michael Ayers, et al. Cambridge: Cambridge University Press, 1998. 1145–1192.
Laursen, John Christian. *The Politics of Skepticism in the Ancients, Montaigne, Hume, and Kant*. Leiden: Brill, 1992.
Laursen, John Christian, and Gianni Paganini, eds. *Skepticism and Political Thought in the Seventeenth and Eighteenth Centuries*. Toronto: University of Toronto Press, 2015.
Lee, Sidney G., ed. *Autobiography of Edward, Lord Herbert of Cherbury*. London: William W. Gibbings, 1892.
Leff, Gordon. *The Dissolution of the Medieval Outlook*. New York: New York University Press, 1976.
William of Ockham: The Metamorphosis of Scholastic Discourse. Manchester: Manchester University Press, 1975.
Leinwand, Theodore B. "Linguistic Intimacy" (unpublished SAA seminar paper, 2016)
Leo, Russ. *Tragedy as Philosophy in the Reformation World*. Oxford: Oxford University Press, 2019.
Leslie, Marina. "Gender, Genre and the Utopian Body in Margaret Cavendish's *Blazing World*." *Utopian Studies* 7.1 (1996): 6–24.
Levine, Alan, ed. *Early Modern Skepticism and the Origins of Toleration*. Lanham, MD: Lexington Books, 1999.
Lewalski, Barbara Kiefer. "Milton's *Samson* and the 'New Acquist of True [Political] Experience." *Milton Studies* 24 (1988): 233–251.
"Milton: Divine Revelation and the Poetics of Experience." *Milton Studies* 28 (1992): 3–21.
Lewalski, Barbara Kiefer. *A Discourse of Constancy: In Two Books*. Trans. Richard Goodridge. London: Humphrey Moseley, 1654.
De constantia. Trans. John Stradling. London, 1594.
Lobsien, Verena Olejniczak. *Transparency and Dissimulation: Configurations of Neoplatonism in Early Modern English Literature*. Berlin and New York: De Gruyter, 2010.

Locke, John. *The Works of John Locke*. London, 1823.
Loewenstein, David. *Milton and the Drama of History*. Cambridge: Cambridge University Press, 1990.
  Representing Revolution in Milton and his Contemporaries. Cambridge: Cambridge University Press, 2001.
Lom, Petr. *The Limits of Doubt: The Moral and Political Implications of Skepticism*. Binghamton: State University of New York Press, 2001.
Long, Michael. *Marvell, Nabokov: Childhood and Arcadia*. Oxford: Oxford University Press, 1984.
Long, Seth. "Excavating the Memory Palace: An Account of the Disappearance of Mnemonic Imagery from English Rhetoric, 1550–1650." *Rhetoric Review* 36.2 (2017): 122–138.
Longinus. *On the Sublime*. Trans. James A. Arieti and John M. Crossett. New York and Toronto: The Edwin Mellen Press, 1985.
Löwith, Karl. *Meaning in History*. Chicago: The University of Chicago Press, 1949.
Lucretius Carus, Titus. *De Rerum Natura*. Trans. W. H. D. Rouse and Martin Ferguson Smith. Cambridge, MA: Harvard University Press, 1992.
Luhmann, Niklas. *Love as Passion: The Codification of Intimacy*. Trans. Jeremy Gaines and Doris L. Jones. Cambridge, MA: Harvard University Press, 1986.
Lupton, Julia Reinhard. *Thinking with Shakespeare*. Chicago: The University of Chicago Press, 2011.
Luther, Martin. *Selections*. Ed. John Dillenberger. New York: Anchor Books, 1961.
Maley, Willy. "Spenser's Languages: Writing in the Ruins of English," in *The Cambridge Companion to Spenser*. Ed. Andrew Hadfield. Cambridge: Cambridge University Press, 2001. 162–179.
Marcus, Leah S. *The Politics of Mirth: Jonson, Herrick, Milton and Marvell and the Defense of Old Holiday Pastimes*. Chicago: The University of Chicago Press, 1986.
Marot, Clément. *Oeuvres Lyriques*. Ed. C. A. Mayer. London: Athlone Press, 1964.
Marotti, Arthur F. "Donne and 'The Extasie,'" in *The Rhetoric of Renaissance Poetry from Wyatt to Milton*. Ed. Thomas O. Sloan and Raymond B. Waddington. Berkeley: University of California Press, 1974. 140–173.
Marshall, David. *The Frame of Art: Fictions of Aesthetic Experience, 1750–1815*. Baltimore, MD: Johns Hopkins University Press, 2005.
Martin, Catherine Gimelli. "The Erotology of Donne's 'Extasie' and the Secret History of Voluptuous Rationalism." *SEL* 44.1 (2004): 121–147.
Martz, Louis L. "Andrew Marvell: The Mind's Happiness," in *Andrew Marvell: Modern Critical Views*. Ed. Harold Bloom. New York and Philadelphia: Chelsea House, 1989. 49–75.
Marvell, Andrew. *The Letters of Andrew Marvell*. Ed. H. M. Margoliouth. 2nd ed. Oxford: Clarendon Press, 1952.

The Poems of Andrew Marvell. Ed. Nigel Smith. Harlow: Pearson Longman, 2007.
Prose Works. Ed. Annabel Patterson et al. 2 vols. New Haven, CT: Yale University Press, 2003.
Matchett, William H. *The Phoenix and the Turtle: Shakespeare's Poem and Chester's "Loves Martyr."* The Hague: Mouton, 1965.
Matytsin, Anton M. *The Specter of Skepticism in the Age of Enlightenment.* Baltimore, MD: Johns Hopkins University Press, 2016.
Mazzeo, J. A. *Renaissance and Seventeenth-Century Studies.* New York: Columbia University Press, 1964.
McCabe, Richard. *The Pillars of Eternity: Time and Providence in* The Faerie Queene. Dublin: Irish Academic Press, 1989.
McCoy, Richard C. "Love's Martyrs: Shakespeare's 'Phoenix and Turtle' and the Sacrificial Sonnets," in *Religion and Culture in Renaissance England.* Ed. Claire McEachern and Debora Shuger. Cambridge: Cambridge University Press, 1997. 188–208.
McDougall, Derek. "Wittgenstein's Remarks on William Shakespeare." *Philosophy and Literature* 40.1 (2016): 297–308.
McDowell, Nicholas. *Poetry and Allegiance in the English Civil Wars.* Oxford: Oxford University Press, 2008.
McGrath, Alister E. *The Intellectual Origins of the European Reformation.* 2nd ed. Oxford: Blackwell, 2004.
McGrath, S. J. *The Early Heidegger and Medieval Philosophy.* Washington, DC: Catholic University of America Press, 2006.
Marvell, Andrew. "The Origins of Aesthetic Value." *Telos* 57 (1983): 63–82.
The Origins of the English Novel 1600–1740. Baltimore, MD: Johns Hopkins University Press, 1987.
"Pastoralism, Puritanism, Imperialism, Scientism: Andrew Marvell and the Problem of Mediation." *The Yearbook of English Studies* 13 (1983): 46–65.
Merchant, W. Moelwyn. "Lord Herbert of Cherbury and Seventeenth-Century Historical Writing." *Transactions of the Honourable Society of Cymmodorion* (1956): 47–63.
Merleau-Ponty, Maurice. "Cézanne's Doubt," in *The Merleau-Ponty Aesthetics Reader.* Ed. Galen A. Johnson. Evanston, IL: Northwestern University Press, 1993. 59–75.
Mersenne, Marin. *Correspondance du P. Marin Mersenne.* Ed. Cornelis de Waard et al. 17 vols. Paris: Beauchesne, 1932–88.
Michaelian, Kourken. "Margaret Cavendish's Epistemology." *British Journal for the History of Philosophy* 17.1 (2009): 31–53.
Milton, John. *Complete Poems and Major Prose.* Ed. Merritt Y. Hughes. Indianapolis, IN: Odyssey Press, 1957.
The Complete Prose Works of John Milton. Ed. Don M. Wolfe. New Haven, CT: Yale University Press, 1953.
Milward, Peter. "'Double Nature's Single Name': A Response to Christiane Gillham." *Connotations* 3.1 (1993): 60–63.

Minazzoli, Agnès. "Formes de penser, manières d'écrire: existe-t-il un style sceptique?" *Papers on French Seventeenth Century Literature* 25.49 (1998): 381–396.
Minor, Vernon Hyde. *The Death of the Baroque and the Rhetoric of Good Taste*. Cambridge: Cambridge University Press, 2006.
Mintz, Samuel I. "The Duchess of Newcastle's Visit to the Royal Society." *The Journal of English and Germanic Philology* 51.2 (1952): 168–176.
Monk, Samuel Holt. *The Sublime: A Study of Critical Theories in XVIII-century England*. New York: Modern Language Association of America, 1935.
Montaigne, Michel de. *The Complete Essays of Montaigne*. Trans. Donald M. Frame. Stanford, CA: Stanford University Press, 1958.
Moriarty, Michael. *Taste and Ideology in 17th-Century France*. Cambridge: Cambridge University Press, 1988.
Most, Glenn W. "After the Sublime: Stations in the Career of an Emotion." *The Yale Review* 90.2 (2002): 101–120.
"The Sublime, Today?," in *Dynamic Reading: Studies in the Reception of Epicureanism*. Oxford: Oxford University Press, 2012. 239–266.
Motherwell, Robert. *The Writings of Robert Motherwell*. Ed. Dore Ashton and Joan Banach. Berkeley: University of California Press, 2007.
Mulhall, Stephen. *Wittgenstein's Private Language: Grammar, Nonsense, and Imagination in Philosophical Investigations, §§ 243–315*. Oxford: Clarendon Press, 2007.
Müller-Sievers, Helmut. "Kyklophorology: Hans Blumenberg and the Intellectual History of Technics." *Telos* 158 (2012): 155–170.
Murphy, Kathryn, and Anita Traninger, eds. *The Emergence of Impartiality*. Leiden: Brill, 2014.
Nauta, Lodi. "A Weak Chapter in the Book of Nature: Hans Blumenberg on Medieval Thought," in *The Book of Nature in Antiquity and the Middle Ages*. Ed. Arjo Vanderjagt and Klaas van Berkel. Leuven: Peeters, 2005. 135–150.
Nelson, Holly Faith, and Sharon Aker. "Memory, Monuments, and Melancholic Genius in Margaret Cavendish's *Bell in Campo*." *Eighteenth-Century Fiction* 21.1 (2008): 13–35.
Neto, José R. Maia, and Gianni Paganini, eds. *Renaissance Scepticisms*. Dordrecht: Springer, 2009.
Netzley, Ryan. "Reading Events: The Value of Reading and the Possibilities of Political Action and Criticism in 'Samson Agonistes.'" *Criticism* 48.4 (2006): 509–533.
Nicols, Thomas. *Arcula Gemmea. A Lapidary: or, the History of Pretious Stones: with cautions for the undeceiving of all those that deal with Pretious Stones*. Cambridge: Thomas Buck, 1652.
Noggle, James. *The Skeptical Sublime: Aesthetic Ideology in Pope and the Tory Satirists*. Oxford: Oxford University Press, 2001.
The Temporality of Taste in Eighteenth-Century British Writing. Oxford: Oxford University Press, 2012.

"The Wittgensteinian Sublime." *New Literary History* 27.4 (1996): 605–619.
Nohrnberg, James. *The Analogy of The Faerie Queene*. Princeton, NJ: Princeton University Press, 1976.
Norbrook, David. "Marvell's 'Horatian Ode' and the Politics of Genre," in *Literature and the English Civil War*. Ed. Thomas Healy and Jonathan Sawday. Cambridge: Cambridge University Press, 1990. 147–169.
  "Milton, Lucy Hutchinson and the Lucretian Sublime: The Sublime Object." *Tate Papers* 13 (2010): online at www.tate.org.uk/research/publications/tate-papers/13/milton-lucy-hutchinson-and-the-lucretian-sublime.
  "Republican Occasions in *Paradise Regained* and *Samson Agonistes*." *Milton Studies* 42 (2003): 122–148.
  Writing the English Republic: Poetry, Rhetoric and Politics, 1627–1660. Cambridge: Cambridge University Press, 1999.
Normore, Calvin G. "Future Contingents," in *The Cambridge History of Later Medieval Philosophy*. Ed. Norman Kretzmann, Anthony Kenny, Jan Pinborg, and Eleonore Stump. Cambridge: Cambridge University Press, 1983. 358–381.
  "Nominalism," in *The Routledge Companion to Sixteenth-Century Philosophy*. Ed. Henrik Lagerlund and Benjamin Hill. New York: Routledge, 2017. 121–136.
  "Ockham on Mental Language," in *Historical Foundations of Cognitive Science*. Ed. J-C. Smith. Dordrecht: Kluwer, 1990. 53–70.
Novarr, David. "'The Extasie': Donne's Address on the States of Union," in *Just So Much Honor*. Ed. Peter Amadeus Fiore. University Park: Pennsylvania State University Press, 1972. 219–243.
Nozick, Robert. *The Examined Life: Philosophical Meditations*. New York: Simon & Schuster, 1989.
Nuttall, A. D. "Spenser and Elizabethan Alienation." *Essays in Criticism* 55.3 (2005): 209–225.
  Two Concepts of Allegory. New Haven, CT: Yale University Press, 1967.
Oakeshott, Michael. *The Politics of Faith and the Politics of Scepticism*. New Haven, CT: Yale University Press, 1996.
Oberman, Heiko A. *The Harvest of Medieval Theology: Gabriel Biel and Late Medieval Nominalism*. Cambridge, MA: Harvard University Press, 1963.
  Luther. 1982. Trans. Eileen Walliser-Schwarzbart. New Haven, CT: Yale University Press, 1989.
  "The Shape of Late Medieval Thought: The Birthpangs of the Modern Era," in *The Pursuit of Holiness in Late Medieval and Renaissance Religion*. Ed. Charles Trinkaus and Heiko A. Oberman. Leiden: Brill, 1974. 3–25.
  "Some Notes on the Theology of Nominalism: With Attention to Its Relation to the Renaissance." *The Harvard Theological Review* 53.1 (1960): 47–76.
  The Two Reformations. New Haven, CT: Yale University Press, 2003.
  "Via Antiqua and Via Moderna: Late Medieval Prolegomena to Early Reformation Thought." *Journal of the History of Ideas* 48.1 (1987): 23–40.

Ockham, William of. *Ockham: Philosophical Writings*. Ed. and trans. Philotheus Boehner. Indianapolis, IN: Bobbs-Merrill, 1964.
  Ockham's Theory of Terms: Part 1 of the Summa Logicae. Trans. Michael J. Loux. Notre Dame, IN: University of Notre Dame Press, 1974.
Orgel, Stephen, and Roy Strong. *Inigo Jones: The Theatre of the Stuart Court*. 2 vols. Berkeley: University of California Press, 1973.
Ormsby-Lennon, Hugh. "Rosicrucian Linguistics: Twilight of a Renaissance Tradition," in *Hermeticism and the Renaissance*. Ed. Ingrid Merkel and Allen G. Debus. Washington, DC: Folger Books, 1988. 311–341.
Ozment, Steven. "Mysticism, Nominalism and Dissent," in *The Pursuit of Holiness in Late Medieval and Renaissance Religion*. Ed. Charles Edward Trinkhaus and Heiko Augustinus Oberman. Leiden: Brill, 1974. 67–92.
Pailin, David A. "Should Herbert of Cherbury Be Regarded as a 'Deist'?" *Journal of Theological Studies* 51 (2000): 113–149.
Palmer, Ada. "Humanist Lives of Classical Philosophers and the Idea of Renaissance Secularization: Virtue, Rhetoric, and the Orthodox Sources of Unbelief." *Renaissance Quarterly* 70.3 (2017): 935–976.
Pankakoski, Timo. "Reoccupying Secularization: Schmitt and Koselleck on Blumenberg's Challenge." *History and Theory* 52 (May 2013): 214–245.
Panaccio, Claude. *Ockham on Concepts*. Burlington, VT: Ashgate, 2004.
  "Semantics and Mental Language," in *The Cambridge Companion to William of Ockham*. Ed. Paul Spade. Cambridge: Cambridge University Press, 1999. 53–75.
Panofsky, Erwin. *Gothic Architecture and Scholasticism*. London: Penguin, 1951.
Parageau, Sandrine. *Les Ruses de l'ignorance: La contribution des femmes à l'avènement de la science moderne en Angleterre*. Paris: Presses Sorbonne Nouvelle, 2010.
Pasnau, Robert. "Abstract Truth in Thomas Aquinas," in *Representation and Objects of Thought in Medieval Philosophy*. Ed. Henrik Lagerlund. Aldershot: Ashgate, 2006. 33–61.
  "Epistemology Idealized." *Mind* 122.488 (2013): 987–1021.
  ed., *Mind and Knowledge*. The Cambridge Translations of Medieval Philosophical Texts, Vol. 3. Cambridge: Cambridge University Press, 2002.
  Theories of Cognition in the Later Middle Ages. Cambridge: Cambridge University Press, 1997.
Patrides, C. A., ed. *Approaches to Marvell*. London: Routledge & Kegan Paul, 1978.
Patterson, Annabel M. *Andrew Marvell*. Horndon: Northcote House Publishers, 1994.
  Marvell and the Civic Crown. Princeton, NJ: Princeton University Press, 1978.
  Pastoral and Ideology: Virgil to Valéry. Berkeley: University of California Press, 1987.
Pavesich, Vida. "Hans Blumenberg's Philosophical Anthropology after Heidegger and Cassirer." *Journal of the History of Philosophy* 46.3 (2008): 421–448.

Peck, Russell A. "Chaucer and the Nominalist Questions." *Speculum* 53.4 (1978): 745–760.
Penn, Stephen. "Literary Nominalism and Medieval Sign Theory: Problems and Perspectives," in *Nominalism and Literary Discourse: New Perspectives*. Ed. Hugo Keiper, Christoph Bode, and Richard Utz. Amsterdam: Rodopi, 1997. 157–189.
Perler, Dominik. "Does God Deceive Us? Skeptical Hypotheses in Late Medieval Epistemology," in *Rethinking the History of Skepticism: The Missing Medieval Background*. Ed. Henrik Lagerlund. Leiden: Brill, 2009. 171–192.
   "Skepticism," in *The Cambridge History of Medieval Philosophy*. Ed. Robert Pasnau and Christina Van Dyke. Cambridge: Cambridge University Press, 2014. 1: 384–396.
Perloff, Marjorie. "Wittgenstein's Shakespeare." *Wittgenstein-Studien* 5.1 (2014): 259–272.
Picciotto, Joanna. *Labors of Innocence in Early Modern England*. Cambridge, MA: Harvard University Press, 2010.
Pierce, Robert B. "Shakespeare and the Ten Modes of Scepticism." *Shakespeare Survey* 46 (1993): 145–158.
Pigman, G. W. *Grief and English Renaissance Elegy*. Cambridge: Cambridge University Press, 1985.
Pippin, Robert B. "Blumenberg and the Modernity Problem." *Review of Metaphysics* 40 (1987): 535–557.
Poole, Kristen. "Naming, *Paradise Lost*, and the Gendered Discourse of Perfect Language Schemes." *English Literary Renaissance* 38.3 (2008): 535–559.
Popkin, Richard H. *The History of Scepticism from Savonarola to Bayle*. Oxford: Oxford University Press, 2003.
Popkin, Richard H., and Charles B. Schmitt, eds. *Scepticism from the Renaissance to the Enlightenment*. Wolfenbütteler Forschungen. Wiesbaden: Otto Harrassowitz, 1987.
Porter, James I. *The Sublime in Antiquity*. Cambridge: Cambridge University Press, 2016.
Povey, Thomas. *The Moderator expecting Sudden Peace, or Certaine Ruine. Directed by Reason, Arising out of the Consideration of what hath already happened, Our present Condition, and the most likely Consequents of these*. London, 1642.
Prakas, Tessie. "'A World of her own Invention': The Realm of Fancy in Margaret Cavendish's The Description of a New World, called the Blazing World." *Journal for Early Modern Cultural Studies* 16.1 (2016): 123–145.
Prescott, Anne Lake. "Spenser (Re)Reading du Bellay: Chronology and Literary Response," in *Spenser's Life and the Subject of Biography*. Ed. Judith H. Anderson, Donald Cheney, and David A. Richardson. Amherst: University of Massachusetts Press, 1996. 131–145.
Price, Bronwen. "Journeys Beyond Frontiers: Knowledge, Subjectivity and Outer Space in Margaret Cavendish's *The Blazing World*." *Literature and History* 7.2 (1998): 21–50.

Bibliography 255

Radley, C. Perrin. "Margaret Cavendish's Cabbala: The Empress and the Spirits in *The Blazing World*," in *God and Nature in the Thought of Margaret Cavendish*. Ed. Brandie R. Siegfried and Lisa T. Sarasohn. Burlington, VT: Ashgate, 2014. 161–170.

Rajan, Balachandra. "The Aesthetics of Inconclusiveness," in *Approaches to Marvell*. Ed. C. A. Patrides. London: Routledge & Kegan Paul, 1978. 155–173.

Ramachandran, Ayesha. "Edmund Spenser, Lucretian Neoplatonist: Cosmology in the *Fowre Hymnes*." *Spenser Studies* 24 (2009): 373–411.

"Mutabilitie's Lucretian Metaphysics: Scepticism and Cosmic Process in Spenser's *Cantos*," in *Celebrating Mutabilitie*. Ed. Jane Grogan. Manchester: Manchester University Press, 2010. 220–245.

The Worldmakers: Global Imagining in Early Modern Europe. Chicago: The University of Chicago Press, 2015.

Rancière, Jacques. *The Names of History: On the Poetics of Knowledge*. 1992. Trans. Hassan Melehy. Minneapolis: University of Minnesota Press, 1994.

The Politics of Literature. 2006. Trans. Julie Rose. Cambridge: Polity, 2011.

Randall, Michael. *Building Resemblance: Analogical Imagery in the Early French Renaissance*. Baltimore, MD: Johns Hopkins University Press, 1996.

Raymond, Joad. *Milton's Angels*. Oxford: Oxford University Press, 2010.

Read, Rupert. "Wittgenstein's *Philosophical Investigations* as a War Book." *New Literary History* 41.3 (2010): 593–612.

Rees, Emma. *Margaret Cavendish: Gender, Genre, Exile*. Manchester: Manchester University Press, 2003.

Reid, Jasper. "The Common Consent Argument from Herbert to Hume." *Journal of the History of Philosophy* 53.3 (2015): 401–434.

Reiss, Timothy J. *Knowledge, Discovery and Imagination in Early Modern Europe: The Rise of Aesthetic Rationalism*. Cambridge: Cambridge University Press, 1997.

Rhetorica ad Herennium. Trans. Harry Caplan. Loeb Classical Library. Cambridge, MA: Harvard University Press, 1953.

Richter, Gerhard. *Thought-Images: Frankfurt School Writers' Reflections from a Damaged Life*. Stanford, CA: Stanford University Press, 2007.

Roberts, Dunstan. "'Abundantly replenisht with Books of his own purchasing and choyce': Lord Herbert of Cherbury's Library at Montgomery Castle." *Library and Information History* 31.2 (2015): 117–136.

Robertson, Geoffrey. *The Tyrannicide Brief*. London: Chatto & Windus, 2005.

Robertson, Kellie. *Nature Speaks: Medieval Literature and Aristotelian Philosophy*. Philadelphia: University of Pennsylvania Press, 2017.

Robertson, Lauren. "Spectacular Skepticism: Visual Contradiction on the Early Modern English Stage." Washington University in St. Louis. Dissertation, 2016.

Rogers, John. *The Matter of Revolution: Science, Poetry, and Politics in the Age of Milton*. Ithaca, NY: Cornell University Press, 1996.

Rorty, Richard. *Contingency, Irony, and Solidarity*. Cambridge: Cambridge University Press, 1989.
Rosin, Robert. *Reformers, The Preacher, and Skepticism*. Mainz: Philipp von Zabern, 1997.
Rossi, Mario M. *La vita, le opere, i tempi di Edoardo Herbert di Chirbury*. 3 vols. Firenze: Sansoni, 1947.
Rothko, Mark. *The Artist's Reality: Philosophies of Art*. New Haven, CT: Yale University Press, 2004.
  Writings on Art. New Haven, CT: Yale University Press, 2006.
Rowse, A. L. "Caroline Philosopher." *History Today* 27.3 (1977): 198–199.
Rumrich, John P., and Gregory Chaplin, eds. *Seventeenth-Century British Poetry: 1603–1660*. New York: Norton, 2006.
Rusch, Pierre. "Hans Blumenberg et la grammaire historique des idées," in *Hans Blumenberg: Anthropologie philosophique*. Ed. Denis Trierweiler. Paris: Presses Universitaires de France, 2010. 141–163.
Rushdy, Ashraf H. A. "'In Dubious Battle': Skepticism and Fideism in *Paradise Regained*." *HLQ* 53.2 (1990): 95–118.
Sacks, Peter. *The English Elegy*. Baltimore, MD: Johns Hopkins University Press, 1985.
Saint Girons, Baldine. "La Peinture et la Nuit," in *Du visible à l'intelligible: Lumière et ténèbres de l'Antiquité à la Renaissance*. Ed. Christian Trottmann et Anca Vasiliu. Paris: Honoré Champion, 2004. 281–299.
Saler, Michael T. *As If: Modern Enchantment and the Literary Prehistory of Virtual Reality*. Oxford: Oxford University Press, 2012.
Sarasohn, Lisa T. "*Leviathan* and the Lady: Cavendish's Critique of Hobbes in the *Philosophical Letters*," in *Authorial Conquests*. Ed. Line Cottegnies and Nancy Weitz. Teaneck, NJ: Fairleigh Dickinson University Press, 2003. 40–58.
  The Natural Philosophy of Margaret Cavendish: Reason and Fancy During the Scientific Revolution. Baltimore, MD: Johns Hopkins University Press, 2010.
  "A Science Turned Upside Down: Feminism and the Natural Philosophy of Margaret Cavendish." *Huntington Library Quarterly* 47 (1984): 289–307.
Saunders, John Turk, and Donald F. Henze. *The Private Language Problem: A Philosophical Dialogue*. New York: Random House, 1967.
Schalkwyk, David. *Literature and the Touch of the Real*. Newark: University of Delaware Press, 2004.
  Speech and Performance in Shakespeare's Sonnets and Plays. Cambridge: Cambridge University Press, 2002.
Schmitt, Carl. *Political Theology: Four Chapters on the Concept of Sovereignty*. 1922/1934. Trans. George Schwab. Cambridge, MA: The MIT Press, 1985.
Schmitt, Charles B. *Cicero Scepticus: A Study of the Influence of the* Academica *in the Renaissance*. The Hague: Martinus Nijhoff, 1972.
  "The Development of the Historiography of Scepticism: From the Renaissance to Brucker," in *Scepticism from the Renaissance to the Enlightenment*. Ed. Richard H. Popkin and Charles B. Schmitt. Wolfenbütteler Forschungen. Wiesbaden: Otto Harrassowitz, 1987. 185–200.

Schneewind, J. B. *The Invention of Autonomy*. Cambridge: Cambridge University Press, 1998.
Schoenfeldt, Michael. "Marvell and the Designs of Art," in *The Cambridge Companion to Andrew Marvell*. Ed. Derek Hirst and Steven Zwicker. Cambridge: Cambridge University Press, 2011. 87–101.
Searle, John. "A Classification of Illocutionary Acts." *Language in Society* 5.1 (1976): 1–23.
Sedley, David L. *Sublimity and Skepticism in Montaigne and Milton*. Ann Arbor: University of Michigan Press, 2005.
Semler, L. E. "Marvell's Mannerist Scepticism: A Reading of 'Mourning.'" *English* 44.180 (1995): 214–228.
Serjeantson, R. W. "Herbert of Cherbury Before Deism: The Early Reception of the *De veritate*." *Seventeenth Century* 16.2 (2001): 217–238.
Sextus Empiricus. *Outlines of Scepticism*. Trans. Julia Anna and Jonathan Barnes. Cambridge: Cambridge University Press, 1994.
Shagan, Ethan. "Beyond Good and Evil: Thinking with Moderates in Early Modern England." *Journal of British Studies* 49.3 (2010): 488–513.
Shakespeare, William. *The Riverside Shakespeare*. Ed. G. Blakemore Evans. Boston, MA: Houghton Mifflin, 1974.
Shami, Jeanne. *John Donne and Conformity in Crisis in the Late Jacobean Pulpit*. Cambridge: D. S. Brewer, 2003.
Shanahan, John. "The Indecorous Virtuoso: Margaret Cavendish's Experimental Spaces." *Genre* 35 (2002): 221–252.
Sharpe, Kevin. *The Personal Rule of Charles I*. New Haven, CT: Yale University Press, 1992.
Sherman, Anita Gilman. "Poland in the Cultural Imaginary of Early Modern England." *Journal of Early Modern Cultural Studies* 15.1 (2015): 55–89.
"The Sceptic's Surrender: Believing Partly," in *The Routledge Companion to Shakespeare and Philosophy*. Ed. Craig Bourne and Emily Caddick Bourne. London: Routledge, 2019. 350–359.
Skepticism and Memory in Shakespeare and Donne. New York: Palgrave Macmillan, 2007.
Shore, Daniel. *Milton and the Art of Rhetoric*. Cambridge: Cambridge University Press, 2012.
Silver, Victoria. "Liberal Theology and Sir Thomas Browne's 'Soft and Flexible' Discourse." *ELR* 20 (1990): 69–105.
"The Obscure Script of Regicide: Ambivalence and Little Girls in Marvell's Pastorals." *ELH* 68.1 (2001): 29–55.
Sim, Stuart. *Empires of Belief: Why We Need More Scepticism and Doubt in the Twenty-First Century*. Edinburgh: Edinburgh University Press, 2006.
Simon, David Carroll. "Andrew Marvell and the Epistemology of Carelessness." *ELH* 82.2 (2015): 553–588.
Skelton, John. *The Book of The Laurel*. Ed. F. W. Brownlow. Newark: University of Delaware Press, 1990.

Skinner, Quentin. *Reason and Rhetoric in the Philosophy of Hobbes*. Cambridge: Cambridge University Press, 1996.

Skulsky, Harold. "Spenser's Despair Episode and the Theology of Doubt." *Modern Philology* 78.3 (1981): 227–242.

Slaughter, Thomas P., ed. *Ideology and Politics on the Eve of Restoration: Newcastle's Advice to Charles II*. Philadelphia, PA: American Philosophical Society, 1984.

Sloterdijk, Peter. *The Art of Philosophy*. Trans. Karen Margolis. New York: Columbia University Press, 2012.

Smith, Hilda L. "'A General War amongst the Men but None amongst the Women': Political Differences between Margaret and William Cavendish," in *Politics and the Political Imagination in Later Stuart Britain*. Ed. Howard Nenner. Rochester, NY: University of Rochester Press, 1997. 143–160.

Smith, Nigel. *Andrew Marvell: The Chameleon*. New Haven, CT: Yale University Press, 2010.

 "The Charge of Atheism and the Language of Radical Speculation, 1640–1660," in *Atheism from the Reformation to the Enlightenment*. Ed. Michael Hunter and David Wootton. Oxford: Oxford University Press, 1992. 131–158.

 ed. *The Poems of Andrew Marvell*. Harlow: Pearson Longman, 2007.

Smith, Plínio Junqueira, and Sébastien Charles, eds. *Academic Scepticism in the Development of Early Modern Philosophy*. Cham, Switzerland: Springer, 2017.

Sommerville, C. John. *The Secularization of Early Modern England: From Religious Culture to Religious Faith*. Oxford: Oxford University Press, 1992.

Sorley, W. R. "The Philosophy of Herbert of Cherbury." *Mind* ns 3.12 (1894): 491–508.

Spade, Paul, ed. *The Cambridge Companion to William of Ockham*. Cambridge: Cambridge University Press, 1999.

Spenser, Edmund. *The Works of Edmund Spenser: A Variorum Edition*. Ed. Edwin Greenlaw, et al. 4th ed. Baltimore, MD: Johns Hopkins University Press, 1966.

 The Yale Edition of the Shorter Poems of Edmund Spenser. Ed. William A. Oram, Einar Bjorvand, Ronald Bond, Thomas H. Cain, Alexander Dunlop, and Richard Schell. New Haven, CT: Yale University Press, 1989.

Spitzer, Leo. "Linguistic Perspectivism in the *Don Quijote*," in *Linguistics and Literary History: Essays in Stylistics*. Princeton, NJ: Princeton University Press, 1948. 41–86.

Spitzer, Michael. *Metaphor and Musical Thought*. Chicago: The University of Chicago Press, 2015.

Spolsky, Ellen. *Satisfying Skepticism: Embodied Knowledge in the Early Modern World*. Burlington, VT: Ashgate, 2001.

Spruit, Leen. *Species Intelligibilis: From Perception to Knowledge*. 2 vols. Leiden: Brill, 1994.

Srigley, Michael. *The Probe of Doubt: Scepticism and Illusion in Shakespeare's Plays*. Vol. 113 of Acta Universitatis Upsaliensis. Upsala: Studia Anglistica Upsaliensia, 2000.

Stark, Ryan J. "From Mysticism to Skepticism: Stylistic Reform in Seventeenth-Century British Philosophy and Rhetoric." *Philosophy and Rhetoric* 34.4 (2001): 322–334.
Stempel, Daniel. "The Garden: Marvell's Cartesian Ecstasy." *JHI* 28.1 (1967): 99–114.
Stephens, Walter. *Demon Lovers: Witchcraft, Sex, and the Crisis of Belief.* Chicago: The University of Chicago Press, 2001.
Stevenson, Gertrude Scott, ed. *Charles I in Captivity.* New York: D. Appleton, 1927.
Stevenson, Jane. "Women and the Cultural Politics of Printing." *The Seventeenth Century* 24.2 (2009): 205–237.
Stevenson, Jay. "The Mechanist-Vitalist Soul of Margaret Cavendish." *Studies in English Literature* 36.3 (1996): 527–543.
Stocker, Margarita. *Apocalyptic Marvell: The Second Coming in Seventeenth-Century Poetry.* Brighton: Harvester Press, 1986.
Stoll, Abraham. *Milton and Monotheism.* Pittsburgh, PA: Duquesne University Press, 2009.
    "Milton Stages Cherbury: Revelation and Polytheism in *Samson Agonistes*," in *Altering Eyes: New Perspectives on Samson Agonistes*. Ed. Mark R. Kelley and Joseph Wittreich. Newark: University of Delaware Press, 2002. 281–306.
Strier, Richard. "Shakespeare and the Skeptics." *Religion and Literature* 32.2 (2000): 171–195.
Stroll, Avrum. *Wittgenstein.* Oxford: Oneworld, 2002.
Stump, Eleonore. "The Mechanisms of Cognition: Ockham on Mediating Species," in *The Cambridge Companion to William of Ockham*. Ed. Paul Spade. Cambridge: Cambridge University Press, 1999. 168–203.
Sugimura, Noel K. "Marvell's Mind and the Glow-worms of Extinction." *The Review of English Studies* ns 62.254 (2010): 241–260.
Suzuki, Mihoko. "The Essay Form as Critique: Reading Cavendish's *The World's Olio* through Montaigne and Bacon (and Adorno)." *Prose Studies: History, Theory, Criticism* 22.3 (1999): 1–16.
Tachau, Katherine H. "The Problem of the *species in medio* at Oxford in the Generation after Ockham." *Mediaeval Studies* 44.1 (1982): 394–443.
Targoff, Ramie. *John Donne, Body and Soul.* Chicago: The University of Chicago Press, 2008.
Tartamella, Suzanne M. *Rethinking Shakespeare's Skepticism.* Pittsburgh, PA: Duquesne University Press, 2014.
Taylor, Charles. *Philosophical Arguments.* Cambridge, MA: Harvard University Press, 1995.
A Secular Age. Cambridge, MA: Harvard University Press, 2007.
Teskey, Gordon. *Allegory and Violence.* Ithaca, NY: Cornell University Press, 1996.
    "'And therefore as a stranger give it welcome': Courtesy and Thinking." *Spenser Studies* 18 (2003): 343–359.

"Thinking Moments in *The Faerie Queene*." *Spenser Studies* 22 (2007): 103–125.
Thomas, Keith. *Religion and the Decline of Magic*. New York: Scribner's, 1971.
Thomson, Iain. "Heidegger's Aesthetics," in *Stanford Encyclopedia of Philosophy*, 2019. plato.stanford.edu/entries/heidegger-aesthetics/ (accessed September 2, 2019).
Thorndike, Lynn. *University Records and Life in the Middle Ages*. New York: Columbia University Press, 1944.
Toulmin, Stephen. *Cosmopolis*. Chicago: The University of Chicago Press, 1990.
Townsend, Dabney. *Aesthetic Objects and Works of Art*. Wolfeboro, NH: Longwood Academic, 1989.
Trierweiler, Denis, ed. *Hans Blumenberg: Anthropologie philosophique*. Paris: Presses Universitaires de France, 2010.
Trinkaus, Charles Edward, and Heiko Augustinus Oberman. *The Pursuit of Holiness in Late Medieval and Renaissance Religion*. Leiden: Brill, 1974.
Trubowitz, Rachel. "The Reenchantment of Utopia and the Female Monarchical Self: Margaret Cavendish's *Blazing World*." *Tulsa Studies in Women's Literature* 11.2 (1992): 229–245.
Tuck, Richard. *Philosophy and Government 1572–1651*. Cambridge: Cambridge University Press, 1993.
"Scepticism and Toleration in the Seventeenth Century," in *Justifying Toleration: Conceptual and Historical Perspectives*. Ed. Susan Mendus. Cambridge: Cambridge University Press, 1988. 21–35.
Utz, Richard J. *Literary Nominalism and the Theory of Rereading Late Medieval Texts*. Lewiston, NY: The Edwin Mellen Press, 1995.
"Negotiating the Paradigm: Literary Nominalism and the Theory and Practice of Rereading Late Medieval Texts," in *Literary Nominalism and The Theory of Rereading Late Medieval Texts: A New Research Paradigm*. Ed. Richard J. Utz. Lewiston, NY: The Edwin Mellen Press, 1995. 1–30.
Van Leeuwen, Henry G. *The Problem of Certainty in English Thought, 1630–1690*. The Hague: Nijhoff, 1963.
Vergil. *The Aeneid*. Trans. Sarah Ruden. New Haven, CT: Yale University Press, 2008.
Von Maltzahn, Nicholas. "The War in Heaven and the Miltonic Sublime," in *A Nation Transformed*. Ed. Alan Houston and Steve Pincus. Cambridge: Cambridge University Press, 2001. 154–179.
Walker, D. P. *The Ancient Theology: Studies in Christian Platonism from the Fifteenth to the Eighteenth Century*. Ithaca, NY: Cornell University Press, 1972.
Walker, Julia M. "John Donne's 'The Extasie' as an Alchemical Process." *ELN* 20.1 (1982): 1–8.
Walsham, Alexandra. "The Reformation and 'The Disenchantment of the World' Reassessed." *The Historical Journal* 51.2 (2008): 497–528.
Walters, Lisa. *Margaret Cavendish: Gender, Science and Politics*. Cambridge: Cambridge University Press, 2014.

Walwyn, William. *The Writings of William Walwyn*. Ed. Jack R. McMichael and Barbara Taft. Athens: University of Georgia Press, 1989.
Walzer, Michael. *The Revolution of the Saints: A Study in the Origins of Radical Politics*. New York: Atheneum, 1974.
Warnke, Frank. "The Meadow-sequence in *Upon Appleton House*: Questions of Tone and Meaning," in *Approaches to Marvell*. Ed. C. A. Patrides. London: Routledge, 1978. 234–250.
Watson, Robert N. *Back to Nature: The Green and the Real in the Late Renaissance*. Philadelphia: University of Pennsylvania Press, 2006.
The way to true happiness leading to the gate of knowledge. London, 1610.
Weaver, Richard M. *Ideas Have Consequences*. 1948. Chicago: The University of Chicago Press, 2013.
Weber, Max. *From Max Weber: Essays in Sociology*. Trans. and Ed. H. H. Gerth and C. Wright Mills. New York: Oxford University Press, 1958.
Werhane, Patricia H. *Skepticism, Rules, and Private Languages*. Atlantic Highlands, NJ: Humanities Press, 1992.
Whitaker, Katie. *Mad Madge: Margaret Cavendish, Duchess of Newcastle, Royalist, Writer & Romantic*. New York: Basic Books, 2002.
Wiley, Margaret L. *The Subtle Knot: Creative Scepticism in Seventeenth-Century England*. Cambridge, MA: Harvard University Press, 1952.
Williams, Raymond. *Marxism and Literature*. Oxford: Oxford University Press, 1977.
Wilson, Bryan R. *Religion in Secular Society: Fifty Years On*. Ed. Steve Bruce. Oxford: Oxford University Press, 2016.
Wilson, Catherine. "Two Opponents of Material Atomism: Cavendish and Leibniz," in *Leibniz and the English-Speaking World*. Ed. Pauline Phemister and Stuart Brown. Dordrecht: Springer, 2007. 35–50.
Wilson, Miranda. "Building a Perfect Silence: The Use of Renaissance Architecture in Margaret Cavendish's *Bell in Campo*." *1650–1850: Ideas, Aesthetics, and Inquiries in the Early Modern Era* 10 (2004): 245–264.
Wittgenstein, Ludwig. *On Certainty*. Trans. Denis Paul and G. E. M. Anscombe. New York: Harper, 1972.
Philosophical Investigations. Trans. G. E. M. Anscombe, P. M. S. Hacker, and Joachim Schulte. Oxford: Wiley-Blackwell, 2009.
Zettel. Trans. G. E. M. Anscombe. Berkeley: University of California Press, 1967.
Wittreich, Joseph. "On Mr. Milton's *Paradise Lost*," in *Approaches to Marvell*. Ed. C. A. Patrides. London: Routledge & Kegan Paul, 1978. 280–305.
Shifting Contexts: Reinterpreting Samson Agonistes. Pittsburgh, PA: Duquesne University Press, 2002.
Wittwer, Roland. "Sextus Empiricus' *Outlines of Pyrrhonism* in the Middle Ages." *Vivarium* 54.4 (2016): 255–285.
Wood, Andy. *The Politics of Social Conflict: The Peak Country, 1520–1770*. Cambridge: Cambridge University Press, 1999.
Woolf, Virginia. *A Room of One's Own*. New York: Harcourt Brace & World, 1929; 1957.

The Essays of Virginia Woolf. Ed. Stuart N. Clarke. Vol. VI. London: The Hogarth Press, 2011.
Worden, Blair. *Literature and Politics in Cromwellian England.* Oxford: Oxford University Press, 2007.
"The Question of Secularization," in *A Nation Transformed.* Ed. Alan Houston and Steve Pincus. Cambridge: Cambridge University Press, 2001. 20–40.
Worsley, Lucy. *Cavalier: A Tale of Chivalry, Passion and Great Houses.* New York: Bloomsbury, 2007.
Yates, Frances A. *The Art of Memory.* Chicago: The University of Chicago Press, 1966.
Yoshinaka, Takashi. *Marvell's Ambivalence: Religion and the Politics of Imagination in Mid-Seventeenth-Century England.* Cambridge: D. S. Brewer, 2011.
Yrjönsuuri, Mikko. "William Ockham and Mental Language," in *Representation and Objects of Thought in Medieval Philosophy.* Ed. Henrik Lagerlund. Burlington, VT: Ashgate, 2006. 101–116.
Zagorin, Perez. *How the Idea of Religious Toleration Came to the West.* Princeton, NJ: Princeton University Press, 2003.
Zerba, Michelle. *Doubt and Skepticism in Antiquity and the Renaissance.* Cambridge: Cambridge University Press, 2012.
Zukofsky, Louis. *Bottom: On Shakespeare.* Berkeley: University of California Press, 1963.
Zweig, Stefan. *The Right to Heresy: Castellio against Calvin.* Trans. Eden and Cedar Paul. Boston, MA: Beacon Press, 1951.

Index

abstraction, 25, 37–41, 49, 54, 56, 58, 69, 181
Academica (Cicero), 5, 8
Act for Removal of Ecclesiastics from Secular Office, 19
Adams, Thomas, 99
Addison, Joseph, 196, 214
Adorno, Theodore W., 30
Aenesidemus, Modes of, 11–12, 29, 106–107, 143, 228
aesthetics
   Cavendish and, 151–152
   framing and, 209–211
   Herbert and, 27, 99, 102–104, 106, 112–114, 116–117, 119–120, 126, 133, 136, 174
   Marvell and, 29, 31, 176, 178–180, 187–190, 193, 195–196, 199, 201–202, 206–215, 217, 219–221, 223
   Shakespeare and, 81
   skepticism and, 3–6, 14, 30, 64–65, 199, 223
   Spenser and, 32, 36, 50, 53–54, 57–58, 60, 63–64, 67–68, 71–72
   sublime and, 6, 64, 78, 186
Agamben, Giorgio, 7, 29, 178–179, 205–206, 209, 213–214, 221, 233
"Al margen de Donne" (Guillén), 90
alienation, 34, 50, 140, 151, 180–181, 201
"Anchoret, The" (Cavendish), 144–146
"Anniversaries, The" (Donne), 28, 55, 213
Anselm, 45, 110
Antony and Cleopatra (Shakespeare), 78
"Apology for Raymond Sebond" (Montaigne), 12, 106, 194
"Apparition, The" (Donne), 210
Aquinas, Thomas, 9, 36, 38–39, 43, 45, 47–48, 54, 57
architecture, 48, 54, 63, 102, 149–151, 153, 172–173, 193
Areopagitica (Milton), 36, 131
Aristotle, 8, 25, 37–38, 47, 94, 104
Arnoldi, Bartholomaeusz, 37

art
   cultural and political role of, 4, 30
   Heidegger and, 25, 34, 53, 63, 69
   Marvell and, 178, 190, 206, 208, 210–211, 218
   skepticism and, 4, 10, 14, 30, 34
   Spenser and, 53, 59–61, 63
As You Like It (Shakespeare), 181
Assman, Aleida, 154
atomism, 29, 156–157, 159, 171
Aubrey, John, 93, 190
Augustine of Hippo, 8, 162
Augustine, Matthew, 223
Aureol, Peter, 41, 110
Austin, J. L., 80, 83
Axiochus (Plato), 36

Bacon, Francis, 9, 27–28, 111–115, 137–138, 147, 166, 223, 229
Barbour, Reid, 107, 111–112, 127
Bardle, Stephen, 29, 215, 222
Baroque, the, 29, 152, 193, 214
Barthes, Roland, 7, 27, 97–99, 135–136, 169
Baxter, Richard, 102
Bayle, Pierre, 102
Bedford, Ronald, 100–101, 109, 111, 121
Bednarz, James P., 84, 89
Bell in Campo (Cavendish), 149
Benjamin, Walter, 26, 201, 229, 234
Bennett, Jane, 176, 182, 185
Berger, Jr., Harry, 49, 58, 70, 73
Berkeley, George, 23
Biard, Joël, 9, 40–41
Biathanatos (Donne), 98
Biel, Gabriel, 37–38, 110
Blazing World, The (Cavendish), 28, 139, 144, 147, 149–153, 156–157, 160–162, 164, 166–169, 173
Blumenberg, Hans, 7, 9, 17–18, 27–28, 64, 67, 139–142, 146–149, 156–161, 163, 168, 170, 172

Bodin, Jean, 121, 130–131
Boethius, 37
Boileau, Nicolas, 30, 78, 199, 222
Bonaventure, 110
Bouhours, Dominique, 199
Boyle, Robert, 13, 167
Brecht, Bertolt, 178
Bredvold, Louis I, 3, 5
Brooks, Cleanth, 89
Browne, Thomas, 48
Bruno, Giordano, 146
Bruns, Gerald L., 70
Bryskett, Lodowick, 35–36
Bunyan, John, 16, 162
Burckhardt, Jacob, 16, 156
Buridan, John, 37
Burke, Edmund, 6, 35, 187
Burke, Peter, 15, 19, 21
Burnet, Gilbert, 120
Butler, John, 111, 121, 130

Calvin, John, 19, 38, 230
Calvinism, 26, 105, 171
Camden, William, 124
"Canonization, The" (Donne), 89
Carroll, Lewis, 181, 214
Cartesianism, 30, 35, 76–77; see also Descartes
Casanova, Jose, 15
Cassirer, Ernst, 6, 141, 199
Castiglione, Baldassare, 30, 36
Cave, Terence, 4, 48
Cavell, Stanley, 5, 7, 10, 77–78, 80, 84–85, 91, 105–106, 176–177, 208, 221, 226
Cavendish, Charles, 137
Cavendish, Margaret (Duchess of Newcastle), 5, 16, 27–28, 99, 115, 137, 139–154, 157–162, 164–175; see also specific works
Cavendish, William (Duke of Newcastle), 28, 99, 146, 154, 164, 166, 168
censorship, 67, 85, 131, 174, 221
Cervantes, Miguel de, 3
Cézanne, Paul, 36
Chappuzeau, Samuel, 165
Charles I (King), 122–123, 127, 130, 148, 205
Charles II (King), 13
Charles V (Emperor), 121, 127–129, 131
Charron, Pierre, 12
Chaucer, Geoffrey, 24, 163
Cheney, Patrick, 6, 58, 78, 81, 89
Chomsky, Noam, 42–43
Cicero, Marcus Tullius, 4–5, 8, 79, 101
Civil Wars, English, 27–28, 92, 133–134, 140, 170, 174, 202
Clarendon Code, 104
Clarke, Samuel, 156

class, 4, 6, 14, 28, 30, 103, 205
Cleveland, John, 221
Clucas, Stephen, 137–138
cogito, 75, 77, 94
cognition, 5, 24, 37–43, 53, 57, 68, 71, 95, 99, 106–107, 112, 115, 117, 179, 183, 188
Coke, Edward, 21
Coleridge, Samuel Taylor, 32
Colie, Rosalie L., 194, 196, 209, 215
colonialism, see imperialism
Common Notions, 27, 100–103, 112, 117, 119–121, 133
Compagnon, Antoine, 37, 48
Complaints (Spenser), 50
Conant, James, 77
conformity, 3, 27, 95, 98–99, 101, 103–122, 124, 126, 130–131, 133–134, 136, 180, 230; see also Herbert of Cherbury
consent, 27, 95, 98–103, 105–106, 112, 119–122, 124–125, 128–131, 133–134, 136
Contra Academicos (Augustine), 8
Conway, Anne, 29
Cooper, Anthony Ashley, 214
Cotton, Robert, 122
Council of Trent, 121, 126–128
Courtenay, William J., 9, 44–46
Cowley, Abraham, 215
Crathorn, William, 41–42
Cromwell, Oliver, 20, 202–207, 211, 220, 230
Cromwell, Richard, 222
Cummings, Brian, 16, 18
Curtius, Ernst Robert, 161

d'Ailly, Pierre, 37–38
Damian, Peter, 45
Dante Alighieri, 143
Daston, Lorraine, 114
Davies, John, 102
Davis, Kathleen, 17–18, 23
De causis errorum (Herbert), 125
De corpore (Hobbes), 111
De principiis (Hobbes), 111
De religione gentilium (Herbert), 103, 125, 133
De religione laici (Herbert), 100, 125
De schismate Anglicano (Sanders), 131
De veritate (Anselm), 110
De veritate (Herbert), 27, 92–95, 99–102, 105, 108–109, 118, 120–121, 126, 129
Dear, Peter, 108
deism, 22, 28, 43
Democritus, 157
Derrida, Jacques, 80, 156

Index

Descartes, René, 9–10, 28, 45, 75, 94, 108, 111, 137, 158–159, 161, 182–183, 199, 208
"Description of an Island, A" (Cavendish), 170
Dialogue Between a Tutor and his Pupil, A (Herbert), 100, 125
Dilthey, Wilhelm, 18, 227
Dioptrics (Descartes), 183
Discours Concerning Ridicule and Irony (Collins), 222
Discourse of Civill Life, A (Bryskett), 35
Discourse on Method (Descartes), 108
disenchantment, 14, 16–17, 29, 43, 71, 176, 226
Dodds, Gregory, 104
Dodds, Lara, 161
Don Quixote (Cervantes), 234
Donne, John, 5, 7, 16, 26–28, 55, 75–80, 86–91, 94, 98, 114, 165, 193, 210, 213
Doran, Robert, 6, 35, 78
"Drop of Dew, A" (Marvell), 177
Dryden, John, 5, 30, 190, 214
Du Bellay, Joachim, 6, 35, 49–50, 52–54, 64, 73, 232
dualism, 86, 157, 179
Dupré, Louis, 9, 43

Ebreo, Leone, 36
Ecclesiastes, 208
Eckhart, Meister, 110
eclecticism, 24, 94, 116, 170–171
"Ecstasy, The" (Donne), 26, 74–75, 78–79, 81, 85–89, 91
Eikonoklastes (Milton), 225
Eliot, T. S., 193
empiricism, 9, 76, 94, 174, 181, 197
enchantment, 3, 71, 176–177, 179–181, 185, 187–188, 219
enlightenment, 14, 17, 29
Enlightenment, the, 5, 223
Epicureanism, 3, 22, 24, 137, 156–157, 159, 172
Epicurus, 101, 157, 191
"Epigramma in Duos montes" (Marvell), 212
Epithalamion (Spenser), 59, 70
Erasmus, Desiderius, 5, 79
Erfahrung, 229, 234
Erlebnis, 227–229, 231, 234
eroticism, 27, 78–79, 82, 176, 180, 182, 193, 197–198, 215–218
eschatology, 18, 47, 50, 52, 63–64, 73, 232
Estienne, Henri, 8
Everett, Barbara, 82–83, 89, 177, 205, 213
Exodus, Book of, 161–162, 194
Expedition to the Isle of Rhé (Herbert), 95, 122, 129

Faerie Queene, The (Spenser), 24, 32, 34–36, 50, 57, 59–60, 62, 64
Fairfax, Anne, Lady, 148
Fairfax, Maria, 213
Fairfax, Thomas, Lord, 193, 195
Fallon, Stephen M., 26
fanaticism, 3, 13, 223
Felski, Rita, 176, 185
Ferry, Luc, 6, 30
Ficino, Marcilio, 26, 36, 86
ficta, 40–41, 44, 53–54, 58
fideism, 48, 82, 90
figmentum, 40–41, 53
"First Anniversary" (Marvell), 220
Fletcher, Angus, 34, 49
Formigari, Lea, 23
Foxe, John, 122
framing, 208–211, 217–218, 221
Friedman, Donald M., 204, 206
Funkenstein, Amos, 18

Gadamer, Hans-Georg, 57, 156
"Gallery, The" (Marvell), 208–211, 217
"Garden, The" (Marvell), 179–187
Gassendi, Pierre, 101, 111
Gauchet, Marcel, 17
gems, 139, 161–169, 173
gender, 138, 141, 144, 148–149, 196, 205, 213, 215–216, 218
Genesis, Book of, 74
Gilbert, William, 113
Gillespie, Michael, 9, 24
Glanvill, Joseph, 13–14, 16, 137, 144, 177, 186
Gorski, Philip S., 15, 20
Gregory, Brad, 22, 43
Griffioen, Sjoerd, 17
Grogan, Jane, 24, 73
Gross, Kenneth, 69–71, 188, 201
Grossman, Marshall, 55, 178, 196, 201, 206, 227
Guicciardini, Francesco, 122
Guillén, Jorge, 90

Hadfield, Andrew, 71
Hadot, Pierre, 69
Hales, John, 177
Halyburton, Thomas, 109
Hamlet (Shakespeare), 1–2, 90
Hamlin, William M., 24
Harry Berger, Jr., 49, 58, 70, 73
Hartlib, Samuel, 94
Hegel, Georg Wilhelm Friederich, 3, 15, 18, 206
Heidegger, Martin, 7, 17, 25, 34–35, 53, 59–63, 69–70, 146, 200, 208
Helfer, Rebecca, 50

Henrietta Maria, Queen, 121, 152
Henry of Ghent, 37–38, 110
Henry VIII (King), 21, 98, 111, 120, 122–124, 126, 129–130
Henry VIII (Shakespeare), 130
Hequembourg, Stephen, 183, 200
Heraclitus, 69
Herbert of Cherbury, 5–6, 17, 27, 89, 92–134, 136, 173–174, 180, 183, 226–227; *see also specific works*
Herbert, George, 16, 94
Herbert, Richard, 98
Herbert, Thomas, 98, 122
Herman, Peter C., 232
Hill, Eugene D., 94, 109, 127
Hirst, Derek, 193, 200–201, 203, 211, 214–215, 220
historiography, 5, 131
History of Jewels (Chappuzeau), 165
History of Philosophy (Stanley), 137
History of the Reign of King Henry VII, The (Bacon), 111
Hobbes, Thomas, 18, 23, 28, 30, 94, 111, 137, 141, 159, 173–174, 183, 214
Holcot, Robert, 42, 54
Holmes, Michael, 109
"Horatian Ode" (Marvell), 179, 202–206, 208, 211, 230
Horkheimer, Max, 30
Hudson, Nicholas, 22, 37, 44
Hudson, Wayne, 170
humanism, 2, 8, 12, 22, 24, 26, 48, 61, 98, 123, 134, 157, 204
Hume, David, 199, 213–214
Husserl, Edmund, 118
"Hymn to Heavenly Beautie" (Spenser), 54
hyperbole, 10, 77–82, 89, 91, 193, 199, 220

iconoclasm, 50, 112, 133, 149
"Idea, The" (Herbert), 116
impartiality, 107–108, 118, 129, 130–131, 133, 201–206, 209, 212, 223
imperialism, 17, 30, 68, 165–166
individualism, 16, 21, 31, 40, 46, 48, 68, 76, 135, 156
intimacy, 7, 26, 58, 75, 77–83, 85–87, 89–91, 200, 211, 217, 226, 228–231
intuitive cognition, 39–40, 43

Jackson, Christine, 111, 121, 123, 131
James I (King), 92, 104, 121
Jay, Martin, 146, 228
Job, Book of, 72
Johnson, Christopher D., 78, 91, 157, 161
Johnson, Samuel, 196

Jones, Inigo, 152
Jonson, Ben, 84, 89, 164–165, 182
Judges, Book of, 99

Kahn, Victoria, 26, 233
kairotic time, 201, 204, 206–208, 223
Kant, Immanuel, 35, 185, 187, 233
Kantorowicz, Ernst, 18
Kripke, Saul, 83
Kuhn, Thomas, 140

La Bruyère, Jean de, 178, 211
Lagerlund, Henrik, 8, 24
Langer, Ullrich, 49, 56, 65
language: *see* mental language; perfect language; private language; public language; universal language
Larkin, Philip, 182
Lee, Sidney, 92, 99
Leff, Gordon, 41
Leibniz, Gottfried Wilhelm, 9, 156
Leinwand, Theodore, 200
Lewalski, Barbara, 225, 229, 232–234
Licensing Act, 174
Life and Reign of Henry VIII, The (Herbert), 95, 100, 104, 120, 122–131
Lipsius, Justus, 104, 133–134
Lobsien, Verena Olejniczak, 177, 180
Locke, John, 16, 23, 37, 44, 75, 94, 101, 120, 133
Loewenstein, David, 225, 233
loneliness, 7, 27, 47, 80, 139, 226, 231
Longinus, 6, 35, 78, 191
Love's Martyr (poetry collection), 84–85, 89
Löwith, Karl, 18, 22, 156
Lucan, 206
Lucian, 12
Lucretius, 3, 11, 29, 67, 137, 191
Luther, Martin, 19–20, 38, 124–125
Lyly, John, 152

Machiavelli, Niccolò, 12
Magnus, Albertus, 152
Marlowe, Christopher, 6, 165
Marot, Clément, 49, 54–58
Marotti, Arthur, 89
marriage, 77–78, 85
Marshall, David, 209
Martin, Catherine Gimelli, 86, 88
Martz, Louis, 177
Marvell, Andrew, 6, 12, 29–31, 169, 176–223, 226, 229; *see also specific works*
Masters, Thomas, 98, 122
Matchett, William, 81, 89
materialism, 29, 156–157, 159

Index

McCoy, Richard, 82
McDowell, Nicholas, 215
McGrath, S. J., 63
McKeon, Michael, 22–23, 29
mechanism, 9, 31, 156–157, 159, 182
medieval
   nominalism, 9, 44, 48–50, 156
   philosophy, 10, 24, 37, 49, 140, 156, 158
   skepticism, 8–10, 24, 37
   theology, 24–25, 45, 183
Meditations on First Philosophy (Descartes), 45, 108, 158
memory, arts of, 52, 149–154, 172, 209
mental language, 9, 25, 37, 42–44, 49, 72, 74
Mersenne, Marin, 108–109, 111
metaphors, 18–19, 40, 86–87, 112, 114, 118, 124, 139–142, 148, 153, 156–157, 159–162, 168, 172–173, 183, 199–200, 206, 215, 217, 220
metaphysics
   Cavendish and, 28, 141, 164
   Heidegger and, 35
   Herbert and, 27, 103–104, 109, 120, 134, 136
   Marvell and, 183, 196, 205, 223
   nominalism and, 47–48, 68
   Ockham and, 41–43
   Shakespeare and Donne and, 26, 55, 79–80, 85, 87–89, 91
   skepticism, 23, 147
   Spenser and, 24, 35, 37, 63, 68, 71–72
Midsummer Night's Dream, A (Shakespeare), 12
Milton, John, 5, 16, 19–20, 31, 36, 66, 132, 184–185, 187–192, 198–199, 201, 215, 225–234
Moderate, The (newspaper), 167
Moderator expecting Sudden Peace, or Certaine Ruine, The (Povey), 97
modernity
   and the sublime, 6, 64, 72, 186
   Blumenberg and, 140, 156–157
   Cavendish and, 139, 143, 149
   nominalism and, 9, 49, 72, 156
   secularization and, 15, 17–18
   skepticism and, 7, 15, 206
Montaigne, Michel de, 4–5, 11–13, 30, 48, 64, 79, 101, 106, 134, 136–137, 194, 234
More, Henry, 137, 144
Most, Glenn, 33, 194
Motherwell, Robert, 25
"Mourning" (Marvell), 177
Much Ado About Nothing (Shakespeare), 1
Mutability Cantos, The (Spenser), 35, 49, 57, 64–73
Myddleton, Thomas, 95–96, 98, 131–132
mysticism, 38, 48, 58, 179

Natural Instinct, 101–103, 105, 115
natural philosophy, 23, 28, 137–138, 141, 145, 147
"Natures House" (Cavendish), 164
Nature's Pictures (Cavendish), 137, 142, 170
Neoplatonism, 24–25, 36–37, 39, 42, 54–55, 89, 116
neo-Scholasticism, 183
neo-Stoicism, 3, 134
Netzley, Ryan, 225
neutrality, 6, 13, 27, 94–95, 97–99, 103, 107–108, 118–121, 129–136, 225
New Atlantis (Bacon), 147, 166
New Organon, The (Bacon), 111–113
"new Philosophy of Beauty, The" (Herbert), 116
Nicholas of Cusa, 86, 160
Nicols, Thomas, 161–162
Nietzsche, Friederich, 3, 16, 34, 156
Noggle, James, 66, 186, 213
nominalism
   Blumenberg and, 27, 139, 156–158
   Herbert and, 103, 105
   language and, 26, 30, 43–44, 74
   Marvell and, 179–181, 183
   Milton and, 226, 231, 233–234
   skepticism and, 6–7, 9, 23–24, 48, 65
   Spenser and, 24, 26, 37–38, 50, 52, 54, 58, 63–65, 68–69, 71–73
Norbrook, David, 191, 204, 206, 233
Normore, Calvin, 9–10, 43
"November" (Spenser), 35, 55–59
Nuttall, A. D., 50, 60, 65

Oakeshott, Michael, 135
Oberman, Heiko, 42, 44, 46–49, 58, 64–65, 68, 110, 231
Ockham, William of, 9, 23, 37–46, 48, 61, 65, 139
"Ode on a Question Moved" (Herbert of Cherbury), 89
"Of Cannibals" (Montaigne), 12
Of Education (Milton), 229
"Of Experience" (Montaigne), 234
Olivi, Peter, 37
"On Mr. Milton's Paradise Lost" (Marvell), 179, 184, 187–192, 201
On the Sublime (Longinus), 6, 78
Orations of Divers Sorts (Cavendish), 147–148
Organon (Aristotle), 37
Othello (Shakespeare), 1, 77, 228
Outlines of Skepticism (Sextus), 8, 11
Ovid, 68, 143, 154
Owen, John, 233
Ozment, Steven, 38, 44, 48

Palmer, Ada, 22
Panaccio, Claude, 41
Panofsky, Erwin, 48, 58
Paradise Lost (Milton), 180, 184–185, 187–188, 190–191, 225
Paradise Regained (Milton), 228–229, 232
Parageau, Sandrine, 138, 170
Park, Katherine, 114
Parliament, 19, 29, 97–98, 121, 123, 132, 167, 187, 222
Pasnau, Robert, 8, 38, 40–41
Patterson, Annabel, 55, 205, 212, 220–221, 233
Paul (Apostle), 19, 119–120
Pearl (Gawain), 162
perfect languages, 74, 180, 198
Perler, Dominik, 37
perspectivism, 3, 5, 7, 10
Petrarch, Francesco, 24, 79
Petrarchism, 55, 181, 187
Philosophical Investigations (Wittgenstein), 74
Philosophical Letters (Cavendish), 137
"Phoenix and Turtle, The" (Shakespeare), 26, 75, 78–79, 81–85, 88–91
Picciotto, Joanna, 181, 183, 212, 223
"Picture of Little T. C. in a Prospect of Flowers, The" (Marvell), 217–220
Plato, 11, 34, 36, 94, 110, 183
Platonism, 55, 101, 116
Playes (Cavendish), 154
Plutarch, 12
"Poem upon the Death of his Late Highness the Lord Protector, A" (Marvell), 211
Poems (Marvell), 6
politics
  Cavendish and, 133, 141, 167, 173–174
  Herbert and, 27, 94–95, 97–99, 120–134, 136
  Marvell and, 29, 178, 188, 191, 195, 204–208, 211, 221
  Milton and, 191, 225, 227, 229
  nominalism and, 10, 45–47, 49
  secularization and, 17–21
  skepticism and, 3–4, 7, 12, 135–136
  Spenser and, 25, 47, 55, 68
  and theology, 12, 14
Pomponazzi, Pietro, 111
Popkin, Richard, 27, 138
Porphyry, 37
Porter, James I., 6, 47, 78, 191–192
Postel, Guillaume, 100
potentia absoluta, 45–47, 49, 64–65, 71, 149, 158
potentia ordinata, 45, 47, 49, 64, 67, 71–72
Povey, Thomas, 97
Prescott, Anne Lake, 54

private language, 6, 26, 74–76, 79–80, 83–88, 90–91
Protestantism, 20–22, 93, 127–128, 149
providentialism, 170–171, 179, 196, 201, 204, 207–208, 212, 229, 233
public language, 84–85, 90–91
Pyrrho, 5, 135
Pyrrhonism, 5, 10, 37, 48, 65, 136, 138, 177

quietism, 95, 135, 177

Ramachandran, Ayesha, 72, 225
Ramism, 4, 26, 149
Rancière, Jacques, 173–175
Randall, Michael, 48
Raymond, Joad, 16
Read, Rupert, 84
reenchantment, 28–29, 178, 185, 223
Rees, Emma, 147, 161
Reformation, the Protestant, 3, 20–21, 24, 53, 100, 120–122, 124–126
Regrets (Du Bellay), 49
Rehearsal Transpros'd, The (Marvell), 207–208, 220, 222
"Relic, The" (Donne), 193
religion
  Cavendish and, 28, 153, 163, 168–171
  Herbert and, 17, 28, 92–95, 99–101, 103, 106, 109, 121, 123–130, 133
  Marvell and, 29, 213
  secularization and, 15–22
  skepticism and, 12, 14, 22–23, 44–47, 49, 135–136, 177–178, 223
  Spenser and, 24, 46, 50, 58, 73
Renaissance
  humanism, 8, 98
  skepticism, 4–5, 7–8, 11, 48–49
reoccupation, 18, 27–29, 139–142, 144–146, 148–149, 153–161, 163, 168, 170, 172; *see also* Cavendish, Margaret
Restoration, the, 153, 166, 168, 186, 188, 208, 215
Revelation, Book of, 50, 161–162
Rhetorica ad Herennium, 150
Richter, Gerhard, 156
Romans, Epistle to the, 119–120
Rorty, Richard, 80, 87, 170
Rossi, Mario M., 97–98, 111, 121, 130
Rothko, Mark, 33–36, 56
"Ruin of This Island, The" (Cavendish), 170–172, 204
Ruines of Rome, The (Spenser), 53

Sacks, Peter, 54, 58
Saint Girons, Baldine, 62

Index

Samson Agonistes (Milton), 31, 225, 229–234
Sarasohn, Lisa T., 138, 144
"Satire II" (Donne), 114
"Satire III" (Donne), 7
Scepsis Scientifica (Glanvill), 13
Sceptical Chymist, The (Boyle), 13
Schalkwyk, David, 83
Schmitt, Carl, 18, 140, 148, 156
Schmitt, Charles B., 4–5, 8
Schoenfeldt, Michael, 209–210, 215
Scholasticism, 9, 26–27, 36–39, 48, 63, 65–66, 82, 113, 119, 158
science, 5, 9, 18, 23, 27, 105, 115–116, 138, 144, 157, 174
Scotus, Duns, 36–39, 45, 63
secularization
   Cavendish and, 28, 144, 154, 164, 169–170
   Marvell and, 29, 178–179, 201, 203, 206–208, 212, 223
   skepticism and, 4, 7, 15–16, 19, 22–23, 223
   Spenser and, 47, 53
   thesis, 16–17, 23, 140
Sedley, David, 6, 64–65, 185, 193, 197, 225, 229
Selden, John, 103, 111
self-assertion, 9, 65, 139, 142, 146–147, 149, 156–158, 170, 172–173, 226, 232
Seneca, 12, 188
Serjeantson, R. W., 101
Sextus Empiricus, 5, 8–12, 106, 137–138, 177, 187, 193, 196, 199, 223
sexuality, 79, 82, 87, 214–215, 217–218
Shagan, Ethan, 104
Shakespeare, William, 1, 5–6, 18, 26–27, 75–85, 88–91, 130, 172, 181, 228; *see also specific works*
Shepheardes Calender, The (Spenser), 35, 54–59
Sidney, Sir Philip, 79, 89, 121
Silver, Victoria, 48, 201, 215
Simon, David Carroll, 202, 223
Skelton, John, 163–164
skepticism
   aesthetics and, 29–31, 54, 176, 178–180, 186–190, 193, 196, 199, 201–202, 209, 212, 215, 223
   and *Hamlet*, 1–3
   and secularization, 15–16, 23, 223
   and the sublime, 6, 14, 31, 35, 58, 64, 66–68, 71, 179, 185–188, 201, 223, 226, 233
   Bacon and, 111–113
   Blumenberg and, 139, 146, 149, 157, 170
   Cavell and, 5, 10, 77–78, 80, 177, 208, 221, 226
   Cavendish and, 27–29, 115, 137–139, 141, 143–150, 153, 159, 168, 170–174

Donne and Shakespeare and, 26, 75, 78–82, 87, 90–91
   enchantment and, 176–180
   first-wave, 12, 138
   Heidegger and, 34–35
   Herbert and, 27, 94–95, 99, 103, 106–108, 111, 115, 119–121, 127, 131, 134, 136, 175
   Marvell and, 29, 31, 176–180, 186–197, 199–202, 204–210, 212–213, 215, 221–223
   Milton and, 31, 225–227, 229, 232–233
   modern, 8–10, 64, 186
   neutrality and, 134–136
   nominalism and, 9–10, 23–24, 44–49, 64–65, 68
   Ockham and, 39–41, 43
   private language and, 26, 75, 77, 80, 87, 90–91
   second-wave, 12–13, 138
   secularization and, 7, 15–17, 19, 22
   Spenser and, 24–26, 32, 35–40, 42, 54–55, 58–60, 62–68, 71
Skinner, Quentin, 4, 173
Smith, Nigel, 12, 189, 205, 207, 217, 220
Sociable Letters (Cavendish), 171
solipsism, 25, 80, 180, 223
Sommerville, C. John, 21
Songe (du Bellay), 50, 73
Songs and Sonets (Donne), 88
Sonnet 111 (Shakespeare), 90
sovereignty, 6, 18, 28, 45, 49, 64–65, 67–68, 147, 153, 161–162, 168, 170, 173
spectator poems, 179, 209, 211–214
Spenser, Edmund, 6, 24–26, 31–44, 46–47, 49–73, 116, 226, 232; *see also specific works*
split subjectivity, 178, 206–207, 209–211, 213, 221, 234
Spruit, Leen, 39–41
Stanley, Thomas, 137, 215
Stoicism, 1, 5, 10, 22, 100, 116, 126, 133–134, 157, 188, 205
Stoll, Abraham, 107, 133, 225–227
Stump, Eleonore, 39
subjectivism, 30, 48, 63, 199
subjectivity, 6, 23, 40, 178, 206–207, 209, 211, 213, 221, 227, 233–234
sublime
   Donne and Shakespeare and the, 79–82, 89, 91
   language and the, 75, 78, 91
   Marvell and the, 29, 179, 184–189, 191–194, 196–197, 199–201, 206, 213–214, 223, 226

sublime (cont.)
  Milton and the, 31, 187–189, 191–192, 227, 231, 233–234
  skepticism and the, 6, 14, 35, 64, 66, 71, 179, 186–187, 213, 223, 226
  Spenser and the, 25–26, 35, 50, 53, 58, 64, 66, 68–73
Swift, Jonathan, 130
Symposium (Plato), 183

Tachau, Katherine, 9, 42
Tacitus, 3, 111, 131
Taylor, Charles, 7, 17, 22, 28, 61, 134, 201, 208
Tempest, The (Shakespeare), 172
Teskey, Gordon, 62, 68, 71
"To His Coy Mistress" (Marvell), 179, 219
"To Mrs. Diana Cecyll" (Herbert), 116
"To Penshurst" (Jonson), 182
Theatre for Worldlings, A (Van der Noot), 50–51, 53
Thomas, Keith, 14
Thomson, Iain, 34, 61
Till, James, 95–96
Timon of Athens (Shakespeare), 6
Tractatus (Wittgenstein), 75, 81
tragedy, 4, 10, 71, 78, 90, 180–181, 206, 225, 234
"Travelling Spirit, The" (Cavendish), 142–144, 165, 167
"True Relation, A" (Cavendish), 154
Tuck, Richard, 111, 134–135

"Unfortunate Lover, The" (Marvell), 221
universal consent, 100–103, 106, 121, 124–125, 129
universal language, 43, 74–75, 183
universalism, 125–126, 133

universals, 23, 25–26, 35–37, 39–41, 43–44, 48, 50, 54, 56, 60, 63, 65, 103, 105, 183, 223
"Upon Appleton House" (Marvell), 169, 178–179, 187, 193–200, 213, 218–219, 223

Van der Noot, Jan, 50–51
Van Helmont, Jan Baptist, 28, 137
Vane, Sir Henry, the Younger, 20, 222
Varro, Marcus Terrentius, 103
Virgil, 142, 170–171, 195
voluntarism, 44, 46–47, 156–157
Von Maltzahn, Nicholas, 188, 191
Vossius, Gerard, 103

Waller, Edmund, 220
Walwyn, William, 12–14
Watson, Robert N., 179–183
Weber, Max, 16–17, 43, 176
Wilkins, John, 183
William of Ockham: *see* Ockham
Williams, Raymond, 46, 109
Wittgenstein, Ludwig, 7, 23, 26, 44, 74–78, 80–88, 91, 105, 176, 200
Wittreich, Joseph, 185, 188, 191, 233
Wood, Andy, 166–167
Woolf, Virginia, 32, 61, 70, 138–139
Worden, Blair, 15, 204
World's Olio, The (Cavendish), 137, 158–159
Wyclif, John, 48

"Young Love" (Marvell), 215–219

Yoshinaka, Takashi, 177
zetetics, 6, 141–142, 201, 205
Zwicker, Steven, 193, 200–201, 203, 211, 214–215, 220

CPSIA information can be obtained
at www.ICGtesting.com
Printed in the USA
LVHW080920030821
694401LV00004B/305